By Jove!

The Meaning of the Astrological Jupiter

Liz Greene

THE WESSEX ASTROLOGER

Published in 2025 by The Wessex Astrologer Ltd
PO Box 9307
Swanage
BH19 9BF
England

For a full list of our titles go to www.wessexastrologer.com

ISBN: 9781916625242

Cover painting: Gustave Moreau, *Jupiter and Semele* (1889), Musée Gustave Moreau, Paris.

Cover design by Fiona Bowring at Bowring Creative
Typeset by Kevin Moore

A catalogue record for this book is available at The British Library

Table of Contents

Part One: 'The Head That Wears a Crown'

It is not possible either to trick or escape the mind of Zeus.

– HESIOD

This seminar was given online for students from the Centre for Psychological Astrology and the Mercury Internet School of Psychological Astrology on 4th September 2021.

Introduction

Jupiter has been known to astrologers for two millennia as the 'Greater Benefic'. We tend to be upbeat about this planet, and its most negative attribute is usually described as 'excess'. Excess can certainly lead to serious problems in our finances, our health, our personal, social, and working relationships, and our encounters with the law. But we're more inclined to give a secret nod and a wink to excess because it can be so much fun. Excess in moderation might sound like an oxymoron, but in the eyes of many, it's not a bad way to live one's life, at least some of the time. And this Jupiterian 'failing' is usually outweighed in textbook descriptions by the planet's reputation for generosity, adventurousness, inspiration, optimism, and faith.

I have no quarrel with keyword descriptions like 'optimism' or 'excess' for an astrological symbol. Although they're often overly simple, these shorthand definitions are valid, up to a point, and they're undoubtedly useful for someone who's beginning to learn astrological language. But any of you with any experience of interpreting charts will know that Jupiter's expression, in an individual life and on a collective level, is rarely simple and sometimes anything but benefic.

In astrology, several planets are associated with complexity and mystery. We might think of Neptune and Pluto as enigmatic, impenetrable, and suspiciously murky; we might view Uranus with trepidation because of its baffling and infuriating unpredictability; and we might struggle to grasp the psychological depth and complexity of Saturn and Chiron. But Jupiter is in some ways the most enigmatic of all the heavenly bodies in our solar system, despite that interpretation of the planet as occasionally a bit theatrical and over the top but nevertheless firmly on the side of 'Right', however we choose to define that term.

Jupiter's complexity and amorality are clearly demonstrated in the many ancient myths about the god's constant shape-shifting, his volatile nature, his foul temper, his appalling behaviour towards women, his envy, paranoia, and sudden bouts of spite and destructiveness, and, in a different and less well-known group of myths, his personification of what was understood in the Greek world of the Orphics, the Platonists, and the Neoplatonists as 'Divine Mind': the essence of an intelligent, all-knowing, and inherently teleological cosmos. Yet many of us persist in assuming that Jupiter always brings 'good luck'. We might wait hopefully for an approaching transit of Jupiter conjunct the Sun or Venus and then find that it's accompanied by unexpectedly painful and challenging experiences. Or we assume something 'good' will happen and then feel deeply disappointed when the transit passes with no recognisable event that enhances our lives in any identifiable way.

I'm not suggesting that Jupiter is really a cleverly disguised 'malefic'. But it seems, even with our increasingly sophisticated understanding of astrological symbols, that we can sometimes be naive in our assumption that every planet can be categorised as either 'good' or 'bad', 'material' or 'spiritual.' This monochromatic approach is an inheritance from older astrologies embedded in simpler and more polarised world-views, and it may be increasingly inappropriate and even destructive to rely on such sharply demarcated categories now.

As an archetypal principle, the astrological Jupiter, like the other planets, is multifaceted and multidimensional. As individuals and cultures are inevitably lopsided and limited, no prevailing world-view, however loudly it proclaims its social, scientific, or religious truths, ever grasps the whole picture. Jupiter reflects archetypal themes that move fluidly along a spectrum from very dark to very light, often with both paradoxically mixed up together. I'm hoping that during the course of our three seminars we'll gain more insight into these underlying archetypal themes reflected by the symbol of Jupiter in the birth chart.

The astronomy of Jupiter

Let's begin with a brief look at Jupiter's astronomy. The astronomical features of a planet can be quite thought-provoking because, like the other heavenly bodies in our solar system, what we now know of Jupiter's physical reality seems to reflect in a strangely synchronous way the attributes of the astrological symbol, even though the ancient cultures that first formulated descriptions of the planet were unaware of many dimensions of its physical reality.

Jupiter is the largest planet in our solar system. Its diameter is eleven times that of the Earth, and its mass is two and a half times that of all the other planets combined. But appearances can be deceptive. Astronomers refer to Jupiter as a 'gas giant' because its vast size reflects an almost entirely gaseous composition. In other words, it's full of hot air. Jupiter lacks an accessible solid surface like that of the Earth; its solid inner core is estimated to be as small as the Earth, and possibly considerably smaller. Size, in this context, really doesn't matter.

Jupiter is also the most visually dramatic of the planets. The striking multicoloured stripes and swirling patterns visible on its surface are comprised of constantly shifting windy clouds of ammonia and water in an atmosphere of hydrogen and helium. These patterns never stay the same; they're like a living, breathing, endlessly mutating abstract painting.

Jupiter has a faint ring system, like the rings of Saturn but much less clearly defined. These rings were formed when chunks of rock and ice crashed into the four small moons – Amalthea, Adrastea, Metis, and Thebe – that now orbit the planet within the rings. Metis and Thebe were named after two of the mythic Jupiter's many lovers; Amalthea and Adrastea were named after the nurses who looked after the newborn god during his infancy. The collisions involving these moons blasted dust into space, and the dust, bound by gravitational pull, encircled the planet and formed its rings.

Jupiter's ring system is composed of three main parts. On the outside is a pair of faint, gossamer rings; the more substantial main ring is in the middle; and a smaller ring known as a halo is closest to the planet itself.

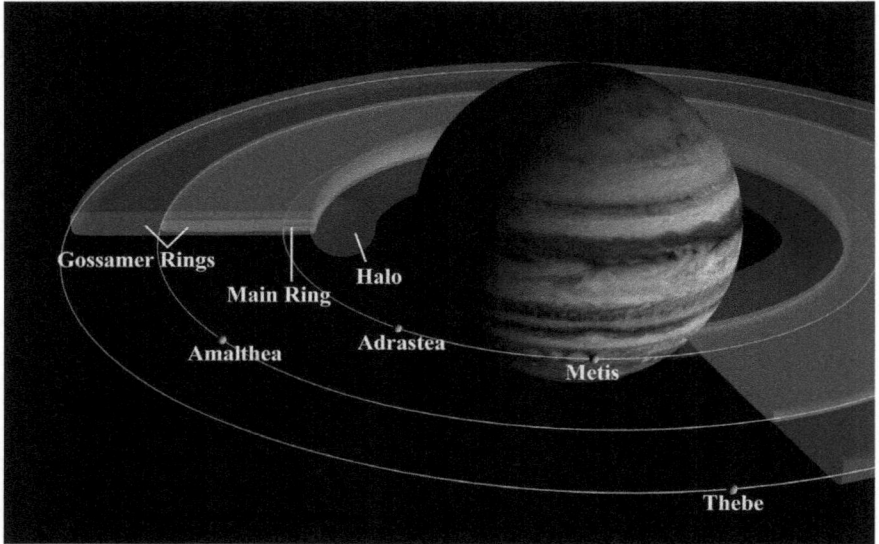

Jupiter's ring system with four of the planet's moons orbiting within it. Image courtesy of NASA, photojournal.jpl.nasa.gov/catalogue/PIA01627.

Jupiter's famous 'Great Red Spot' is a centuries-old anticyclonic storm raging on the planet's surface. This storm is much larger than the Earth and is constantly mutating and changing shape. If and when it finally clears, another storm will probably take its place. We can see from its astronomical features that this heavenly body isn't what it seems. Its size is deceptive, with proportionally very little solidity at its core, and it's in a state of constant flux. The nature of the astrological symbol with its accompanying myths faithfully echoes these fundamental features of the physical planet.

The 'Jovian year' – the planet's cycle around the Sun – takes approximately twelve years, so despite its size, Jupiter is surprisingly nimble. It moves far more quickly around the Sun than any of the smaller planets beyond its orbit, taking less than half the time of Saturn's cycle. And it has an impressive number of satellites. Jupiter has more than seventy known moons, and there may be many more still undiscovered.

As the diagram indicates, four small moons are embedded in the ring system. The four largest moons, which orbit beyond the rings, were discovered by Galileo in 1610 and were named after four more of the mythic Jupiter's lovers: Io, Europa, Ganymede, and Callisto. Io is the most volcanically active body in the solar system. Europa, roughly the size of our own Moon, has an ice-water surface and an atmosphere primarily composed of oxygen; it's currently considered to be the most likely candidate in the solar system to support some form of extraterrestrial life. In some ways Jupiter comprises an entire mini-solar system in itself, and the physical planet's multitude of moons, presaged in the ancient world by stories of the god's extensive catalogue of paramours, faithfully reflects an important dimension of the meaning of Jupiter as an astrological symbol.

The mythology of Jupiter

As the mythic ruler of heaven, Jupiter, like the other planetary gods, has ancient antecedents that vanish in the mists of prehistory. In common with sky-gods from many other early cultures, the Greek Zeus was portrayed as a king, a lawmaker, an arbiter of Fate, a demiurge or world-creator, and a cosmocrator or ruler of the universe. He was frequently referred to as 'All-Father'. 'Our Father Who Art in Heaven' is one of the latest epithets in a long line of these divine celestial rulers.

The origins of the name

The name 'Zeus' is derived from an ancient Indo-European sky-god called Dyeus or Djeus: a name whose root means 'to shine'. The Roman name Jupiter is a contraction of *djeus*, which in archaic Latin became *iovis*, with *pater*, the Latin word for 'father'. 'Jupiter' literally means 'father of light' or 'shining father'. According to the early 20th-century scholar Arthur Bernard Cook, who produced an impeccably researched and illustrated but now virtually forgotten three-volume work on Zeus, the name Djeus can also be translated as 'The Bright One', reflecting the planet's dominance in the night sky.[1] The Latin words *deus*, meaning 'god', and *divus*, meaning 'divine', are also derived from this name, and the modern French *dieu*, also meaning 'god', in turn comes from the Latin, as does the Italian *dio* and the English words 'deify' and 'divine'. Although Zeus may have all but vanished from the religions of our modern world, he's alive and well in our languages.

Zeus shares many attributes with other Indo-European sky- and thunder-deities such as the Norse Thor and the Hindu Indra. The alternative Roman name for the god, Jove, was pronounced 'yo-weh' and, in Latin, spelled with an 'i' rather than a 'j' (there's no 'j' in the Latin alphabet). From this name we derive the adjective 'jovial', a quality often associated

---

1   Arthur Bernard Cook, *Zeus: A Study in Ancient Religion* (Cambridge, 1914), Vol. I, p 1.

with the astrological Jupiter. Jove, pronounced as the Romans pronounced it, is phonetically close to the Hebrew Iaweh (the Christian Jehovah, whose name, in Latin, is pronounced 'ye-o-wah'), who is also understood as the heavenly All-Father. On Greco-Egyptian magical amulets from the late Hellenistic period, the names of Jove and Iaweh are conflated in the name Iao. Hellenistic magic was cosmopolitan and perceived no significant differences between the two deities. Jove, Yahweh, and Jehovah share a wide range of attributes, some positive and some unpleasant, although not surprisingly, many modern scholars are vociferously insistent that the similarity of these names is merely 'coincidence'.

The infancy of Zeus

Zeus was the youngest child of the Titan Kronos, king of the gods, and his sister-wife Rhea. Kronos, whom the Romans knew as Saturn, swallowed his other children – Hestia, Demeter, Hera, Hades, and Poseidon – at the moment of their births because an oracle had prophesied that he would be overthrown by one of his offspring, just as he himself overthrew his own father Ouranos.

These two paintings, both well-known representations of the myth, were created two centuries apart. The one on the left is by Rubens and the one on the right by Goya. Although Hesiod's *Theogony* tells us that Kronos swallowed his children whole, both artists chose to portray him biting and tearing at their flesh. This distinction has been duly noted by art historians, and various theories have been offered about the meaning of the cannibalistic savagery portrayed in the paintings, ranging from a portrayal of the horrors of war to a general statement about how dreadful life and human nature can be. Whatever the artists intended, the images convey a horrific sense of threat that may tell us something about what it might have felt like to be the infant Zeus, and what might lie hidden at the roots of Jupiter's touchy pride and explosive unpredictability.

This mythic tale also offers an instructive example of the wonderful Greek grasp of paradox: for their concrete fulfilment, prophecies usually depend on strenuous attempts to avoid them. Understandably, Rhea wasn't wildly enthusiastic about having her children eaten by their father, and on the advice of her mother Gaia, the primal Earth-goddess, she devised a plan to save them. She handed Kronos a stone wrapped in swaddling

Left, Peter Paul Rubens, *Saturn* (1636-38). Right, Francisco de Goya, *Saturn Devouring his Son* (1820-23). Both paintings, Museo del Prado, Madrid.

clothes which, assuming it was the infant Zeus, he promptly swallowed. One might assume the immortal king of the gods would notice the difference, but evidently Kronos wasn't the sharpest knife in the drawer or, more likely, he was so accustomed to being obeyed that it never occurred to him that his wife would dare to thwart him.

Meanwhile, the infant Zeus was hidden in a cave on Mount Dikte in Crete and was cared for by a mountain nymph called Adrasteia, whose name means 'inescapable' – she was sometimes equated with the goddess Nemesis, whom I'll talk about more later – and a goat-nymph called Amalthea, whose name means 'nourishing goddess' and who suckled the baby with her milk.

Nine warrior-dancers called Kouretes, daimons of the wild mountains of Crete, were appointed by Rhea to guard the cave. They shouted, clashed their cymbals, banged their spears on their shields, and played lots of heavy

Rhea hands Kronos a stone wrapped in swaddling clothes. Karl Friedrich Schinkel, *Cronos and Rhea*, 19th c., Reichsministerium für Volksaufklärung und Propaganda, Berlin. The painting is based on a Greco-Roman bas-relief now at the Capitoline Museums, Rome.

Jakob Jordaens, *The Childhood of Zeus* (c. 1640), Musée du Louvre, Paris.

metal music at all hours of the day and night to mask the sound of the baby's cries.

Once Zeus reached manhood, which divine babies tend to do very quickly, the Titan Metis, goddess of guile and wisdom, secretly gave Kronos an emetic at the request of her sister Rhea that forced him to vomit up the stone he had swallowed. All of

Kouretes guarding the infant Zeus, drawing based on an ancient Greek terracotta plaque, in Jane Ellen Harrison, *Themis: A Study of the Social Origins of Greek Religion* (Cambridge, 1912), p. 23.

Zeus' siblings were regurgitated as well. Together with some of the more sympathetic Titans as well as the Kyklopes and the Hundred-Handed Giants (also the children of Gaia, and therefore Zeus' uncles and aunts), they formed a small army, overthrew Kronos, and cast him into Tartarus.

After the battle, Zeus and his brothers, Hades and Poseidon, chose lots to decide which realms they would govern. Zeus received rulership over the heavens, Hades became lord of the underworld, and Poseidon presided over the seas. To express his gratitude to the goat-nurse Amalthea who had fed him in infancy, Zeus placed her in the heavens as the zodiacal constellation of Capricorn. He further honoured her – or not, depending on your point of view – by creating his thunder-shield, known as the *aigis*, from her hide. And he formed the horn of plenty, the cornucopia or *keras amaltheias*, capable of providing endless nourishment, from one of her horns, which he'd accidentally broken off in a temper tantrum while he was still a baby.

Gaia, his grandmother, retained her primal rulership over the Earth, but Zeus and his brothers were permitted to govern portions of the earthly realm according to their natures. Zeus presided over mountains, Poseidon ruled the waterways under the earth, and Hades governed volcanoes and sulphureous hot springs as well as the subterranean realms where the souls of the dead resided. But the brothers weren't equal. As king of the gods, Zeus enjoyed superiority over his siblings.

The three divine brothers in classical ceremonial pose. Left to right: Zeus/Jupiter with his thunderbolt, from Smyrna, c. 250 CE, Musée du Louvre; Poseidon/Neptune, who probably originally held a trident, from Melos, 2ⁿᵈ c. BCE, National Archaeological Museum of Athens; Hades/Pluto with Cerberus, the three-headed canine guardian of the underworld, mid-2ⁿᵈ c. CE, Archaeological Museum of Heraklion.

When we look later at some of the psychological patterns connected with the astrological Jupiter, it's worth remembering this mythic tale of the god's birth and early life. It's a colourful story with an apparently satisfactory ending. But if this were a human child, we wouldn't expect him to be especially trusting or well-adjusted. A psychiatrist might even consider conditions reflecting severe emotional damage, such as 'post-traumatic stress disorder' or 'narcissistic personality disorder'. After all, Zeus' father tried to eat him and then he had to be hidden in a cave with a goat for a mother and a crowd of very noisy guards constantly banging and crashing about outside who prevented him from getting a decent night's sleep.

Pathology notwithstanding, the endangered childhood, in which the child is threatened by a tyrannical father or father-figure, is an archetypal theme which we can find in many stories about gods, demigods, and heroes, including the story of Jesus. And it's also been played out many times throughout history in ruling families in which fathers murder sons, sons murder fathers, and siblings plot together to destroy their parents or each other. Archetypal patterns tend be expressed not only as core dynamics within the individual psyche, but also as repeating events in human history.

The Orphic Zeus

This classical tale about Zeus' birth and childhood will probably be familiar to any of you acquainted with Greek myth. So will the stories about the god's promiscuity. But there are other, more obscure portrayals of Zeus that can tell us a good deal more about the complex nature of this deity and his astrological symbol. In early Orphic religious currents, which emerged in the archaic Greek world as early as the 8th century BCE, Zeus was the child of Kronos, as he was in classical myth. However, the details of the story and the nature of the god are somewhat different.

In some Orphic texts as well as in classical versions of the story, the first deity to emerge from primal Chaos was Ouranos, the 'starry heaven'. But the Orphic *Rhapsodies*, a late antique compilation of earlier Orphic poems, refers to a primal god called Phanes, who preceded Ouranos. Phanes' name is derived from the Greek word *phainein*, which means 'to reveal' or 'to bring to light'. From this root we get English words such as 'hierophant', 'phantasm', and 'diaphanous', all of which refer to something hidden that's partly revealed.

Phanes emerged from a fire-filled cosmic egg which emanated from Nyx (Night) and Chaos. Also called Protogonos, which means 'first-born', Phanes had no parents. He's an image of the life-force itself: eternal, endlessly creative, invisible and incomprehensible, and revealed only in glimpses through the forms it emanates and inhabits. The Stoics believed this life-force was the essence of a single, all-encompassing godhead, embodied on every level from the material to the spiritual.

Phanes can be roughly equated with what the 1st-century BCE Stoic-Platonic philosopher Poseidonius of Apamea called the 'vital force', and what the early-20th-century French philosopher Henri Bergson referred to as '*élan vital*'. Jung was deeply interested in this idea, and when he named Phanes as the incoming god of the new astrological aion in *Liber Novus*, he seems to be suggesting that humans will finally begin to recognise that the divine is not somewhere 'up there', transcendent and outside creation, but is inherent in life itself on every level of existence, including the human psyche. Although Phanes was invariably portrayed in ancient iconography as a male deity, he was also described in the *Orphic Hymns* as a beautiful, golden-winged hermaphrodite because he was capable of generating new life from within himself. From his own creative power he emanated Ouranos, the 'starry heaven', and Gaia, the Earth.[2] They in turn produced the Titans, including Kronos, who then fathered Zeus and his siblings.

Fig. 909.

Engraving of Phanes in A. B. Cook, *Zeus*, Fig. 909, based on a Greco-Roman bas-relief from the 2nd c. CE. Phanes as cosmocrator is shown surrounded by the zodiacal constellations. His androgyny is suggested by his fiery solar crown and male genitals combined with the lunar crescent behind his shoulders. His cloven hoofs suggest a connection with Pan, the god of Nature, whose name means 'all'.

So far, the story follows classical myth, except for the presence of Phanes, who is uniquely Orphic. But then the narrative takes a bizarre turn that scholars researching Orphic currents in the early decades of the 20th century believed was somehow 'un-Greek', and which they attributed to 'Oriental influences' (the term then used to describe the Middle East as well as India). This same blinkered assumption about the 'rationality' of early Greek culture in contrast to the 'irrationality' of the 'Orient' was also made about astrology by some scholars at the time. Franz Cumont, one of the most important

---

2   See *The Orphic Hymns*, trans. Apostolos N. Athanassakis (Scholars Press, 1977), Hymn V, *To Protogonos*.

early-20th-century researchers into Greco-Roman religions, was particu-larly culpable; he was an impeccable scholar but suffered from what's now known as 'researcher's bias'. He evidently couldn't accept the idea that such 'mystical' beliefs might have emerged organically and simultaneously in disparate cultures without necessarily being 'imported'.[3]

Zeus, once he became king of the gods, devoured the phallus of his great-grandfather Phanes so that he could acquire the primal god's creative potency. Orphic myths exhibit a predilection for cannibalism not usually found in the stories presented by Homer and Hesiod, although I suppose the theme of Kronos eating his children is cannibalistic enough. After this dubious meal, Zeus raped his brother Hades' wife Persephone and fathered the god Dionysos, also known as Zagreus, who was born in the underworld.

This myth contradicts the classical story of Zeus fathering Dionysos on the Theban princess Semele. Because Zeus had swallowed his great-grandfather Phanes' phallus, the Orphic Dionysos, son of Zeus, inherited the creative power of the primal god, and the child's undisguised radiance inevitably aroused envy and resentment among the earthbound Titans. Encouraged by Hera, who had her own grievance against this splendid, shining child who was her husband's progeny by someone else, the Titans distracted the infant god with sparkling toys and then, in an outburst of violent rage and envious spite, proceeded to dismember and eat him. I did warn you about the cannibalism in Orphic myths.

In revenge, Zeus blasted the Titans to ashes with a lightning bolt. In classical myth, humans were created by Prometheus out of earth and water. But in Orphic teachings, they were created from these ashes. Because the Titans had already digested and absorbed Dionysos, the ashes combined the earthy, greedy, envious Titanic nature, equated with the physical body (*soma*) and its passions, and the creative divinity of Dionysos-Phanes, equated with the immortal soul (*psyche*). This dualism of body and soul is unique in Greek myth and is elegantly articulated in inscriptions on the Orphic *lamellae*: small funerary tablets, usually made of gold or bone, that were placed over the mouths of the dead. These tablets provided instructions to the soul of the deceased about what to say to the underworld guardians

---

3   For Cumont's views on astrology, see Franz Cumont, *The Oriental Religions in Roman Paganism* (1911); Franz Cumont, *Astrology and Religion Among the Greeks and Romans* (1912). Most of Cumont's works have been published in more recent editions in both French and English, and some are available online.

in order to escape the endless cycle of rebirth, referred to as 'the sorrowful, weary Wheel'.

On one of the *lamellae*, the soul is advised to avoid drinking from the underworld Pool of Forgetfulness, and must say to the guardians:

I am a child of Earth [Gaia] and Starry Sky [Ouranos], but my race is of heaven alone.[4]

Orphic gold *lamella* from Thessaly, 4th c. BCE, J. Paul Getty Museum, Malibu, CA.

The echoes of this dualism of *soma* and *psyche*, with *soma* invariably cast as the villain, have continued to resonate through the centuries, especially in Christian beliefs about the endemic sinfulness of the mortal body and the essential purity and heavenly origin of the human soul. These ideas are also relevant to our understanding of the astrological Jupiter, which I hope will become clearer over the course of our seminars. Despite

---

4   From an Orphic *lamella* from Petelia, Italy, 4th c. BCE, in Fritz Graf and Sarah Iles Johnston, *Ritual Texts for the Afterlife: Orpheus and the Bacchic Gold Tablets*, Routledge (2007), p. 7.

his penchant for sexual encounters with beautiful women and boys, Zeus was not a friend of the Earth-world.

Orphic currents never comprised a formal religion. They were a loose collection of beliefs and ritual practices united by specific themes, and there's still a great deal that scholars don't understand about the Orphics and how their ideas developed and spread. According to classical scholars writing in the mid-20th century, late classical quotations from Orphic poems such as the *Rhapsodies* were merely inventions by the Neoplatonists, who purportedly then falsely attributed these poems to 'Orpheus'. The Neoplatonic quotations from 'Orpheus' were no longer considered by these scholars to be genuine renditions of much older religious texts, and the reality and importance of pre-classical Orphic currents were effectively cancelled.

This dismissive scholarly perspective was forcibly altered by the discovery in northern Greece in 1962 of an early 4th-century BCE Orphic text known as the Derveni Papyrus.[5] This extraordinary document was written by an Orphic initiate who belonged to a category of ancient writers known as 'allegorists'. These authors made it their business to examine older texts and reinterpret them according to the philosophical and scientific perspectives of their own time. The Derveni Papyrus was intended by its author as an up-to-date analysis of a much older Orphic poem. Not much has changed in the scholarly world since then, as it seems we're still attempting to interpret and reinterpret older systems of thought through the lens of our own current religious, sociological, scientific, and moral paradigms.

---

5   For a translation of this papyrus with commentary, see Gábor Betegh, *The Derveni Papyrus: Cosmology, Theology and Interpretation*, Cambridge University Press (2004). For other works on the papyrus, see André Laks and Glenn W. Most (ed.), *Studies on the Derveni Papyrus*, Oxford University Press, Vol. 1 (2001) and Vol. 2 (2022); T. Kouremenos, G. M. Parassoglou, and K. Tsantsanoglou (eds.), *The Derveni Papyrus*, Libri Antichi Arezzo (2006); Marco Antonio Santamaria Alvarez (ed.), *The Derveni Papyrus: Unearthing Ancient Mysteries*, Brill (2019). New books continue to be written about the Derveni Papyrus, attesting to its enormous importance in understanding Orphic religious currents and their impact on later developments in Judaism, Christianity, occult and esoteric currents in the late 19th and early 20th centuries, and so-called 'contemporary spiritualities'.

The Orphic poem cited by the Derveni author assigns a special role to Zeus that's strikingly different from the petulant, lascivious son of Kronos who rules the heavens from Olympus. In the poem, Zeus is described as 'Divine Mind' or *nous*. His 'Immortal Breath' or *pneuma* is called 'Fate' or *moira*; and he has always existed, long before he was given a name. The Derveni author quotes the following passage from the poem, which, based on its language structure, is understood by scholars to have been written in the 5th century BCE or possibly even earlier: at least a century before the Derveni author himself was born.

> Now Orpheus named this breath Moira...For before Zeus received his name, Moira was the wisdom of the god always and through everything.[6]

Fate is thus the 'wisdom' of Zeus, his Divine Breath, and according to the Derveni Papyrus, it's inherent in all things and shapes their nature, their limits, their purpose, and their ultimate destiny according to the divine plan.

In the work of the 5th-century BCE philosopher Empedocles, who seems to have been strongly influenced by Orphic ideas, Zeus is one of the four 'roots' or primal cosmic powers. He's equated with the 'root' of air. Air, in Orphic thought, isn't the same as the Aristotelian sub-lunar element of air which comprises one of the four astrological triplicities we use in chart interpretation. Orphic 'air' is the Divine Mind: the essence, intention, and plan of the cosmos and everything within it. It's roughly equivalent to the Christian idea of Divine Providence. Because everything is part of and infused by his Divine Breath, Zeus is and knows everything, past, present, and future.

Fate or *moira* in this context is identical to teleology: the unique nature of a thing, its essence, its boundaries and limits, its purpose, and its destiny to become what it innately is. This idea was expressed by the 6th-century BCE Greek philosopher Heraclitus, who stated, "A man's character is his fate"; by the late 18th-century German Romantic poet Novalis, who declared that "fate and character are the same conception"; and in modern times in James Hillman's 'acorn theory' about the development of the human

---

6   *DP* Col. 18, in Betegh, *The Derveni Papyrus*, p. 39.

personality.[7] An acorn can only become an oak tree, not a cherry tree or a cabbage, because that's its intrinsic nature, and its nature is the same as its destiny. Each of us can only become what we essentially are, which is both our fate and our teleology.

> For air existed even before the things that are now were set together and always will exist. For it was not born, but existed...The wisdom of Zeus ordains how the things that are and the things that come to be and the things that are going to be must come to be and be and cease...Zeus the king, Zeus who rules all with the bright bolt.[8]

Although air, in Orphic thought, isn't an astrological element, and the Orphic gods aren't planetary, we can gain a lot of insight into the astrological Jupiter from the Orphic portrayal of Zeus. If we want to delve into the deeper meaning of the planets, we need to move beyond Ptolemy's Aristotelian model, in which Jupiter is 'hot', 'moist', and 'temperate' and serves as the 'Greater Benefic' of the solar system.[9]

When we look later at Jupiter's placement in the natal chart, it might be helpful to remember this idea of the 'wisdom of Zeus', which describes a plan or design of unfoldment inherent in every living thing. We can sometimes get an intuitive glimpse of a hidden pattern in our lives – even when things go badly pear-shaped – that seems to offer us meaning, hope, and a sense of connection with a larger, wiser, and more meaningful universe. This glimpse is one of the ways in which the astrological Jupiter as an inner dynamic reveals to us the 'wisdom of Zeus' at work in our own lives. It isn't foreknowledge in the sense of predicting a future determined by some external fate. It's a recognition of what we are and what we need to become, which is also the part we're meant to play in an endless unfolding story.

---

7   Heraclitus, *The Fragments of Heraclitus* 121, trans. G. T. W. Patrick, Harvard University Press (2013); Novalis, quoted in Hermann Hesse, *Demian*, Boni & Liveright (1923). For Hillman's 'acorn theory', see James Hillman, *The Soul's Code: In Search of Character and Calling*, Random House (1996).
8   *DP* Col. 17 and 19, in Betegh, *The Derveni Papyrus*, pp. 37 and 41.
9   For the origins and development of the four astrological elements, see Dorian Gieseler Greenbaum, *Temperament: Astrology's Forgotten Key*, Wessex Astrologer (2005).

Whether or not this meaningful universe is an objective reality or a subjective inner experience is a question that's been argued in psychological and philosophical circles for a very long time, and the answer for each of us seems to depend on our own individual experiences and world-view. Perhaps it really doesn't matter whether we generate a sense of meaning from within ourselves and project it onto a non-sentient universe, or perceive the objective reality of a meaningful, intentioned cosmos. Either way, our lives are changed and enriched. This intuitive perception of life as meaningful has always been experienced and described by humans across cultural and historical boundaries, embedded in different religious, philosophical, and cultural frameworks but reflecting a psychological impetus or mode of perception symbolised by the astrological Jupiter.

In conventional astrology we associate Jupiter with fire because of its rulership of Sagittarius, and with water because of its rulership of Pisces, encapsulated in Ptolemy's description of the planet being 'hot' and 'moist'. Jupiter is traditionally in dignity in Sagittarius and Pisces, in detriment in Gemini and Virgo, in exaltation in Cancer, and in fall in Capricorn. But in Orphic myth Zeus isn't a planet. He's the divine essence of air, which isn't the kind of air we associate with Gemini, Libra, and Aquarius. It's air as *pneuma*, Divine Breath, emerging from *nous*, Divine Mind, and breathed into everything in the form of *moira* or Fate.

The element of air is related to the thinking function, communication, connection, conceptualisation, rationality, and the realm of ideas. That's not the same as Divine Mind, and people with lots of planets in air signs aren't necessarily attuned to the *nous*. Sometimes it's quite the opposite, since hyper-rationality is often entirely resistant to the hidden dimensions of life. The element of air is limited to its own specific domain, although vitally important in understanding the dynamics of an individual personality, and it emerges from Aristotle's division of the sub-lunar realm into the four categories describing the 'stuff' of which this world is made. In contrast, Zeus as Divine Mind is the source and symbol of the order, purpose, and meaning of the universe and everything in it. As the Derveni Papyrus states, it has always existed, everywhere and in everything.

We can't ever fully grasp an archaic world-view like that of the Orphics because our modern consciousness is so different. As a collective, the Western world has lost, and often wilfully denigrates, a spontaneous and intuitive sense of the interconnectedness of everything on every level of life, although we might theorise about it through various ecological movements and contemporary spiritualities. In consequence we may idealise cultures like the Aboriginal Australians because they seem to have retained that intuitive sense of the unity of life. But we can't recreate this through an act of will because other modes of perception and evaluation have gradually taken its place. Yet each of us might suddenly have a brief but powerful inner experience that seems to come from an altogether different level of reality – although these experiences, like the god Phanes, reveal something and then vanish, stubbornly refusing to return when called.

Even if we've moved too far away from the Orphic world-view to ever fully recapture it, we might open the door to a glimpse of this archaic idea of Zeus if we use the imagination and work with astrology as a symbolic rather than a literal model. The idea of Zeus as *nous* is much broader and more complex than Aristotle's categories. Zeus isn't the 'root' of fire, although the astrological Jupiter rules a fiery sign. According to Empedocles, the 'root' of fire is the underworld god Hades, also called Aidoneus, who personifies the divine fire that lies at the core of the universe and destroys and regenerates all things.

Zeus isn't the 'root' of water either, although in astrology Jupiter rules Pisces, a water sign. The 'root' of water, according to Empedocles, is the goddess Persephone, mother of Dionysos, whose tears of grief and mourning for her son's dismemberment and death at the hands of the Titans form the essence of the world's grief, suffering, and compassion. These tears are inherent in all things because all things ultimately die, even the planets and stars, and grief is an archetypal experience. Empedocles called Persephone by the name Nestis, which means 'the fasting one', or 'the one deprived of nourishment' because she lost her only child. Persephone isn't one of the planetary gods, nor is she associated with any zodiacal sign. And the 'root' of earth is Hera, Zeus' sister-wife, who is also not a planetary god. There are two asteroids called Hera and Persephone, and many astrologers work with these in the chart. But modern astrological interpretations of these asteroids, however valid they might be in their own context, don't seem to have any real parallel with Empedocles' 'roots'.[10]

---

10 For the four divine 'roots', see *Empedokles: Fragments and Commentary*, trans. Arthur Fairbanks, K. Paul, Trench, Trubner (1898); Peter Kingsley, *Ancient Philosophy, Mystery and Magic: Empedocles and Pythagorean Tradition*, Clarendon Press (1995).

Fate, fortune, and luck

The Orphic portrayal of Zeus equates his Divine Breath with fate and teleology. Teleology implies an entwined relationship, or even a hidden unity, between fate and free will. We're fated to become what we've always potentially been, but we can choose to align ourselves with our *moira* consciously and contribute our creative efforts to its unfolding. As Jung put it, "Free will is the ability to do gladly that which I must do." The operative word here is 'gladly', because we can't do what we 'must' do – in other words, fulfil our *moira* – willingly unless we intuitively grasp, accept, and consciously support its meaning and purpose.

In a psychological context, we can choose to cooperate with and actively encourage the individuation process that unfolds in our lives with or without our consent. Our active participation makes it richer and more rewarding. Considering the idea of teleology can give us insight into the connection between Jupiter and fate in a sense quite different from the way we normally think about fate. The more deeply we explore this, the closer we get to some understanding of Jupiter's mystery. The sphere of life where we could intuitively sense our lives being shaped by our teleology is suggested by the sign and house placement of Jupiter in the birth chart.

'Good luck' and 'bad luck' are both related to Jupiter because both are part of the teleology of an individual life. Jupiter's 'luck' – which is not the same thing as the apparently random turns of the Wheel of Fortune – is related to the gambling instinct, which can sometimes become an addiction as destructive as an addiction to heroin or alcohol. When we take serious risks – with money, with career choices, with the law, with the lives of others, or with our emotions and our bodies – we're 'testing' the god to see whether he favours us. It's a compulsive displacement of the Jupiterian need to feel connected to a purposeful pattern. It's interesting that we use the term 'winning streak' to describe a run of good luck, as though Jupiter's 'bright bolt' has streaked through our lives. The word 'luck' is Middle Dutch in origin, derived from *gheluc*, which means 'good fortune'. A strong natal Jupiter is often experienced as a feeling of being 'lucky' or 'fortunate' because the rewards of our risk-taking can inspire an intuitive sense of a special connection to a higher or deeper source.

In Jupiter's realm our experiences of luck, whether 'good' or 'bad', are bound up with what we are and what we necessarily need to become. The concept of luck is far more profound than we might imagine. Experiencing ourselves as lucky may imply that unconsciously we feel uniquely chosen for a particular reason. We recognise ourselves as an important part of a larger pattern, even if we don't consciously believe in any god at all. When Jupiter is prominent in the birth chart, the person may feel especially favoured, although sometimes that feeling can provoke guilt because others haven't enjoyed the same divinely bestowed benefits in life. 'Lucky' people can also inflate and begin to believe they can get away with almost anything, and sometimes they do. And sometimes the luck runs out.

Why should we feel these things? The belief that we're lucky may reflect an intuitive sense that there's a meaning in everything, a connection to a bigger pattern or plan. If we feel connected to that pattern, we feel relevant, special, and confident in our future, and this can encourage us to pursue opportunities that others might miss or reject. The potion known as *Felix Felicis* or 'Liquid Luck' in *Harry Potter and the Half-Blood Prince* makes the imbiber 'lucky'. But J. K. Rowling's description is subtle and psychologically astute. The potion's luck ultimately comes from Harry's faith in his intuitive hunches and his willingness to trust and act on those hunches, rather than from a literal rearrangement of events through the intervention of an invisible external power. 'Liquid Luck' might as well be called 'Liquid Jupiter'.

Jupiter's feeling of being special is different from the Sun's sense of specialness because it isn't about 'me' as a unique entity. It's about our place in a much larger, eternally unfolding scheme or design – a conviction of meaning and purpose rather than a sense of personal self-esteem. This conviction can be reflected in a belief that we're lucky – or unlucky, if we feel that somehow the gods have singled us out for punishment. The idea of a hostile divine finger pointing exclusively at us also implies the sense of a higher plan or a design, even though it's a less pleasant experience. Sometimes we may hear deeply religious people declare that their suffering has been imposed on them by God as a 'test' of faith or a necessary trial to build character. Despite the implicit assumption in such declarations that God can be petty, spiteful, and vindictive – which, to be fair, the mythic Zeus often was – this attitude still reflects the longing to feel part of a meaningful pattern.

Zeus' battles: the Titanomachy

The mythic Zeus was embroiled in many battles, some forced on him and some created by his own defensiveness and bad temper. This mythic theme can give us some insight into the astrological Jupiter. Zeus was no more peaceful than his planet, buffeted by its incessant storms and constantly shifting gaseous surface. Not only was Zeus' childhood fraught with the danger of annihilation; as ruler of Olympus he was perpetually threatened by enemies, real or imagined, that had to be conquered, punished, or destroyed. We don't usually think of Jupiter's zodiacal signs, Sagittarius and Pisces, as being particularly belligerent or defensive. These two signs are mutable, adaptable, and kindly – up to a point. But sometimes myths about the planetary gods, especially older versions of the stories, can reveal dimensions of a sign that we might tend to overlook.

The struggle between Zeus and his father Kronos was known as the Titanomachy, from the Greek root *maché,* which means 'battle'. Kronos was a Titan, and the fight pitted the six Olympian children of Kronos and Rhea – Zeus, Hades, Poseidon, Hera, Hestia, and Demeter – against the

Cornelis van Haarlem, *The Fall of the Titans* (1588-90), Statens Museum for Kunst, Copenhagen

Titans, the offspring of Ouranos and Gaia. Not all the Titans fought against the Olympians. Some, like Okeanos, abstained from voting, while others, such as Themis and Prometheus, actively aided Zeus and his siblings. The result was the overthrowing of Kronos and the triumphant ascension of Zeus to the throne of Olympus.

Zeus' battles: The Gigantomachy

Zeus and his fellow Olympians also fought against the Giants, who, along with the Erinyes or Furies, had sprung from the blood and semen of Ouranos when it fell to the earth and fertilised Gaia after his son Kronos castrated him. Although the Giants had helped the young Olympian in his fight against Kronos, they later became his enemies. Zeus won the battle, and the vanquished Giants were buried under the earth; they were believed to be the source of volcanic eruptions. Although the early Greek poets Pindar and Bacchylides described the Giants as arrogant and violent, no specific reason for the battle is described in any early texts. It seems to have just 'happened'.

The Gigantomachy, Greco-Roman bas-relief, 2nd c. CE, Aphrodisias, Turkey; Istanbul Archaeological Museum. The Giants were usually portrayed as hybrid creatures with serpents' tails instead of legs.

The Roman poet Ovid described an effort by the Giants, led by their king Eurymedon, to overthrow Zeus and seize Olympus as the reason for the war. Ovid, when he couldn't find any original Greek sources, simply invented his own stories, often with great elegance and ingenuity. But Zeus didn't always need a reason for his battles, other than his perennial sense of being threatened.

Zeus' battles: The fight with Typhon

As with humans, so with the gods: violence begets more violence. Typhon was a sea-monster created by the Earth-goddess Gaia to avenge Zeus' victories over her chthonic children, the Titans and the Giants. Typhon, portrayed in archaic iconography as a winged monster with serpent legs, attempted to overthrow Zeus and claim supremacy over the heavens. But Zeus' thunderbolts proved too powerful, and Typhon was hurled into Tartarus or, according to other sources, buried beneath Mount Etna in Sicily. Like the Giants, the buried monster was associated with earthquakes and volcanic eruptions.

These three mighty battles which Zeus fought and won are connected through the kind of enemy he struggled with. The stories reflect his hostility

Typhon, pictured as a winged monster with serpent legs. Greek black-figured *hydria*, 540-530 BCE, Staatliche Antikensammlunge, Munich.
Photo: Bibi Saint-Pol.

towards the creatures born from the womb of his grandmother Gaia, the Earth, and their hostility towards him. It isn't coincidental that both the Giants and Typhon were portrayed with serpent legs, as the serpent belongs to the mythic domain of the Earth, the underworld, and the Great Mother. As a sky-god whose nature was symbolised by the eagle, Zeus was in eternal conflict with earthly beings, especially those he perceived as potential threats to his power.

Once Zeus had established his unassailable rule, the threats came from a different quarter. They were usually directed towards his illegitimate children by Hera, who hated these offspring because they were the humiliating evidence of his infidelity. Hera, in Empedocles' world-view, is the 'root' of Earth, and astrologically, although she isn't traditionally associated with any planet, she seems to reflect a dimension of Saturn as Earth-mother. Although Zeus defeated Kronos, he couldn't defeat Hera. As both Zeus' sister and his wife, she was eternally bound to him and he to her, no matter how high he flew or how many romantic escapades he pursued. Ultimately she couldn't harm him, but she could try to destroy what he created. She never fully succeeded, but she never stopped trying.

The beings Zeus felt threatened by also included the human race, towards which the god seems to have harboured an enduring sense of anger laced with fear – although he also sometimes offered aid and good fortune to selected humans like Philemon and Baucis, faithful worshippers who devotedly tended one of the god's shrines. Humans, like the Titans and the Giants, were described as creatures of earth; in Orphic myth they were created from the ashes of the dead Titans, and in classical myth they were formed by Prometheus out of earth and water. Zeus' propensity to treat the Earth-world and its inhabitants as enemies might offer us some insight into the difficulties that the astrological Jupiter, and its zodiacal signs Sagittarius and Pisces, often have with the mundane world. We'll look at this theme in more detail later.

The love-life of Zeus

Now I'd like to spend some time on the stories of Zeus' many lovers, because one of the god's most prominent characteristics in myth is his irrepressible promiscuity. This quality is central to the ways in which the astrological Jupiter is expressed on various levels. For those of you who think the exploration of myth in relation to the planets is irrelevant, I hope you'll think again. Myth can offer immense insight into the dynamics of the planets, and this kind of understanding tends to elude rational definitions and lists of keywords. Stories are always more powerful in conveying deeper internal truths than didactic explanations. It's why we often learn more about human nature from novels, plays, and films than from psychology textbooks. If you can enter into the stories imaginatively and try to glimpse the characteristic human behaviour patterns that are peeping through, you might be rewarded with lots of 'Aha!' moments.

The mythic Zeus was immensely fertile as well as immensely promiscuous. Only one night with a lover invariably resulted in a pregnancy and a semi-divine child. This combination of promiscuity and fertility might be telling us something about an archetypal pattern of constant restless movement, the ceaseless creation of new possibilities, the pursuit of endless new desires, a really low boredom threshold, boundless inspiration, and a profound reluctance to be fettered to any concrete responsibility for the consequences.

With Hera, Zeus fathered five 'legitimate' divine children: Ares, the god of war; Hephaistos, the divine smith and artisan; Eris, the goddess of discord; Eileithyia, the goddess of childbirth; and Hebe, the goddess of eternal youth. Interestingly, Ares' parentage is portrayed differently in Ovid's later Roman version of the divine family history. Rather than being the son of Zeus, he was said to have been engendered parthenogenically by Hera in retaliation for Zeus giving birth to Athene from his own head. But apart from Ovid, the war-god was invariably described as the son of Zeus from Homer onward, and that included his Roman version, Mars.

Zeus also fathered a long list of demigods, heroes, and founders of dynasties and city-states, of both sexes and by different mothers. Each of his children was special in one way or another, semi-divine like Herakles and Perseus or fully divine like Hermes, Athene, Apollo, and Artemis. Further myths developed around the lives of each of these children, who often ended up marrying their divine relations. The impossibly complicated family dynamics that ensued would baffle even the most brilliant of family therapists. Some of the god's children by mortal women, such as Perseus, accomplished great achievements in the world; others were catalysts for destruction resulting in a new order. An example of the latter is Helen, the daughter of Zeus and Leda. Helen was portrayed by the Greeks not only as the most desirable woman in the world but also as the cause of the destruction of the great kingdom of Troy and the rise of the Greek city-states as the embodiment of a more civilised and enlightened culture.

One of Zeus' most important characteristics in terms of his chequered romantic life was his love of disguises, expressed through his inclination to transform himself into an animal, a bird, a poor traveller, a shepherd, his chosen lover's husband, or even an inorganic substance like a shower of gold or a cloud of darkness, in order to achieve his various seductions and rapes. Each of these transformations involves specific imagery that might give us some clues to the different levels of life in which the astrological Jupiter operates and expresses its fertility.

This deity was constantly in motion, impregnating a succession of different women and always moving on to a new conquest. He never visited the same lover twice, although he remained with some of them for several nights rather than just one. And there was always a gestation period between the sexual act and the birth of his offspring which was often fraught with great danger to the mother as well as the child. This seems to be a particularly important feature of this group of stories about Zeus. The impact and meaning of Jupiter's transits aren't always discernible at the time, and the gestation period as well as the birth may be profoundly uncomfortable, as these stories illustrate.

Another important dimension of Zeus' romantic escapades was his tendency to have no involvement with the birth and upbringing of his children, other than occasionally keeping a distant watchful eye on some of them as they matured and fulfilled their own destinies. He sometimes sent help their way through other agencies, human or divine, but he never turned up to read them a bedtime story or take them to a football match or discuss their university choices or give them the keys to the car. We might see Zeus as the archetypal absent father, unavailable to his children for everyday practical care and support yet passing on to them an inherent sense of destiny that reflected his continuing life within them in the form of inspiration and intuitive vision. Variations on this theme appear in many current religious beliefs about God as Heavenly Father; he isn't available for coffee and a chat and doesn't usually respond to prayers in any obvious way, but he keeps a watchful eye on his faithful from an invisible heavenly domain.

Now let's look at a few of Zeus' many loves.

Zeus and Danaë, mother of Perseus. Zeus transforms into a shower of gold.

One of the best-known children of Zeus was the hero Perseus, whom even the mythologically challenged might recognise from films such as *Clash of the Titans*, released in 1981, with Laurence Olivier playing Zeus, and its 2010 remake, this time with Liam Neeson as the king of the gods. While the latter film and its 2012 sequel, *Wrath of the Titans*, have shamelessly tampered with the original story to placate modern ideological sensibilities – Perseus is presented as more of a left-wing political agitator than a Greek hero, and important elements of the original myth have been drastically altered or abandoned entirely – nevertheless we can see how captivating the figure of this son of Zeus has remained over the centuries. His exploits have inspired artists of every historical period, especially his conquest of the monster Medusa. His mother Danaë's seduction has also inspired many painters; this one is by Titian, who produced several versions on the theme.

Perseus was the mythic founder of the great city-state of Mycenae and the ancestor of the Perseid Dynasty. He was the half-brother, the brother-in-law, and the great-grandfather of Herakles, the first through both of them being sons of Zeus, the second through Perseus' half-sister, the goddess Hebe, marrying Herakles (her half-brother), and the third through

Titian, *Danaë* (1545-46), Museo di Capodimonte, Naples.

Herakles' mother Alkmene being Perseus' granddaughter. The therapeutic term 'enmeshed family' doesn't even begin to describe this entanglement, and don't even think of trying to draw up a family tree. These divine family dynamics suggest the interconnection of archetypal patterns as a kind of endless woven tapestry. Ultimately no single event, no single level of life, and no single individual is entirely separate or independent of the others.

Perseus' mother Danaë, whose name comes from a root meaning 'to judge', was a mortal woman, the daughter of King Acrisius of Argos. Acrisius had been warned by the Delphic Oracle that he would one day be killed by his grandson. Like so many figures in Greek myth, he tried to prevent the prophecy from being fulfilled, thereby unwittingly ensuring its fulfilment. He imprisoned his daughter in a bronze chamber open to the sky but securely locked on all sides to keep her chaste. Naturally it proved impossible to keep the impassioned god out of the chamber. Zeus transformed himself into a shower of gold which fell from the heavens through the open roof and magically impregnated Danaë.

Acrisius, still fearful of the oracle but even more fearful of angering Zeus once he discovered the truth, stopped short of having his daughter put to death. Instead, he placed Danaë and her newborn child in a locked chest and cast them into the sea. Naturally they didn't drown – Uncle Poseidon stepped in to lend a helping hand – and after many adventures during which he was assisted by various deities at the behest of his divine father, Perseus beheaded the snake-haired gorgon Medusa, rescued the princess Andromeda from the sea monster Cetus, married her, returned to Argos, architected the death of his grandfather Acrisius (thus fulfilling the oracle Acrisius had tried so hard to dodge), became King of Tiryns, and founded his dynasty.

Perseus typifies the archetypal myth of the hero because, first of all, his existence, even before his birth, threatened the established order, so his infancy was spent in grave danger. This is an echo of Zeus' own birth, faithfully mirrored in the prophecy given to Kronos that one of his children would overthrow him. This motif of the endangered childhood of the archetypal hero, whose faith in his future part in a divine plan helps him to snatch victory from the jaws of defeat, is especially relevant to the astrological Jupiter.

If you're interested in this theme, find a copy of Joseph Campbell's *The Hero With a Thousand Faces*, first published in 1949, reissued in several

Detail of Perseus wearing the winged helmet loaned to him by Hermes and brandishing the head of Medusa. Benvenuto Cellini (1545-54), Loggia del Lanzi, Florence.

editions, and denigrated in recent years by many academics opposed to Campbell's ideas about the archetypal and 'universal' nature of mythic motifs rather than the 'cultural specificity' now demanded by much of the academic establishment. The archetypal patterns that lie behind culturally specific myths *are* universal, despite strenuous efforts to ignore this fact or explain it away through 'transmission'. These two perspectives – the universality of mythic patterns and their unique cultural adaptations – are not mutually exclusive, and we can honour both the creative ingenuity of a particular culture and the commonality of our shared human experience at the same time.

Zeus' particular transformation in this story – the shower of gold – can tell us something about the astrological Jupiter. Each of the god's seductions involves a different metamorphosis and reflects a different manner through which the deity enters human experience to generate his progeny. These symbols may also tell us something about the nature of the children he fathers. In other words, the way in which we experience a transit to or from Jupiter – even if it's very difficult at the time – may suggest something about its meaning and what might eventually come out of it.

The shower of gold implies material good fortune, and this dimension of Jupiter seems to be expressed quite literally in many lives. We might hope that Jupiter's 'good luck' will come to us in concrete form, like winning the lottery or achieving advancement in our career. Sometimes it does. But it's worth looking at what else gold might symbolise, since it appears as a central motif in so many myths and fairy tales as well as in the imagery of alchemy. Gold is traditionally the Sun's metal; Jupiter's is tin.

Gold is accorded the highest value in many cultures and has been associated with royalty and divinity for millennia. Of course gold is beautiful, but more importantly, it doesn't corrode. From a mythic perspective, it's eternal and incorruptible. This may be why wedding rings are traditionally made of gold, perhaps as a demonstration of the triumph of hope over experience.[11] Silver, the Moon's metal, oxidises quickly, as do copper, which belongs to Venus, and iron, which belongs to Mars. Lead, which is Saturn's metal, also oxidises, and so does quicksilver, which belongs to Mercury.

Tin, Jupiter's metal, resists oxidisation for longer, but it too eventually corrodes. And tin doesn't have the beauty of gold, although it was essential during the Bronze Age – the period when most of these myths first emerged – for the creation of weapons. Bronze is an alloy of tin and copper, but bronze too will corrode over time. Gold coins and jewellery can remain buried in the earth for thousands of years and come out just as brilliant and unspoiled as they were when they were first made. In the ancient world gold was viewed as immortal and indestructible, as it was in alchemy, and so it was equated with the divine.

We might view this particular transformation by Zeus as a fertilisation of the imagination, and perhaps also of material life, through an experience of inner divinity – a solar conviction of essential uniqueness. Jupiter injects a sense of confidence in our individual value as part of a greater plan or purpose. This pattern of appropriating the symbols of another god appears in several myths about Zeus' amours. He seems to have enjoyed clothing

11 This phrase was attributed to Samuel Johnson in James Boswell's *Life of Samuel Johnson*, written in 1791. Johnson used it after hearing of a man who had remarried soon after the death of a wife to whom he had been unhappily married.

himself in the attributes of other deities, and this can give us a hint about one of the ways in which the planet 'works' and engenders meaning: by mobilising or 'constellating' the expressions of other planets in the chart.

Zeus and Leda, mother of the twins Castor and Polydeukes and the twins Helen and Klytaemnestra. Zeus transforms into a swan.

The story of Leda and the Swan portrays another transformation by Zeus linked to solar symbolism. In order to seduce Leda, an Aetolian princess who married King Tyndareus of Sparta, Zeus transformed into a swan and, to gain Leda's sympathy, pretended he was fleeing from an eagle's attack. I would suggest that you read William Butler Yeats' poem, *Leda and the*

Gustave Moreau, *Leda* (1875), Musée Nationale Gustave Moreau, Paris.

Swan, for an extraordinarily beautiful and explicit invocation of this divine coupling.[12]

Leda's name means 'queenly woman'. Zeus seduced her on a night during which she had also made love with her husband, and she became pregnant by both. Instead of giving birth in the usual fashion, she produced two eggs. When they hatched, each egg contained one semi-divine child, the progeny of Zeus, and one mortal child, the progeny of Leda's husband, King Tyndareus. From the first egg emerged the Dioscuri twins, Kastor and Polydeukes, known to the Romans as Castor and Pollux. Polydeukes, whose name means 'very sweet', was semi-divine, taking after his father Zeus, while Kastor, whose name means 'shining', was mortal, taking after his father Tyndareus. When Kastor died, Polydeukes begged his father Zeus to allow his twin to share his immortality, so Zeus transformed them into the constellation of Gemini, and they became the divine patrons of sailors and horsemen.

From the second egg came Helen, the semi-divine daughter of Zeus, and Klytaimnestra, the mortal daughter of King Tyndareus. Helen, whose name, appropriately for a daughter of Zeus, means 'torch' or 'light', married King Menelaos of Sparta. Because of her unearthly beauty and, taking after her father, her propensity for infidelity, she became the catalyst for the Trojan War. Klytaimnestra, the mortal child of Tyndareus, whose name means 'famous for her suitors', married King Agamemnon of Mycenae and

Robert Fagan, *Castor and Pollux* (1793-95), National Trust Collections, Attingham Park, Shropshire.

---

12 The poem is available on a number of websites; see www.poetryfoundation.org/poems/43292/leda-and-the-swan. See also *The Collected Poems of W. B. Yeats*, Wordsworth Editions (2000).

Left: Dante Gabriel Rossetti, *Helen of Troy* (1863), Hamburger Kunsthalle, Hamburg. Right, John Collier, *Clytemnestra* (1882), Guildhall Art Gallery, London.

then, enraged by his sacrifice of their daughter Iphigeneia at the outset of the Trojan War, murdered her husband and was murdered in turn by her son Orestes. Klytaimnestra's story forms the basis for Aischylos' great tragic trilogy, *The Oresteia*, one of the most powerful works of literature ever written.

Zeus presented himself to Leda as a poor frightened swan fleeing from an eagle's attack. This deception reflects the god's darkly ironic sense of humour, since the eagle is Zeus' own bird. The joke was on Leda, which is rather cruel, but the ironic humour is typical of this deity, and of the astrological Jupiter as well. The swan is Apollo's bird, so once again Zeus adopted a solar symbol to disguise himself. In Plato's dialogue *Phaedo*, Socrates declares that swans sing most beautifully before their deaths because they know they are returning to the Sun-god Apollo, the divinity to whom they belong. This is the origin of our colloquial term 'swan song'.

> And you seem to think I am inferior in prophetic power to the swans who sing at other times also, but when they feel that they are to die, sing most and best in their joy that they are to go to the god whose servants they are. But men, because of their own fear of death, misrepresent

the swans and say that they sing for sorrow, in mourning for their own death. They do not consider that no bird sings when it is hungry or cold or has any other trouble…Since they are Apollo's birds…they have foreknowledge of the blessings in the other world, and they sing and rejoice on that day more than ever before.[13]

Like the shower of gold, the swan may hint at a prescient knowledge of solar immortality which Zeus passed on to his children. They didn't necessarily use it wisely. Helen generated chaos and destruction when she ran away with the Trojan prince Paris and triggered the Greek invasion of Troy. But she herself survived the conflagration, returned to her furious but eventually forgiving husband, and lived happily with him until her death, after which they both earned entry into the Isles of the Blessed. She was clearly lucky.

Perhaps, if we view the mythic Zeus through Orphic eyes as the embodiment of the teleology of Divine Mind, the destruction of Troy was necessary to generate a new order and a new chapter in history. From the ruins of the demolished city came Aeneas, the semi-divine child of Aphrodite and the Trojan prince Anchises, whom the Romans believed to be their forefather. The Roman Empire eventually absorbed Greek culture, art, philosophy, mathematics, and law, and spread them throughout the known world. And in the story of Orestes, Klytaimnestra's son, we find an entirely new social concept: the first human jury, set up by Athene and Apollo to judge whether Orestes was right or wrong in murdering his mother to avenge his father's death at her hands.

Every semi-divine child that Zeus fathered seems to have made some kind of contribution to the future of humanity, not always earth-shattering and sometimes ethically questionable, but invariably inventive and inspired. These mythic children, who were often amoral by modern standards, seem to be part of the vision of an intricate pattern that takes many centuries, or even millennia, to come to fruition. And the 'bad' children are as essential as the 'good' ones to the fulfilment of the story. In the mythic tales they influenced history, but at the time that Zeus performed his seduction, none of the characters in the story, human or divine – except, perhaps, Zeus himself – knew how the story was going to unfold. The future is inherent

---

13 Plato, *Phaedo* 85a, in *Plato in Twelve Volumes*, Vol. 1, trans. Harold North Fowler, William Heinemann Ltd. (1966).

at the moment of Jupiter's symbolic impregnation – the oak tree inherent in the acorn – but it's usually a complete mystery from the human point of view, and the real denouement may take place many generations after the individual's own demise.

Zeus and Leto, mother of Apollo and Artemis. Zeus appears to Leto as himself.

Leto, known to the Romans as Latona, was the daughter of the Titans Coeus and Phoebe, and was therefore herself an immortal. Her name means 'hidden'. Perhaps because she was divine like him, Zeus felt he didn't need to appear as anything other than himself. Also, there was no suspicious husband or furious father lurking in the background. But Zeus had to contend with Hera's spite. When Leto became pregnant with twins, Hera was so enraged that she commanded all lands to shun the expectant mother, and Leto could find no place to find shelter and give birth to her children. Eventually, after wandering all over the Earth, she arrived at Delos, an island which the Greeks believed floated rather than being attached to the ocean floor, and which was therefore beyond Hera's command. Here, surrounded by the swans who guarded the island, she gave birth to Apollo the Sun-god and Artemis the Moon-goddess, in the shade of a palm tree.

Francesco Pozzi, *Leto with the infants Apollo and Artemis* (1824), Sculpture Gallery, Chatsworth House, Derbyshire.

Incensed still further by the failure of her efforts to prevent the birth, Hera kidnapped her own daughter Eileithyia, goddess of childbirth, to ensure that Leto's labour was hard. Apollo's birth took an agonising nine days. But it all ended well; Leto was eventually accepted on Mount Olympus and, according to Hesiod, she was the gentlest and kindest of all the Olympians, granting any wish asked of her.

The importance of these divine twins, both planetary deities themselves, seems to reflect the description of the Orphic Zeus as cosmocrator: the creator and governor of the planets and constellations.

Zeus and Metis, mother of Athene. Zeus appears to Metis as himself, but then turns himself into a giant fly and swallows her.

Metis, whose name means 'wisdom', 'skill', or 'craft', was another Titan, the goddess of wise counsel, deep thought, and magical cunning. She was the daughter of Okeanos and Tethys, primordial rulers of the sea before the advent of Poseidon. Metis was on Zeus' side from the beginning: she was responsible for giving Kronos the emetic potion that made him regurgitate Zeus' siblings, allowing Zeus to rally them, defeat Kronos, and take the throne of Olympus. But an oracle declared that she would bear Zeus a daughter wiser than her mother, and a son more

Athene, Roman, 1st c. CE, copy of a Greek original, c. 4th c. BCE, Musée du Louvre, Paris.

powerful than his father who would one day overthrow him. Apparently learning nothing from family history, Zeus, in order to cheat the oracle, turned himself into a giant fly and swallowed Metis. But even gods can't fight their *moira*. Zeus was too late to prevent half the prophecy; Metis was already pregnant with Athene.[14]

While inside Zeus' stomach, Metis, undeterred by whatever else he might have eaten, began forging a suit of armour for her unborn child. This gave Zeus terrible migraines because of all the banging and hammering. In desperation the god demanded that his son Hephaistos, the divine smith,

split his forehead open with an axe. This released Athene, who sprang forth fully armed as the goddess of wisdom, craftsmanship, and battle strategy. As with Zeus and Leto, this coupling of immortals resulted in a new divine power. But Athene took a subtle revenge on her father. As we've seen, she was responsible for breathing life and sentience into humans, conferring on them her father's Divine Breath.

Zeus and Mnemosyne, mother of the Nine Muses. Zeus transforms into a humble shepherd.

Mnemosyne was yet another Titan, daughter of Ouranos and Gaia, sister of Kronos, and therefore Zeus' aunt. She was the goddess of memory, which is what her name means in Greek. Although she was a deity in her own right, Zeus disguised

Dante Gabriel Rossetti, *Mnemosyne* (1876-81), Delaware Art Museum, Wilmington, Delaware.

14 There are several mythic variations on the theme of Zeus swallowing Metis. See Timothy Ganz, *Early Greek Myth: A Guide to Literary and Artistic Sources*, Johns Hopkins University Press (1993), pp. 51, 84, 743.

himself as a mortal shepherd in order to seduce her. He made love to her for nine consecutive nights – an unusually long period for the god to retain his erotic interest – during which time the Nine Muses were conceived. In Orphic teachings, Mnemosyne presided over the Pool of Memory in the underworld, which allowed souls who drank from it to recall their divine origin and avoid the wheel of rebirth.

The Nine Muses included Calliope (epic poetry), Clio (history), Euterpe (music and lyric poetry), Erato (love poetry), Melpomene (tragedy), Polyhymnia (hymns), Terpsichore (dance), Thalia (comedy), and Ourania (astrology). Astronomy as a science independent of astrology didn't exist when these myths were first recorded, so if you read anywhere that Ourania was the Muse of astronomy, take that with a pinch of salt. The Muses, sources of inspiration for the arts, were born from a mother associated with the recollection of the soul and the memory of its divine origin. This myth raises interesting questions about what we define as art, and about the deeper purpose of human artistic creativity.

I have no explanation for why Zeus chose to appear as a simple shepherd to generate these divine sources of creative vision, nor how Mnemosyne managed to keep him interested for so long. Perhaps he knew

Gustave Moreau, *Hesiod and the Muse* (1891), Musée d'Orsay, Paris. As Hesiod was one of the greatest Greek epic poets, the Muse portrayed is probably Calliope.

the importance of the Muses for the future of human creativity. His disguise might be related to the humble but important nature of an ancient shepherd's role as guardian of a vulnerable flock, and the enduring power of that symbol.

In Christian teaching, the shepherds were the first to receive the revelation of Jesus' divine birth, and Jesus himself has been portrayed as the 'Good Shepherd' for two millennia. In Psalms 77:21, God is described as a shepherd who leads his flock through the wilderness. And David is presented as a humble shepherd boy who was chosen by God to conquer the giant Goliath and become not only the next King of Israel but also the creator of the Psalms. Maybe it's when we're closest to our ordinary humanity and genuinely responsive to our own and others' vulnerability that we're particularly receptive to Jupiter's creative inspiration.

Zeus and Maia, mother of Hermes. Zeus transforms into a cloud of darkness.

Maia, from whom the month of May takes its name, was another Titan, eldest of the Pleiades, the seven daughters of Atlas and Pleione. Maia was a nymph of the mountains, and her official job description was to bring rain. Her name in Greek is an honorific for an older woman and means 'mother'

Hermes with his mother Maia, Greek red-figure vase, c. 500 BCE, Bavarian State Collection of Antiquities, Munich. Hermes wears his ubiquitous 'traveller's hat' and holds the 'pan-pipes' which he invented and which became the favoured musical instrument of shepherds.

or 'midwife'. Disguised as a cloud of darkness, Zeus seduced her in her solitary cave on Mount Kyllene, where she lived apart from her sisters. Their child was Hermes, one of the most important of Zeus' divine progeny and, like Apollo and Artemis, a planetary god.

Hermes can't be defined by the rulership of any single sphere of life. He's the god of connections, and his conception in darkness seems to reflect the mysterious and hidden manner in which these connections between different domains and levels of life exist and are themselves secrets whose revelation can transform consciousness. Alchemy, which was sometimes referred to as the Great Secret, places Hermes-Mercurius at the centre of the alchemical work: the invisible transformative agent that unites opposing substances in the darkness of the alembic and transmutes them into a single divine essence, the Philosophers' Stone or elixir, that always secretly existed in embryonic form at their core.

It seems that Hermes' mother Maia was truly a 'midwife' in the most profound sense. It also seems that Zeus could not only adopt the symbols of the Sun, like gold and the swan; he could also appear through his progeny in the guise of what Jung called the 'transcendent function', which can unite the opposites within the personality, spur the development of consciousness, and allow a glimpse of the inner core, the Self, which embodies the essence and teleology of the individual.

Zeus and Semele, mother of Dionysos. Zeus transforms into his full and lethal divine glory.

In Orphic texts, the goddess Persephone was the mother of Dionysos. But in classical myth the god's mother was Semele, a mortal princess of Thebes. Interestingly, her name means 'Earth'. When Zeus began courting her, Hera, indulging in a predictable hissy fit, disguised herself as an old nurse and persuaded Semele that, if the god promised her a gift in return for her favours, she should ask him to reveal himself in his full glory.

In her naivete Semele obeyed the old nurse's instructions and held Zeus to his promise to give her anything she asked for. She demanded that he reveal his divinity to her. He protested, knowing the dreadful result, but she insisted, so he complied. As a result she was burned to death, because no mortal could survive the full impact of Zeus' immortal radiance. But at the moment of her passing, she conceived his child. The embryonic Dionysos was rescued from her dead womb by Hermes, his half-brother, and sewn into Zeus' thigh. Eventually Zeus gave birth to the child. After this unusual entry into the world, Dionysos was known as 'twice-born'.

It's tempting to speculate on the symbolism of this strange story. Are we humans unable to grasp the full implications of Jupiter because we would be overwhelmed by so much prescient knowledge? This myth might give us some insight into what a powerful religious experience can do to the recipient, especially if they lack the capacity for conscious reflection and don't possess a vocabulary of their own, verbal or visual, which might provide grounding and a creative container for the encounter.

Perhaps Hera, the 'root' of Earth, will always take her revenge if we're foolish enough to display such *hubris* and assume we have a right to such knowledge. Semele's name tells us that she, like us, is a creature of Earth. We may get intuitions of some kind of meaningful pattern or plan in life, but we

Gustave Moreau, *Jupiter and Semele* (1889), Musée Gustave Moreau, Paris.

can never grasp the entirety; it would certainly drive us mad. Fantasy and science fiction novels and films often tap deep archetypal patterns, often without meaning to. Some of you might remember the dramatic conclusion of the 2008 film *Indiana Jones and the Kingdom of the Crystal Skull*, when the Russian commander Irina Spalko, played by Cate Blanchett, demanded to 'know everything' from the interdimensional entities and was destroyed when her request was granted. It's a modern rendition of Zeus and Semele, although there's no pregnancy and no Dionysos afterwards.

Zeus and Europa, mother of King Minos of Crete. Zeus transforms into a bull.

Europa was a Phoenician princess from Tyre. Her name means 'wide-seeing', and she enjoys the distinction not only of bearing three semi-divine children to Zeus, but also of having the continent of Europe named after her. Her liaison with the god is mentioned in Homer's *Iliad*, but the story is much older and originates in Crete. Zeus saw Europa, immediately desired her, and came up with a plan.

The god transformed himself into a pure white bull and mingled innocently with her father's herds. Europa admired the magnificent creature and went over to caress its flanks, and then, rather naively, climbed onto its back. Clearly no one had warned her not to speak to strange bulls. Zeus, still in his bull-shape, instantly rushed to the sea and began to swim, with the terrified girl still clinging to him. He took Europa to Crete, where he fathered three sons on her, of whom Minos, the eldest, whose name means 'king', was the greatest.

Minos, living up to his name, grew up to become the most powerful of all the kings of Crete. Zeus, to commemorate his union with Europa, placed the white bull in the heavens as the constellation of Taurus. After their deaths, Minos and his younger brother Rhadamanthos became judges of the souls of the dead in the underworld. This mythic role continued into the Christian era; Michelangelo, Gustave Doré, and William Blake all portrayed Minos as a human figure entwined with serpents, judging the souls of the damned in Hell.

Although in astrology we associate the astrological sign of Taurus with its planetary ruler Venus, in myth the goddess Aphrodite's animal counterpart was the dove. In the archaic Greek world, the bull was the main

Europa on the bull, while a friend tries to stop the animal's rush to the sea. The bull in this Roman fresco is brown, but Homer described it as pure white. House of Jason at Pompeii, 1st c. CE, Museo Archeologico Nazionale, Naples.

animal form of Poseidon, reflecting the raw power of nature when the god, abiding in subterranean waterways in his bull-shape, became angry, shook the earth, toppled cities, and flooded the land with tidal waves. Once again Zeus seems to have appropriated the symbol of another deity, in this case his brother Poseidon: not just as god of the sea, but also as the embodiment of the destructive power of the waters erupting from within the earth itself. If we're psychologically minded, we might see this as a strikingly apt symbol of a psychotic break: sub-terranean emotions, long buried, erupt and flood the earthbound rational ego. The bull as a symbol of sexual power and fertility is also relevant. I don't think anyone would argue with the fact that powerful sexual desire can be one of the most potent instruments that drives us to become what we are meant to be – often at great cost and the risk of a metaphorical earthquake or tidal wave in our personal lives.

Like Helen, King Minos was a child of Zeus who behaved badly, resulting in his personal humiliation, the destruction of his kingdom, and the rise of Athens as a great power. Minos' error was due to *hubris*. For a long time he ruled his kingdom wisely and, according to Homer's *Odyssey*, consulted with his father Zeus every nine years and received his laws straight from the god. Poseidon, Minos' divine uncle, also favoured him and gifted him a magnificent white bull to keep in his herd until the moment when it had

Minos judging the souls of the damned. Engraving by Gustave Doré (1861-65)
for his late 19th-century edition of Dante's *Inferno*.

to be sacrificed to the god. The white bull was a commemoration of Minos'
own conception, and along with it came the gift of Cretan dominance over
the Mediterranean and all the lands bordering on it.

But Minos, when the time came to offer the bull back to the god,
decided to cheat Poseidon and keep the animal for himself, to enhance
his prestige and breed valuable bovine offspring from it. Deeply offended,
Poseidon called on Aphrodite to afflict the king's wife Pasiphaë with an
obsessive passion for the bull. They mated and the result was the Minotaur,
half-human and half-bull: a monster that fed on human flesh and had to be
contained within the Labyrinth.

This not only shamed Minos but resulted in the Athenian hero
Theseus slaying the monster and taking the throne of Crete after a great
earthquake, accompanied by a tidal wave, overwhelmed the island. Unlike
Helen, Minos was unlucky. But apparently he was forgiven; Zeus honoured
him and his brother Rhadamanthos by making them judges of souls in the
underworld. However, it can't have been a pleasant job, and the brothers
could never get any paid holidays or permission to work from home. Zeus'
'honouring' may have been ironic.

Zeus and Alkmene, mother of Herakles. Zeus transforms into Alkmene's husband Amphitryon.

Alkmene was the granddaughter of Perseus, and therefore Zeus' great-granddaughter. Her name means 'strength from wrath'. She married Amphitryon, a prince of Tiryns, and always behaved as a loving and loyal wife. But a woman's fidelity to her husband never deterred Zeus, nor did an incestuous liaison with his own great-grandaughter. He just needed the right disguise. While Amphitryon was away on a military expedition, Zeus transformed himself into the absent prince's likeness and seduced Alkmene. The god enjoyed it so much that he commanded Helios to keep the Sun from rising for three days.

Detail from Nicholas Tardieu, *Alcmene and Zeus disguised as Amphitryon* (c. 1730), British Museum.

Amphitryon returned from battle immediately afterwards and made love to his wife on the same night, so Zeus managed to get away with the deception – at least for a while – even after she became pregnant by the god. The result of their union was Herakles, the greatest of the Greek heroes. Hera, predictably, remained Herakles' bitter enemy for the entirety of his life.

The 'Farnese' Herakles, 3rd c. CE Roman copy of a Hellenistic Greek original by Lysippos, Museo Archeologico Nazionale, Naples.

Zeus and Ganymede, who became cupbearer of the gods. Zeus transforms into an eagle.

Ganymede was the son of Tros, a great-grandson of Zeus. The great city-state of Troy had not yet risen to power, but this family is described in the *Iliad* as the founding dynasty of the later Trojan kingdom. Ganymede's attractions were so great that Zeus was determined not just to seduce him,

Roman mosaic of Jupiter and Ganymede, 2nd c. CE,
Museo Nazionale Romano, Rome.

but to possess him permanently. According to the *Homeric Hymn to Aphrodite*, the god "carried off golden-haired Ganymedes because of his beauty, to be amongst the Deathless Ones and pour drink for the gods in the house of Zeus".[15]

To accomplish the abduction, Zeus transformed himself into an eagle, his avian *alter ego*. Like many Greek deities, Zeus enjoyed lovers of both sexes. In this story there is no progeny. But Ganymede's ascension to immortality suggests a permanent connection with the divine, portrayed as an act of eternal service to it.

---

15 *Homeric Hymn to Aphrodite*, 5:202-205, in *Hesiod: The Homeric Hymns and Homerica*, trans. H. G. Evelyn-White (William Heinemann, 1914).

The 'purpose' of Zeus' liaisons

These are only a few examples from a very long list of Zeus' lovers. Many of them have provided creative inspiration for artists and poets for many centuries. The range of Zeus' choices, from mortal women and young boys to Titans, nymphs, and goddesses, reflects the vast range of his potential for seeding. But only a few of Zeus' love affairs had no destructive consequences, even if the ultimate outcome was a happy one.

Often these amours invoked great rage and spite in his wife Hera, with ugly results. Herakles, for example, was driven mad by Hera, and in his deranged state murdered his own wife and children. And Io, an Argive princess whom Zeus desired, was transformed into a cow by Hera, who then sent a gadfly to torment the creature with constant stings. Danger to the life of the mother as well as the child is a common theme, as well as families torn apart by suspicion, jealousy, and fear. We should never assume that Jupiter's 'benefic' potentials are invariably or immediately accompanied by fun, good fortune, and happiness. Some potentials may involve a difficult gestation, a great deal of suffering, and a hard birth.

There might be subtler reasons why Zeus was drawn to a particular mortal woman, a particular youth, or a particular goddess, beyond simple sexual desire aroused by physical beauty. Sometimes the name of the desired object can give us a clue. I mentioned earlier that the name Maia, the mother of Hermes, means 'midwife'. Hermes not only played this part quite literally in the birth of the infant Dionysos out of Zeus' thigh, but was also, in his alchemical role, the midwife of consciousness and trans-formation. The name Alkmene, mother of Herakles, means 'strong from wrath'. Herakles was certainly capable of misplaced destructive wrath – he seems to have inherited his father's foul temper – but he also possessed the immense courage that springs from justified rage, allowing him to serve as protector of the people and the destroyer of deadly creatures like the Lernaean Hydra and the Nemean Lion, enemies of human life.

But if we think about a 'purpose' for each of Zeus' mythic liaisons, it would have been impossible for any mortal to know, at the time, what his intentions were. Perhaps the god didn't know himself – unless we think of him in the Orphic context, in which case he would have known everything. Jupiterian teleology may well be benefic in terms of the unfolding of a meaningful design. But what it feels like at the time may be surprisingly painful. Jupiterian experiences vary enormously. They might be fortunate, happy, and joyful. Or they might involve a lot of unhappiness and a teleology that the brevity of a single human lifespan prevents us from knowing. As with anything involving Jupiter, we can only trust in the ultimate meaning of what we can't foresee.

When we get swept along by that "Yes, I really must do that!" moment of Jupiterian inspiration, it isn't simple desire. It's not an equivalent to Martial passion or Plutonian obsession or Venusian delight, although aspects to natal Jupiter from other planets can involve other levels of experience. But with Jupiter there's always something else at work. Just beneath the surface is a sense that there are wider possibilities inherent in our choices at that moment. Something important could come out of that hunch, that vision, that longing. It's more complex than mere gratification or simple excess.

It's interesting to consider whether the mythic Zeus' romantic escapades were driven by teleology – the knowledge that the child of that particular union would found a kingdom, slay monsters, or lead to the destruction of a city – or whether the god was simply pursuing the desires of the moment without any thought of collateral damage or seeding the future. Perhaps the answer is, 'Both'. There seems to be an intent shrouded in mystery, spurred by the promise of instant gratification.

Hindsight might reveal a sense of the intentions of the god. But astrology can sometimes give us a clue. Natal Jupiter can offer hints about the area in our lives where we're likely to be presented with a succession of doors opening onto a path into the future. And a natal planet transited by Jupiter might tell us something about what dimension of our lives is being inspired and fertilised. Although this may not offer any clarity about the precise course of events in the concrete world, it can inspire a strong sense of hope and a faith in future possibilities.

The vengeful Zeus: Prometheus' theft of fire

The mythic Zeus could be vengeful and unforgiving if crossed, and sometimes even when he merely imagined he was being crossed, or thought that he might be crossed at some time in the future. This is one of his most pronounced attributes, although we don't usually associate this kind of vindictiveness with the 'Greater Benefic'. Although he was known in the Greek world as Zeus *Soter* (Saviour), Zeus *Meilichios* (Gracious

One), and Zeus *Epidotes* (Giver of Good), he could display cruel, spiteful, and vindictive behaviour. One of the most unattractive examples of this tendency can be found in the myth of the Titan Prometheus.

Prometheus, who was responsible for creating humans, was convinced they had far more potential than they were able to express. He made his creatures from earth and water, and Athene breathed life and mind into them. As they were now equipped with three of the four elements – earth, water, and air – perhaps Prometheus, whose name means 'forethought', could envisage that they could be godlike if they possessed the element of fire as well. The Titan stole some of Zeus' divine fire from the god's lightning-bolt, brought it to Earth in a hollow fennel stalk, and gave it to human beings. This might not have been a good idea.

Heinrich Füger, *The Creation of Man by Prometheus* (1817), Palais Liechtenstein, Vienna.

In his great epic tragedy, *Prometheus Bound*, Aischylos, writing in the 5th century BCE, equated Zeus' stolen fire with knowledge allied with vision, and with the revelation of the crafts and sciences of building, carpentry, agriculture, navigation, metallurgy, mathematics, writing, and astronomy.[16] Forethought, ingenuity, and creative inventiveness help us to face the future with hope and make the best use of our potentials. Aischylos' idea of Zeus' fire as the source of creative vision in the sciences complements the Nine Muses, Zeus' daughters, as the source of creative vision in the arts, hinting at the astrological Jupiter's relationship with inspired imagination on every level of life.

Zeus' punishment of Prometheus was swift and ruthless, and certainly earned him another, less complementary epithet: Zeus *Labrandios*, 'The Raging One'. He had Prometheus chained to a rock in the Caucasus mountains. Each day Zeus' eagle would peck out Prometheus' liver, and each night the liver would regenerate. Because Prometheus was an immortal, he couldn't die, but was condemned to suffer this agony daily for eternity, until Chiron's sacrifice of his own immortality released the Titan from his bondage.

Prometheus' release didn't sweeten Zeus' animosity towards humans. Whether he feared their future power or foresaw their potential for destruction, the god decided to make them suffer by instructing Hephaistos to create Pandora, a composite creature whose name means 'all-gifted'. She was equipped with impressive qualities, each one donated by a different deity. When she descended from Hephaistos' workshop to Earth, she brought a jar with her as Zeus' gift to humans. But as Homer insisted, we should beware the Greeks bearing gifts. The jar – it was never described as a 'box' in ancient sources – contained every possible evil that could afflict human beings. It also contained Hope, which is generally interpreted as a good thing. However, Friedrich Nietzsche once declared that hope "is the worst of all evils, because it prolongs man's torments".[17] Perhaps the inclusion of Hope in Pandora's jar is another example of Zeus' dark sense of irony.

Although she was instructed not to open the jar, one of Pandora's attributes, which she received from Hermes, was curiosity, a trait of which

---

16 See Aeschylos, *Prometheus Bound*, trans. E. H. Plumptre, David McKay, London (1931), pp. 102-109.
17 Friedrich Nietzsche, *Human, All Too Human: A Book for Free Spirits* (2012), p. 53.

Zeus was fully aware. Hesiod, who seems to have disliked women, referred to Pandora's curiosity as 'a shameless mind and a deceitful nature'.[18] Inevitably Pandora pried the lid off the jar and inadvertently released all the evils contained inside.

Pandora's jar seems to reflect the preordained lot of humans. We're gifted creatures blessed with Promethean inspiration, but we exist in mortal bodies and each of us has a shadowside. Therefore, thanks to Pandora, we suffer, feel physical pain, injure and kill each other and ourselves, experience envy, pride, greed, wrath, hatred, spite, and cruelty, become sick, feel despair and desolation, become

John William Waterhouse, *Pandora* (1896), private collection. Waterhouse appears to have adopted the common misconception of a box.

old and frail, and then die without knowing what will become of us afterwards. Yet we also have hope, no matter how bad it gets – although, as Nietzsche suggested, disappointed hope is one of the chief sources of bitterness and depression. Zeus' revenge through Pandora describes everything that makes us suffer as living beings. Yet it seems that the

18 Hesiod, *Works and Days*, trans. Hugh G. Evelyn-White, William Heinemann, London (1914), 67-68. There are numerous variations in the early myths of Pandora; see Ganz, *Early Greek Myths*, pp. 155-58 and 162-65.

enigmatic god ensured that, despite his vindictive punishment, we would find the optimism to keep going anyway.

The vengeful Zeus: The Great Flood

All that Zeus feared after humans received the gift of fire began to unfold as he had foreseen. They became increasingly arrogant and full of *hubris*, failed to honour him, and began to treat the worship of all the deities with disrespect. Like Yahweh in the Old Testament, Zeus decided to finally destroy these recalcitrant creatures by sending a Great Flood. But as in the Biblical story, and the earlier Babylonian myth on which that story was based, humans managed to survive.

According to Genesis 6:11-9:19, Noah and his family were allowed to escape the Flood because God judged them as virtuous and deserving of life. Zeus, on the other hand, apparently couldn't find anyone worth saving. The elderly couple who survived Zeus' Great Flood were rescued not through his mercy but through the agency of Prometheus, who had his own investment in humanity's eventual success. The couple were called Deucalion and Pyrrha, and they were too old to bear children. But Deucalion was the son of Prometheus, and the Titan wasn't prepared to see his own progeny, let alone the entire human race, destroyed.

Prometheus warned Deucalion about the Flood and, like Yahweh in the story of Noah, instructed him in how to build a huge boat, so the couple managed to escape the inundation of the waters. Afterwards Zeus relented and allowed them to repopulate the Earth – an ambiguous act of kindness, rather like inserting Hope into Pandora's jar – by throwing 'the bones of your mother' (the stones that form the backbone of the Earth) over their

Domenico Beccafumi, *Deucalion and Pyrrha* (1520), Museo Horne, Florence.

shoulders. Deucalion's stones became men, Pyrrha's stones became women, and human beings once again began to go forth and multiply.

This spiteful quality highlights an aspect of Jupiter that we might rather not think about. We could view the god's distaste for humans as a kind of spiritual superiority; he is, in a way, a kind of religious or ideological zealot who must stamp out any person or attitude that isn't aligned with his own truth. Zeus could be capricious, arrogant and, using a more modern term, narcissistic. He couldn't bear competition and he didn't want humans to have any real freedom to develop, in case they became his equals and challenged his plans for the future. We can see some of the same qualities in Yahweh, who can also be a problematic deity, unpredictable and apparently impervious to human suffering. A disturbing example is his behaviour in the *Book of Job*.

When we look later at the psychology of narcissism, which has a strong connection to the astrological Jupiter, we'll see how this unforgiving aspect of the deity can relate to certain destructive psychological patterns. Yet paradoxically, Zeus still allowed Hope to be included in Pandora's jar and permitted Deucalion and Pyrrha to survive the Flood and repopulate the earth. Giving the god the benefit of the doubt, we might say that his spite and vindictiveness were paradoxically balanced by his compassion and generosity.

Jupiter as heavenly psychopomp

In Roman myth, Jupiter, in the form of his eagle, carried the soul of a deified hero or emperor to the heavens. The role of psychopomp, which means 'conductor of souls', was in earlier Greek myth fulfilled by Hermes the Traveller. The Roman ascent of the soul to the heavens was known as catasterism, from the Greek *katasterismos*, meaning 'to place among the stars': the transformation after death into a star or constellation or, viewed another way, eternal heavenly life. Catasterism occurs in Greek myth as well. Herakles was transformed into the constellation we know as Hercules; Amalthea became the constellation of Capricorn; the white bull of Minos became the constellation of Taurus; the seven Pleiades, one of whom was Maia, mother of Hermes, became the cluster of stars still called by that name; Kallisto, another of Zeus' lovers, became the constellation we know as Ursa Major; and the Dioscuri twins, Castor and Pollux, became the constellation of Gemini. Many other mythic demigods, hybrid beings, and even inanimate objects like Orpheus' lyre, were transformed into heavenly constellations.

In Roman times, ordinary mortals too could achieve celestial glory and deification, if they were sufficiently worthy – which usually meant emperors and their wives, or important military leaders. Julius Caesar was catasterised after his murder, and a number of later Roman emperors were deified and were believed to be carried up to heaven by Jupiter after their deaths. This image is a bas-relief of the emperor Antoninus Pius and his wife Faustina from the 2nd century CE, showing the newly catasterised couple taken up to their heavenly abode by a winged *daimon* or god and accompanied by Jupiter's eagles.

Detail of a column base portraying the celestial apotheosis of the Roman emperor Antoninus Pius and his wife Faustina, 2nd c. CE, originally in the Campus Martius, Rome; Musei Vaticani.[19]

---

19 The figure on the lower left of the bas-relief, holding an obelisk, represents the Campus Martius, the site of imperial deification ceremonies. The figure on the lower right is the goddess Roma, who was usually portrayed, like Athene (the Roman Minerva), complete with shield and battle helmet. Her shield depicts the twins Romulus and Remus, founders of the city of Rome, being suckled by a she-wolf.

No scholar has so far been able to declare for certain the identity of the winged figure in the bas-relief. It could be a *genius*, the spirit-protector of the individual, roughly equivalent to the individual *daimon* in Platonic literature. It's sometimes been described as Aion, the personification of Eternity. It might be Mercury-Hermes in his role as psychopomp. Or it might even be Jupiter himself in youthful form. But the god's presence is made clear through his eagles, and Antoninus Pius bears a sceptre with an eagle at its head. The fig leaf, by the way, is a later Vatican addition.

We don't usually think of the astrological Jupiter as a significator of death. But the planet can often be seen making an important transit, or being transited, in the natal chart at the time of an individual's passing, and sometimes it may be active in a person's chart at the time of the death of a loved one. In themselves, such transits don't indicate death, which is difficult if not impossible to predict in a literal way. But if death does occur when Jupiter is active in the chart, it may reflect the experience as an experience of release, a freeing of the soul from the burden of the suffering body. Equally, when Jupiter is active in the chart during a painful crisis or time of loss, like the death of a loved one, there's often an underlying theme of release or freedom from some kind of worldly or emotional burden, although it may not feel that way at the time.

The psychology of Jupiter

Jupiter and the *puer aeternus*

Now I'd like to explore the psychology of Jupiter, which may help to clarify why all those myths I've been discussing can be so helpful in understanding the astrological symbol. I'll start with the archetypal figure known in psychological circles as the *puer aeternus*, the 'eternal youth'. The quintessential character in Western literature most characteristic of this figure is Peter Pan. When Captain Hook asks him, "Pan, who and what art thou?", Peter replies: "I'm youth, I'm joy... I'm a little bird that has broken out of the egg."[20]

Edward Mason Eggleston, *The Paradise of Peter Pan* (1932), published as a calendar print (1934) by Thomas D. Murphy Co., Red Oak, Iowa.

Mercury and the *puer*

The term *puer aeternus* means 'eternal youth'. Although the Latin word *puer* is masculine in gender, the psychological dynamic it describes is applicable to any human being. The figure is usually imaged as a beautiful boy or young man, not because it's limited to men, but because it reflects a quality of youthful energy that's dynamic rather than receptive. This figure is sometimes associated with Hermes-Mercury, and Eggleston's painting of

---

20 J. M. Barrie, *Peter and Wendy [Peter Pan]* (1904), Chapter XV.

Peter Pan, if a pair of winged sandals was added, could easily be a portrait of the god.

Some female deities display many of the characteristics of the *puer*, either occasionally or as a fundamental part of their nature. Artemis and Helen of Troy, both the children of Zeus, might be viewed in this way, and Aphrodite also exhibits *puer* behaviour, making her a *puella*, the feminine gender of the Latin noun. There are also solar elements in the *puer*, symbolised by the motif of the Divine Child and the sense of specialness and immortality that this image conveys. However, Hermes is the mythic figure most commonly associated with the *puer*, especially as he's portrayed in alchemical texts and images, where in his guise of Mercurius he symbolises the elusive transformative agent responsible for the generation of the Philosopher's Stone or alchemical gold.

Jupiter and the *puer*

But the *puer aeternus* is more multidimensional than the astrological Mercury or any other single astrological significator, and Jupiter is also related to this figure and as relevant as Mercury in understanding the psychology of the *puer*. In ancient Roman texts, the god Jupiter was described as *iuvenis*, an adjective on which our word 'juvenile' is based and which encompasses a range of qualities including 'youthful', 'adolescent', 'callow', and 'immature'. While there are certainly attributes that are Mercurial and solar in the *puer*, the Jupiterian qualities are equally obvious, especially in the mythic Zeus' perennial restlessness and inclination to shape-shift. Exploring this archetypal figure as it's understood in psychology can give us a lot of insight into the astrological Jupiter.

Jung referred to the archetype of the *puer* as the opposite face of the *senex*, the 'old man', who is portrayed as a specifically Saturnian figure in alchemical engravings, right down to the long beard, the lame or missing leg, and the scythe. Jung understood the polarity of *puer* and *senex* to comprise half of a fourfold masculine archetype, completed by the polarity of the warrior and the poet. Among the traditional planets, the warrior seems to be an obvious image of Mars. But the poet is less easily equated with a planetary symbol, unless we relate him to the Sun-god Apollo, patron of music and poetry. Although we might be inclined to associate the astrological Neptune with Jung's description of the poet as a masculine archetype, the sea-god in Roman myth had no inclination for poetry, nor did his Greek antecedent, Poseidon.

Archetypes and individual psychology

In his early writings, Jung, who was still constrained by the world-view of his cultural milieu, viewed the psychology of the *puer* as entirely problematic, interpreting it as an immature psychological state that needed to be outgrown. Perhaps he had difficulty at the time in dealing with his own *puer* inclinations. In the original version of *Symbols of Transformation*, first published in German in 1912 – just at the time he parted ways with Freud – he stated:

> The lovely apparition of the *puer aeternus* is, alas, a form of illusion. In reality he is a parasite on the mother, a creature of her imagination, who only lives when rooted in the maternal body.[21]

Jung's later interpretations of the *puer*, especially after he'd begun to explore alchemy more deeply, became less judgemental and less linked to a mother-complex. But some later descriptions of the *puer* by Jungians focused on the psychological expression of this figure as emotionally deficient and lacking in the capacity for empathy and deep commitment. Chief among these writers was Marie-Louise von Franz, whose book on the theme, called *The Problem of the Puer Aeternus* – the title immediately reveals her perspective before you've even opened the book – is full of rich insight, but also full of value judgements that could distort our under-standing of this mythic figure.[22]

Von Franz acknowledges the *puer*'s attractiveness and magnetism, as well as 'a certain kind of spirituality': "Many have the charm of youth and the stirring quality of a drink of champagne." But she emphasises the *puer*'s reluctance to take responsibility for the consequences of personal choices and actions or tolerate a committed emotional bond. These behavioural patterns certainly seem to be on blatant display in some individuals in whom the archetypal pattern, often reflected by a strong Jupiter and its

---

21 C. G. Jung, *Symbols of Transformation*, CW5 (1952), a revision of *Wandlungen und Symbole der Libido* (1912), ¶393.

22 Marie-Louise von Franz, *The Problem of the Puer Aeternus* (Spring Publications, 1970).

zodiacal signs, appears to dominate other aspects of the personality. But the 'pathological' elements may, like beauty, sometimes be in the eyes of the beholder.

James Hillman's work on the theme, *Senex and Puer*, offers a necessary balance to von Franz' approach, and it's a good idea to read both of them.[23] Viewing the *puer* as an archetypal image rather than a reflection of problematic behaviour, Hillman has far more empathy with this figure. If we want to understand the *puer* as an important facet of the astrological Jupiter, we may need to separate the archetypal pattern from its expressions in any particular individual, just as we need to separate the astrological Jupiter as a general symbol from its expressions in a particular individual's birth chart. The complex nature of an individual chart – with every planetary aspect, sign, and house placement each contributing to the story, combined with the often underestimated capacity for individual choice and shifts in conscious awareness – can contradict any general moral judgement on the *puer*. So can cultural norms, which vary not only from place to place, but from century to century and even from decade to decade.

Jupiter can reflect the best and the worst of the *puer*. It depends on an individual's capacity – and willingness – to integrate this archetypal pattern according to how it 'sits' in the birth chart and relates to other natal planets and the balance of elements. And measuring a capacity for commitment may also depend on the specific needs of others. Whether someone is 'appropriately' committed can sometimes be a highly subjective judgement, depending on the level on which the commitment is felt and expressed.

Sexual fidelity, for example, many not always reflect emotional commitment, and emotional commitment may be deep and enduring despite sexual infidelity. A partner's, parent's, child's, or friend's apparent callousness and lack of empathy may appear to someone else as a refreshing willingness to allow breathing space in a relationship. It's interesting how the *puer* seems to polarise so many analysts, who feel they need to side with or oppose the archetypal figure depending on their own individual natures.

---

23 James Hillman, *Senex and Puer: Uniform Edition of the Writings of James Hillman*, Vol. 3:03 (Spring Publications, 2005). This book is a compilation of several published papers on the theme.

Literature is full of characters who reflect the *puer* archetype. In addition to Peter Pan, the Little Prince in the novella of that name by Antoine de St Exupéry is often mentioned by analysts. And some of Shakespeare's non-human characters, like Ariel in *The Tempest* and Puck in *A Midsummer Night's Dream*, portray many of the elusive, spiritually or imaginatively focused, arrogant, mischievous, and apparently amoral attributes of the *puer*.

As there's often an acute receptivity to the deeper levels of the unconscious in those in whom the archetypal pattern is dominant, the psychology of the *puer* involves living in a realm of endless intuitive possibilities, free of the limitations and responsibilities of ordinary everyday life. The pasture is always greener and the imagined potentials of the future are always more compelling than the tiresome routines and restrictions of the present. The *puer* can't tolerate the dreariness and indignity of an ordinary mortal fate. Puck makes clear his disdain for ordinary human foibles when he declares: "Lord, what fools these mortals be!"

Some of the most creative dimensions of the *puer* expressed through the human personality are displayed in the inspirational nature of intuitive vision, the capacity to see through and around obstacles, the gift of grasping paradoxes, the joy and humour that transform others' monochrome lives into landscapes full of colour, and the ability to pursue hopeful possibilities even in the darkest circumstances. For the *puer* there's always light at the end of the tunnel, even if more sensible people insist that it's really an oncoming train. Peter Pan gives it away when he says, "I am youth, I am joy." "Tomorrow", Scarlett O'Hara declares hopefully in *Gone With the Wind*, "is another day."

One of the more challenging facets of the *puer* expressed through human behaviour lies in a difficulty in honouring long-term commitments, completing any task that requires patience and attention to detail, and dealing with any worldly reality – emotional, financial, physical, sexual – once it's begun to become monotonous and spoils the joyful fantasy of the ideal image that always beckons just around the corner in a possible future. Callousness and insensitivity to the feelings of others can be a destructive trait, and feeling bored, trapped, and stifled is a characteristic response to any sense of constraint in relationship. Relationships often provide the arena for the *puer*'s pursuit of the impossible, the unobtainable, the illicit, and the endlessly new, and many individuals who are perfectly capable of carrying responsibilities in their working environment find they can't deal with such limits in their personal lives.

You can see how all this relates to the mythology of Zeus, with his volatility and his endless amours. Perhaps this is one of the reasons why the *puer* so often polarises psychologists attempting to describe the archetype. If we've been deeply hurt, betrayed, or abandoned by a *puer* lover, partner, friend, parent, or child, we'll be more likely to view the archetype as pathological. We all have Jupiter somewhere in the birth chart, and there's a bit of the *puer* in every one of us. Some people are terrified of the instability implied by this volatility, and try to stifle it. Others project it and repeatedly become involved with people who seem to embody the *puer*'s pattern. Still others identify with it at the expense of their loved ones and the stability of their everyday lives.

Like anything else in the birth chart, Jupiter as *puer aeternus* can be mobilised as a defence against other, more painful and vulnerable dimensions of the personality. The person with Venus conjunct Saturn in Scorpio square Pluto, for example, may fear the potential hurt and humiliation of too deep an attachment, and may unconsciously adopt *puer* behaviour as a form of protection if Jupiter and its signs are also strong in the natal chart. The *puer* poses a particular kind of psychological dilemma, and often the person seeking help for that dilemma may admit, "I have a problem with commitment." Equally often they might project the *puer* and complain, "My partner has a problem with commitment." We'll look at this pattern more closely later in some example charts.

Although the excesses of the *puer* may sometimes be related to apparently intractable conflicts in personal life that are echoed in the birth chart, the archetypal pattern is not in itself pathological. Archetypes aren't inclined to bow to our definitions of 'normal' or 'abnormal', and they always reflect paradoxes and a broad spectrum of expressions. The *puer* is a symbol of the joy and potential of youth, the inspired pursuit of future possibilities, and the endless fertility of the creative imagination. These Jupiterian qualities fuel our will to live, and they're essential if we hope to find joy and meaning in life.

If we view the *puer*'s pattern only as a psychological problem, we may as well declare that all young people are pathological. Some might even agree with that assessment; as Oscar Wilde once declared, "Youth is wasted on the young." But viewing the *puer* solely as a problem also means not only writing off youth, but also condemning all older people to a grey, twilight existence in which they're expected to 'act their age'. They're not supposed to take risks, spend their money on themselves, drive a sexy car, dress flamboyantly, have exciting sex, or enjoy any real fun unless it involves sitting around the table playing card games in a care home. Generational divides are exacerbated and made corrosive by this kind of polarising. Humans of any age, background, and situation need a good dose of the *puer* in some shape or form to feel life is worth living.

Jupiter and narcissism

We're looking at something much darker when we explore the theme of narcissism. But the word is often misused. Accusing someone of being a 'narcissist' has become quite fashionable lately as a term of abuse used, often indiscriminately, against politicians and celebrities we don't like, as well as against people we know personally who have been selfish enough to ignore our own needs and wishes. Ambrose Bierce, an American journalist writing during the Civil War, produced a darkly satirical work called *The Devil's Dictionary*, first published in 1875, in which he defined an egotist as "a person of low taste, more interested in himself than in me".[24]

Narcissism is commonly associated with callous insensitivity and a propensity for boasting and self-aggrandisement: in other words, too much self-love. But that can be a misleading assessment. We need to understand the complexities of narcissism before we can make sense of its close relationship with the astrological Jupiter. 'Narcissistic personality disorder', as a clinical term, isn't rooted in an excess of self-love. It reflects exactly the opposite: a profoundly and sometimes irrevocably damaged sense of self-worth.

No astrological symbol 'causes' a problematic psychological pattern. Astrological significators may reflect or hint at such patterns, but one of the great advantages of being a psychological astrologer rather than a psychiatrist is that the roots and creative possibilities of these patterns, as well as likely expressions of both a creative and destructive kind, are implied by the astrological symbol without having to apply social assumptions of

---

24 Numerous editions of this work have been produced since its original publication in 1875. For a more recent edition, see Ambrose Bierce, *The Devil's Dictionary*, Bloomsbury, 2004.

'normal' or 'abnormal', 'healthy' or 'pathological'. With any planetary expression, including the tough ones, we're looking at a spectrum of possibilities ranging from dark to light, rather than a single fixed behaviour pattern.

Jupiter doesn't 'cause' narcissism, nor is a strong Jupiter an infallible indicator of it. But if an inner wound or intractable internal split is deep enough – usually suggested by painful Saturn or Chiron aspects to personal planets, or an apparently irreconcilable conflict between radically different dimensions of the personality – and the conscious ego is too weak, brittle, or loosely wrapped to contain and work with the tension, Jupiterian attributes can be mobilised as a defence. Some of Jupiter's most characteristic defences are reflected in what we think of as the typical behaviour patterns of narcissism: self-aggrandisement, lack of empathy, the need for everyone's focus to be on oneself, the inclination to be spiteful and vindictive in response to a perceived slight, and the inability to cope with any form of rejection, criticism, or failure.

John William Waterhouse, detail from *Echo and Narcissus* (1903), Walker Art Gallery, Liverpool.

The myth of Narcissus

The Greek tale of Narcissus portrays the psychological roots of narcissism with disturbing precision. Narcissus was a hunter from Boeotia, famous for his great beauty. In one version of the story he's the son of the mortal youth Endymion and the Moon-goddess Selene; in another version, he's the child of the river-god Cephissus and the nymph Liriope. He isn't fully mortal in either of these versions, since at least one of his parents is a divinity.

In Ovid's *Metamorphoses*, which follows the second version of the story, Narcissus' mother Liriope was told by the blind seer Tiresias that her beautiful son would have a long life provided he never recognised himself. Although Tiresias, like all good oracles, tended to speak in metaphors, Liriope interpreted this prophecy literally and, as so many figures in myth seem to do, tried to cheat the oracle by preventing the child from ever seeing his own reflection in a mirror or a pool of water. Narcissus grew up with no idea of what he looked like, and therefore no awareness of his own beauty. Since he could never acquire self-understanding through contemplating himself, he could never develop genuine self-love; and without self-love, he couldn't love anyone else. He rejected every amorous advance and treated every suitor, male or female, with coldness and contempt.

Eventually this behaviour angered the goddess Aphrodite, especially his callous treatment of the nymph Echo (or, in some versions of the story, the youth Ameinias). Through Aphrodite's contrivance, Narcissus, after a hunt, stumbled across a still pool in the forest. When he knelt to drink, he glimpsed a beautiful face in the water and spoke to it. But the beautiful stranger never replied. When Narcissus attempted to touch the image, the face vanished in ripples. The more he stared, the more deeply in love he fell. Unable to eat or sleep, he eventually starved to death gazing at his own reflection. Or, in other versions of the story, he drowned himself in despair.

Mirror, mirror on the wall

Liriope's fear that her son would die young if he recognised himself tells us a great deal about the kind of parental dynamic that's often linked with what's known as a 'narcissistic wound'. It relates to a process known as 'mirroring'. The parent can't allow the child to develop a sense of self – whether because of anxiety for the child's future (as in the myth) or because of possessiveness, or a combination of the two. If he recognised himself and acquired too much confidence and self-sufficiency, Narcissus might encounter danger and be harmed; or he might go off with a lover and abandon his over-doting, jealous parent.

Either way, the child with a narcissistic wound hasn't been adequately 'mirrored'. This means there's no encouragement to become an individual through parental mirroring of the child's unique personality with its own individual values and feelings; instead, the child must mirror the parent's demands and become what they need their offspring to be. I'm sure you can grasp the implications. How can we develop real self-confidence and a sense of our own special value when we aren't allowed to become an independent self, but must always live up to an image of what our parents need us to be?

Another way of looking at this dynamic is that, in a disturbing reversal of roles, the parent needs the child to become the parent, mirroring back the parent's own feelings, longings, needs, and sense of worth. When this happens, the child is robbed of any sense of a solid core of identity. No feeling of self-worth can develop because the child grows into an adult who feels of value only when mirroring others, who may themselves then feel understood and valued and can say, "You're so wonderful and sensitive, and no one has ever understood me like you do." Later relationships then become a constant repetition of the original parental pattern; we're convinced we're loved not because of who we are, but because of what we're able to give the other person. Obviously that's not a recipe for living happily ever after.

The child learns to perform – often with great skill – in order to obtain love, without any real inner conviction of being lovable and worthwhile as a unique individual. Others' love must always be earned by becoming what they require. And praise and approval have to be renewed constantly because there isn't any enduring inner sense of worth. The moment the external mirror is removed, the sense of self-value collapses and another source of love and affirmation must be found.

Narcissism is often accompanied by an acute sensitivity to what others need and want us to be. The psychoanalyst Alice Miller referred to the 'gifted' child who possesses a high degree of intuitive and emotional sensitivity and will therefore be more damaged by such an upbringing.[25] Everything becomes a performance, and the performances, if they're accompanied by genuine talent, can sometimes be very impressive. Yet despite all that bravado and apparent self-confidence, the narcissist is a bit like a Polo Mint. There's a hole, an empty space, hidden at the core of the personality.

The underlying feeling, which is usually entirely unconscious, is that one is nothing and nobody, unlovable and worthless. Desperate defence mechanisms are needed to stifle the loneliness and self-loathing emanating from that empty core. Sometimes these defence mechanisms involve great rage when someone doesn't respond to the performance as planned. Narcissists can be relentlessly unforgiving if the show has failed to convince, and they usually know instinctively when someone's apparent appreciation isn't entirely wholehearted.

The narcissist's deepest hatred is directed towards those who can see through the defences, even when the seeing is also accompanied by compassion. It isn't difficult to understand why criticism is so unpalatable to the narcissist, why deep and corrosive envy of those who are more genuinely self-confident can present such a problem, and why the narcissist so often uses manipulation and gaslighting to convince the other person that *they* are the one suffering from an emotional problem. 'Malignant' narcissism describes a willingness – or even an intention – to harm or destroy others, emotionally and sometimes even literally, in order to preserve that fragile self-image.

In psychiatry, narcissism isn't considered a 'mental illness'. It's classified as a 'personality disorder', meaning that there is underlying structural damage to the integrity of the personality. That doesn't mean it can't be worked with therapeutically. But sadly, extreme narcissism is usually accompanied by an equally extreme reluctance to explore that dark hole at the centre of the personality and face and work through the depression, isolation, humiliation, rage, pain, and despair that it secretly contains.

As I said, Jupiter doesn't 'cause' narcissism. But if we're wounded deeply enough and early enough, Jupiter – especially if it dominates the natal chart through its signs or a conjunction with an angle or strong

---

25 Alice Miller, *The Drama of the Gifted Child: The Search for the True Self* (Basic Books, 2008).

aspects to other planets, especially Sun and Moon – may be mobilised as a defence against the corrosive feeling of being worthless and unlovable. Lots of placements in the element of fire in the natal chart can heighten Jupiter's compensatory inclinations because the fire signs tend to dwell in a world of limitless possibilities and don't always find it easy to face ordinary human limits and conflicts. The usual suspects, Saturn and Chiron, may often be found in strong aspect to the personal planets, especially Moon and Venus.

It's as though there are two entirely different people in the natal chart: the apparently overconfident Jupiterian and the severely wounded child. Jupiter may rush in with its grandiosity, brashness, boldness, inventiveness, and showmanship in order to conceal the feeling of emptiness at the centre of the personality. Lack of empathy is typical, as Narcissus shows us in the myth. How could there be empathy for others when they don't really exist except as extensions of oneself? Others are there to mirror, not to be seen and valued as separate individuals. And their compassion is felt more as an insult than an expression of love and understanding. Compassion, which may be perceived by the narcissist as pity, doesn't bolster the ideal self-image that the person struggles so hard to maintain.

Narcissists must be in the limelight at all times. Being ignored is a crushing and humiliating experience. They need to be the most important person in the relationship, the family, the circle of friends, the company, the community, the political party, or even the country. Other people's devotion is constantly required, so genuine friendship is difficult; narcissists require acolytes, not equals. Like the mythic Zeus, if they're crossed or challenged they can be frighteningly vengeful, even to those they refer to as friends, and they can react spitefully to even the faintest hint of an insult, a slight, or a lack of appreciation. Narcissists don't cope well with rejection, real or imagined. We can see the mythic Zeus revealing himself in these descriptions, and we need to remember the story of the god's own childhood to put the pieces together.

From this brief description, we can get some idea of what constitutes 'narcissistic personality disorder'. But even psychiatry has a problem in defining exactly who is a narcissist, especially since the psychiatrist may suffer from the same problem, expressing it in a different way. The most gifted therapists, according to Alice Miller, often carry the same narcissistic wound as their patients, but they've turned it into a powerfully effective tool for helping others. It might seem a long way from the healer's attentiveness and sensitivity to the politician, CEO, or social influencer who's more concerned with being important and admired than with the lives and livelihoods of those in their charge. Yet the ability to read cues and mirror others' needs, and the compulsion to be seen as a person of value, may spring from the same root.

We all have Jupiter in our charts, and we've all been wounded in one way or another because we also all have a natal Saturn and a natal Chiron. And no chart is perfectly balanced. Every one of us has an element of narcissism because we all need to be mirrored in order to bolster flagging self-esteem. There's no such thing as a perfect parent who can give us perfect mirroring. But it's a question of degree as well as of self-honesty. Our inherent narcissism isn't intrinsically bad or harmful. Because it's linked to Jupiter, it can provide the incentive to develop a potential talent and work to become more of what we potentially need to become. The narcissistic wound can also be a spur to self-understanding, if we're honest enough to recognise our own internal unhappiness. That can allow us to move beyond the compulsive self-absorption of narcissism and begin to enjoy the pleasure of others' recognition of our efforts without mistaking it for a true measure of our worth. None of us had an idyllic childhood in the Paradise Garden, and we've all been bruised.

Clinical narcissism describes a state in which demanding others' mirroring has become the only method of relating and the only way of interacting with the world. The extreme narcissist can't bear being seen as a fallible human. They don't want to be imperfect, flawed, and needy, nor be seen as an 'ordinary' human living what they perceive as a boring, insignificant life. They must be the ruler of Olympus: important and special, not simply because it's nice to be appreciated but because they feel they'll cease to exist if they aren't always fed by others' adulation.

Narcissists can't bear to lose. If such a horrific event occurs, they will always find someone to blame. If a relationship fails, it's always because of the other person's emotional problem. If they're ignored, it's because of the other person's self-centredness. If they lose an election, the polls must have been rigged by the opponent, or the ignorant voters were duped by misinformation or simply too naïve and stupid to make the right choice. You can see how narcissism, when it's unleashed in the political arena, can lend itself to conspiracy theories, whether one imagines one is the victim of them or one deliberately tries to create the conspiracies oneself. Extreme narcissists can become abusive in close relationships, and sometimes they're violent. More often they excel at gaslighting, which is the favoured technique of the threatened narcissist attempting to undermine the other person's confidence in order to hide desperate insecurity.

Sadly, if we unconsciously identify with an archetypal figure, we tend to be fated by the story's outcome, metaphorically and sometimes even literally. Narcissus died of starvation and exhaustion because he was so obsessed by his own reflection that he ignored the most basic human needs. Or, alternatively, he drowned himself because he could never achieve the full love and recognition he craved. Some extreme narcissists end their lives lonely and bitter, abandoned by friends and family because those close to them have grown tired of being manipulated and treated like mirrors rather than real people. Other narcissists might suffer a tragic early death through an 'accident' that involves a secret unconscious choice. It may seem preferable to go down in flames and be remembered at one's peak, rather than living quietly to a ripe old age, unnoticed by the wider world.

Narcissism is one of Jupiter's most painful and problematic dimensions, although the planet in itself isn't the 'cause' of the distress. If we can find the courage to face the complex feelings that lie behind the narcissistic pattern, some healing and integration is possible. But without consciousness, there isn't any healing. Narcissists can go to their graves still blaming the world for their unhappiness, not least because they're unlikely to undergo psychotherapy. And if they do, they're rarely inclined to accept anything interpreted as a criticism from the therapist, and they'll do anything, including lying, to avoid being seen.

The worlds of politics, fashion, entertainment, and business are full of people displaying this psychological pattern in obvious ways. But anyone can suffer from a narcissistic wound, and it might be obvious only to their partner and family. The wound is often accompanied by considerable intelligence and impressive talent. In some ways talent can make it worse, and so can the power achieved through high public office, wealth, or fame. The gifts and rewards help to conceal the inner wound from others and from oneself. When we look at some example charts later, hopefully you'll see how this might have bearing on the behaviour of so many individuals in the public eye, past and present.

Hubris, nemesis, and the refusal to acknowledge limits

The themes of *hubris* and *nemesis* form the core of Greek tragedy. The protagonist is culpable of *hubris* and inevitably invokes a destructive fate, not because they're evil – often these characters are fine and noble – but because they can't accept the limits placed on them by the gods or, put another way, by their own *moira*. We might also see these limits as the natural laws of the universe: the archetypal patterns of which the gods are symbols and to which even the gods are subject. The immortals too can be afflicted by *hubris*. Prometheus is a good example, and so is the healer-god Asklepios, who overstepped his boundaries by bringing a dead man back to life, and incurred the fatal wrath of Zeus.

Ananke or Necessity holding her spindle at the centre of the cosmos, with the three Moirai beneath her. Illustration by Edmond Lechevallier-Chevignard of the relevant passage from the Myth of Er in Plato's *Republic*, in *Magasin Pittoresque* (1857).

There's *hubris* in the belief that we can 'overcome' or 'transcend' the natal chart, which is a psychological map of who we are. We might want to believe that we can send back our Chiron or Saturn and get a Venus replacement from Amazon, if we could just find the right political, social, psychological, spiritual, dietary, or medical formula. We fantasise that we can overcome our limits, achieve perfection, and live forever. Self-development isn't the same as *hubris*, unless we imagine that it will cure our fundamental humanness.

More commonly known these days as a sense of 'entitlement', *hubris* involves the belief that we really shouldn't have to suffer any limitations in life, even if the gods themselves – or life's tough and often unfair realities – have imposed them. *Hubris* is a special form of arrogance: a refusal to accept one's *moira*, the teleology that ensures that we cannot become other than what we are. We might hopefully achieve the best version of ourselves, and accepting limits doesn't mean passively bowing to 'fate' or grimly putting up with one's lot without effort or complaint. But we can't transform into someone else. No individual, no community, and no collective is above the archetypal patterns symbolised by the planetary gods.

If we're consumed by *hubris*, Nature – including our own nature – strikes back in the form of *nemesis*. Portrayed in the ancient world as a goddess, Nemesis is a personification of natural law and reflects the cosmic response to a destructive imbalance.

Nemesis is closely allied with *ananke* or Necessity, who's likewise portrayed as a goddess and symbolises *moira* as natural law. Necessity, who in Orphic texts was, like the primal god Phanes, believed to have emanated out of Chaos, is usually portrayed with a spindle. Plato, in the *Republic*, described her holding her spindle and seated at the centre of the cosmos, while the three Moirai weave, measure, and cut the threads of all living things, and the heavenly bodies circle around her.

This ancient concept, personified as a goddess in Greek iconography, isn't interchangeable with the Abrahamic idea of divine punishment for 'sin', which is specifically focused on human transgressions as defined by a particular culture at a particular epoch of history. 'Sin' is a very personal idea, and the divine retaliation it invokes is likewise highly personal as well as being a pragmatic tool utilised by some religions to control the anarchic and heretical elements in society. Necessity, in contrast, is impersonal and applicable not only to humans and gods, but to the heavenly bodies as well. The Greek philosopher Heracleitus wrote in the 5th century BCE, "Sun will not overstep his measures; otherwise the Erinyes, ministers of Justice, will find him out."[26]

Sometimes God's punishment for sin and the retaliation of Nemesis are in accord across cultures. The abuse and murder of a child, in Greek myth, was guaranteed to invoke Nemesis and usually resulted in a terrible

---

26 G. S. Kirk, J. E. Raven, and M. Schofield (eds. and trans.), *The Pre-Socratic Philosophers* (1983), p. 201. The Erinyes are the avenging Furies, born from the blood of Ouranos as it fell to the earth after his castration. Like the three Moirai, they are expressions of the central idea of Nemesis/Necessity.

family curse that passed down through the generations. Today the same crime may result in a lengthy prison sentence or even, in some countries, the death penalty. But the sense of a profound cosmic violation represented by this offence transcends cultures and historical epochs.

'Sin' is all too often in the eyes of the beholder, who can display a resentful envy and pettiness unique to humans. *Nemesis*, in contrast, is, like *moira*, intrinsic to and embedded in every living thing. Although portrayed as a goddess, *nemesis* exists within us along with our potential for *hubris*; they are two sides of the same coin. *Nemesis* can retaliate against gods as well as humans and can be unleashed on a collective as well as on an individual.

This small sculpture is Roman and dates from the 2nd century CE. It portrays the goddess Nemesis crushing an arrogant human with her right foot and holding a Wheel of Fortune in her left hand, conflating her with the Roman goddess Fortuna. But Fortuna's actions are random, while those of Nemesis are concerned with divine retribution against *hubris*.

The next image is a portrayal of the goddess in an engraving titled *Nemesis* by the 16th century artist Albrecht Dürer. Like the Romans, he conflated her with Fortuna; the engraving is also known as *The Great Fortune*. Dürer's version of Nemesis, winged like the Roman figure, stands on the Wheel of Fortune. In her right hand she brandishes a triumphal cup symbolising reward, while in her left she holds a bridle, presumably to restrain those who are arrogant enough to strive beyond their limits.

The goddess Nemesis, Roman sculpture, c. 150 CE, Getty Villa, Los Angeles.

Albrecht Dürer, *Nemesis* (1502), Metropolitan Museum of Art,
New York.

In Greek myth, entire cities could be struck down as the result of one individual's *hubris*, particularly if the transgressor was a ruler, since the ruler was viewed as the representative of the people and the intermediary between them and the gods. In the myth of Oedipus, the whole population of the city-state of Thebes was terrorised by the Sphinx because of Oedipus' *hubris*. We might even speculate that the Earth itself can strike back at the transgression of natural law, invoking Nemesis in the form of plagues, earthquakes, floods, and tidal waves. The Greeks certainly thought so. It might seem as if that's exactly what's happening in our present world. Blind to our *hubris*, we humans may have inadvertently invoked the vengeful goddess.

Nemesis could also pursue human beings after death, inflicting ongoing punishment in the underworld. Tantalus, from whose name we get the word 'tantalise', was condemned to an eternity in Tartarus (the high-security prison of the underworld), tempted by food and drink that he wasn't allowed to swallow or even touch because he'd been arrogant and stupid enough to try to trick the gods into eating human flesh.

Ixion was bound to a fiery wheel because he was so full of *hubris* that he believed he could seduce Hera. As you might imagine, this infuriated Zeus, who punished Ixion by hurling him into Tartarus, where he was tied to the wheel forever.

Gioacchino Assereto, *Tantalus*, c. 1640s, Schloss Eggenberg, Graz.

Jules Elie Delaunay, *Ixion Falling into the Underworld* (1876),
Nantes Museum of Art.

Arachne, according to Ovid, was arrogant enough to challenge the
goddess Athene to a weaving contest, boasting that she possessed greater
skill. Although Athene could find no fault with Arachne's work, the
goddess was so incensed by the mortal woman's *hubris* that she turned her
into a giant spider – not because Arachne was gifted, but because she'd
claimed she was more gifted than the very deity who had originally taught
the skills of weaving to humans.

These mythic figures were all afflicted by *hubris*. They weren't intrinsically bad, or at least they didn't start off that way. They often began their
lives as gifted individuals favoured by the gods. Pentheus, the protagonist in
Euripides' tragedy, *The Bacchae*, was a fine king, ethical, loyal, courageous,
and fiercely protective of his people. But he, like so many of the central
characters in Greek tragedy, couldn't accept his mortal limits. He refused
to recognise and respect the truth of divinity when the god Dionysos
arrived on his doorstep, especially since the laws of this deity, including
the necessity of periodic ritual states of ecstasy, differed from Pentheus'
own human-made laws.

Rather like an ancient version of Oliver Cromwell, or certain political leaders in the modern world, Pentheus stubbornly doubled down on his own rigid ethical stance rather than acknowledging the paradoxical nature of human beings and the necessity of an element of disorder to fully understand the true nature of order. In retaliation, Dionysos sent his maenads – including Pentheus' own mother Agave – to tear the king to pieces while they were in a state of god-induced ecstatic madness.

All these mythic characters secretly wanted to be divinities themselves. Some, like Pentheus, were unconscious of their *hubris*, while others, like Arachne and Tantalus, actively boasted about their superiority over a god. They knew what they were doing, but they tried it on anyway. They couldn't

Pentheus torn apart by maenads, Roman fresco, c. 1ˢᵗ c. BCE-1ˢᵗ c. CE, Casa dei Vetii, Pompeii.

accept the fact that they were mortals who must live within the limits of natural law.

We might view the astrological Jupiter as the chief contributor to *hubris*. Yet Jupiter also contains its own *nemesis* because we overreach our boundaries and then inevitably invoke a backlash, internally and sometimes in the external world as well. In some myths focused on the theme of *hubris*, like the stories of Prometheus and Ixion, Zeus himself became enraged and imposed punishment. The words 'glass houses' and 'stones' come to mind. But Zeus himself, as he was portrayed in Orphic myth, is the embodiment of *moira* as Divine Breath emanating from Divine Mind. He himself is *nemesis*. If we think about Zeus' many battles, we can trace a common theme. Zeus' most relentless enemy was the Earth-world and the chthonic creatures that symbolise it. He forever devalued and antagonised this domain – the instinctual realm of his grandmother Gaia and his wife Hera – and it forever fought back.

Kronos the Titan, although he was vanquished by Zeus, remained an indestructible immortal, and we might view the astrological Saturn as the obvious *nemesis* of Jupiter, working against him from the domain of concrete reality. In mundane life, Jupiter's power is curtailed because of the limits of mortal incarnation. But we might also think of Hera, the divine 'root' of Earth, who invariably retaliated against Zeus' infidelities and curtailed the boundless potentials of his offspring. Hera is Zeus' *nemesis*, and as an inseparable dyad, both are inherent in the astrological Jupiter.

Hera's wrath often fell on his lovers and not on the god himself, partly because his immortality protected him and partly because, in her view, it was all the fault of these treacherous women, who were arrogant enough to believe themselves worthy of his passion. But many of Zeus' lovers were deceived or coerced into his embrace and were free of *hubris* themselves. They, like us, seem to reflect the collateral damage arising from a universe that's imperfect, still in formation, and full of divisions, polarities, and constant creative conflict and change. The realm of spirit and the realm of matter seem to be forever coupling, generating new progeny, quarrelling, separating, injuring each other, reconciling, and coupling again.

Hubris and inflation

The astrological Jupiter easily lends itself to *hubris* if it's been mobilised as compensation for a sense of limitation or damage. In this sense *hubris* has a direct relationship with narcissism because it can be a form of defence against feeling insignificant, worthless, and impotent in the face of life's challenges. The psychological term 'inflation', which is often the response to a narcissistic wound as well as one of the main weaknesses of the *puer aeternus*, is a psychological synonym for *hubris*, because it describes a state in which the individual identifies with an archetype rather than accepting their flawed human limits.

A large catalogue of historical and current figures – dictators, leading politicians, CEOs of international conglomerates, plutocrats, celebrities, influencers, extremists of various political and ecological persuasions, and religious leaders steeped in self-righteous fanaticism – fit this description. And each time we confront their propensity for destructiveness, we're astonished, horrified, and full of judgement, failing to recognise where each of us as an individual may be culpable of exactly the same propensity, albeit in a smaller and less obvious way.

It's very difficult, when in the throes of an inflated Jupiterian vision of potential – one's own or that of a collective – to say to ourselves, "I might be wrong," or "I might be in too much of a hurry," or "I might need a bit more realism," or even, "I might need to listen to other people." When the Roman Senate awarded a successful military commander a triumphal march honouring his victories, it was customary for a slave to ride behind him in his triumphal chariot, chanting repeatedly in his ear: "Remember you are mortal." As Jupiter was their chief deity as head of the Capitoline Triad of gods, the Romans, despite their many failings as a culture when viewed through the lens of today's values, may have understood the god's dangerous propensity for *hubris* and its inevitable invocation of *nemesis* far better than we do today.

Faith, optimism, and meaning

By this time you'd all be forgiven for thinking that Jupiter is really Saturn in disguise. After all, they're a father-son duo, and the apple, as they say, never falls far from the tree. To cheer you up, it might be a good idea to consider the planet from a happier perspective and think about the well-known

Jupiterian themes of faith and optimism. These keywords are often used in relation to Jupiter, and while they might not reveal the full complexity of the planet, they do seem to reflect important dimensions of its deeper meaning. These encouraging themes may turn out to have a dark side too. But by now we should expect that of Jupiter.

Jupiter might be understood to symbolise an archetypal potency or pattern within us that longs for a connection with a greater, higher, or deeper reality. We need to know that life – our own lives, the life of humanity, and the life of the planet itself – has a meaningful teleology and isn't just a series of random blips in a pitiless and soulless material universe. Put another way, if we go back to the Orphic idea of Zeus, the astrological Jupiter reflects our need to feel related to the Divine Mind. Yet another way of looking at it might be that Jupiter symbolises our efforts to find a connection with the intelligence of Nature and with the inherent purposefulness of life itself.

'Divine' doesn't necessarily mean a transcendent power 'outside' or 'above' incarnate life. That might be the viewpoint of some religious doctrines, but it isn't everyone's perspective or experience, and it can be deeply unhelpful to view the astrological Jupiter as simply 'transcendent'. 'Divine' may connote life itself – Poseidonius' 'vital force' or Bergson's '*élan vital*' – with its infinite interconnections between different levels of reality from the material to the spiritual and everything in between, which the Stoics understood to be the essence of deity. This is a form of pantheism, a word which derives from the Greek and means 'all is god'. The Kabbalist Moshe ben Jacob Cordovero, writing in the 16th century, echoed this perspective within a Jewish religious framework:

> The essence of divinity is found in every single thing – nothing but it exists... Do not attribute duality to God... Do not say 'This is a stone and not God'. God forbid! Rather, all existence is God, and the stone is a thing pervaded by divinity.[27]

We could also understand Jupiter as a way of describing what Jung called the religious instinct: the intuitive sense, conscious or unconscious, that the universe is meaningful and imbued with pattern and design,

27 Moshe Cordovero, *Shi'ur Qomah*, Modena MS 206b, cited in Daniel Matt, *The Essential Kabbalah: The Heart of Jewish Mysticism* (Castle Books, 1997).

a unified living entity that's still unfolding and possesses infinite intelligence, purpose, and creativity. If there is indeed something within us that experiences this web of connectedness – and whether it's 'objective' or 'subjective' might be the wrong question to ask – we will long for it and seek it, sometimes quite compulsively, even if we don't recognise that a link between our mundane reality and something bigger and wiser that gives our lives meaning is what we're really looking for. We may project our intuitive perception onto some surprising and often appallingly unsuitable objects. But underlying Jupiter's worldly compulsions is something far more complex than an excessive desire for pleasure or personal satisfaction.

Even a tiny glimpse of that greater reality, by whatever name we call it and in whatever form we perceive it, encourages us to have faith in the future. We discover that we can tolerate even horrific circumstances because we have a sense of hope rooted in meaning; we experience a feeling that it all counts for something and that, as Paul declared in Romans 8:28, "We know that all things work together for good". Viewed through Jupiter's lens, the events that happen in our lives point to something meaningful; life's vicissitudes aren't random; and our experiences, however difficult and painful, might ultimately lead us to something better because it's all part of a larger pattern. Even if we don't understand the pattern, we have faith in it.

The 'will to meaning'

This dimension of Jupiter is different from the Sun's sense of self-esteem. The astrological Sun is concerned with the individual self, the core of the personality. Who am I as a unique individual? What makes me special? How do I express myself in my own unique way? Jupiter isn't really interested in 'I' as a unique individual. It's more concerned with other questions. What is my contribution to life? What is my purpose in the greater scheme of things? What is my role in the unfolding of the bigger picture? What can I offer that's significant? Life is full of joy, beauty, humour, fellowship, and love, but it's also full of pain, darkness, unfairness, loneliness, and tragedy. The astrological Jupiter asks: Is there a larger pattern behind it all? Is there some deeper meaning that can help me make sense of it? And if so, what part am I meant to play? These are Jupiter's, rather than the Sun's, most urgent questions.

The Austrian psychiatrist, philosopher, and Holocaust survivor Victor Frankl focused his life's work on the human quest for meaning. He stated in his autobiography, *Man's Search for Meaning*, that he had survived four different concentration camps, including Auschwitz, along with the loss of his father, his mother, his brother, and his wife at the hands of the Nazis, by finding personal meaning in the experience. According to Frankl, this gave him the will to live through it. In later life he created his own form of therapy, which he called 'logotherapy', insisting that the underlying motivator in human life is 'the will to meaning', even in the most terrible circumstances.[28]

Even a small conviction of meaning can support the sense that our individual lives and efforts are worth something, despite suffering, loss, and failure. Our lives have significance, even if we never receive any recognition of that significance in the eyes of others or in our own lifetimes. Jupiter's natural inclination, displayed most noticeably in the psychology of the *puer aeternus*, is to avoid the dreary monotony and pain of an ordinary human fate. But it's also Jupiter that infuses that 'ordinary' fate with meaning and allows us to experience contentment without the necessity of fireworks, applause, and celebrity status.

Our Jupiterian longing can be a spur to make something more of ourselves, and to become the best possible version of ourselves as a commitment to the future. And even if we aren't able or willing to acknowledge the longing for what it is – an inevitable dilemma for those who are intractably wedded to the rational intellect or the evidence of the senses – that won't stop Jupiter. We'll seek the connection anyway, through surrogates that are secretly symbols of what we really seek but which we call by other names.

Surrogates and 'tokens'

Often our surrogates are concrete objects, or abstract concepts such as 'society'. We may be driven by the compulsive pursuit of something – sex, money, food, travel, social position, success – and we feel we *must* obtain the object of our desire because a meaningful future seems dependent

---

28 Victor Frankl, *Man's Search for Meaning* (Beacon Press, 2006). This book was originally published in 1946 as *Ein Psychologe erlebt das Konzentrationslager* (*A Psychologist Experiences the Concentration Camp*).

on it. We feel so much better after we've gratified ourselves, even if we're hungry again an hour later. But the object of our longing may be a mask for something else hidden behind it. We look for our meaning in concrete things and we turn them into magical talismans that can bring us luck and affirm the favour of the god.

Some people turn a football team into a religious object. According to recent statistical analyses, there's a direct link between whether our favoured team wins and how we feel about the current government and the nation's prospects for the future. Other people find their talismans in the latest fashion in clothing or interior design, the latest celebrity trend, the latest piece of technology, or the latest 'progressive' ideology. We can turn our homes, our families, and our communities into talismans, and our determination to keep loved ones within our grasp and under our control isn't always an expression of simple emotional need.

Viewed through this lens, 'identity politics' might be seen as a kind of surrogate religion in which the group identity becomes a deity who offers meaning to our small, insignificant lives. We chant slogans as though they were prayers, and we march through the streets with talismanic banners as though we were on a medieval religious crusade. We focus on ideas, objects, and sometimes people, and through them we try to get the sense of a deep connection with a greater design. Much of the time we may have no idea that a feeling of contact with a higher or deeper reality is what we're really looking for. We may feel repeatedly bewildered and disappointed because the magical meal only satisfies briefly, and we may fail to find the sense of genuine hope and faith that we long for so much. The more people we can convert and the more unbelievers we can 'cancel', the more we feel supported in our faith. It's really a form of addiction, although we don't always recognise our dependency.

Paradoxically, religions themselves – especially the highly dogmatic ones – can be surrogates for Jupiter's longing. It's another example of Jupiter's dark irony. Sometimes a political ideology becomes a form of religion, offering the same reassurance that we're fulfilling a divine purpose even when we loudly proclaim we're agnostics or atheists. Beliefs that are based solely on rules, texts, concepts, and sacred objects may offer a replacement for a genuine interior sense of religiosity.

All the planetary gods, as symbols of archetypal patterns, were for millennia understood to be embedded in what the Neoplatonists called 'tokens' or *sunthemata* – objects and images that are talismanic containers for and embodiments of the gods. Putting a sprig of myrtle in your wedding bouquet didn't just mean you sought the favour of Aphrodite. Because myrtle was deemed to be Aphrodite herself in floral form – divinity everywhere and in everything – you weren't merely praying to an invisible deity for blessing and support. You were bringing the goddess to the wedding. This is the ancient idea behind the law of *sumpatheia* or 'sympathies', also known as 'correspondences'. But if we can't understand the nature of symbols as bridges and gateways, we may take these 'tokens' entirely on a literal level.

We can also seek our Jupiterian connection by projecting it onto a spiritual teacher who promises enlightenment, or a secular guru who promises perfect health and longevity through dietary or exercise regimes. People as well as objects, images, and ideas can become our *sunthemata*. In consequence we may fail to find the courage to pursue the stormy internal journey to the hidden core of Jupiter. Given the turbulence and unreliability of the mythic Zeus, this trepidation isn't at all surprising. None of us wants to become Semele and wind up burned to ashes.

I'm not suggesting that any of these ways in which humans pursue the Jupiterian longing is 'wrong'. They're projections, but projecting our internal life is what the human psyche does. We can't come to a conscious recognition of what's within us before we've first projected it outside and then painstakingly internalised it. And our different 'tokens' reflect the many different forms in which the mythic Zeus disguises himself in order to sow his seed.

The god never repeats himself, and each of us receives our Jupiterian inspiration in different ways. The challenge isn't to try to pin Jupiter down to one 'legitimate' path. It's to try to do our best to ensure that our pursuit is life-enhancing rather than life-destroying. Natal Jupiter can be in any of the twelve zodiacal signs and the twelve houses, and it can form aspects to all, some, or none of the other planets. If our symbolic talismans can spark that longed-for connection while enriching and benefitting our own and others' lives, the 'tokens', however mundane they might be, are expressing the planet with just as much validity as more recognisably psychological or spiritual pathways.

But there are times when Jupiter's unacknowledged longing can become a destroyer. We can see this in the compulsive behaviour of narcissism, and in the sometimes catastrophic results of *hubris* when it afflicts those who seek social, political, or financial power at the expense of those they claim to represent and serve. We'll look at an example of this darker Jupiter later, as well as examining the charts of people who seem to have lived the natal planet in creative ways that have enhanced their own and others' lives, sometimes without ever realising that the driving force behind their aspiration was the search for meaning and a connection with a greater reality. Although Jupiter reflects the human religious instinct, we don't have to be conventionally religious to express Jupiter in creative and constructive ways.

The reality of the symbol

Jupiter reflects our capacity to experience symbols as meaningful gateways to a sense of connectedness. This planet is our built-in symbol-reader. The 3rd-century Neoplatonic philosopher Plotinus, expressing his disdain for literal thinking about the so-called 'influence' of the stars and planets, declared:

> All teems with symbol; the wise man is the man who in any one thing can read another.[29]

The planets, in Plotinus' view, aren't causes, and they don't make events happen. They symbolise those events and correspond with them. Plotinus described the planetary movements as celestial writing rather than a source of 'influence'; we read the heavenly script to understand the nature and intention of the Divine, and then we can choose how to work with it. But responding to the symbolic dimension of life requires a willingness to deal with paradoxes, and the human ego doesn't handle paradoxes well. We want life's contradictions to be one thing or the other, and not a secret unity. We want the luxury of taking sides without the pain of uncertainty.

The word 'symbol' comes from the Greek root *sumbolon*, which means 'throw together'. Symbols contain opposites 'thrown' together: an outer form or image that embodies and points towards an inner meaning. That meaning reveals apparently irreconcilable opposites that are mysteriously and impossibly one, portrayed in a web of connections that make no logical causal sense but together hint at a unity that defies rational analysis. When

---

29 Plotinus, Ennead II:3:7, in *Plotinus: The Enneads*, trans. Stephen MacKenna (Faber & Faber, 1969).

Jupiter's capacity for symbolic understanding is hampered, we can interpret symbols in an overly literal way. Then, of course, they aren't symbols any more, and the gateways are closed.

This is often the case with literal, fundamentalist approaches to religious experience. It isn't accidental that Jupiter, although fluid and constantly changing, is also traditionally associated with religion in its most dogmatic forms. Contrary to popular opinion, Jupiter and its zodiacal signs aren't always overflowing with tolerance. Both Sagittarius and Pisces can, on occasion, display an intransigence that's startling in its self-righteous certainty. We might associate Capricorn with rigid restraint and Taurus with stubborn intractability, but Jupiter's signs, when they become doctrinal, can make these earthy signs look like the most chilled of stoned hippies at Woodstock.

The capacity to perceive religious imagery symbolically can be hampered by narrow, concrete interpretations that can easily generate intolerance and fanaticism. 'Truth' becomes inflexible and bound to 'historical' events, sometimes factual but sometimes embellished or imagined, that can't ever be questioned. Irreproachable sacred texts demand complete acceptance rather than flexible interpretation. And fixed formulae created by humans are believed to be written by a divine hand. As the English novelist and philosopher John Cowper Powys once wrote, "The Devil is every God who exacts obedience."[30]

This kind of literal-minded perception of life isn't, of course, limited to religion. It can be found in many spheres of life that are related to the 9th house. 'Scientism' as dogmatic truth is an obvious example, although genuine scientific inquiry, not an 'ism' in itself, has adopted many paradigms over history, some of them open to a symbolic understanding of material reality. We can find literal thinking in political and social ideologies, and in various schools of psychology and psychiatry, some of which can be disturbingly and sometimes destructively narrow-minded. And we can also find it in astrology. It's possible to interpret astrological symbols with a deadly literalness, and then we see nothing in the chart except concrete manifestations. This event will happen, that event will not happen, and the psyche with all its depth, complexity, and nuance is completely overlooked or vehemently denied.

---

30 John Cowper Powys, *Porius: A Romance of the Dark Ages* (1951), Chapter XV.

Gustave Moreau, *The Head of Orpheus* (1865), Musée d'Orsay, Paris.

That doesn't mean concrete reality has no place in Jupiter's realm. Symbols can be expressed on many levels, including the material world. And valuable insights and benefits in practical terms can be our reward if we embrace and reflect on the earthy level of symbolic expression. But dismissing the other levels destroys our receptivity to the symbol, and we severely limit ourselves – and, if we're practising astrologers, our clients – because there's no longer a spectrum of different levels of reality through which an astrological significator can be expressed. Then we might wind up creating our own fate because we can't see any option other than the literal one, or any choices other than concrete ones.

Messiahs, acolytes, and the 'elect'

Paradoxically, it's in the religious sphere, usually considered as Jupiter's domain, that we can often see with clarity the fruits of a constipated Jupiter's intolerance and dogmatism. Political ideologies are often disguised religions, and religions are often the vehicle for a disguised hunger for worldly power. Over the millennia, wars have been fought over the interpretation of symbols as literal facts, and immense suffering and countless deaths have resulted from a rigid insistence on inflexible doctrines. This is still an ongoing problem in the current world, including the Western world, where we like to think of ourselves as enlightened, progressive, and tolerant. Somewhere, perhaps disguised as a fox or a magpie, Zeus is laughing his ironic laugh.

Jupiter's dogmatism isn't the same as Saturn's, although sometimes in a natal chart Jupiter's role as symbol-reader and symbol-generator can be hampered by a rampantly dominant Saturn. But Jupiter, as we've seen in the mythic Zeus' stubbornness, is capable of great inflexibility in perception and understanding. We might think about Zeus' unrelenting antagonism towards those annoyingly rebellious humans, resulting in the Great Flood and Pandora's jar of human woes. We shouldn't always blame Saturn for our problems. Our intolerance often arises from the belief that we've discovered the Real Truth. That makes us one of the elite, a member of the 'elect': we alone have a special connection with the godhead, and we alone can understand and implement God's will. We become petty little messiahs puffed up with virtue, intent on saving the world whether or not it wishes or even needs to be saved.

An example of this kind of religious elitism can be found in the doctrines of the religious group known as Jehovah's Witnesses. Many of us are familiar with this group through their periodic visits to private homes, inviting residents to discuss religious issues if they're interested. The individuals themselves are almost invariably pleasant, decent, and well-meaning. They're rarely aggressive or intimidating, and they don't bully or harangue. But the teachings themselves are redolent of Jupiter's elitist inclinations. One of the doctrines of the Jehovah's Witnesses claims that, from the time of Christ, only 144,000 anointed souls can be truly saved and can rule with Christ as saints in the Kingdom of God. It's unclear who's doing the counting, or what happens when the quota has been filled.

Lutherans, Calvinists, Mormons, and Universalists also believe in this kind of 'elect', and an element of predestination has coloured some of these religious approaches. According to Calvin, the 'elect' are chosen by God long before their birth, regardless of whether they live virtuous lives. It takes all the fun out of being a sinner. The Gnostics of late antiquity also believed they were 'elect', although there was no fixed number of elect souls and salvation was based on *gnosis* or inner knowledge. This was achieved through individual rituals and practices in accord with the doctrines of the particular Gnostic sect, rather than through preordained divine favouritism.

To be convinced we're one of the 'elect', especially if election isn't dependent on our moral and ethical choices, is an unmistakeable form of *hubris*. For that matter, so is any form of belief in a spiritual elite, since the determination of who does or doesn't merit entry into the holy clubroom depends not on gods but on humans, who will inevitably impose their own personal agendas. We're back to the issue of inflation and identifying with an archetype – in this case the archetype of the Divine Child who grows up to become a Messiah.

I'm sure you can see the link between this kind of inflation and the grand dreams of the *puer aeternus*, and more obviously in the self-aggrandisement of narcissism. We're favoured by the divine because we know divine secrets that the unenlightened don't, and that makes us godlike and, at best, entitled to look down with contempt and pity at the spiritually ignorant. At worst, we may feel justified in persecuting those we perceive as heretics. Ironically, the word 'heresy' comes from the Greek *hairesis*, which means 'choice' or 'option'. A heretic is someone who has made an individual choice about how to live and what to believe, rather than obeying an official doctrine.

When we inflate in this way, we may claim divine authority because we alone are the true children of the divine. This seems to give our lives significance, and anyone who challenges our conviction must be rooted out and silenced. Substitute the word 'politics' for 'religion' and we can see exactly the same process at work, and it's happening all around us now. No discussion is possible because we can't tolerate an alternative or relative truth, and respect for the validity of diversity of thought and speech becomes impossible. That's what happens when a literal mind experiences the revelations of a strong Jupiter but can't or won't recognise the gateway of the symbol.

Art and symbol

Audience: Liz, what's the significance of the image of the woman with a head on a tray that you showed us before?

Liz: The image of the woman with a head on a tray is a painting by the 19th-century French Symbolist artist Gustave Moreau. It's called *The Head of Orpheus*, also known as *Thracian Girl Carrying the Head of Orpheus*, and the 'tray' is Orpheus' lyre. The painting portrays the final chapter of the Orpheus myth, in which the poet was torn to pieces by the maenads, the worshippers of Dionysos, because he tried to reform their mysteries and make them more civilised. He sought a balance in worship of the god between the rational and the nonrational, and was rewarded by having his head ripped from his body in much the same way Dionysos himself was ripped apart by the Titans in Orphic myth, and King Pentheus was dismembered by the god's maenads in Euripides' *The Bacchae*.

The severed head went on singing, revealing cosmic secrets despite the poet's death, and as it floated down the River Hebrus it was found by one of the Muses. That's the subject of Moreau's painting. The Muses gathered up the severed fragments of Orpheus' body and buried them at the foot of Mount Olympus, and his lyre was taken up to the heavens and transformed into the constellation of Lyra.[31] I don't know which Muse Moreau is showing us, although it's most likely to be Calliope, the Muse of epic poetry, who in some sources was Orpheus' mother. That would make Orpheus the grandson of Zeus. As for why she's called the 'Thracian Girl', the Muses, the daughters of Zeus and Mnemosyne, were said to have come from Thrace, where Orpheus himself was born and died.

The image is relevant to Jupiter's relationship with symbols because Moreau is known as one of the most important of the Symbolist painters. His

---

31 Several ancient sources describe this story, including Apollodorus, Pausanias, Eratosthenes, Virgil, and Ovid. The Maenads were offended not only because of Orpheus' Apollonian predilections but also because he spurned their advances.

use of mythic images is enigmatic, evocative, and sometimes deliberately mischievous. We can read lots of things into his paintings, and probably all these different perceptions are in some sense valid. That's a characteristic of symbols: they resist single definitions and interpretations. Jung devised a technique he called 'amplification' to help illuminate symbols; this is a way of expanding our understanding by looking at other associated symbols and ideas to evoke an intuitive sense of the elusive, paradoxical core.

I don't know what Moreau was trying to say in this painting. I'm not an art historian. But being an art historian doesn't necessarily guarantee an understanding of symbols; some art historians are terribly literal and unimaginative in their interpretations. Perhaps Moreau was hinting at the suffering of the artist dismembered by an aesthetically impoverished and insensitive world, or the link between art and prophecy, or the immortality of aesthetic vision even if the artist has failed to communicate that vision in their individual lifetime. Or maybe all three interpretations apply, along with many more.

In several of his works, Moreau seems to be making a statement about the cruel price, inwardly and in society, that the artist must pay for the gift of creative vision. Moreau was a man on a crusade, despite the surreal calm of his paintings. In his birth chart, the Moon makes an exact conjunction with Pluto at 4° Aries, and Sun, Chiron, and Venus are all conjunct between 16° and 22° Aries. These five Aries planets are in the 11th house, and the Sun-Chiron-Venus configuration squares a Uranus-Neptune conjunction in Capricorn. Born with the Sun involved with a major outer planet config-uration, Moreau was unusually receptive to shifts occurring at a deeper level of the collective psyche. He wasn't especially interested in painting the objects, people, and everyday experiences of ordinary French life.

Jupiter is in Virgo in the 4th house, conjuncting the IC. This suggests that Moreau found his connection with a higher reality through developing and perfecting his craft, which drew its inspiration not only from his family background but also from a deeper historical past rooted in the land of his birth. There's a grand earth trine between Jupiter in Virgo, Mercury in Taurus, and Neptune in Capricorn. Moreau's challenging intuitive visions are portrayed as physical realities in his paintings, articulated in perfect detail with a kind of dreamlike hyper-realism. But each of his figures, objects, and landscapes is itself a symbol, as are the myths, legends, and religious themes on which almost every one of his paintings is based.[32]

The symbolic theme of the singing head of Orpheus was shared by two other late 19th- and early 20th-century Symbolist painters, Odilon Redon and Franz von Stuck. Each of them used the same mythic image to express his own individual ideas and perceptions. The head of Orpheus is a powerful symbol. It helps to know the myth of the poet, but that knowledge isn't necessary to respond emotionally to Moreau's painting. Try to get an intuitive sense of what this particular image might mean to you, and what thoughts and memories it might trigger. The painting can offer us an exercise in looking at symbols with the intuition rather than the intellect, which is also what we try to do in order to make sense of an image from a dream. The ability to respond to symbols in this way is one of the most important functions of Jupiter.

The cosmic comedian

Jupiter has an important relationship with humour, and the word 'humour' has an interesting history. It's derived from the Latin word *humor*, which means 'moisture', and it was originally related to bodily fluids. The Greco-Roman physician Galen, writing in the late 2nd to early 3rd centuries CE and borrowing from typological theories offered by the Greek physician Hippocrates seven centuries earlier, described four different kinds of fluid he believed were found in the body: blood, phlegm, yellow bile, and black bile. Galen developed a theory of four basic temperaments – sanguine, phlegmatic, choleric, and melancholic – based on the balance of these fluids in the body. These temperaments in turn echo Aristotle's four 'sublunar' elements and Ptolemy's descriptions of the seven planetary rulers of the zodiacal signs.

Humour and the humours

The 'sanguine' temperament, related to Jupiter and, interestingly, the element of air, is warm and moist and based on blood, which Galen believed was produced exclusively by the liver, traditionally ruled by the 'warm and moist' Jupiter. Although 'sanguine' suggests a relaxed, tolerant, easy-going

---

32 Moreau was born on 6 April 1826 at 9.00 am in Paris. His birth chart, given a Rodden Rating of AA (very high level of accuracy), is available at astro.com.

nature, an excess of blood, according to Galen, causes a person to be too enthusiastic, bombastic, and theatrical. The idea of excessive sanguinity as a source of illness persisted through the medieval period into the late 19th century and provided the basis for the medical practice of 'bloodletting', performed when the patient was overheated or feverish.

The 'phlegmatic' temperament, related to the Moon and the element of water, is cold and moist and based on phlegm, also fondly referred to as mucus or catarrh. Phlegm serves as a lubricant in the body to stop the tissues from drying out and, in the nasal passage and the throat, it moistens and warms the air we inhale, and filters out dust and allergens. The term 'phlegmatic' suggests calm, stolidity, and a patience bordering on meekness. But an excess of phlegm, according to Galen, results in laziness, apathy, inactivity, and a weak pulse.

The 'choleric' temperament, related to Mars and the element of fire, is hot and dry and based on yellow bile, which Galen believed came from the gall bladder. Unlike the sanguine and phlegmatic temperaments, the choleric temperament has never enjoyed an especially good reputation. An excess of yellow bile, according to Galen, causes a state of constant rage and aggression. Galen didn't get its source quite right: yellow bile (it's actually greenish-yellow) is in fact produced by the liver, although it's stored in the gall bladder. Its job is to break down fats in the food we eat. We still refer to 'bilious attacks', expressed through symptoms like indigestion, stomach cramps, nausea, and vomiting, although there can be many causes for these symptoms and physicians no longer attribute them to an excess of yellow bile.

The 'melancholic' temperament, related to Saturn and the element of earth, is cold and dry and based on black bile, which Galen associated with the spleen. Today we know that there's no such thing as black bile in terms of the fluids the human body produces. The bile produced by the liver and stored in the gall bladder is greenish-yellow, not black, and it isn't a good sign if 'black bile' appears in vomit because it's usually an indication of internal bleeding. But from Galen's time to the early modern period, melancholics were perceived as suffering from a whole range of psycho-physical diseases – depression, gastrointestinal problems, muscle pains, and arthritis, to name just a few – that caused or corresponded with their unhappy mental state.

Galen's description does make a certain amount of sense; depression is now linked with a number of conditions that often elude specific physical diagnoses. Jung was deeply interested in this ancient medico-psychological typology and its links with astrology, and the two together formed the main basis of his theory of the four psychological types – although without the focus on blood, phlegm, and bile.

The theory of the humours might seem to bear no relationship to humour in the sense of what we find funny. It seems a long way from black bile to *Monty Python's Flying Circus*, although we might view the ironic vignettes created by this brilliant 20th-century team of comedians as a definitive example of the 'melancholic' end of the humour spectrum. But perhaps the apparent distance between humour and the humours isn't as great as it seems. To humour someone means catering to their whims according to their temperament, and certainly each of us finds different things amusing. Humour has a wide range of expressions, just as Zeus does in his myriad transformations, and what one person finds hilarious might bore someone else or deeply offend them. Offence at someone else's humour appears to be an increasingly common response in our current climate, and sometimes it seems that soon there won't be any real humour left at all.

Humour and joy

Humour can be ironic and subtle, with a dark cutting edge. Equally, it can be expressed as gross slapstick and buffoonery, often scatological and sexually suggestive; we can giggle at 'lavatory' humour and 'dirty' limericks even if we loudly proclaim that we find it all terribly puerile. But one of the qualities of humour as a reflection of Jupiter is that, whether it's darkly ironic or simply gross, there's an element of joy in it. We might recall how Zeus presented himself to Leda when he was seducing her: he was just a poor swan fleeing from an eagle's attack. Although the joke was on Leda, it's also Zeus laughing at himself. Whether or not we find something funny seems to depend on our individual temperament. Perhaps this is related, in part, to natal Jupiter's sign, house, and aspects. But there's general medical agreement that laughter, whatever triggers it, benefits the heart, lungs, and muscles, and releases all those 'happy' endorphins that alleviate stress.

Our individual response to humour may be influenced by our political beliefs, our personal emotional experiences, our cultural background, and our individual values. Collectives seem to favour certain kinds of humour, and what's funny in one country might be viewed as tacky, tasteless, or offensive in another. Language can also shape humour through idioms and subtle social references that can be entirely lost in translation. In Zürich I once watched the Monty Python sketch about the dead parrot dubbed in German, and the German translation, although deserving ten out of ten points for effort, was simply incapable of communicating the English idioms, regional accents, and sly cultural references. I'm sure the same applies the other way as well. And humour also follows fashion, like clothing and interior design. What matters is that whatever our culture and background, we're able to laugh, especially at ourselves.

A sense of humour reflects our ability to see the absurdity in life and in our own behaviour. That in turn requires the ability to cope with paradoxes, since life is both sublime and ridiculous, dark and brutal as well as joyful and bright, all at the same time. If we can manage to countenance life's innate contradictions, we might be able to laugh. Comedians who specialise in cruelty and mockery in order to score political points or destroy someone's reputation aren't in the least bit funny. There's no joy or absurdity in spite. This might be why literal thinking is so rarely humorous, and why fanatics of any persuasion always miss the punchline and never know how to laugh at themselves.

Humour is not the same as wit, although they often overlap. Wit seems to be related to Mercury, and without Jupiter's sense of meaningful connectedness, wit can be sharp, biting, scathing, and often brilliant, but may be entirely devoid of joy and whimsy. If wit lacks absurdity, then it lacks joy, and the only people laughing are those who feel their own agenda is being vindicated.

At the best of times, wit and humour supplement each other. But often wit is nothing but cleverness that masks envy and the desire to hurt. The kind of mockery that accompanies bullying and scapegoating isn't remotely funny, and Jupiter's joyfulness plays no part in it. Once again, J. K. Rowling's psychological insights are astute. The shapeshifting, soul-destroying Boggart in the Harry Potter novels takes the form of a person's greatest fear, but it can be driven away with the 'Ridikkulus' spell, which forces it to assume an absurd, laughter-provoking shape. Humour, like Jupiter, is one of our best antidotes to fear.

Gluttony: the Second Cardinal Sin

There's one more theme related to the psychology of Jupiter that's worth exploring: the Cardinal Sin known as Gluttony.

The origin of the Seven Cardinal Sins

The Seven Sins in Christian theology originate in the much older idea of the soul's descent from its heavenly home through the seven planetary spheres into physical incarnation. In the ancient Greek world, the descending soul was believed to be encased in a 'soul-vehicle', the *ochema pneuma*, whose purpose was to act as an organ of transmission and communication between the mortal body and the immortal soul. We've already encountered that word *pneuma* in relation to the Orphic Zeus. It's the Divine Breath of the god permeating the cosmos as *moira*: in other words, the World Soul, of which each individual soul is a part. Theosophical doctrines appropriated this ancient idea of the soul-vehicle in their descriptions of the astral body, bound to the physical body by a silver cord that breaks at the time of death.

References to the *ochema pneuma* can be found in Plato and the Neoplatonists, and it wasn't perceived as negative in any way; it was the necessary link between body and soul. But the Gnostics of late antiquity weren't quite so appreciative of it. They interpreted the idea of the soul's descent into incarnation as a journey through the domains of the seven malign planetary archons, who tainted the pure soul with the specific vices belonging to each of their realms.

The Gnostic planetary archons were generally viewed as nasty pieces of work. Each archon attached a layer like a malignant envelope around the soul, and each layer was subject to that planet's malevolent compulsions. The soul-vehicle thus became the carrier of *heimarmene* or astral fate. This negative view of the soul-vehicle as the source of seven unsavoury vices was reinterpreted in early Church doctrine as the Seven Cardinal Sins. Although the Gnostic planetary archons have never been part of the Church's official doctrine, their continuing presence in the guise of the seven Cardinal Sins is unmistakeable.

In Gnostic literature, which drew some of its ideas about the dualism of body and soul from the Orphics, the *ochema pneuma* was known as the 'counterfeit soul'. Unless the individual could break free from its planetary compulsions, there could be no return to the heavenly realm of the transcendent God; the soul would be trapped in an endless cycle of miserable earthly incarnations. We've inherited this idea of freeing ourselves from planetary 'compulsions' in the belief that it's possible to 'transcend' the natal chart, at least in our spiritual lives, as though the planetary configurations represent a fateful bodily imposition on our otherwise free souls. This idea, elaborated by Thomas Aquinas in the 13th century as a justification of astrology within the parameters of Catholic doctrine and appearing in more modern form in the work of 20th-century astrologers such as Margaret Hone, comes straight out of the Gnostic textbook.[33]

The Roman authors Cicero and Macrobius also took up the idea of the descent of the soul through the planetary spheres, but they weren't Gnostics and they wrote about the descent in a more positive way, associating the seven planets with benign as well as unpleasant attributes.[34] Mars, for example, doesn't only confer wrath, violence, and an inclination to war and bloodshed; it also confers courage, heroism, honour, and an aspiration to excellence. But Pope Gregory I, appropriating the ancient idea in the 6th century CE, stuck to the Gnostics' unattractive view of the planetary gods, presenting them as compulsions to sin rather than divine potencies with a creative as well as a destructive face.

On the Gnostic scale of unpleasantness, Gluttony (*Gula*), Jupiter's sin, took second place, following Envy (*Invidia*), Saturn's sin, which was deemed to be the worst one. Pope Gregory disagreed with the original Gnostic order, which was planetary, and placed Pride (*Superbia*), the Sun's sin, at the top of the list. Among those Christian authors willing to mention the planets, there was inevitable disagreement about which planet governed which sin.

---

33 Thomas Aquinas, *Summa theologica* I.115); Thomas Aquinas, *Summa contra gentiles* III.82-94. Both texts are available online in various editions and translations. For the 20th-century version of the idea, see Margaret E. Hone, *The Modern Textbook of Astrology* (Fowler & Co., 1972).

34 Macrobius, *Commentary on the Dream of Scipio*, trans. William Harris Stahl (1990); M. Tullius Cicero, *Somnium Scipionis*, in *De re publica and De legibus*, trans. C. W. Keyes (1928).

Avarice (*Avaritia*), for example, might be assigned to either Mercury or Jupiter, depending on how it was defined; it was sometimes called Greed, which might be viewed as Jupiterian, but it was also called Deceit, which might be more Mercurial.[35] In fact several of the sins might be applicable to the mythic Jupiter, including Pride, Lust, and Wrath. But Gluttony seems to epitomise the planet best.

Jupiterian Gluttony isn't simple greed, nor is it avarice. It's far more subtle and complex. Depictions of Gluttony in later literature and art are usually of clinically obese people stuffing themselves silly. Some of you may recall the nausea-inducing scene in the 1983 film, *Monty Python's Meaning of Life,* in which a very large man seated at a restaurant table eats so much that he literally explodes. This kind of depiction is misleading and unfortunate because there's often a deeper layer underlying displays of

Georg Emanuel Opiz, *The Glutton* (1804), private collection

---

35 For the history of the Seven Cardinal Sins and their origins, see Morton W. Bloomfield, 'The Origin of the Concept of the Seven Cardinal Sins' (*Harvard Theological Review*, 1941), and Morton W. Bloomfield *The Seven Deadly Sins* (1952).

gluttony which may reflect a profound unconscious aspiration: an urgent inner quest that we haven't yet recognised and which we blindly act out through substances such as food. We're back to the Jupiterian theme of the way in which we use physical objects and substances as symbols without realising it.

Obsession, addiction, and aspiration

Gluttony has a relationship with both obsession and addiction. There's something we feel we *must* have; we can't be happy or even survive without it. But obtaining the object of desire is only momentarily satisfying. We're hungry again soon afterwards and need another fix. Perhaps Zeus felt like that when he suddenly noticed someone new who took his fancy. He had to possess the object of his desire and nothing could stop him, not even Hera's dire threats. But once satisfied, nothing could induce him to stay; he had to find a new lover to pursue. Given the long-term results of his matings and their hidden teleology, this suggests more than simple greed. When it's disguised and unconscious, Jupiter's gluttony can feel overwhelming and shameful. But it can also make us intolerant of those who don't share our particular craving.

Gluttony is often focused on material things like food, drugs, sex, money, or beautiful objects. The compulsive collector of *objets d'art*, rare books, or precious gemstones is as much an addict as the compulsive gambler. But gluttony can also be focused on less identifiable objects, such as worldly position or power over others. Obsessive ambition is a form of gluttony, although it's often admired rather than recognised as an addiction. The worlds of politics, finance, and business are full of this kind of gluttony, highlighted in the 1987 film *Wall Street* in which Gordon Gekko, played by Michael Douglas, made his infamous pronouncement: "Greed is good."

Gluttony can also take emotional forms. Our compulsion might be to be needed, and we *must* have people around us who depend on our nurturing. Without it, we fear our lives will be meaningless and we'll simply disappear. This form of gluttony often isn't recognised for what it is because it can appear so caring and so hard to challenge. But if taken to excess, it can impel us to devour other people through emotional manipulation, negating their potential strength and right to an independent life. In the end we can destroy ourselves in an orgy of self-sacrifice that ultimately doesn't benefit anyone. We may also be addicted to being victimised, and may unconsciously pursue multiple situations where we can feel crushed by a soulless, cruel oppressor. Like addiction to power, with which it bears a certain secret relationship, addiction to victimisation often presents itself as virtuous.

There's also a form of intellectual gluttony: we *must* have all the answers and *must* discover absolute scientific or social or philosophical truths: we *must* know everything. We can't live without stuffing ourselves with more and more knowledge, regardless of whether it improves our own or others' lives. Admitting that we simply don't know the answers to everything and then getting on with our lives is tantamount to a negation of life.

And we can also be spiritual gluttons. We *must* find the absolute Truth, we *must* know the will of God, and we *must* preach it so that more and more people are converted to our beliefs. I'm sure you can think of many examples of all these subtler forms of gluttony, which are often collectively valued because they appear attractive or selfless and may have the added bonus of achieving concrete rewards. The dangers of these subtler forms of gluttony to one's own body and psyche are often ignored, as are the people who are damaged along the way by our own cravings.

As you can see, Gluttony is a versatile sin. Like the mythic Zeus, it can appear in many guises. Spiritual gluttony is closely related to fanaticism because the glutton hungers to be one of those superior, elite beings who alone know the will of the Divine. Gluttony is also related to narcissism if, because of deep and gnawing insecurities, we become gluttons for other people's adulation and the stream of praise pouring into the empty place inside. We desperately want to be seen as wonderful, special, and terribly important in the eyes of others, and the craving overshadows everything else. If we fall out of the limelight or our popularity ratings slump or we don't get enough 'likes' on Facebook, we may fall into a profound depression or an overwhelming rage towards those who aren't showing us the right degree of appreciation.

We tend to experience our gluttony through longing for an object – material, emotional, intellectual, spiritual – but often we don't realise that we're projecting something much more elusive and profound onto the object. We think it's the object itself that we crave, and it's difficult to break free of that conviction. But until we can get some sense of the deeper symbolic roots of our gluttony, we'll never feel full. We'll always be hungry, no matter how much we keep stuffing ourselves.

Since we all have a natal Jupiter, we all have a place within us where we're gluttons for something. A moderate degree of gluttony may do no harm and could offer a lot of pleasure as well as a road leading us to deeper insights into who we are and what we really seek. And a bit of excess may sometimes be just the right antidote to Saturn's gloomy austerity, reminding us that life can be joyful. But if gluttony begins to breach our limits and elbows other planetary needs aside, then we can get into a lot of trouble, materially, emotionally, physically, socially, and legally. We can make ourselves physically and emotionally sick, and we can injure and even destroy other people as well as ourselves. For obvious reasons, it's important that we try to face as honestly as we can that deeper level of our Jupiterian gluttony and what it might actually mean.

Questions and comments: Jupiter and envy

Audience: Liz, what do you think about all the angry people who follow in the wake of someone else's Jupiterian good fortune? They're the 'haters'. A lot of jealousy can follow someone else's luck, even if the lucky person has really worked hard to earn it. Is this part of Jupiter too?

Liz: Yes, what you're describing does seem to come with the Jupiter kit. Just as Zeus was envious of the potential power of human beings, other, more chthonic immortals like Typhon and the Giants were envious of Zeus and tried to overthrow him. Envy on both sides is a theme in Jupiter's story. The people you're calling 'haters' resemble the husbands, parents, and suitors of the mortals whom Zeus seduced. These mythic characters felt threatened and enraged because the resultant progeny might eventually take away their status, power, or love-object, just as Zeus' own father Kronos felt threatened by Zeus himself before he was even born. Zeus' seductions always left a trail of extremely angry people in their wake, and this often posed a great danger to the newborn child.

When the astrological Jupiter has symbolically impregnated us with a new vision, a new idea, a new inspiration, or a new possibility, others may sometimes feel anger because they wish they could have that kind of vision themselves, along with the sheer nerve to pursue it. They would prefer it if everyone remained unlucky, unfortunate, and uninspired. In Britain we sometimes refer to it as the 'politics of envy': if I can't have it, you shouldn't have it either. And that doesn't apply only to wealth.

The 1984 film *Amadeus*, directed by Milos Forman, was based on a 1979 play by Peter Shaffer, which in turn was inspired by an 1830 play by Alexander Pushkin. The film portrays this problem concisely, and although it's decades old, it's one of those films whose underlying theme is archetypal and never loses its relevance. At the end of the film, the composer Antonio Salieri, whose envy of Mozart's ebullient and apparently undeserved genius ultimately destroys his rival, declares, "I speak for all mediocrities in the world. I am their champion. I am their patron saint." Envy often follows people who shine with too much solar light, but it can also follow people who have the imagination and verve to transform themselves into someone else and fly off in pursuit of a Jupiterian inspiration – even if they fail in their quest.

There's always an aura of the chancer about Jupiter. We have to take a chance of some kind if we're hoping to experience that deeper or higher connection we seek. The chance may be material, emotional, intellectual, or spiritual, but there's always a risk. We can't have an adventure if we know exactly where we're going and what the outcome will be. Then it isn't an adventure any more; it's just another daily commute. J. R. R. Tolkien expressed this beautifully in both *The Hobbit* and *The Lord of the Rings* when he wrote about the reluctance of the hobbits to enter into adventures, and the danger of stepping out of our front door onto a road that could sweep us away and whose end we can't foresee.

Jupiter is incapable of being predictable. It's just not in the nature of the planet. In some ways it's more unpredictable than Uranus, which may be expressed suddenly and unexpectedly but remains highly predictable in the fixity of its progressive views. We can always be sure the new Uranian idea for reform is accompanied by the insistence that it may be painful but it's 'for the good of all'. We're back again to the mythic Zeus, whose behaviour is always surprising, not only in his loves and the transformations he undergoes to fulfil them, but also in his volatile temper. Will he be benign and reward us, or will he just hurl a thunderbolt at us because he's in a bad mood that day?

Those you call the 'angry people' will often try to block the mysterious intuitive spark in us that generates the faith to strike out into the unknown as we strive to connect with a bigger pattern. Even if we fall on our faces, at least we had the boldness and vision to try, which in itself can arouse envy in others. And sometimes we ourselves are the ones who unwittingly become the 'angry people', not only towards others but also towards our own adventurous spirit. Aspiration, like Gluttony, can sometimes be perceived as a sin.

There isn't any point in blaming other people for feeling angry when we display the Jupiterian spirit. When Jupiter is at work and we take a leap, it's not simply because we're reckless, selfish, and irresponsible, although someone else is sure to point that out. It's that something is changing inside us, and a door is opening. A lot of the anger that often surrounds Jupiter, like the storms always erupting on the physical planet, lies not only in other people's responses, but also in our anger towards ourselves because we may be forced out of our 'comfort zone' and asked to make a leap, take a chance, follow a hunch, or recognise and gamble on an opportunity. We don't know whether any of it is going to work. We may fail dismally, injure others, and lose everything. It's the not knowing that can generate anger as well as anxiety. We humans aren't very well equipped to deal with uncertainty any more than we're equipped to deal with paradoxes, and Jupiter is nothing if not uncertain.

On the astronomical Jupiter, nothing is stable, and the physical attributes of the planet mirror the psychological patterns we experience internally. If we try to look for solid earthy ground, we won't find any, because there's no accessible surface to stand on. There's no proven method of knowing whether our intuitions and leaps of faith will work, or whether the opportunity was merely a narcissistic fantasy. The only way we can find out is to pursue Jupiter's vision with as large a dose of realism as we can muster and a willingness to read the small print before we jump. If we never jump, we may spend the rest of our lives full of regret, wondering why life has somehow passed us by. The proverbial sadness of old age often reflects remorse over our mistakes. But equally, it may reflect the sorrowful realisation that we lacked the courage to make those mistakes, and failed to fulfil our potential because we couldn't find the optimism to believe in a meaningful future and take the risks required.

Is Jupiter 'controllable'?

Audience: Would you say that Zeus's uncontrollable sexual urges are a good illustration of the excess and bad judgement that people with a strong Jupiter sometimes show?

Liz: I understand your question, but no, I wouldn't say that. I'm not sure I would call Zeus' urges 'uncontrollable'. He's an archetypal image, not a human being, and his sexual proclivities are symbolic. They point to a fundamental facet of the archetype, which must continuously sow new seeds and generate new possibilities to fulfil a meaningful future. The astrological Jupiter also reflects an important dimension of the individuation process, reflected in the capacity to recognise that there *is* an individuation process, a teleology unfolding in our lives.

Your choice of words implies that Jupiter's 'uncontrollable urges' could somehow be mastered or made more temperate. But they're like Mars' need to engage in battle. It's not helpful to suggest that the archetypal principle we associate with the astrological Mars ought to master its warlike, competitive nature and become a team player. Mars' 'uncontrollable' impetus to fight and win is symbolic: a necessary dimension of the life process ensuring its survival and its continuing independent development. It's a necessity, and its expression in human life depends on how the individual chooses to work with it, rather than on something intrinsically wrong with the impetus itself. Mythic attributes like these can't be judged as though they were literal. They're symbols of the necessity of an archetypal potency and its need to fulfil its own nature.

As far as 'excess' and 'bad judgement' are concerned, you're right in one sense: a strong Jupiter can certainly reflect a tendency to abandon moderation and an inclination to act before considering consequences. But that doesn't always end badly. It depends not only on the specific situation but also on the individual's own choices and the degree of their self-awareness. You seem to be suggesting that if we try hard enough, we can learn to control Jupiter's excesses. But working with the planet's problematic expressions isn't an issue of ego-mastery or will power. Problems arise from the way in which an individual chooses to respond to what Jupiter symbolises, rather than with the nature of the planet itself. Every planet is 'excessive' in the pursuit of its own fulfilment.

Excess, like beauty, can also sometimes be in the eyes of the beholder. The chief objector to Zeus' promiscuity is his wife Hera. But from Zeus' point of view, it could be argued that she's impossibly possessive, which can be a form of excess in itself. Jealousy and love triangles are ubiquitous in mythic stories. But Hera's rage is primarily directed at her husband's illicit offspring and the fact that he could generate all those exceptional semi-divine children without her. That's envy rather than jealousy: the deep envy sometimes expressed by those who feel unable to generate creative vision themselves, and who then attack another person's creative work in the hope they'll feel better about themselves. The psychoanalyst Melanie Klein wrote an entire volume on the problem of envy of the creative power of others.[36] Unfortunately the density of her psychoanalytic language could cure even the worst case of insomnia, but her central theme is deeply important.

The mythic Zeus' promiscuity doesn't reflect 'bad judgement'. Is there a cosmic rulebook that states exactly how many sexual partners the god is allowed to have before his sexual meanderings are deemed 'excessive'? Zeus isn't averse to rape, which in human life is a vile and inexcusable act. But as I said, when we explore mythic stories, we're looking at symbols, not actual people. Archetypal patterns, when they erupt into our lives, can do so forcibly and without our conscious consent, and we may feel emotionally violated by events, inner forces, and compulsive patterns we don't understand. Try to think more symbolically. You have a valid point on one level, but your choice of words conveys a particular moral approach that might not always be the best one for working with the astrological Jupiter's challenges.

We can certainly make florid blunders through arrogance and inflation. These blunders are often referred to as 'bad judgement', and sometimes they're destructive to others as well as to oneself. Sometimes they're

---

36 Melanie Klein, *Envy and Gratitude* (1957). This was one of Klein's last works and probably her most controversial. She discusses the 'primary envy' felt by the infant towards the mother who possesses the power to create new life. Although Klein's approach is characteristically Freudian and specifically related to infancy and the parent-child relationship, the idea, if it's extracted from its reductive framework, has great relevance to more general expressions of destructive envy towards those who are perceived to have the fertility to create something solely from their own imagination.

inexcusable and even unforgiveable. But *why* do we become arrogant and inflated? Jupiter itself isn't at fault; it's usually because we're trying to hide from wounds and insecurities we don't want to face, and we enlist Jupiter – our sense of connection with a greater purpose in life – as a defence. Although we need a moral conscience when dealing with Jupiter, we don't need the morality police. And sometimes our blunders are the best thing that could happen to us because we get knocked off our perch and learn some hard lessons that otherwise we might do our best to avoid. We don't always know which blunders will be unforgivable and which will lead to the enhanced awareness that comes from facing our shadow-side and learning to laugh at our often insufferable moral rectitude.

I'm not suggesting that we should never try to exercise reflection and restraint, especially when the consequences of our choices damage the lives of others. Conscious awareness is the only effective tool we possess to engage with and mediate the archetypal potencies. But mediating, reflecting, and exercising restraint aren't the same thing as control, and Jupiter, like all the planets, is an archetypal principle, not a bad habit that can be kicked through will power or a stay in rehab.

If we identify with the archetypal principle Jupiter symbolises, then we may become uncontrollable because consciousness is no longer able to mediate. Believing that we can do whatever we like, and justifying it through our emotional needs, religious beliefs, or political ideologies, reflects a state of being out of control, and our *hubris* will sooner or later invoke *nemesis* in one form or another. But it's the individual who chooses how to express a strong Jupiter, and it's the individual, not the planet, who unleashes Jupiter's most destructive dimensions. Planetary symbols don't make bad judgements. It's humans who try to appropriate the planetary potencies for their own purposes, usually unconsciously. If we want to work with Jupiter in the most creative way, control isn't a helpful approach. Humility, a sadly misunderstood and underrated attribute, is right at the top of the list of qualities we might do well to cultivate, along with that precious Jupiterian ability to laugh at life and at ourselves.

The astrology of Jupiter

The meaning of Jupiter

Can we summarise the meaning of the astrological Jupiter? Probably not. But a workable hypothesis may be embedded in the question: Jupiter symbolises our quest for meaning. The best clue is given by the portrayal of Zeus in the Orphic descriptions of *nous*, *pneuma*, and *moira*: Divine Mind, Divine Breath, and Fate as teleology. These themes, in whatever terminology we choose to couch them, form the core of the planetary symbol in the birth chart. Jupiter reflects our need to discover meaning and the ways in which that meaning emerges from the intuitive perception of a greater design at work in life.

Jupiter's natal placement isn't only a pointer to how we can expand and benefit our lives, although that's often the reward of finding the courage and faith to pursue a vision. This planet reflects a particular kind of joy which springs from the sense that we're in exactly the right place at exactly the right time. Through natal Jupiter we somehow 'know' we're connected to a bigger pattern. We feel our lives matter and that events are 'meant' and hold a deeper significance, even if we can't rationally explain how or why. We long to feel a connection with this mythic portrayal of Zeus as the divine power that permeates everything and reveals that everything is interwoven and in a process of intentional development. Something much greater than us is felt to be constantly creating, transforming, shape-shifting, fertilising, emerging. We get closest to a sense of it through the sphere of life symbolised by Jupiter's placement in the natal chart.

The idea that life might be meaningful is viewed by many people as an infantile concept that reflects the existential human fear of insignificance, powerlessness, and inevitable death. This is essentially a Marxist perspective, which views the religious instinct solely as a product of socio-economic forces: the 'opiate of the masses'. But all we achieve by espousing that perspective is to replace the idea of 'god' with ideas of 'society', 'economic forces', and 'cultural constructs', which then appear as universal potencies as powerful and tyrannical as any deity.

Such people aren't likely, if they experience Jupiter strongly on an inner level, to talk about meaningful patterns and the teleology of the soul. Instead, they feel vindicated in the absolute rightness of their beliefs, and they may swell up with *hubris* because the universe apparently favours them. And why shouldn't they see it that way? There's no concrete proof that our lives have any meaning at all; we perceive life through the lens of our own individual nature, and we interpret it accordingly.

A conscious pursuit of meaning is usually the fruit of suffering and consequently asking the big questions that arise only when more rational explanations and solutions have failed. But would any of us wish to suffer, or see suffering inflicted on others, just so that humans can develop greater consciousness? Does suffering always make a person one of the spiritual elite? I doubt it. Sometimes our pain just twists us and makes us bitter, and we learn nothing at all. We can choose to work with Jupiter in many different ways, some more creative and some more destructive. Jupiter points to the perception of a larger pattern at work in life, and it might be a good idea to explore that pattern, whether it's objective, subjective, or both, and learn what we can without believing we can learn it all and know what Zeus knows. Socrates once said that the beginning of wisdom is the realisation that we really know nothing at all.

Centaurs and Fishes

Let's look briefly at the two signs that Jupiter governs, Sagittarius and Pisces. If any of you wish to use Neptune as the ruler of Pisces, that's entirely valid – there's no hard-and-fast rule about this, and astrologers will probably always disagree about outer planet rulerships as well as many other things. But if this is your preference, it might be helpful to think of Jupiter and Neptune as co-rulers of Pisces, rather than abandoning Jupiter entirely. Sagittarius and Pisces both seem to reflect, with unerring accuracy, many important dimensions of Jupiter's nature.

Jupiter's signs thrive on connections, Sagittarius mentally and Pisces emotionally. They move across boundaries and are most at home in liminal realms, and neither will stay in their own or anyone else's boxes. In this sense, both signs are innately subversive when faced with rigid intellectual, emotional, spiritual, or material boundaries, unless they unconsciously succumb to their own potential fanaticism. Both Sagittarius and Pisces perceive links that other signs tend to miss between all kinds of events, experiences, ideas, spheres of knowledge, feelings, and apparently unrelated dimensions of life.

Mercury and its signs, Gemini and Virgo, are also mutable and also gifted at making connections, but neither of these signs is impelled to put the pieces together to discover a complete story and experience the sense of an overall meaning. The information alone is sufficiently satisfying to Mercury, especially if it's interesting as well as useful. Sagittarius and Pisces can perceive invisible relationships, and in the pursuit of the connections, suddenly something clicks. It's like a treasure hunt, or the fascination of putting together a complex jigsaw puzzle when the underlying picture suddenly becomes clear even if only a few pieces are in place. Both signs are involved in this process, although they do it in different ways.

Both signs can also suffer from Jupiter's more problematic side. They're predisposed to put vision before reality, belief before logic, and perceived truth before facts, and they're easily inclined to gluttony, inflation, and fanaticism, especially as a defence against more difficult natal placements that neither sign is well equipped to face. Both Sagittarius and Pisces, along with Gemini, used to be referred to in older astrological texts as 'double-bodied' signs, as there are two fishes in the image of Pisces and a hybrid of human and horse in the image of Sagittarius. This suggests that neither of these mutable signs is amenable to sticking to a single purpose, goal, or mode of response to life. They're more interested in discovering bridges. The American poet Walt Whitman was born with the Sun in Gemini trine Jupiter in Aquarius, and a Uranus-Neptune conjunction in Sagittarius in the 9th house (the natural house of Jupiter) square a Saturn-Pluto conjunction in Pisces in the 12th (also the natural house of Jupiter). In *Song of Myself*, he wrote, "I am large, I contain multitudes."

Sagittarius

The image for Sagittarius is that of a centaur, but it isn't clear which one, as there are quite a few mythic centaurs to choose from. A constellation called Centaurus, located in the southern hemisphere, is one of the largest constellations in the heavens, although not found on the ecliptic and therefore not part of the zodiac. Centaurus was portrayed in ancient Babylon not as a centaur, but as either a bison with a human head or an even stranger creature with a man's head and torso attached to the rear legs and tail of a bison. This being belonged to the Sun-god Shamash.[37] The Babylonians linked the constellation of Sagittarius with the war-god Nergal, whose planet was Mars and who was portrayed as a winged centaur with two heads, one human and the other that of a panther, shooting an arrow from his bow. Nergal also boasted a scorpion's stinger above his horse's tail. You can't get much more mutable than that.

Some Greek authors equated the constellation of Centaurus with Kentauros, the mythic child of Nephele, a cloud-nymph, and Ixion, whom Zeus hurled into Tartarus because of his *hubris*. Kentauros was born with a twisted body; in an effort to escape the misery of constant mockery and loneliness, he fled to Mount Peleion and mated with the wild horses living there, fathering the race of centaurs. In ancient Rome, the constellation of Centaurus was associated by Ovid with a centaur we're more familiar with in astrology: Chiron, the divine healer, teacher, and hunter, fathered by Kronos on the Oceanid nymph Philyra.[38] But many present-day astrologers assume that the constellation of Sagittarius, not that of Centaurus, is a representation of Chiron.

To confuse us even further, the Roman writer Hyginus associated Sagittarius with a hybrid creature called Krotos, son of Pan the goat-god and Eupheme, nurse of the Nine Muses. Krotos, who was raised by the Muses, was a great hunter who invented the bow. He was also an accomplished musician.[39] Although Krotos was a satyr rather than a centaur, the Muses asked Zeus to set him among the stars as the constellation of Sagittarius. His bow represents his archer's gift; his equine half reflects his skill on horseback; and his goat's tail reveals his true satyr's nature.

You can see from these various mythic references that we really have no idea which centaur is depicted by the constellation of Sagittarius

---

37 Gavin White, *Babylonian Star-lore* (2008), p. 57.
38 Ovid, *Fasti*, V, 379.
39 Hyginus, *Fabulae*, 224; Pseudo-Eratosthenes, *Catasterismi*, 28. Pseudo-Eratosthenes is the name given to an unknown author who summarised *Epitome*, a lost work by the 3rd to 2nd c. Greek astrologer and poet Eratosthenes, under the title *Catasterismi*. Both Hyginus and Pseudo-Eratosthenes cite a 3rd-century BCE Greek tragedian called Sositheus as the source for the story of Krotos.

because several different mythic beings were associated with it in different ancient cultures. Whichever one it might be – healer, hunter, patron of the arts, solar deity, or war-god – or even if it's really a centaur at all and not some other form of hybrid creature – the 'double-bodied' shape suggests a bridge, although not necessarily an easy one, between the instinctual and divine worlds.

All the various mythic attributes associated with the constellation could be seen as a reflection of Sagittarius' multifaceted nature, and these diverse qualities are all relevant to the mythic Zeus as well as the astrological Jupiter. Despite its reputation for frankness, Sagittarius, like Pisces, indulges regularly in shape-shifting. Some of you may recall the controversial astrological research of the French statistician Michel Gauquelin, whose work spanned the period between 1949 and 1973. Gauquelin, although not an astrologer, was interested in the underlying character traits of eminent professionals and athletes and, as a result of his research, came to the conclusion that particular planets placed within orb of conjunction of the angles in the natal chart, especially the Ascendant and the MC, might reflect the individual's chosen profession as a reflection of innate abilities. Jupiter culminating near the MC turned up with surprising

Sidney Hall, *Sagittarius*, Plate 24 in *Urania's Mirror* (1825), restored by Adam Cuerden.

frequency in the chart of actors and politicians. Both, to achieve success, must be consummate shape-shifters, and they're often indistinguishable from each other.

Pisces

The Piscean fishes aren't as difficult to identify as the Sagittarian centaur. One of the myths associated with Pisces is the story of Aphrodite and her son Eros (the Roman Venus and Cupid) provided by the Roman poet Ovid. He wrote that the divine pair, when threatened by the monster Typhon, tied themselves together with a rope, jumped into the Euphrates River, and transformed themselves into two fishes in order to escape.

The Roman author Hyginus, writing slightly later than Ovid in the 1st century CE, offered an earlier Greek version of the story. Aphrodite and Eros, when Typhon tried to attack them, jumped into the Euphrates and were rescued from the monster by two fishes, who were then rewarded by being placed in the heavens as the constellation of Pisces. Hyginus also described another, even older version originating in Babylonian myth. A mysterious cosmic egg rolled into the Euphrates, and two fishes nudged it ashore to rescue it from the waters. Some doves then sat on the egg to warm

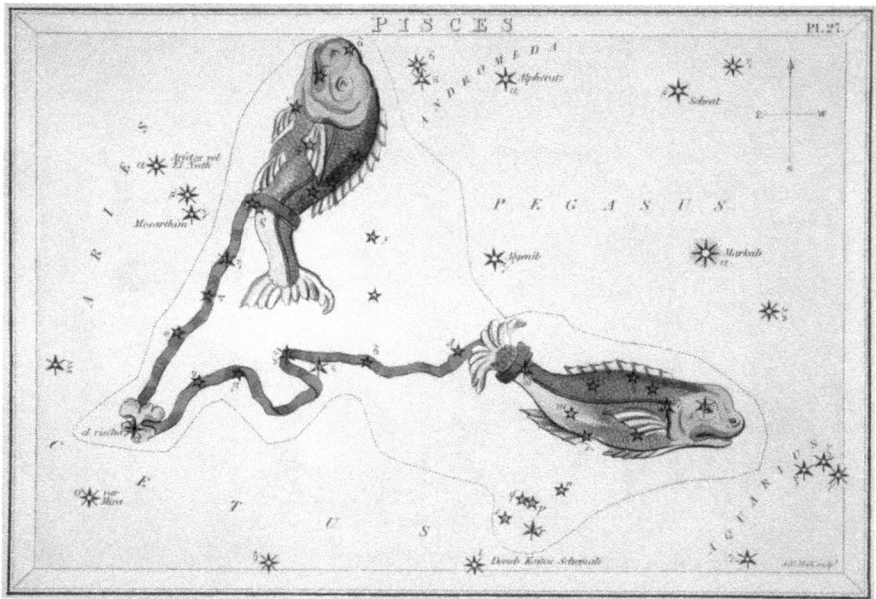

Sidney Hall, *Pisces*, Plate 27 in *Urania's Mirror* (1827); original image restored by Adam Cuerden.

it until it hatched, and Aphrodite, known in ancient Babylon as Ishtar, rose from it. She rewarded the fishes by turning them into the constellation of Pisces.[40]

A relationship between Aphrodite and Pisces is evident in these stories about the constellation, perhaps reflected in astrology's traditional description of Pisces as the sign of Venus' exaltation. The theme of rescue or salvation is also common to all three versions of the myth. This theme reflects Jupiter as *Agathos Daimon* ('good spirit'), the saviour and bringer of luck. And perhaps we should also include Zeus *Skotitas* ('the murky one'), as befits the darker side of this enigmatic zodiacal sign which excels in the evasion and obfuscation so vividly displayed in Zeus' constant shape-shifting.

Jupiter in the natal chart

Jupiter's natal house placement suggests the sphere of life in which we instinctively seek a connection with a greater pattern, and where we strive to experience meaning and significance. It's also where we may genuinely receive an inspired glimpse of our own teleology, perhaps more than once during the course of life. Jupiter's natal house describes the domain where we'll focus our longing to discover the bigger story and our individual place in it, whether or not we're consciously aware of the longing. And Jupiter's natal sign tells us something about the manner, mode, or style in which we tend to pursue and interpret the quest for meaning.

When we think about natal Jupiter's sign, it's helpful to remember Jung's model of the four functions of consciousness, which he linked with Galen's four humours and the four elements of astrology. Thinking is related to the element of air, feeling to the element of water, intuition to the element of fire, and sensation to the element of earth. We all experience Jupiter's joy and Jupiter's cravings differently, and we're inspired by different triggers. Jupiter's sign by element can tell us a lot about what function we're characteristically likely to use the most, even if it's neither well-adapted nor sophisticated, to seek a connection with what we sense as a greater unfolding pattern.

Jupiter's natal aspects to other planets can reveal the ways in which our yearning for meaning will interact with other, equally valid needs

---

40 Hyginus, *Poeticon astronomicon* 2:30; Ovid, *Fasti*, 2:457; Hyginus, *Fabulae*, 197.

within us. It may be misleading to assume that hard aspects will bring out the worst side of Jupiter and soft aspects the best, because it doesn't really matter what the aspect is. It's the connection between the two planets that seems to be the most important factor. And it's up to individual consciousness to work with the combination in the most creative and life-enhancing way we can.

The nature of the aspect may tell us more about how we experience and cope with our own responses. A square between Jupiter and another planet can hint at the feeling that we're doing something wrong, or that we have to struggle or take one side against the other. There's always a sense of tension, and the stress can push us into extremes of behaviour. Oppositions can reflect the conviction that we're the victim of something or someone 'other' who disrupts our lives. Or we may depend on that 'other' to provide us with a sense of meaning which we'll eventually need to discover within ourselves. Trines may reflect a feeling of lazy self-satisfaction: "Oh, that will be easy. I don't have to reflect on it or do any hard work." Sextiles may reflect a feeling of wanting to understand something: "Yes, that's going really well (or badly), but *why*?" The nature of the aspect won't tell us whether we're experiencing the creative or destructive side of Jupiter, because both expressions can emerge with any aspect, alternatively or simultaneously.

Example charts

Now let's look at our first example chart. Despite its complexity, there's something satisfyingly literal about Jupiter in the birth chart. That literal quality can be quite amusing in an ironic sort of way. Jupiter might be viewed as the most enigmatic of the planets because of its symbolic dimension, where everything is perceived as paradoxical and imbued with hidden meaning. But at the same time, the planet may be expressed in a strikingly concrete and obvious way.

Example 1: Florence Nightingale

This is the natal chart of Florence Nightingale, with Jupiter in the 6th house in Pisces. Where else could it possibly be? But there's a catch. The birth data for this chart isn't reliable. The rating originally given by Lois Rodden was DD ('Dirty Data'), meaning there are two conflicting birth times, neither of which was officially verified. At astro.com the rating is X, meaning no birth time, because the official birth record gives only the date and the two birth times therefore can't be considered valid. They may be entirely speculative, rectified, or derived from hearsay, but the absence of official documentation or written family records means we can't rely on either of them.

The first birth time, 2.00 pm LMT, is the one I've used for the chart given below. It fits the known facts of Florence Nightingale's life so well that it's difficult to challenge. The second birth time, 8.45 am LMT, results in 21° 52' Cancer on the Ascendant, with a Sun-Moon conjunction in Taurus in the 11th house and Jupiter in Pisces in the 9th. Arguments could be made on behalf of this chart too, although perhaps not as convincing. Some of you may want to work only with firm birth data, which is fair enough, and if you find Florence Nightingale's life interesting you should set up a noon chart

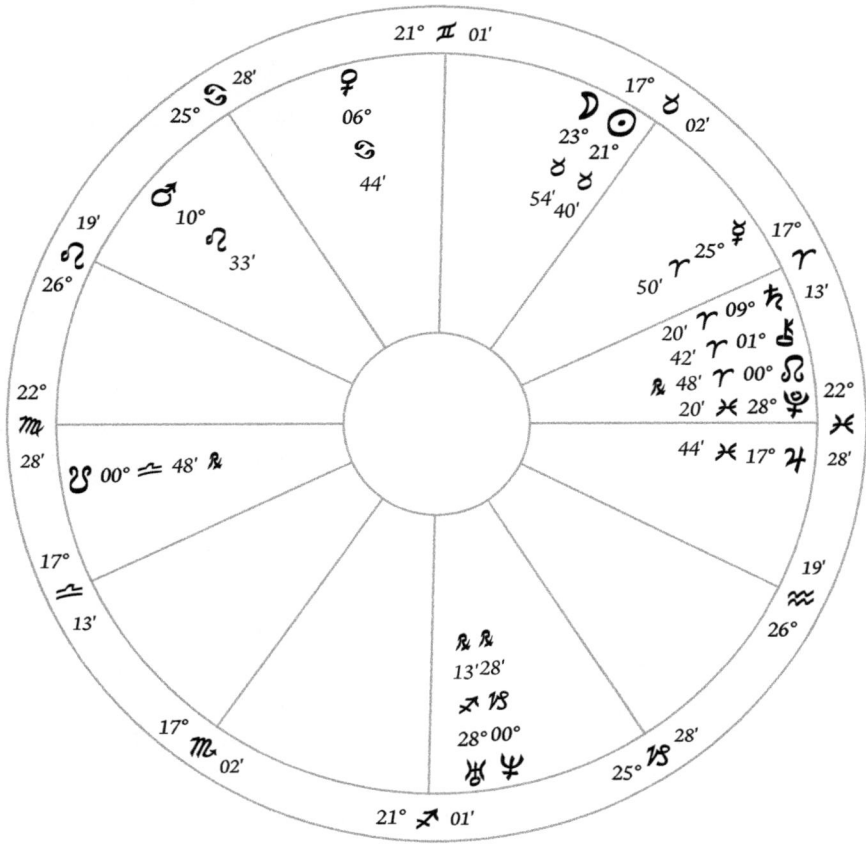

Florence Nightingale
12 May 1820, 2.00 pm, Firenze, Italy

or a flat chart with 0° Aries on the Ascendant. These are both valid ways of presenting a chart with no birth time. You could then avoid debates about the validity of house placements, angles, and house cusps. The aspects between Jupiter and the other planets, and the interpretations I'll be suggesting, would remain the same.

For those of you who might not be familiar with her, Florence Nightingale was a 19th-century British social reformer and statistician who became a nurse. Now viewed as the founder of modern nursing, she reached

Florence Nightingale c. 1860. Photo by Henry Hering, National Portrait Gallery, London.

the peak of her career during the Crimean war, during which she trained and managed nurses and organised the care of wounded British soldiers in Constantinople. After the war, she founded the first secular nursing school in the world at Saint Thomas' Hospital in London. During her lifetime, Victorian society idolised her and projected an idealised image on her; she became known as 'The Lady with the Lamp' and 'The Ministering Angel'. However, she wasn't always the most comfortable of personalities to deal with. According to some of her contemporaries, she could be a demanding termagant who, in today's climate, would probably be accused of bullying her staff and her patients. In other words, she was a perfectionist with high standards and an absolute, unflinching dedication to her vocation.

Florence Nightingale was also involved in a number of social reforms, including attempting to improve healthcare for the whole of British society, advocating hunger relief in India, and trying to abolish the existing prostitution laws. The size of these aspirations is unmistakeably Jupiterian, but her approach to implementing them was practical. She was deeply committed to what now might be understood – or misunderstood – as feminism, but she didn't perceive herself as a feminist because no such concept existed at the time. She didn't experience herself as 'oppressed' just because she was female. Rather than believing there was some kind of fundamental gender-based social injustice that she had to battle against, she felt the existing laws were ignorant and inefficient in terms of their benefits to society because too many women's individual skills and abilities were not being utilised. A pragmatist rather than an idealogue, today's identity politics would have meant little to her.

Florence Nightingale was a remarkable figure, in part because of the tenacity with which she pursued and found her meaning in life, and also because she wasn't battling for an overarching ideological cause. Her projects were always specific and practical despite their Jupiterian scope, and her methods were geared towards what could be done every day for actual people. She felt she should try to improve the world around her on a realistic level by using the abilities she was born with and the skills she had developed; and that was exactly what she did, without any fanfare.

This quality reflects the realistic, earthy attitude of a strong sensation type, reflected in the chart by the intense focus of a new Moon in Taurus in the 9th house and the efficiency and attention to detail of a Virgo Ascendant. It also reflects the lack of any planet in the element of air: she tended to look closely at what was in front of her, but found it harder to step back and detach from the immediate demands of the present. She couldn't see any point in pursuing anything other than the service to which she was dedicated, fuelled by her immovable religious convictions.

Florence Nightingale was also a prolific writer, and she authored a number of short texts based on her medical knowledge and experience. She deliberately wrote them in simple language because she wanted everyone to be able to understand them. A poor family with a sick child could read one of these texts and get clear advice on how to provide basic home treatment for a fever or a rash because the language was accessible rather than impossibly erudite and technical.

She was born into wealth but was brought up in an apparently liberal, humanist household, so it was easy for her to ignore the traditional female role models of her time because she hadn't imbibed them in early life. She had many friends of both sexes, including colleagues in powerful positions. We don't know, and probably never will, whether any of these people became her lovers. But she refused to marry because she believed her vocation was a call from God – which is what the word 'vocation' implies – and marriage might interfere with her calling and force her to compromise it. She was deeply religious but not intolerant, and she opposed religious discrimination of any kind. She explored Eastern religions with enthusiasm and was convinced that all religious systems had something to offer and contained something of truth in them.

Natal Jupiter is in the 6th house, traditionally associated with service and with improving, integrating, and healing the body and the material environment. Jupiter is also in dignity in its own sign of Pisces. This sign is traditionally linked with compassion, empathy, and the gift of being able to identify with another person's suffering. It's also associated with self-sacrifice in the name of an artistic, spiritual, or humanitarian ideal. Meaning comes from merging with others and sharing the universal emotions common to all human beings. In some ways this natal Jupiter placement couldn't be more obvious in its expression in her life. Concerning herself with social causes, working as a nurse in a war zone, and tending to the suffering of others, comprise as literal an expression of Jupiter in Pisces in the 6th house as we're likely to see.

Jupiter also conjuncts the Descendant, so the need to find meaning and a connection with a greater design through her work also involved her relationships with others. Her commitment couldn't be satisfied by working in a research lab or quietly writing books at home; she had to be out there in the field, relating all the time, training other nurses and engaging emotionally as well as practically with injured soldiers. Her pursuit of meaning lay not only in service but also in relationships, and she was prepared to sacrifice – and, equally importantly, also avoid – the fulfilment as well as the challenges of a personal romantic relationship and the rewards of family life in order to pursue her calling.

Natal Jupiter isn't challenged by any other planets. Its only major aspects are sextiles to the Sun-Moon conjunction in Taurus in the 9th house. These are comfortable aspects, so there's no inner confusion or conflict between her work and her beliefs. Although she explored many different religions, she was more inclined to perceive the common ground between them rather than their incompatibilities. Although a deeply committed Christian, she was uninterested in evangelism and never tried to convert others to her beliefs. The feeling of living a meaningful life was found through 6th-house practical service in a way that expressed

Piscean empathy and identification with others while harmonising with her immoveable faith in a higher power.

Florence Nightingale's earthy nature suggests she was entirely realistic about the inevitability of war with its concomitant suffering and death. But her sense of vocation was unshakeable. Nursing and teaching were not merely a job; they fulfilled a demand from a higher power. But at the same time we can see her dedication as a kind of gluttony. She was compulsively addicted to her work at the expense of any personal emotional and sexual fulfilment and, like the mythic Zeus, she obviously enjoyed giving orders and running the show.

Earlier I suggested that she avoided personal relationships as well as sacrificing them to fulfil her vocation. Like any other human, Florence Nightingale was complex and seems to have experienced deep fear and self-doubt, despite the comfortable certainty of the Jupiter-Sun-Moon configuration. The 7th house is quite tricky. Pluto in the 7th conjuncts the Descendant in Pisces, and Chiron in Aries in the 7th, in an out-of-sign conjunction with Pluto, conjuncts Saturn in Aries, also in the 7th. It isn't surprising that she shied away from marriage, and who could blame her? On a personal level, Pluto, Saturn, and Chiron all in square to Venus in early Cancer reflect deep shyness, loneliness, and vulnerability. Her sense of self-worth as a loveable individual seems to have been severely undermined. As a woman, she didn't feel she was of any value, despite her confidence in her abilities and her certainty about her vocation. That liberal, humanist background might not have been quite as liberal as it seemed.

This is an excellent example of the way Jupiter can be mobilised to compensate for more difficult configurations in the natal chart. Jupiter is always ready to act as a compensation for pain, as well as providing meaning and context for the pain. Florence Nightingale's confidence may only have extended to the belief that her life had significance in the greater scheme of things, and that she was meant to serve others. But as a woman who might be fulfilled in love, she didn't believe she deserved or could ever enjoy that kind of contentment. Perhaps she also feared she would be controlled, undermined, humiliated, or abandoned in any close relationship she allowed into her life. The Saturn-Chiron-Pluto configuration reflects great depth and insight, which she certainly expressed in her work. But it seems she also projected that power onto any person with whom she might have become emotionally and sexually involved.

The configurations involving these 7th-house planets suggest a deep wound that Jupiter helped to conceal and compensate for. Florence seems to have been a deeply unhappy person who felt painfully isolated and unable to connect with others unless she was needed and in control. I'm not suggesting that this kind of Jupiterian compensation is 'wrong'. From Jupiter's teleological perspective, perhaps she was 'meant' to be denied a rewarding personal life because the deprivation allowed her to fulfil a deeper purpose in a story that's still unfolding long after her death. And Jupiterian compensations are characteristic of what we all do to cope with being human. Our gifts and aspirations balance, conceal, and provide meaning for our feelings of fear and inadequacy and, looking at it through Jupiter's lens, perhaps this is how it's meant to be, as long as the compensation is sincere and contributes something creative to life. Unfortunately, as we'll see later, this isn't always the case.

Along with those painful squares from Venus in Cancer to Saturn, Chiron, and Pluto, Florence's Venus is in an out-of-sign opposition with Uranus in Sagittarius, which in turn is in an out-of-sign conjunction with Neptune in Capricorn. These two outer planets are square to the Pluto-Chiron-Saturn conjunction. Venus is the only personal planet in this T-cross, and it's painfully beleaguered. Jupiter's apparently literal expression is starting to look more complex than it first appears. If we want to understand natal Jupiter, we need to look at everything else in the chart, because we humans will always seek to alleviate the pain of intractable wounds through finding something meaningful that makes sense of our suffering. Jupiter will often come into play as a response to areas of the chart where we experience a feeling of damage, injury, limitation, or deprivation.

There is a profound paradox in this because we don't tend to pursue meaning unless we're suffering, yet often we suffer because we persist in seeking meaning rather than living in the moment and valuing what we have. In Florence Nightingale's case, the paradoxical role that Jupiter plays contributed a great service to her own life as well as to the generations that followed, since her work formed the basis for what we now understand as modern nursing. Whatever she might have been like as an individual – and it seems she could be highly unpleasant, pernickety, stubborn, and domineering – she made a contribution that continues to generate fertile progeny. Today's nursing profession owes a great debt to her. Well beyond her lifetime, Jupiter seeded something through its natal 6th-house placement which at the same time helped her to cope as a deeply damaged person, allowing her to feel that the damage had been transformed into a creative contribution.

Audience: I'm curious what other factors in her chart helped her make the lifetime commitment that seems to be so difficult for a lot of people with a strong Jupiter.

Liz: Perhaps the most important factor was her own individual choices. But the most powerful astrological contribution may be the new Moon in Taurus in the 9th. When a person is born at a new Moon, the solar sense of individual specialness tends to occlude lunar emotional responses to the outside world. It's the dark of the Moon, so there's an intense laser-beam solar focus that can sometimes appear as a kind of imperviousness to any external interference. Even if the new Moon is in an empathetic sign, the person can sometimes display a surprising insensitivity and self-absorption. It isn't as simple as being 'selfish'; often people born under a new Moon are capable of great self-sacrifice, as Florence Nightingale was. But there's a kind of insularity, an immovable faith in one's own path.

That can be both problematic and immensely creative. The new Moon in this chart is in a fixed sign, in a house concerned with one's religious and intellectual world-view. However volatile Jupiter might be in itself, especially in mutable Pisces, Florence Nightingale was immovable in her belief in her calling. Jupiter's volatility seems to have been reflected in the variety of causes she was involved with, ranging from writing, teaching, and nursing to the wide range of social projects she supported. She was probably easily bored and needed a varied array of outlets through which she could express herself.

Jupiter's tendency to mobilise and sometimes inflate in the face of pain links it with narcissism, and a deep narcissistic wound can sometimes result in identifying with the Olympian archetype and needing to be seen as the most important person in the world. I don't believe this applies to Florence Nightingale – perhaps she escaped it because of the weight of planets in earth and the self-critical tendencies of the Virgo Ascendant – but it's common enough in professions such as politics and the arts. The narcissistic wound, reflecting a corrosive sense of being insignificant and worthless, may become intolerable, and Jupiter compensates for the suffering in a variety of ways both dark and light.

We're back to one of the main conundrums underpinning this planetary symbol. The mythic Zeus' relationship with what the Greeks understood as Divine Mind is reflected in our human need to experience joy and meaning through discovering some kind of intelligent plan at work in life. That's pretty straightforward and 'natural'. But the inevitable disappointment and injury that result from the collision between that need and the limitations of concrete reality can in themselves mobilise Jupiter's quest for meaning as well as its potential for bombastic and explosive destructiveness. Jupiter symbolises an innate archetypal pattern, but its activation depends on experiences that seem to deny the fulfilment of that need. There isn't really any answer to the conundrum. An abiding sense of connection to a deeper pattern in life, rather than a descent into narcissism or a compulsive flight into the fantasy-world of a *puer* on the rampage, depends on our ability to cope with the paradox.

Audience: You mentioned Florence Nightingale's wound in relation to Venus. What about her Chiron? Is there any relationship between Chiron and Jupiter?

Liz: In her natal chart, Jupiter and Chiron aren't in aspect. But there's a relationship between the two on a deeper level, in terms of the way in which suffering can provoke Jupiter into action and can stimulate a quest for meaning. In Florence's chart, Venus and Chiron are in square and Chiron is in Venus' natural house, the 7th. Jupiter isn't involved in this configuration. But it does conjunct the Descendant, and this suggests a contradiction between great expectations in relationship and Chiron's assumption that all personal relationships will end in pain and tears. I'm certain that Florence Nightingale didn't expect to be loved as an individual; she assumed she would be rejected and abandoned because she felt that somewhere deep down, she was ugly, unlovable, and doomed to loneliness.

This may reflect a lonely childhood, especially if we consider the neediness and vulnerability of Venus in Cancer, and it may describe her experience of her parental background. Uranus and Neptune are conjunct in the 4th house, related to the father, and Venus is under fire in the 10th, related to the mother. I would guess there was an unhappy parental marriage with an emotionally absent but highly idealised father and a needy and perhaps destructively jealous mother who couldn't cope with the competition of an attractive daughter. The parental background is connected to Florence

Nightingale's feelings of abandonment and rejection. That isn't an unusual situation and it happens often enough in families, Victorian or otherwise.

In order to feel her life had any significance, she turned to natal Jupiter to give her a sense of meaning because she couldn't solve the problem by working on her personal relationships. That would have been unbearably risky and painful, and depth psychology as we know it now didn't exist, at least during most of her lifetime. Florence died in 1910 and Freud had already published several major works by then. But even if she was familiar with psychoanalysis, she would probably have rejected it on religious grounds, as do many committed Christians today. And the new Moon in Taurus, along with Saturn, Chiron, and Pluto in the 7th, suggests far too much pride and suspicion of others' motives to bare one's soul to a stranger.

The unhappiness reflected by Chiron and the other planets forming hard aspects to Venus mobilised Jupiter in a way that might never have happened if those difficult aspects weren't present in the birth chart. We might even speculate that the teleology of this individual life wasn't based on living and dying as a lonely, disappointed woman; it was centred on creating and embodying an idea that has generated fertile progeny for two centuries and changed the course of how we understand healing. The lonely, disappointed woman was, in Jupiter's context, a necessary and meaningful spur to fulfilling a teleology stretching beyond a single lifetime.

Audience: Could the 7th house indicate the many relationships where she took care of people?

Liz: Yes, I think so. The 7th house, with Jupiter conjuncting the cusp and Pluto, Saturn, and Chiron as well as the Moon's north Node placed there, seems to reflect her need to constantly engage with people, whether they were the wounded and sick patients in her care, the nurses she trained, the unknown readers towards whom she directed her books, the welfare of the various social groups whose lives she attempted to improve, or the military authorities with whom she had to deal during the Crimean War.

Her entire life was focused on other people, and they all embodied in one way or another each of the 7th-house planets: an opportunity to pursue an inspired vision (Jupiter); a confrontation with wounded, suffering humanity (Chiron); an engagement with death and the will to survive (Pluto); and the limits and hardships inherent in mortal life (Saturn). Behind that focus is the new Moon in the 9th house and the sense of a divinely given calling that could only be fulfilled through the symbolism of Jupiter in Pisces in the 6th house.

Example 2: Mick Jagger

Florence Nightingale's chart offers us a good example of natal Jupiter in the element of water. In this next example, natal Jupiter is in the element of fire. It's also another demonstration of how Jupiter can be expressed in obvious, literal ways in an individual's life, but with much deeper levels at work beneath the surface.

Mick Jagger's career has spanned more than six decades, and he's one of the most successful and influential figures in the history of popular music.

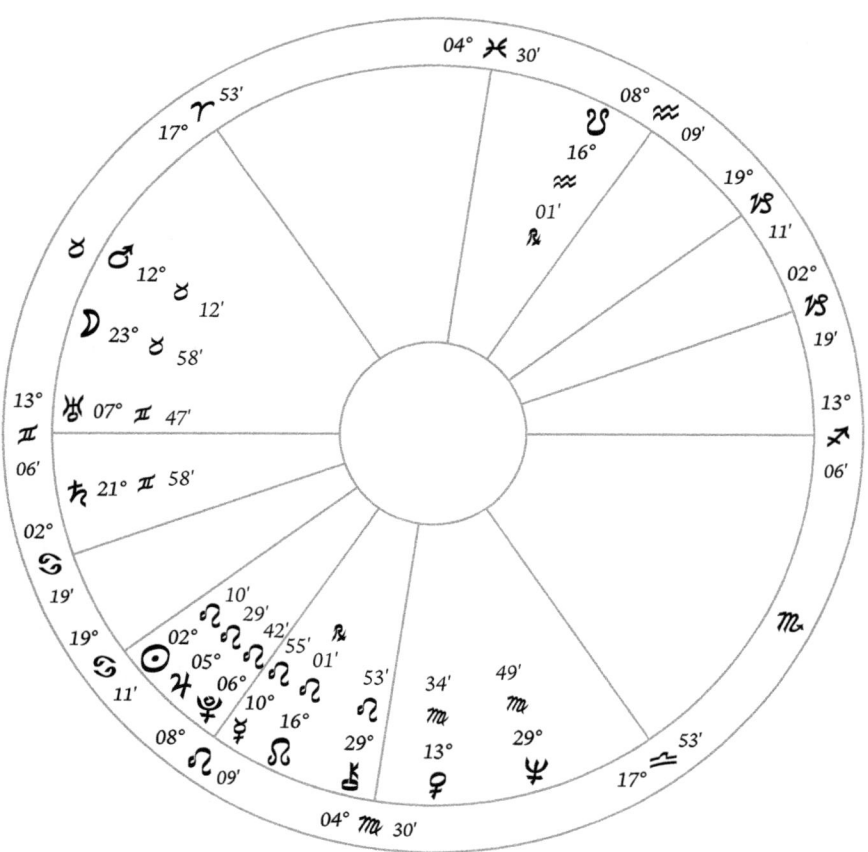

Mick Jagger
26 July 1943, 2.30 am, Dartford, England

Mick Jagger at a Rolling Stones concert at Zuiderpark in The Hague, Netherlands, 29 May 1976.

I don't need to provide a lengthy biography; all the information is available online if you don't know it already. Briefly, he grew up in a middle-class family in Dartford, Kent. His father was a gymnast and physical education teacher who 'would have preferred him [Mick] to become a sportsman'.[41]

Mick Jagger attended the London School of Economics before abandoning his studies to join the Rolling Stones. He gained notoriety not only for the flamboyant and sexually suggestive (and often explicit) style of his music and performances, but also for his colourful romantic career, his involvement with drugs, his collisions with authority, and his position of dominance in the 'counterculture' of the 1960s. He's been formally married and divorced only once, but he's fathered eight children with five different women. His most recent child, a son called Deveraux Octavian Basil Jagger, was born in 2016 when Mick was 73. He was knighted by Queen Elizabeth II in December 2003, although rumours circulating at the time, which might or might not be true, claimed the Queen didn't want to hand him the award in person because she felt he was an 'unsuitable' candidate. I can't imagine why. Formally, he's now Sir Michael Philip Jagger, and I have no doubt that he, more than anyone, appreciates the irony.

Natal Jupiter is at 5° Leo in the 3rd house, conjunct natal Sun at 2° Leo, Pluto at 6° Leo – both also in the 3rd house – and Mercury, the chart ruler, at 10° Leo in the 4th house. Sun, Jupiter, and Pluto, although technically in the 3rd, are conjunct the IC at 8° Leo, close enough to merit being interpreted

---

in both the 3rd and 4th houses, assuming the birth time is accurate. Jupiter also squares natal Mars at 12° Taurus in the 12th house.

There are no surprises here. Even if the birth time is a little off, if you've seen him perform and didn't have any birth data you might readily guess that stellium in Leo.[42] The 3rd house is the house of expression, communication, and movement. The 4th is concerned with family background, father, and roots. Although the closeness of the Sun-Jupiter-Pluto to the 4th house cusp implies considerable complexity in his family background and his relationship with his father – especially in light of his need to kick against authority – it's also relevant to think about what the idea of 'roots' might mean on a deeper, inner level, particularly in terms of the kind of music Mick Jagger is immersed in.

In his personal life, with all those children fathered with different mothers, Mick Jagger has behaved a lot like the mythic Zeus. It would be easy to label him a narcissist, but I don't think that perception is either helpful or accurate. We should use the term carefully. Being a narcissist in the clinical sense doesn't mean someone is simply vain, flamboyant, and prone to showing off. If the two were identical, every extraverted person born with an emphasis in the element of fire, especially those with Jupiter in Leo, could be accused of narcissism. Clinical narcissism reflects a profound wound and a compulsive compensation for feelings of emptiness and worthlessness. One giveaway is that narcissists don't usually have real friends; they have either acolytes or enemies. Mick Jagger has sustained deep friendships with both men and women over many decades.

There are certainly painful aspects in the chart, although the same might be said of all of us. Venus at 13° Virgo squares Saturn at 21° Gemini, and Moon at 23° Taurus squares Chiron at 29° Leo. Early feelings of loneliness, isolation, and the expectation of being rejected, used, or abandoned in close relationships have undoubtedly played their part in Mick's chequered personal life. These kinds of feelings can easily fuel the need to be loved by as many people as possible, and the aspects aren't uncommon among

42 The chart data, as with all the charts in this seminar volume, is available at astro. com. Jagger's birth time is listed as Rodden Rating A, which means 'accurate' based on data quoted by the person, kin, friend, or associate. Because the data comes from someone's memory, family legend, or hearsay, we shouldn't expect 100% to-the-minute accuracy. In this case the birth time was provided by Mick Jagger himself.

those who seek fame in spheres like music, theatre, fashion, and film. Hard aspects from Saturn and/or Chiron to Moon and/or Venus can be found in the charts of Elvis Presley, Marilyn Monroe, Michael Jackson, and a whole host of other gifted artists who have tried to assuage their loneliness and lack of self-esteem by becoming famous and desired by a global audience.

But that doesn't equate with clinical narcissism. And Sun conjunct Jupiter in Leo isn't an aspect inclined to feelings of worthlessness. The person may be an exhibitionist and a *prima donna*, and temperamental behaviour is usually *de rigeur*, especially if there's a secret underlying shyness and lack of self-value. But with Sun-Jupiter in Leo there's also a deep confidence in one's uniqueness and the ultimate value of one's gift, and this can provide the person with a sense of connection to a deeper meaning in life. Talent, however modest, is something that must be developed and contributed as part of a larger design.

In Mick Jagger's case, it's likely that such perceptions are intuitive and felt rather than rationalised through a philosophy or an ideology, but I believe they're nevertheless a powerful motivation. With Jupiter in Leo, meaning is pursued through authentic self-expression, and that requires honestly assessing one's abilities and limits and developing one's talents to the best of one's capacities. Trouble can arise when an individual isn't honest and realistic about those abilities and limits, and they try to become something they're not. Envy of others' gifts may also make it hard to value and develop one's own.

Mick Jagger's way of experiencing his life as meaningful is to be one of the brightest lights in the heavens, and to get everyone dancing. With Pluto involved in the conjunction, that light may also be dark, subversive, and even sinister. But Mick has to shine and make an impact, and he may also, because of the emphasis at the IC, unconsciously carry the unspoken dreams of earlier generations of the family who weren't able to express their own creative gifts. If we think about the roots of the music that serves as a vehicle for his self-expression, it weaves together blues, jazz, gospel, R&B, and early rock and roll – genres that in turn have their own roots in Black America and its historical oppression, poverty, and suffering. Some of the impact of the Stones' music lies in the power of these early sources, welded together by the band to form a unique sound that draws on the past but is entirely contemporary.

Mick Jagger has to communicate, but with Mercury conjunct Pluto, clear verbal communication isn't his first language. Self-expression becomes a kind of obsession because Jupiter conjuncts Pluto. It constitutes his survival and is quite literally a matter of life and death on the psychological level. There's no universe in which he could have stayed at the London School of Economics and pursued a career in business; nor could he have followed his father and become a gymnast, although the way he uses his body in performances might be seen as his own version of it. Lots of people over the decades, including some close to him, have voiced critical comments – no doubt often justified – about the flawed aspects of his personality. But he's been loyal to his daimon and followed his inner necessity regardless of the cost, reflecting the authenticity demanded by Sun conjunct Jupiter in Leo.

What is the nature of his talent? Mick Jagger isn't a great composer. He's not Beethoven or Mozart, nor is he a true poet like Bob Dylan or Leonard Cohen. Many of the most popular tunes in the Stones' repertoire were written jointly with, or solely by, Keith Richards. So how has he acquired such power as a collective icon? What is it we respond to through that angular Sun-Jupiter-Pluto conjunction? In a way he's managed to invoke and give us a taste of Zeus in his rowdier, darker guise, showing us that a human can embody a very badly behaved god and get away with it.

Planets closely conjuncting angles tend to convey an unadulterated archetypal punch, connecting us with a planetary potency in distilled form. Willingly or unwillingly, consciously or unconsciously, the individual incarnates the mythic figure on some level. These angular planets have great importance in terms of how we're perceived by the world. This is what Michel Gauquelin discovered in his research, which I mentioned earlier. The angles are related to embodiment, and a planet on an angle embodies its archetypal nature, often in an obvious way.

It's interesting that Mick Jagger could write and record a song called *Sympathy for the Devil*, especially if we remember the violence that erupted at the Altamont concert in 1969, when Hell's Angels were employed as security guards and four people died after the song was performed. It's likely that no one else at the time would have dared to create such a song, which couldn't be a clearer expression of Sun-Jupiter-Pluto in Leo. The Devil has been given many names in folklore and religious teachings; the one Mick Jagger chose for *Sympathy for the Devil* is Lucifer, which means 'bearer of light'. Even if you loathe him and his music, he remains not only a colossus in the music world, but also a vivid embodiment of Jupiter in the element of fire.

Why then did *nemesis* not hunt him down for his *hubris*? Mick Jagger has somehow managed to avoid dying in a plane crash like Buddy Holly, Jim Croce, John Denver, and Otis Redding, or overdosing like Brian Jones, Janis Joplin, Jimi Hendrix, and Jim Morrison, or destroying his body slowly and relentlessly like Elvis Presley and Michael Jackson. So many gifted figures in the popular music world have encountered a tragic fate, often – although not always – through their own agency. How did he escape it? Did his strong natal Jupiter 'protect' him in some way?

Apart from its conjunctions to the Sun, Pluto, and Mercury, Jupiter squares natal Mars in Taurus in the 12th and sextiles Uranus, also in the 12th. Mick Jagger, consciously or not, has been persistently angry for most of his life: angry towards the establishment, angry towards the 'normal' society of his generation, and angry towards authority figures, beginning with his father. His behaviour reflects that of quite a few of Zeus' children in myth. With Mars in Taurus in the 12th, this slow-burning anger draws on a deep pool of familial and collective rage that carries a very long history.

This may be related to the kind of music he's chosen to write and perform, rooted in a history of darkness, rage, and suffering that finds its redemption through a quality of joy that makes people want to move instinctively to the rhythm. Jupiter in hard aspect to Mars is a 'bad boy' aspect, always spoiling for a fight. But somehow Mick Jagger has got away with it, unlike so many of his 'counterculture' contemporaries. It's interesting to ask *why*. Is he just lucky? And if so, what does Jupiter's 'luck' really mean?

Audience: Is it charisma?

Liz: Charisma doesn't really help someone escape *nemesis*. Often charisma is the very thing that invokes *nemesis*, if the person identifies with the archetype and the adulation of the audience that so often follows. Identification with an archetype is an essential definition of *hubris* and it's never a good idea, especially if a planet is on an angle in the natal chart. Identification leads to inflation, and the individual personality, along with personal choices, is subsumed. But I suspect Mick Jagger doesn't really take the archetypal image all that seriously. He might be vain and self-centred, but he isn't truly hubristic because he can laugh at himself. Although he knows how to embody and invoke the archetype, he doesn't identify with it. We should always remember Jupiter's irony. This planet reflects our ability to see the utter absurdity of life at the same time as its profound meaning.

Mick's performances are a kind of caricature of himself. His sense of the absurdity of life may allow him to connect with the deeper level of Jupiter that helps us to recognise that the gods are laughing at us as well as cherishing us, and that we would be wise to laugh with them. However famous and important we may believe ourselves to be, each of us, like every other human, will eventually get old and die. Mick Jagger hasn't truly identified himself with the Jupiterian archetype. He unashamedly enjoys it, opportunistically capitalises on it, greedily feeds himself from it, and has gleefully made a great deal of money from it. But he doesn't seem to have made the mistake of thinking that he *is* Jupiter.

Perhaps this is also why he's managed to maintain friendships with his ex-wife and his various lovers. Zeus had a jealous, furious Hera to contend with, but Mick Jagger has somehow managed to avoid this dilemma and hasn't had to endure Hera's form of bitter, relentless retaliation. It seems he's been perceptive enough to know intuitively that if we're given a gift, we can enjoy it, share it, and profit from it, but we aren't its creator. We're its vessel. We can express it and benefit from it, but it's there for a reason bigger than ourselves. Jupiter can connect us with the divine, whether or not we choose to use that term, through the sense of a meaningful life. But we ourselves are humans, not divinities.

Audience: Is this part of the meaning of the 3rd house? Does it make us mortal and relatable?

Liz: That's an interesting question. Relatable, yes. A good metaphor for the 3rd house is breathing. We breathe in and we breathe out, and we transmute what we've taken in and communicate it to others in a different form. The 3rd house, as an airy house, is one of the houses concerned with relationship, in this case the relationship of one idea to another, and the relationship with others through the communication of ideas. The impact of speech is a remarkable thing, whether we understand 'speech' as actual words or as other forms of language such as music, painting, sculpture, or dance, or systems of knowledge rooted in symbols, such as astrology, Tarot, or alchemy. Ideas need a language, and language is both symbolic and a form of relationship. As for the mortality part, I don't think that's the concern of the 3rd house. The experience of our mortality is the ambiguous gift of Saturn and Chiron, and also of the Moon, which reminds us that everything moves in waxing and waning cycles. And the houses that bring us face to face with our mortality most powerfully are the 4th, the 8th, and the 12th.

Jupiter in the 3rd can reflect the joy of discovering what happens when we communicate something and someone else really hears it. We sing a song and others begin to sing along. We say something and it changes someone else's view of reality. And we experience the same transformation as the recipients who participate in the conversation. The 3rd house is Mercury's natural house, and Mercurius, in alchemical symbolism, is the agent of transmutation. It's a magical process.

When Jupiter is in the 3rd, that deeper level of communication reveals meaning to the individual as well as to those with whom they communicate. Perhaps this is why the Stones – those who are left – are still making albums and still touring. I doubt they need the money. But I'm sure Mick Jagger loves those live performances. He would never have survived as a studio musician with no direct contact with an audience. The magic of being on stage, and the sudden spark when the audience has connected, provide the meaning. And with a Gemini Ascendant, Jagger not only knows how to embody Zeus; with Mercury, the chart ruler, conjunct Jupiter on an angle, he can also embody Hermes the Trickster.

Audience: Can Jupiter conjunct Pluto indicate an exaggeration of the need to regenerate? And the promiscuity as well?

Liz: Pluto reflects our survival instinct, and because it moves so slowly, it symbolises the survival instinct of an entire generation. When Pluto is angular or makes strong aspects to personal planets, we're plugged into a collective sense of threat and a collective determination to survive. We're impelled to change or destroy everything we feel is rotten, spoilt, and past its sell-by date, or we will get sick and die. We destroy the world, or a small part of our own personal world, in order to regenerate it so we can perpetuate life. The urge to regenerate is the urge to live, through the constant purging or transforming of anything that threatens life.

The Pluto in Leo generation has expressed this survival instinct by focusing on the importance of the individual. Mick Jagger is no exception; in fact, he's a fine example of his generation. This group, which spans a period of nearly twenty years, is sometimes known as the 'me' generation, but it's not simple selfishness. The individual matters, the individual is worth something, and individual self-expression is necessary for the collective to survive. It's the great solar declaration expressed in the English folk song, *Green Grow the Rushes O*, "One is one and all alone and ever more shall be so." Pluto in Leo isn't interested in 'we' as a collective cooperative. It's not a team player. It's concerned with the survival of the creative 'I' so that life itself may survive.

The Pluto in Leo generation is also known collectively as the 'baby boomers'. The operative word here is 'baby', not just because there was a boom in births just after the Second World War – in fact Pluto was already in Leo during the war years – but also because the archetype of the divine child infuses the collective psyche of this generation. Survival depends on asserting one's individuality and individual potential against the dreary uniformity of social norms and conventions and the noxious fumes of 'groupthink' personified by the kind of unreflective, destructive mass movements that triggered the war in the first place. As the American social philosopher and comedian George Carlin was purported to have said, "Never underestimate the power of stupid people gathered in large groups."

As for promiscuity, it depends on how you define the term and what moral judgements you make about it. We've already looked at the issue of Zeus' promiscuity earlier. Promiscuity can sometimes be a person's response to the terror of becoming involved too deeply and then suffering humiliation and abandonment because they love too intensely and fixedly. I wouldn't associate Pluto with promiscuity in the sense of a constant succession of casual lovers in pursuit of transient sexual satisfaction, unless it's a defence against a fear of the price one might have to pay for loving too deeply.

Nor is Jupiter in itself necessarily a contributor to promiscuity, despite the mythic figure's endless amorous pursuits. As I said earlier, mythic images are symbols, not actual people. Jupiter-Pluto in Leo can sometimes describe an almost obsessive loyalty, especially if other chart factors collude, such as Venus in Scorpio or a strong Venus-Pluto aspect. Mick Jagger's apparent promiscuity may have more to do with natal Venus square Uranus, which doesn't enjoy being confined by conventional codes, and with his Gemini Ascendant, which sometimes just gets really bored with the same conversation – and sex can be a form of conversation – with the same person all the time. It may also reflect his natal Venus square

Saturn, which fears and expects rejection and may follow the precept that there's safety in numbers. And if you have thousands of attractive young people hurling themselves at you after every public performance, it might be an offer too tempting to refuse. Are you certain you could?

The question of promiscuity is complex, and there may be many psychological and astrological factors involved. Also, it depends on the cultural values of the time and place. "Thou shalt not commit adultery" is specific to the Abrahamic religions but not to every culture at every epoch of history, and what we call promiscuity may mean something entirely different in another cultural context. And the mythic Zeus' promiscuity isn't that simple either, since it almost always involves the engendering of a significant child who furthers some kind of deeper pattern or design.

Let's look at another example, this time with natal Jupiter in the element of earth.

Example 3: Adolf Hitler

Adolf Hitler presents us with one of the darkest expressions of Jupiterian inflation that any of us is ever likely to encounter. Jupiter isn't the 'culprit' here; no planet 'makes' anyone behave in a particular way. A planet is a symbol of a particular psychological dynamic embedded in a complex web of other, equally important dynamics in the birth chart. And if there is a 'culprit', it may lie in our individual choices, which depend on our willingness to develop a modicum of consciousness and self-reflection. We can learn a lot from this chart because, at first glance, it displays what looks like an apparently benign conjunction of Jupiter and the Moon. Although Jupiter is in Capricorn, the sign of its fall, and the Moon in Capricorn is in its detriment, Moon-Jupiter contacts are usually interpreted as positive – perhaps a bit theatrical and excessive, but nevertheless fundamentally big-hearted. So what's wrong with this picture?

As in Mick Jagger's chart, Hitler's Jupiter is in the 3rd house, although it's nowhere near the IC. But we're looking once again at the theme of communication as a source of meaning: the experience of a connection with the audience, the spark that leaps across the divide between separate individuals when an idea has been expressed and received. Hitler loved to give speeches to a huge audience. But the ideas in his case were cruel, violent, malign, and destructive, as was their medium of expression.

Jupiter at 8° Capricorn not only conjuncts Moon at 6° Capricorn but also opposes Chiron at 6° Cancer in the 9th house. The Moon and Chiron are in exact opposition. This is a deeply injured Moon, placed in a sign in which it tends to feel cramped and constricted. That isn't because there's something 'wrong' with Moon in Capricorn. As usual, everything depends on what the person does with such feelings. But even in its happiest expressions, pride, fear of emotional vulnerability, habitual self-control, and the horror of being too dependent on other people tend to incline Moon in Capricorn to maintain a show of strength and endurance at all times.

We mustn't reveal weakness; we mustn't display neediness; we must never break down in floods of tears and ask for help. We must always be the person who supports and guides others, even to the point of controlling

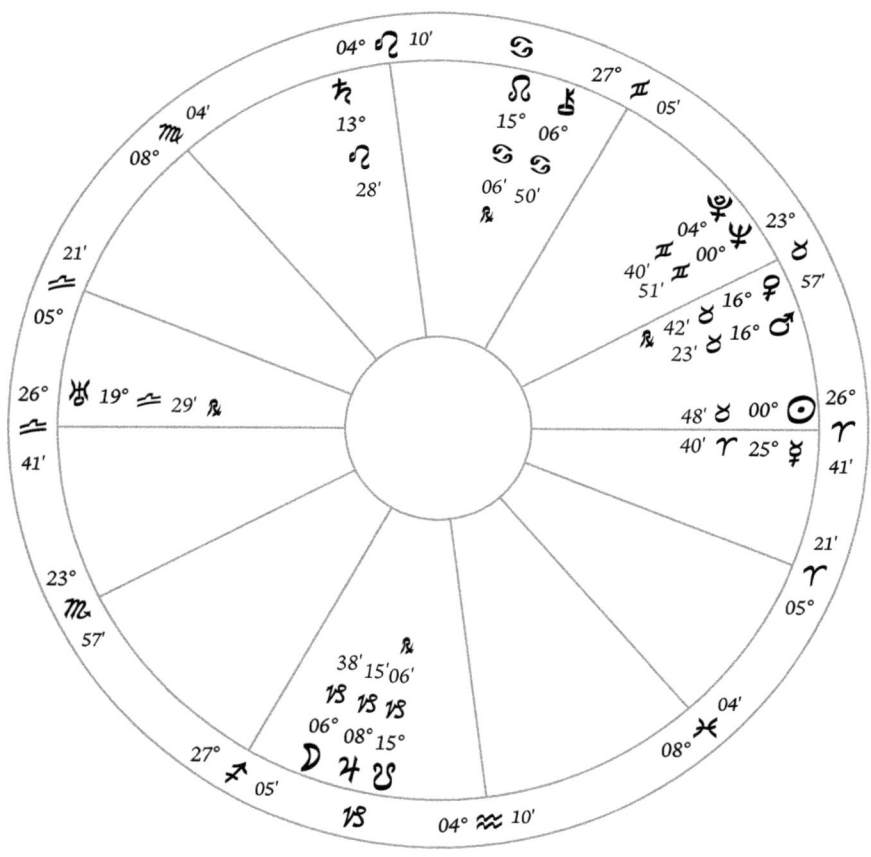

Adolf Hitler
20 April 1889, 6.30 pm, Branau am Inn, Austria

Hitler in 1938. Photo by Heinrich Hoffmann, German Federal Archives.

them as well as ourselves. Too much of that, and it's easy to begin to believe that our own feelings are a burdensome interference. Eventually we might not register any feelings at all. It's easier to simply turn off the phone so that we don't have to hear it ring. And that can happen very early in life.

The Moon is our avenue of empathy and emotional connection with others, especially through shared vulnerability. If the Moon can't allow itself to show any hint of vulnerability, a deep internal disconnect may occur. A similar situation can occur with Moon in hard aspect to Saturn. Taken to its extreme, a painful sense of emotional constriction and isolation may, in some people, result in a chronic tendency to blame others for one's loneliness.

This uncomfortable Moon may express profound resentment at being victimised or abandoned, and without any consciousness of the mechanism of projection, self-righteous blame may lead to some rather unpleasant results – especially if Jupiter rides to the rescue to compensate for all that bitter self-pity. In Hitler's case, with Moon in Capricorn exactly opposite Chiron, the feeling of being the victim of others' cruelty and harsh control was so firmly entrenched that it became impossible to engage in any sort of self-reflection. Jupiter's tendency to self-aggrandisement then became the inevitable compensation.

Jupiter's sign can tell us about the manner in which we seek to achieve a sense of meaning and a connection with a greater design. Jupiter in the element of earth will usually pursue the experience of meaning through worldly channels. That doesn't necessarily mean an unbridled pursuit of money or material success. Sometimes people with an earthy Jupiter may reject worldly wealth in the name of a spiritual goal or a political aspiration to change society. If Jupiter is in Taurus, the experience of meaning may come through sensual pleasure and encounters with beauty in nature, music, and art. It might also come through building something that endures: a home, a school, a solid family unit, a company, a system of ideas. In Virgo, Jupiter may pursue practical knowledge or craftsmanship as a means of experiencing a sense of usefulness in the world. Jupiter in earth longs to do something practical, to make something happen and, especially when it's in Capricorn, to claim authority and respect. Through concrete achievements, we might experience the sense that our individual lives have meaningfully influenced the future.

Jupiter in Capricorn is known as an ambitious placement. Ambition in itself is not a negative thing. It can be immensely creative, positive, and beneficial to others; without it, there would be no social or scientific advances and we would probably still be living in caves gobbling raw meat and clubbing each other to death fighting over a mate or a mammoth bone. It might seem as though we're still doing exactly that, with marginally more sophisticated weaponry, dating apps, and an air fryer to cook the meat. But ambition – on behalf of others as well as oneself – has allowed us to live longer and more fulfilling lives than we did at the end of the last Ice Age, and, in some parts of the world at least, life is considerably safer and better than it was a century ago, however loudly we might complain.

With Jupiter in Capricorn, everything depends on what the individual chooses to do with their ambition, and what kind of motives lie behind it. If the motive is self-serving power in the world, and ambition and control of others become a compensation for the Moon's feelings of emotionally isolation and abandonment, then Jupiter's inclination to inflation will kick in, and we might see the behavioural pattern known as 'malignant narcissism'. I mentioned earlier that I didn't feel it was appropriate to suggest that Mick Jagger suffers from clinical narcissism. But I think it's entirely appropriate to apply that term to Hitler. Extreme malignant narcissism seems to be related to what we call psychopathy and sociopathy. I won't attempt to answer the perennial question of whether such an individual is 'made' through environmental pressures or simply born that way, or a combination of the two: character interacting with environment in an unpleasant alchemical mix. I'm inclined to agree with the latter perspective.

It may be worth looking at a bit of Hitler's history to get a sense of how the Moon-Jupiter-Chiron configuration might have been reflected in, and symbolises his response to, his childhood. He was the fourth of six children. Three of his siblings died in infancy, but Hitler had to share his home with two half-siblings from his father's second marriage (Hitler's mother Klara was his father Alois Hitler's third wife). So little Adolf was surrounded by other children, with parents who never had any time at all for him. A naïve, well-intentioned social worker might feel terribly sorry for the poor little boy, who was regularly beaten by his father. A large proportion of the world's population has suffered over the centuries, and continues to suffer, from precisely this kind of domestic environment. But for Hitler, no one else on earth had ever suffered as much as he did. This is where we see the self-aggrandising fantasies of extreme narcissism kicking in.

Hitler constantly fought with his father and rebelled against the disciplines of his school. He was morose and detached and argued constantly with his teachers. He had aspirations to become an artist, but his father wouldn't allow it, and the extent of his talent was questionable anyway. He was constantly thwarted, but he didn't seem to have the capacity to find a way through his frustration, other than to build up a reservoir of hate.

I can't answer the question of whether this kind of behaviour is something that emerges as a response to childhood experiences, or if it's already inherent. Childhood experiences may be relevant because they can either mitigate or inflame what's already present from birth. Hitler seems to have nursed with obsessive care every early experience of disappointment. No one would ever be forgiven for the fact that he had suffered. The Jupiterian need to feel relevant and important in the grand scheme of things seems to have exaggerated these hurts to grandiose proportions. His remedy was equally grandiose: he believed he was destined to rule the world and had the right to destroy anyone who stood in his way.

Jupiter in Capricorn can reflect a healthy need to find meaning through being effective in the world. One can make a difference by reoganising or reshaping the social or material environment. In the 3rd house, this can be achieved by communicating ideas. In itself, that's a gift, and there's nothing inherently negative or destructive about it. We might imagine someone who teaches at or founds an innovative new school, or contributes to new ideas in scientific research, or pursues innovative designs or techniques in architecture or industry, or enters the world of politics in the hope of generating a better future through targeting educational change. They sometimes say of Capricorns that they always find it preferable to marry the conductor than the second violin; but if the conductor is willing, why not?

When Jupiter forms a strong aspect to the Moon, Jupiter will enlarge and inflame whatever the Moon is feeling. If we're feeling sad, Jupiter insists that it's not mere sadness; it's heart-breaking tragedy. If we're feeling happy, Jupiter insists that it isn't simple happiness; it's ecstasy. Every emotion is enhanced, and everything becomes a drama, huge and larger-than-life. The volume was turned up on everything Hitler felt, including his rage, his vindictiveness, and his spite. It's likely that all humans feel envy and anger at one time or another, but Hitler's envy and anger were a thousand times greater.

Moon-Jupiter aspects have a reputation for being theatrical and over-the-top, whatever signs are involved. That can be delightful because of the richness and intensity of feeling and the ability to enthuse others. It can also be exhausting for other people. Hitler was certainly theatrical; everything, from the absurd moustache and the uniform decked in gaudy medals to the parades and rallies, was staged to the last detail, and he was adept at manipulating the emotions of his audiences through the use of visual symbols. But what was the object of the performance?

I've talked quite a lot about Jupiter being mobilised to compensate for wounds. We saw this process in Florence Nightingale's chart with her Venus square Saturn, Pluto, and Chiron, and in Mick Jagger's chart with his Venus square Saturn and Moon square Chiron. In Hitler's chart the Moon opposes Chiron, and Venus and Mars are both square Saturn. With the Sun, Saturn, Venus, and Mars all in fixed signs, there's a stubborn resistance to change, and the sense of damage, loneliness, frustration, and impotent rage – the latter particularly related to the Mars-Saturn square – can become entrenched. Florence Nightingale must have experienced painful feelings of loneliness and damage, but she did something quite different with it. She certainly compensated through her Jupiter, but she became a healer. Hitler projected his feelings of damage and became a destroyer. He had to find a human group that he could claim was inferior and could then justify exterminating in the name of transforming society. But what was he really trying to eradicate?

The enemy lurking inside this narcissistic black hole is a profound self-loathing, and the millions of people whom Hitler murdered had

Hungarian Jews forced onto the ramp of the Auschwitz-Birkenau concentration camp in 1944. Unknown photographer. The Auschwitz Archive, Yad Vashem, Jerusalem.

to carry the projection of what he secretly felt about himself. This is the most terrible extreme of malignant narcissism, and it's a corrosive void that twists gifts into weapons and swallows up empathy, remorse, and compassion. We might think about the vengeful Zeus, who tried to destroy the entire human race because he felt threatened by them and envious of their potential to become as creatively powerful as him. This is Jupiter stretched to its darkest extreme because there's no capacity to acknowledge inner pain, no empathy, and no capacity for self-reflection.

I'm inclined to believe this man was born with the potential to become a psychopath, and wasn't turned into one by nasty parents. But his family background and cultural matrix probably helped to tip the scales. Was it nature or nurture? Hitler's parents were probably no worse than most of the rest of Europe's parents in that generation. Fathers, and sometimes mothers, did regularly beat their children – many still do – and while we might now understand this as abuse and report it to social services or the police, Hitler's parents' generation understood it as necessary discipline.

Mothers who had no access to birth control – and in a Catholic family they might not have availed themselves of it anyway – had more children than they could look after. Only a fortunate few children were allowed to pursue their vocations as they wished. In our current determination to incessantly berate our society for its failings and find someone 'outside' to blame for extreme violence, cruelty, and sociopathy, we tend to forget how far we've come from the world as it was during Hitler's childhood. Or have we really come that far at all?

Social factors aren't always the culprit. We clamour loudly for our right to freedom, yet we often fail to acknowledge the role our own free choices play in how our lives unfold. I'm not convinced that environment, whether parental or social, is the whole story, or even the major part of the story, when we're dealing with someone like Hitler, who was so utterly incapable of experiencing remorse. Sociopathy, psychopathy, and malignant narcissism may be appropriate terms. Yet we won't find the signatures neatly defined in the birth chart – only a hint of possibilities that may never come to a malign fruition.

Aspects like those in Hitler's chart are not particularly rare or exceptional, and perhaps it's sheer good luck that humanity doesn't cough up too many people who live out those aspects on the world stage in the way Hitler did. And perhaps the ones who do are acting as conduits for the destructive potential that exists in every one of us. Hindsight comes cheaply, and we can see how Hitler's Jupiter played an important part in the ways he acted out his nature. But planetary configurations won't tell us whether someone is a psychopath. They can only suggest the forms through which the person is most likely to express this kind of pathology, and the nature of the psychological factors that might encourage and inflame it.

From this chart we can get a sense of how Jupiter in its most destructive form was mobilised to compensate for the emotional wounds reflected by the Moon-Chiron and Venus-Mars-Saturn configurations. With even the smallest modicum of reflection, compassion, and remorse, Hitler might have been able to avail himself of some kind of help. After all, he was well aware of Freud, but he drove him out of Vienna under threat of death because Freud was a Jew. But Hitler could never have countenanced therapy because he never acknowledged that anything in him was in need of healing. There seems to have been a fundamental psychological piece missing, and because of that, his Jupiterian search for meaning transformed into something deeply and intractably malignant.

Example 4: Mata Hari

This next example is the chart of Margaretha Geertruida Zelle, known to history as Mata Hari. She was a Dutch exotic dancer and courtesan, convicted of being a German spy during the First World War and executed by a French firing squad in 1917, at the age of forty-one. Of course she had Jupiter in Scorpio in the 1st house. Where else would it be? Mata Hari enjoyed a highly successful career as a seductress, and to this day no one knows for certain whether she really was a double agent. Her life remains a mystery, and there is even a mystery around what happened to her body after her execution. Her remains vanished and have never been found.

Margarethe Zelle was the eldest of four siblings, with three younger brothers. When she was a child the family was affluent, and she attended exclusive private schools. But when she was thirteen, her father went bankrupt, her parents divorced, and her mother died soon afterwards. Eventually she went to live with her uncle, but she found life with him intolerably oppressive. Ever alert to new opportunities and, with Sun conjunct Mars in Leo square Jupiter, never lacking in courage – or foolhardiness, depending on one's point of view – at the age of eighteen she responded to a newspaper advertisement placed by a Dutch army captain called Rudolf MacLeod, who was seeking a wife. She married him and moved with him to Java.

The marriage brought her wealth and status. But MacLeod was an alcoholic who beat her regularly and openly kept a concubine. Margarethe eventually ran off with another Dutch officer and became an exotic dancer, performing under the stage name of Mata Hari. In 1903, at the age of twenty-seven, she moved to Paris and began to accrue fame for her dancing. During her time in Paris she lived a thoroughly promiscuous life, claiming to be a Javanese princess of priestly Hindu birth. This constant reinventing of herself reflects her Jupiter in Scorpio in the 1st house; her past died completely with each successive and entirely opportunistic incarnation.

In 1916, her lover at the time, Vadim Maslov, a Russian pilot serving with the French forces during the First World War, was shot down in Germany. Margarethe, who was a Dutch citizen and therefore entitled to cross national borders – the Netherlands had remained politically neutral during the war – requested permission from the French government to visit Maslov in the German hospital where he was recovering. The French

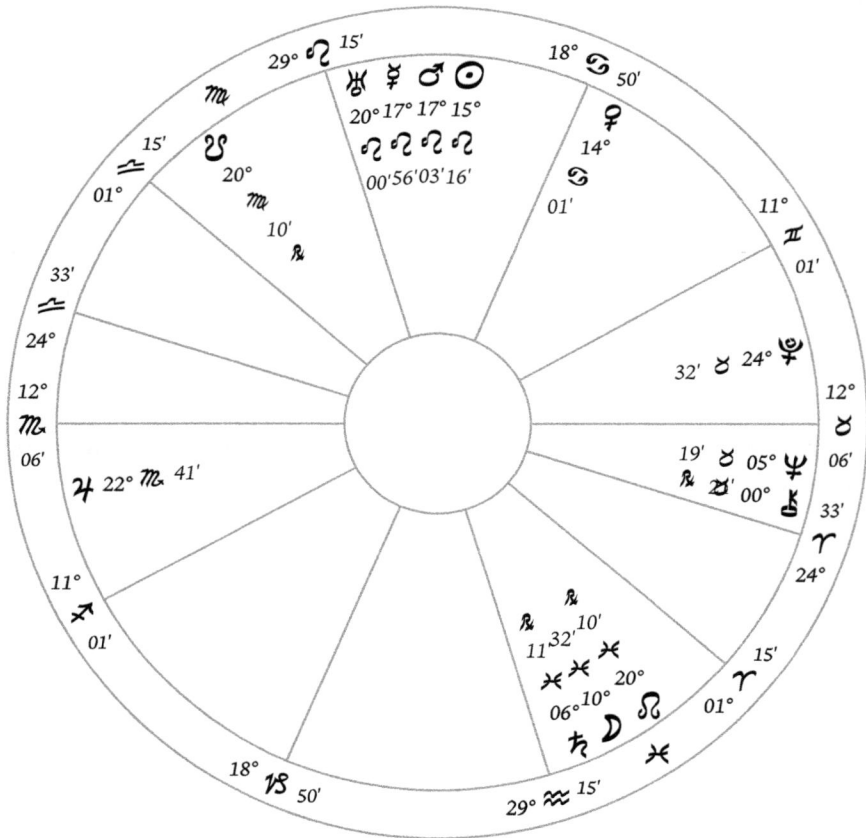

Mata Hari
7 August 1876, 1.00 pm, Leeuwarden, Netherlands

Duexième Bureau granted permission but naturally wanted something in return: she had to agree to work for them as a spy. They offered her a million francs to seduce Crown Prince Wilhelm, eldest son of the Kaiser, to extract military secrets from him, as he was nominally a senior German general on the Western Front. To gain access to Wilhelm, Margarethe told the Germans she would provide them with French military secrets, but she demanded that they give her a considerable sum of money as well.

She did indeed pass on French 'secrets' to the Germans, but these tidbits of information turned out to be Paris gossip about the sex lives of French politicians and army officers. Furious at being duped, the Germans reported her to the French as a double agent. The French put her to the test by ordering her to obtain information about six Belgian agents who

Mata Hari in 1906. Unknown photographer.
Photo, France Culture.

were suspected of secretly working for Germany. When one of them was summarily executed by the Germans, the French assumed she had passed his name to the Germans to warn them and concluded that this was proof she was working for the enemy. Although neither French nor British intelligence agencies ever found any actual evidence, she was accused of being instrumental in the death of 50,000 French soldiers. At her trial she consistently declared she was innocent of the charges. At her execution, Jupiterian to the last, she refused a blindfold and defiantly blew a kiss to the firing squad.

No one claimed Margarethe Zelle's body, so it was duly turned over to the State for medical study. Her head was embalmed and kept at the Museum of Anatomy in Paris. But some time during the 1950s, the head vanished and has never been found. Although the Museum was recorded as receiving the rest of the remains in 1918, a year after her death, these also vanished. Debate continues about whether Margarethe Zelle had truly been a spy or whether she was a scapegoat for the ineptitude of both the French and German governments The entire story couldn't be more redolent of the ironic humour of Jupiter in Scorpio.

Jupiter squares a tight stellium of planets in Leo in the 9th house: Sun at 15°, Mars and Mercury both at 17°, and Uranus at 20°. Jupiter also opposes Pluto in the 7th at 24° Taurus and forms a trine to Venus at 14° Cancer in the 8th. The Leo planets in a T-cross with Jupiter and Pluto certainly suggest a great deal of what we know of her character, including the theatricality, the brazenness, the boldness and courage, the self-absorption, the shamelessly deceitful cleverness, and the refusal to live according to the conventions of the time. Jupiter's involvement with these Leo planets exaggerated their expression, making her a kind of caricature of herself.

But Jupiter also needs to be viewed as the way in which Mata Hari tried to find meaning in her life. Her quest might not seem to be particularly spiritual or aspirational; a lot of her actions sprang from her determination to survive and remain loyal to her real passions, chief of which was, in her own words, her injured Russian pilot, whom she consistently declared to be the great love of her life. Jupiter opposing Pluto in Taurus in the 7th and trine Venus in Cancer in the 8th suggests that she was telling the truth, that she was, at heart, an incurable romantic, and that loyalty to her passions was both an obsession and an act of survival. In her own way, she remained entirely loyal to her daimon.

The 1st house is concerned with our sense of who we are in the world, which determines the ways in which we interact with others. It's how we appear to other people, how they appear to us, and accordingly, how we wish to appear in order to assert our own individuality. Of all the zodiacal signs, Scorpio is the least inclined to hide from the deeper levels of human nature, including its capacity for boundless hypocrisy and self-deceit. Mistrust is built into this sign because every human being carries a shadow, regardless of how virtuously they present themselves. Mata Hari had no illusions about the world and the people in it, especially the Great and the Good: those 'heroic' individuals who led in government and the military during the Great War. She had experienced brutality and abuse in her marriage and regular exposure to the seamier aspects of human sexuality, as well as ample affirmation of the time-honoured observation that truth is always the first casualty of war.

We might identify Jupiter's narcissistic inclinations in Mata Hari, and view her Moon-Saturn conjunction in Pisces in the 4th house as the source of a deep and intractable sense of loneliness, hurt, and abandonment, for which Jupiter's larger-than-life dramas offered compensation. We might also look at the lack of the element of air in the natal chart and come to the conclusion that the ability to step back, detach, and analyse her own behaviour was not something she could achieve without immense effort. Jupiter in the 1st house in Scorpio suggests that she took delight in being an enigma, found pleasure in deceiving the deceivers, and discovered meaning in being able to navigate the darkness, play it with skill, and survive it.

It might be hard for us to see anything positive or creative in this, although Mata Hari's enduring fame suggests that nevertheless, we're secretly drawn to those who unashamedly refuse to endure the indignity and tedium of an ordinary life.[43] But we can't expect Jupiter in the 1st, regardless of the sign and the public persona, to be found wandering about in sackcloth in pursuit of a selfless life, unless it's onstage in a play. The enlarged personality becomes the means of forming a connection with something greater that gives one's life significance, despite the fact that it might sometimes appear self-centred or amoral by others' standards. But the mythic Zeus was never troubled by human moral judgements. As divine ruler of the universe, he created his own moral laws to suit himself.

Example 5: Carl Gustav Jung

The last natal chart we'll look at today is that of C. G. Jung. I won't go into much detail about his life at this point, since I want to discuss his chart in the next seminar in the context of the twelve-year cycle of the Jupiter return.

In Jung's chart, natal Jupiter is at 23° Libra in the 8th house. Jung found meaning through exploring the hidden depths of human nature and creating a psychological system of ideas that could make his experiences and discoveries comprehensible within a rational framework. His theories were focused on integration and conscious cooperation with the unfolding life-pattern he called individuation. As an explorer of the hidden dimensions of the psyche, he felt impelled to formulate and elucidate what he found there. His psychological theories are based almost entirely on the concept

---

43 Mata Hari's life has provided a continuous stream of inspiration for film and television. A German silent film entitled *Mata Hari: The Red Dancer* was released in 1927, ten years after her death; an American film, *Mata Hari*, directed by George Fitzmaurice and starring Greta Garbo, was released in 1931; an Italian film titled *Mata Hari: Agente Segreto H21*, starring Jeanne Moreau, was released in 1964; a Dutch mini-series about her life, *Mata Hari*, was released in 1981; an erotic American film called *Mata Hari*, directed by Curtis Harrington and starring Sylvia Krystal, was released in 1985; and, most recently, a Russian-Portuguese TV series, *Mata Hari*, directed by Julius Berg, was released in 2016. Margarethe Zelle would no doubt have found all of it highly entertaining.

of opposites and their integration – how Libran can one get? – through digging as deeply as he could in the mysterious realms, both dark and light, described by the 8th house. Once again, Jupiter is strikingly obvious in its expression, even in a house known for its obscurity.

From an early age, Jung experienced extraordinary dreams, intuitions, and visions which he later interpreted as communications, instructions, clarifications, or interventions from a hidden source. Zeus as *nous* arrived disguised as the unconscious psyche, the matrix of individual and collective teleology. These interventions from the unconscious, in Jung's view, always attempted to balance and often opposed the individual's conscious attitudes; the more lopsided and extreme the ego's stance, the more powerfully the unconscious would push against the imbalance. This is the

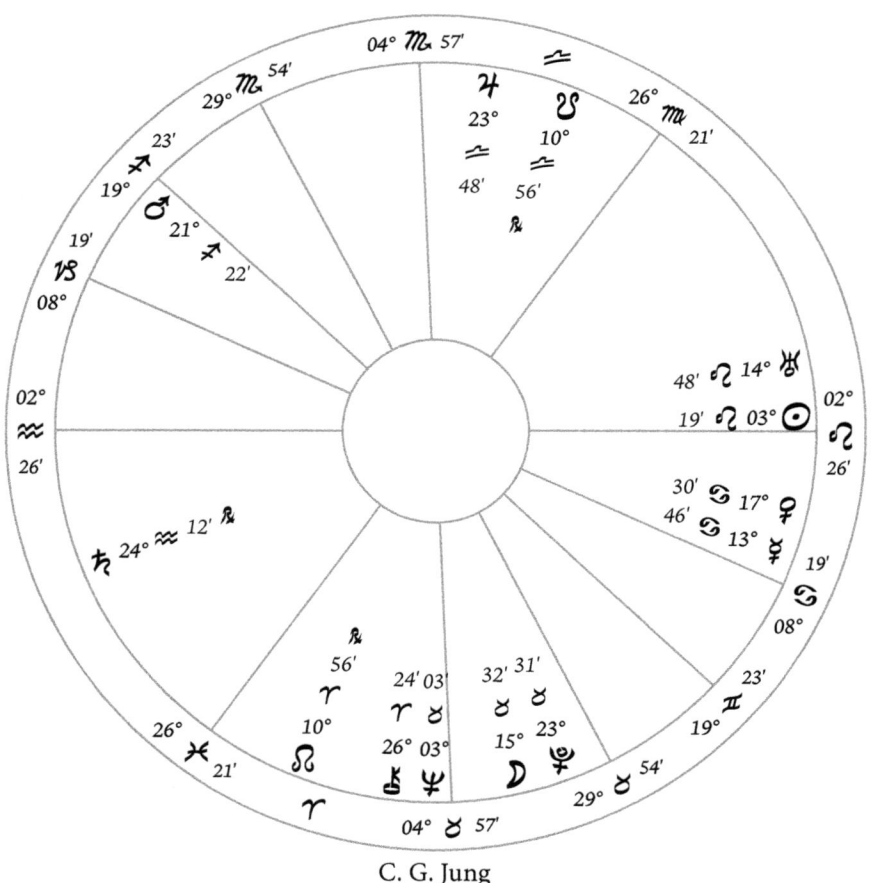

C. G. Jung
26 July 1875, 7.27 pm, Kesswil, Switzerland

ancient idea of *hubris* and *nemesis*, internalised and clothed in the garb of modern depth psychology.

Jung was deeply religious in his own way, but he found it difficult to accept the stern and unforgiving nature of his family's Swiss Protestant Christianity with its lack of visual images. During the iconoclastic eruptions of the Protestant Reformation in the mid-16th century, the cathedral in Basel lost all its religious paintings and statues. If any of you have visited the Grossmünster Church in Zürich, built between the 12th and 13th centuries, you'll be aware of the great beauty and symmetry of the architecture contrasting with the disturbingly bare white walls, with not a single religious icon in sight. The Grossmünster, like Basel Cathedral, lost all its religious statues during the Reformation. Jung felt this form of Christian worship lacked an important element provided by Catholicism, Eastern Orthodox Christianity, and the ancient pagan religions: the rich array of archetypal images through which the individual could connect on emotional and intuitive levels to the realm of the divine.

Although he still considered himself a Christian, Jung was more inclined to understand religious stories and images, including those of Jesus, on a symbolic rather than a literal level. This allowed him to be receptive to ideas from a wide range of religious sources, including Buddhist, Hindu, Platonic and Neoplatonic, Stoic, Orphic, Kabbalistic, and pagan ideas as well as the occult movements of the late 19th and early 20th centuries, in particular H.P. Blavatsky's Theosophy and Rudolf Steiner's Anthroposophy.

He delighted in making connections between all these approaches to the mysteries in order to find their common archetypal ground. Despite working as a psychiatrist in the Swiss

C. G. Jung in 1936, at the age of sixty-one.
ETH-Bibliothek, Zürich.

medical establishment of the time, his early visionary experiences led him to engage passionately throughout his life with esoteric studies, including astrology, Tarot, the *I Ching*, ritual magic, and ancient mystery religions.

Jung also inherited and married wealth. That's one of the 'perks' often associated with an 8th house Jupiter, since the 8th house is traditionally linked with inheritance and shared resources. Although not rampantly promiscuous, Jung had several extra-marital involvements, the most important being with his former patient, Toni Wolff. But his marriage remained solid throughout his life. The need for sexual variety is often one of the expressions of Jupiter in the 8th, perhaps because each new experience can reveal new and meaningful emotional insights and transformations. And there's always that issue of gluttony.

Jung suffered throughout his life from a painful conflict between his rational, scientifically trained intellect and his intuitive understanding and experience of what he called 'the spirit of the depths'. He expressed his visions and ideas through paintings and sculptures as well as written works, focusing on the nature of symbols and their power to transform the psyche, as well as the 'individuation' process by which a person's unique life unfolds as a meaningful journey towards integration and wholeness.

Although not angular, Jupiter is nevertheless very busy in Jung's chart. It's closely trine Saturn at 24° Aquarius in the 1st house. It also forms a wide out-of-sign square with the Sun at 3° Leo in the 7th and opposes an out-of-sign conjunction of Chiron at 26° Aries and Neptune at 3° Taurus in the 2nd, forming a T-cross. Jupiter also widely squares a conjunction of Mercury at 13° and Venus at 17° Cancer in the 6th, closely sextiles Mars at 21° Sagittarius in the 11th, and forms an exact quincunx with Pluto at 23° Taurus in the 3rd house. Finally, Jupiter forms a wide out-of-sign square with the Ascendant. The only planets Jupiter doesn't aspect are the Moon and Uranus. Not surprisingly, friends and colleagues sometimes referred to him as 'jovial'. Entangled as it is with so many other planets, perhaps it's to be expected that Jupiter, in its role as a symbol of the religious instinct and the quest for meaning, seems to have played such a profoundly important part on every level of Jung's life and thought.

Some concluding thoughts on Jupiter in the natal chart

We might understand Jupiter as one of the two core significators of the sense that we have a deeper purpose in life. The other significator is the Sun, which is concerned with individual uniqueness and self-expression. Jupiter isn't personal in quite the same way. Although it's sometimes viewed as a 'personal' planet in contrast to the outer planets, it reflects the individual's experience of being part of a greater design. Jupiter's sense of having a part to play in a larger story can give us the conviction that our individual lives mean something in the context of the unfolding of life; that we're here for a reason because we have something of our own to contribute; and that things happen to us and in the world according to some unknown intelligent design in which, willingly or unwillingly, we're participants.

What is the teleology of an individual life? That isn't something any of us can define in a few sentences, like filling out a census form. Our teleology isn't fulfilled until the moment of our death, and perhaps not even then. Nor is it static and unchanging. It communicates itself as an inner conviction, a powerful intuition, or a deep feeling of participating in a never-ending story. And it might be impossible ever to articulate because it's so elusive. But for those who have experienced it, it can't be ignored or denied without painful psychological consequences.

Many people wish they had a 'real' vocation rather than an unloved job that pays the bills. They don't know why they're here. They either strive to make the best of it, motivated by love of family and friends or the satisfaction of transient desires, or they give themselves over to resentment and self-pity. Or they do both. Some individuals who haven't experienced a sense of vocation feel disappointed because they mistakenly believed that vocation is the same as a certain kind of work in the outer world, like being an engineer or a doctor. Then they feel let down when they achieve success in that field while an inner sense of meaning continues to elude them. In Western societies we're often pushed into making decisions about our future profession too early in life. Those youthful choices, made due to family expectations or practical considerations like 'employability', might not be a true reflection of what we need to become. Social and economic pressures can make it difficult to value our own inner timing, which varies from one person to another. Like plants, some of us flower early, some flower late, and some have more than one flowering season.

Vocation is an elusive creature. It may not be reflected in work that gives us a healthy bank balance, and we might need a job to support ourselves in the world while we pursue a vocation that's entirely different and perhaps materially unrewarding. Sometimes the two can overlap, but a lot of the time they don't. We might get clues about our vocation from the Sun, but Jupiter in the natal chart is equally important. If we reject any intuition of a meaningful journey that we need to pursue 'gladly', we can make a sad mess of our lives because we start chasing surrogates on which we project our Jupiterian longing. But the good news is that, since gods don't age, Jupiterian inspiration can strike us at any time in life. For Jupiter, there's no such thing as 'too old' or 'too late'.

Jupiter, like the mythic Zeus, is inconstant. Even if we get a glimpse of a meaningful pattern, it can vanish ten minutes or a week or ten years later and reappear in an entirely different form. If we try to nail it down because we can't put our faith in its reality, it slips through our fingers and leaves us feeling empty and depressed. We can't control this elusive Jupiterian vision with the ego. We can only provide the conditions in which we're receptive to it, and then hope for the best.

If we want to work creatively to embed the sense of a deeper connection in our everyday lives, it might be wise to let our visions go and allow ourselves to become ordinary and earthbound again. The real problem of the *puer aeternus* isn't that this archetypal figure is incapable of commitment; it's that, when this pattern dominates us, we may refuse to relinquish 'never-never-land'. We keep trying to make Jupiter an on-demand service, rather than allowing ourselves to be inspired and then get on with embedding the inspiration in everyday life as best we can. If we can let the vision go, and return to earth to do the hard work of giving it form, we might be joyfully surprised and delighted when suddenly Zeus appears again as a shower of gold, a swan, or a humble mortal shepherd. It's not a good idea to sit around waiting for Zeus to come back, like Hera does in myth. He isn't likely to ring up to let her know he's going to be late. Her eternal resentment springs from her inability to accept the fact that she'll never find him in the same place she last saw him.

We need to let the god be free, work as constructively as we can with the fruits of his inspirations, and hope without expectations that he comes back again in another form as we ourselves change over time. Zeus never repeats himself; he transforms into different shapes according to his own inner requirements. Our capacity to express Jupiter creatively tends to be intermittent and sporadic rather than consistent, echoing the nature of the mythic deity.

Jupiter reflects where and how we might experience our greatest joy. The word 'joy' comes from the Old French *rejoir*, meaning 'to rejoice', and that word derives from the Latin *gaudere*, also meaning 'to rejoice'. Although we might associate joy with sensual delight, emotional fulfilment, or the rewards of worldly achievement, we might also think about rejoicing in the context of religious festivals, where it plays a prominent part in the lyrics of so many carols and hymns. We rejoice because we know that a gift – something extraordinary, ineffable, and inexplicable – has been freely and generously given to us, and it confers meaning on our human suffering and mortality. I'm not suggesting that we have to follow any particular religion to experience this. No religion is required. Rigid religious doctrines can actively destroy joy and replace it with fear, and there isn't much left to rejoice about.

Jupiter's natal house, sign, and aspects can help us to understand where we might experience both joy and the impulse to rejoice. This might not reflect our choice of work, although sometimes it does; we saw examples of this in the charts of Florence Nightingale, Mick Jagger, and C. G. Jung and, in a darkly distorted form, in the chart of Adolf Hitler. Florence Nightingale's work couldn't have been much fun, but it offered her a meaningful connection with what she understood as the divine. Jung didn't have a lot of fun when he descended into a prolonged psychotic breakdown, resulting in the visions he eventually recorded in *Liber Novus*. But he emerged with a sense that at last he had understood the meaning of his life's work.

Jupiter's natal placement can point to vocation in a deeper sense: an activity that connects us with the feeling that our life has meaning. As with everything in the chart, so very much depends on how much self-awareness we're prepared to cultivate, and how willing we are to explore not only our gifts but also our wounds and our limits. Paradoxically, although Jupiter can open doors to future possibilities and potentials, it also hints at where we may have to face and accept what we can't become. The more self-honesty we can cultivate, the better we can work with Jupiter and keep our faith in the future, our sense of humour, our ability to laugh at ourselves, and our capacity to truly rejoice.

Part Two: 'When You Wish Upon a Star'

Zeus does not bring all men's plans to fulfilment.

– HOMER

This seminar was given online for students from the Centre for Psychological Astrology and the Mercury Internet School of Psychological Astrology on 2 October 2021.

Introduction

Today's seminar is the second in our series on Jupiter, and our focus will be on Jupiter on the move. We're going to be looking at the Jupiter return as the planet moves through its twelve-year cycle, and we'll explore its transits to other planets in the natal chart. We'll also consider other planets transiting natal Jupiter, Jupiter in the progressed chart, and Jupiter in synastry and in the composite chart. So there's a lot to cover and a lot to piece together.

Although I'll be focusing mainly on example charts today, many themes from Jupiter's mythology, which we looked at during the first seminar, will keep coming up, and these stories might help to reveal the deeper meaning of Jupiter's transits. In myth, this deity is like a rock band: he's constantly on the road and he's addicted to shape-shifting. We can never really know how Jupiter's transits will be reflected in our lives on a concrete level. All we can be certain of is that we can't be certain.

The Jupiter return

Jupiter takes approximately twelve years to make one circuit of the zodiac. When we're studying its cycles in an individual chart, it's helpful to remember that the time of the Jupiter return, in interpretive terms, isn't a specific moment. We don't suddenly wake up one morning every twelve years and experience the Jupiter return precisely on the date of its exact conjunction. The planet's retrograde cycle means that it can hang about for nearly a year within orb of conjunction to its natal place.

The year before the exact return is often the most revealing time, as all the relevant pieces are being set up on the board, even if we don't recognise this prologue as an essential part of the story. The Jupiter return may begin after only eleven years, with a runover into the year following its exact conjunction. This can vary from one person to another depending on its retrograde cycle. We need to track the entire period of time the planet is transiting within orb of natal Jupiter, and reflect on what's going on in our lives, internally as well as externally. And it's especially helpful to look at the connections between successive Jupiter returns. Although the external circumstances may be entirely different each time, if we look more deeply we might discern a common thread of meaning beneath the surface.

Suddenly, nothing happened again

A frustrating feature of Jupiter's cycle for those who think astrology is solely about concrete happenings is that the planet's return may not coincide with any specific event at all. It might sometimes seem that Jupiter's eagerly awaited rendezvous with its natal position doesn't 'do' anything. And if events do occur, they may not always be happy or fortunate ones. Equally, we might not register their significance at the time, just as we might not notice a tiny oak seedling which will eventually grow into a large tree. I've heard quite a few astrologers say with great irritation, "Jupiter just came back to its own place in my chart, and nothing happened!" Once upon a time I said this myself. With any transit involving Jupiter, nothing may 'happen' in the sense of a concrete occurrence. Unless we're making an effort to understand our inner development process, it may seem that the transit has gone by without a significant experience of any kind.

But there will usually be a *seeding* of some kind. Something is planted, even if it's simply a vague idea, a nascent feeling that begins to develop in a relationship, a hunch that pursuing a particular new project might turn out to be interesting and fruitful, or a chance meeting with someone who might later become important in one's life. Even if we nurture that seed and pursue the hunch or the new opportunity, we might not see any tangible results until the next Jupiter cycle, or even two or three Jupiter cycles later. It's pointless to try to pin down these cycles in terms of concrete happenings, which might or might not manifest. Jupiter fertilises us in some way, even if the seed takes a long time to sprout and come to fruition. And we can't always anticipate what the fruit will look like.

However, we always have choices under Jupiter transits. The growth and fruition of a seed depends in large part on the care, or lack thereof, given to it by the gardener. We can refuse to participate in the planting. In myth there are many stories about the numerous women Zeus seduced, and the eventual progeny that resulted from these unions. But we never hear about the women who might have turned him down. It's entirely possible that quite a few said, "Well, I'm flattered, but I don't think so, I'm committed elsewhere," or, "Sorry, it's the wrong time of the month."

Admittedly, if there were such women, Zeus would probably not have taken 'No' for an answer. But since we're not mythic characters, we can choose to ignore an opportunity or a sudden intuition, and we may have entirely valid reasons for doing so – although ignoring the *meaning* of that opportunity or intuition might not be the cleverest way to move through life. And sometimes we don't even realise there *was* an opportunity, unless life makes clear to us later what we've missed. A seed can be planted but we might not bother to water it, or we drown it in too much water. We let it get smothered by weeds, or we accidentally step on it, or we allow the cat to dig it up. We might not recognise the seed for what it is, or we choose to pass it by because we'd rather opt for stability and material guarantees rather than taking that scary leap of faith that could land us in trouble as often as it reaps rewards.

Another disturbing thing about Jupiter is that when the planet's cycles do coincide with events, the events can sometimes be deeply painful or unpleasant. The term 'benefic' starts sounding like an ironic joke. Of course a lot depends on what planet Jupiter is transiting, and what natal aspects are triggered. But even when we might reasonably expect 'good fortune' from a Jupiter transit, in myth this god doesn't always engage in courtly seduction with flowers and a candlelit dinner. Sometimes he's a rapist, and we may feel violated by experiences we didn't ask for and which cause us suffering. Jupiter's seeding can be painful and may sometimes involve illness, separation, or loss. The release of life and the opening of a door to a more meaningful future might not be recognisable at the time because we're hurting too much emotionally. That's an entirely valid human response. Only with hindsight can we put the pieces together and glimpse the teleology of the pattern.

Sometimes a very difficult period which coincides with a Jupiter return or a Jupiter transit over another natal planet may turn out to be the overture of a process that will unfold over time to unlock profound meaning on an inner level, and the suffering may be necessary for our development in some way, even though we can't initially see what the result might be. Sometimes the opposite is true and we're led on the proverbial wild goose chase, because Jupiter can inflame and inflate any planet it touches, including its own natal place. We may get wildly excited about something that seems to be a good idea at the time, and then we find ourselves in a serious mess.

Given this uncertainty, how do we constructively approach a Jupiter return, or a Jupiter transit over another natal planet? It's often helpful to study Jupiter's cycles in our own chart, and in the charts of the people who are closest to us, to see whether we can catch a glimpse of a connecting thread of meaning. This can help us to make more sense of what an approaching transit of Jupiter might symbolise.

Jupiter's morality

In myth, Zeus is entirely amoral when judged by our human standards of right and wrong. But the gods aren't very interested in the modern religious and ideological frameworks we try so hard to impose on them anachronistically, and we can't force a rigid moral framework on Jupiter. That doesn't mean we should abandon our own individual moral convictions and act according to Jupiter's less attractive impulses. But we might need to examine with great care the moral judgements we try to force on ourselves and others when Jupiter is loitering nearby, so we don't inadvertently stifle our own or others' development in the name of a preconceived and inflexible set of ideas. As individuals, how we experience and judge 'goodness' or 'badness' depends on many things, including our cultural background, our personal beliefs, what Jupiter is doing in our natal chart, and how we cope with the dichotomies and paradoxes symbolised by the planet. Perhaps most importantly, we can ask ourselves how aware we are of the need for meaning in our lives.

Jupiter doesn't sit alone in a natal chart. It will always be connected to the whole chart through its aspects with other planets. Even if natal Jupiter is entirely unaspected, it will still be connected through its dispositor – the ruler of the sign in which it's placed – and through the houses where Pisces and Sagittarius fall on the cusp. The meaning of those houses, as well as Jupiter's natal house, will be brought into focus during its transit cycle around the chart. Even if natal Jupiter is in one of its own signs and unrelated to any other planet at birth, transits to and from other natal planets will connect it to the larger story of our lives.

Because of these connections, more things are triggered by the Jupiter return than natal Jupiter itself. We can learn a lot by studying all the aspects it forms to other natal planets during its transit cycle, as well as the phases of its own cycle. This kind of close observation, although it can seem tedious, is a form of internal diary, and it can highlight the thread of meaning that runs through the twelve-year Jupiter cycle.

Example 1: C. G. Jung

In the first seminar I mentioned that we'd be looking at Jung's chart in greater detail as an example of the Jupiter return. I'm going to follow the sequence of his first four Jupiter returns because he's a good example of someone who paid more attention to inner events than he did to outer happenings. In a sense he's done a lot of our work for us in terms of exploring the symbolic meaning of Jupiter. His experiences under these Jupiter returns were often disturbing and strange, and not what we might expect if we took a more conventional approach to the astrological Jupiter.

In Jung's autobiography, *Memories, Dreams, Reflections*, there are few descriptions of the important events that happened in his life. *Memories, Dreams, Reflections* is a deeply interior narrative which has annoyed some readers hoping for a detailed chronicle of Jung's mundane life. The book was heavily edited – some might even say 'censored' – by Aniela Jaffé, an analyst whom Jung trained, who worked as his personal secretary from 1944 to the time of his death in 1961, and to whom he dictated the material. She had her own agenda, and we may never know how many of Jung's original statements were deliberately altered or omitted.

Jaffé's selective editing notwithstanding, the work reveals enough to give us plenty to examine. What we get instead of a narrative of events is made clear

C. G. Jung. Photo, World History Archive/Ann Ronan Collection.

in the title: Jung's dreams, visions, and compulsions; his memories of psychological events; his insights and realisations; the development of his ideas and beliefs; and some of the inspirations behind his work. We might not view him as a typical Jupiterian, since neither Sun, Moon, nor Ascendant is in Sagittarius or Pisces and Jupiter isn't angular. But the planet is very busy in his birth chart through its aspects to almost all the other planets. He's a useful person to explore through the framework of the Jupiter cycle because his experiences take us much closer to the core of what Jupiter might really symbolise.

Jung's natal Jupiter is at 23° Libra in the 8th house. It aspects most of the other natal planets as well as the Ascendant. Only the Moon and Uranus aren't connected to it, so Jupiter is well integrated in the chart. It opposes an out-of-sign Chiron-Neptune conjunction in the 2nd house and it's in an out-of-sign square to the Sun at 3° Leo in the 7th, so it's part of a T-cross with those planets. Jupiter is also closely trine Saturn, the chart ruler, at 24° Aquarius, and it sextiles Mars at 21° Sagittarius. Mars is in turn sextile Saturn, forming, with Jupiter and Saturn, what's sometimes called a 'minor grand trine' or 'talent triangle'. Jupiter widely squares Mercury and Venus

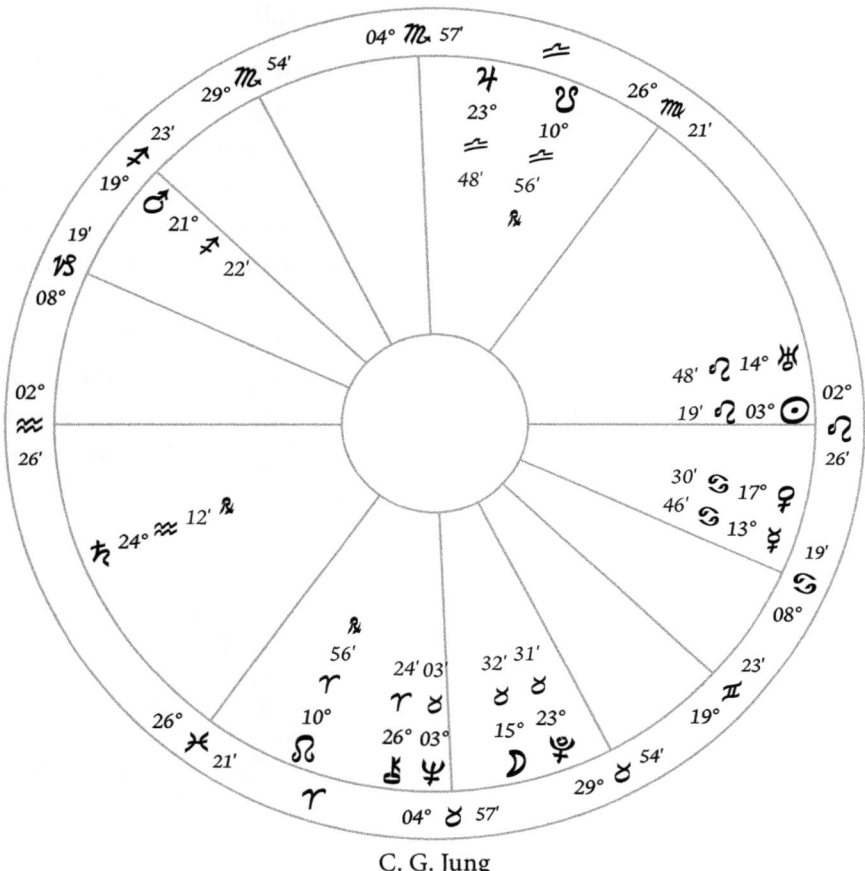

C. G. Jung
26 July 1875, 7:27 pm, Kesswil, Switzerland

in Cancer, it's in exact quincunx to Pluto in the 3rd house, and it forms an out-of-sign square with the Ascendant in early Aquarius.

This is an active and engaged Jupiter, but it's concealed in the mysterious depths of the 8th house. We might expect experiences of meaning and teleology to emerge repeatedly in Jung's life through 8th house matters. In other words, meaning arises from the deeper levels of the psyche through dreams, visions, direct encounters with and eruptions of the unconscious, compulsions, sexual experiences, and family secrets. A sense of teleology is most likely to develop from close encounters with the underworld of the unconscious, which might repeatedly reveal hints of a greater pattern or design.

John F. Kennedy: a different kind of 8th house Jupiter

Not every 8th house Jupiter is expressed in the same way. For someone more extraverted and outwardly focused than Jung, an 8th house Jupiter might convey meaning in very different ways. In myth the god seems to choose different women according to the child each of them will bear, since behind his apparently spontaneous behaviour lies the foreknowledge of the Divine Mind. As a contrast to Jung, it's interesting to look at the chart of John F. Kennedy, who also had an 8th house Jupiter.

Kennedy's Jupiter is at 23° Taurus, conjunct Mars and Mercury in the 8th house. It makes quite a few aspects to other planets, including two planetary connections absent in Jung's chart: Kennedy's Jupiter is exactly square Uranus in Aquarius and trine Moon in Virgo. Unlike Jung's chart,

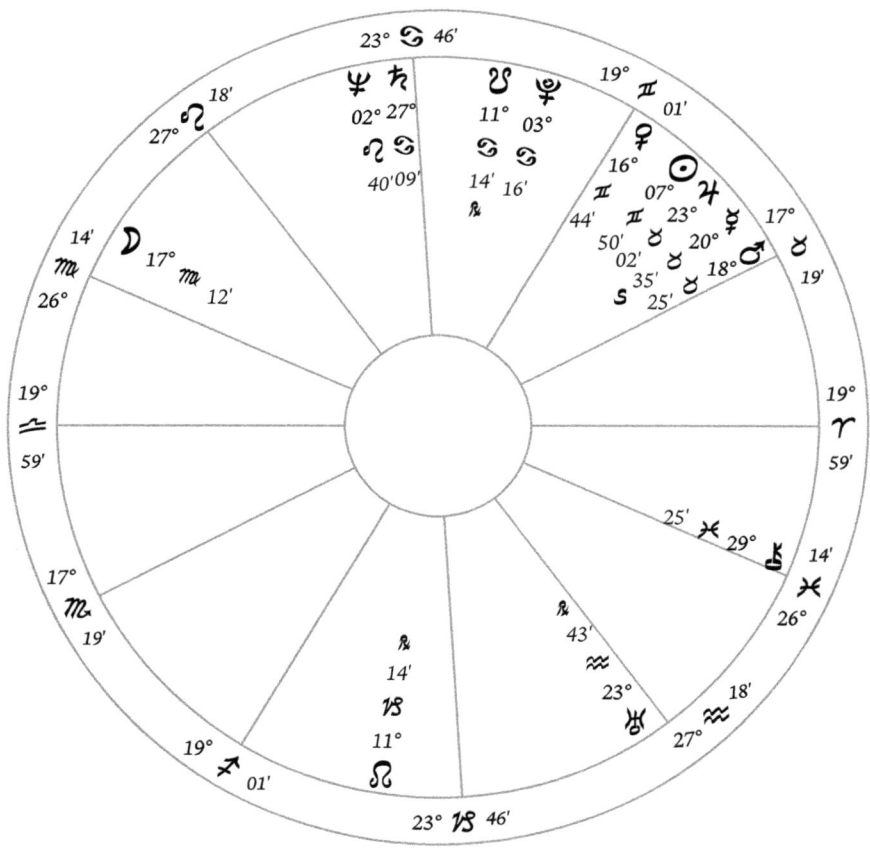

John F. Kennedy
29 May 1917, 3.00 pm, Brookline, Massachusetts

this chart is weighted in the elements of air and earth. The Moon is in Virgo; Mercury, Mars, and Jupiter are in Taurus; Sun and Venus are in Gemini; Uranus is in Aquarius; and the Ascendant is in Libra. Saturn and Pluto are both in Cancer and Chiron is in Pisces, so the element of water is also quite strong.

But the only planet in the element of fire is Neptune in Leo in the 10th house, a singleton by element and therefore unusually powerful but in an unsophisticated and unpredictable way. From the element balance alone, this chart doesn't suggest an individual inclined to focus on intuitive perceptions. His strengths and limits and his contribution to life – or, put another way, his *moira* – were entirely different from Jung's, and the 8th house revealed itself in very different ways.

Kennedy, like Jung, was a highly intelligent and perceptive man. But his intelligence was directed towards the outer world and what he could achieve in it. He was a consummate politician, and he seems to have lived his Jupiter mainly through political machinations, sensual appetites, and a compulsive need to fulfil the enormous expectations of his deeply dysfunctional family. Kennedy was driven by what's now referred to as a 'sex addiction'; he couldn't stay away from women and had to have different lovers on a frequent and regular basis. Sexual release apparently offered him a few precious moments of escape into oblivion, or into an Otherworld in which he could find a modicum of inner peace and perhaps a connection with a deeper pattern that his conventional Catholicism couldn't provide.

Kennedy was also addicted to a variety of different drugs, including demerol, methadone, barbiturates, amphetamines, and anti-anxiety medications. Some of these were prescribed because he was in chronic physical pain; he suffered from Addison's disease and spastic colitis along with spinal problems and osteoporosis. But perhaps he also took the medications because some of them, like the constant stream of women he pursued, offered him a form of escape. His encounters with the 8th house realm, including the mystery surrounding his death, were experienced through concrete objects and events rather than through inner happenings revealing hidden dimensions of life.

Although some of Jupiter's more traditional meanings in the 8th house were enacted in obvious ways in his life, like the wealth provided by a substantial family inheritance, Kennedy wasn't temperamentally inclined to follow Jupiter's golden thread through the doorway into the inner world. Perhaps he might have done if he'd been able to break free of the overwhelming pressure of his family with all its dark 8th house secrets. But if he had parted ways with family expectations, he might never have entered politics. It could be argued that the path he followed was entirely appropriate, not only for him personally and for the impact he had on his country during his brief time in office, but also for the Jupiterian symbol he's become for many people as his nation's history has unfolded in the decades following his untimely and still ambiguous death.

In contrast, Jung *was* inclined to follow Jupiter's golden thread into the depths, partly because his introverted intuitive temperament was inherently inclined that way. Jung also had a deep bond with his enigmatic mother who, according to his own description, seems, appropriately for his Moon-Pluto conjunction, to have had one foot perpetually through the doorway into a magical Otherworld. Kennedy's father was driven by political ambition; Jung's father, a clergyman, was driven by spiritual aspiration. Kennedy's mother, like his father, was devoted to politics; she was also a socialite who didn't involve herself in the traditional pursuits of motherhood, passing those tasks to servants. Jung's mother was eccentric, often depressed, and believed spirits visited her at night. In *Memories, Dreams, Reflections*, Jung wrote that she "cooked wonderfully", but was "like one of those seers...like a priestess in a bear's cave". The different ways in which each of us navigates Jupiter may depend not only on innate temperament, but also on what kind of support, tacit or overt, the natal planet receives in early life.

The first Jupiter return

At the time of Jung's first Jupiter return, when he was approaching his twelfth birthday, he experienced a vision which had a major impact on his lifelong quest for meaning through encounters with the unconscious psyche. According to his description in *Memories, Dreams, Reflections*, he had no idea what the vision meant at the time, but he found it disturbing, shocking, and shameful. He knew instinctively that it had to be kept secret.

The vision occurred as he was walking home from school. He passed through the square of the great medieval cathedral in Basel, admired its spire pointing to the sky, and imagined God sitting high above it in heaven on a golden throne. Then a 'yawning dark chasm' suddenly opened in his mind, and he was convinced he mustn't think any further about the cathedral or something horrible and sinful would emerge. After days of struggling against a feeling of impending dread, physically exhausted and unable to eat or sleep, he finally allowed the forbidden vision to emerge:

Jung in the early 1880s.

> I gathered all my courage as though I were about to leap forth into hell-fire and let the thought come. I saw before me the cathedral, the blue sky. God sits on His golden throne and from under the golden throne an enormous turd falls upon the sparkling new roof, shatters it, and breaks the walls of the cathedral asunder.[44]

Jung intuitively 'knew' that he had been shown a great secret of tremendous import, reflecting "a dim understanding that God could be something terrible". As his father was a clergyman, we can understand how this might have been an unsettling experience for a devout child brought up in a strict Protestant Christian household. But the vision offered the first clue to an idea that emerged later in Jung's life and began to dominate his psychological theories: divinity is whole rather than perfect, the opposites are secretly one, and God, like all of life, has a shadow.

The second Jupiter return

Four years before his second Jupiter return, when he was twenty, Jung made a decision to pursue medicine and psychiatry, rather than following in his father's footsteps by studying philosophy and theology. He duly began his medical studies at the University of Basel. But at the time of the Jupiter return, just before his twenty-fourth birthday, he suddenly decided to move

44 C. G Jung, *Memories, Dreams, Reflections* (Vintage Books, 1965), p. 39.

to Zürich because he'd heard about a clinic in the city, the Burghölzli, and a professor of psychiatry working there, Eugen Bleuler, who was involved in interesting and unusual research into the psyche.

Bleuler was known for his unusual contributions to the understanding of mental illness. He coined a number of terms now firmly embedded in the vocabularies of psychiatry and psychology, including 'schizophrenia', 'autism', and 'depth psychology'. Jung had decided to act on a hunch. At the Burghölzli, he began working under Bleuler's supervision, and it seems the hunch paid off.

Bleuler had been studying Freud's work and duly introduced Jung to Freud's writings, encouraging his pupil to focus his studies on unconscious psychological phenomena. He also helped Jung to research and develop what's now known as the 'word association test'. If any of you have ever formally taken this

Eugen Bleuler, c. 1900, National Library of Medicine, Bethesda, Maryland.

test, which isn't fashionable in today's more reductively minded psychiatric establishment, you'll know that it can be surprisingly revealing as a method of uncovering unconscious conflicts that have been stifled or suppressed.[45]

At the time of his first Jupiter return, Jung experienced a powerful vision, and he had no choice about whether to receive it or not. It was a kind of psychic rape by the unconscious, and it struck him like Zeus' mythic lightning-bolt. At the time of his second Jupiter return, he was an adult and could make his own choices. His decision to move to Zürich was a conscious decision to follow a hunch, as was the decision to accept Bleuler's tutelage and involve himself in research furthering his understanding of

---

45 C. G. Jung, *Studies in Word-Association: Experiments in the Diagnosis of Psychopathological Conditions* (Heinemann, 1918). A number of editions are available. The book is also available at Internet Archive, archive.org/details/studiesinwordass00jung/page/n15/mode/2up.

the unconscious psyche. An opportunity presented itself and he grasped the opportunity, although at the time he had no idea where it would lead.

But two other incidents happened during this second Jupiter return that didn't involve any choice. Planets in the 8th house often seem to emerge through compulsion or eruption rather than through a conscious decision. These two incidents exposed Jung to what could be called telekinetic phenomena. At the time of the first event, Jung was at his family home in Basel, studying his textbooks. Next to his bedroom was the dining room, which contained a large antique walnut table. Suddenly he heard a loud crack like a pistol shot. His mother had been sitting in an armchair in the dining room near the table, and she cried out in terror at the sudden noise. When Jung rushed into the room, he found that the table, made of thick, seasoned wood, had split of its own accord, cracking from the edge right through the middle – an apparent impossibility which baffled Jung as well as his mother.

Two weeks later, a similar event occurred. Another loud crack resounded from the dining room. Once again, his mother had been in the room, this time with his younger sister Johanna, and they were both terrified. After determined searching, Jung discovered that a large knife, which had been used earlier during a meal and had then been washed and put away in the drawer of the sideboard, had snapped into four precise pieces. Jung took the pieces to a cutler, who informed him that the steel wasn't faulty in any way. Like the splitting of the walnut table, the splintering of the knife had happened without any discernible physical cause.

These incidents infuriated Jung because he couldn't find a rational explanation for either of them. At that time in his life, as a scientist he depended on reason and concrete evidence to understand and evaluate his experiences. The table was thick and solid, and the knife had been sound. Eventually, because he was involved at the time with Bleuler's research into unusual psychological phenomena, Jung decided that the explosions were telekinetic and reflected some kind of unconscious disturbance. Since the events occurred when he was at the family home in Basel, he assumed the disturbance must be his own and was connected with the powerful emotional and erotic undercurrents that had been developing between him and his cousin, Hélène Preiswerk, who was a natural psychic. She came from Jung's mother's side of the family and, like his mother, sensed supernatural presences around her.

Hélène was a medium, and Jung had been experimenting with her in seances since he was in his teens. He had stopped these experiments when he began his medical and psychiatric studies, but after the mysterious events of the table and the knife, he encouraged Hélène to begin the seances again, and immersed himself in research into what happened to his cousin when she experienced one of her psychic trances. Eventually Jung wrote his dissertation on the subject of Hélène's mediumship, which was published under the title *On the Psychology and Pathology of So-Called Occult Phenomena*.[46]

Hélène Preiswerk (1881-1911), unknown photographer, date unknown.

Jung's response to these two inexplicable occurrences which, like his vision at the age of twelve, seemed to open a gateway into another realm, was to try to understand them and embed them in a rational framework of ideas. His natal Jupiter is in Libra, an air sign, in trine to Saturn in Aquarius, another air sign. We tend to respond to Jupiter's trail of clues not only through its house and aspects but also through the sign and element in which it's placed in the natal chart.

The third Jupiter return

At the time of Jung's third Jupiter return, just before his thirty-sixth birthday in 1911, he once again experienced a powerful revelation. This time it wasn't a vision or a telekinetic event; it was a transformative intuitive insight that seemed to clarify his future path, giving him the sense that the path was meaningful and that he had correctly read the signposts revealing an inner intelligent design. In 1955, when Jung was eighty, he wrote a letter to an American friend, the writer Upton Sinclair. By the time he sent the

46 C. G. Jung, *On the Psychology and Pathology of So-Called Occult Phenomena,* in C. G. Jung, *Psychiatric Studies,* CW1 (1957).

letter, he had had a lifetime to put together the clues scattered like a trail of breadcrumbs through those early Jupiter returns. He wrote:

> The ruler of my birth, old Saturnus, slowed down my maturation process to such an extent that I became aware of my own ideas only at the beginning of the second half of life, *i.e.* exactly with 36 years.[47]

Jung referred to 'Old Saturnus' as the 'ruler of my birth' because Saturn is the traditional ruler of his Aquarian Ascendant. Jung was well aware of Uranus – he had inserted its glyph, along with those of Neptune and the seven traditional planets, into his first diagram of the 'Systema Munditotius', drawn in 1916 and included in published form in the Appendix of *Liber Novus*. He had also been reading Alan Leo's astrological works since 1904, roughly the time of his first Saturn return, and Leo highlighted the significance of Uranus as the 'higher octave' of Mercury but not as the definitive ruler of Aquarius. As Jung had considerable respect for Leo's work, he evidently viewed Saturn as the ruler of the sign.[48]

There's no significant Saturn transit to its own place at the age of thirty-six; the second outgoing square of the Saturn cycle occurs for all of us a couple of years later. Nor did Jung refer to any specific transit to or from either Saturn or Jupiter in his own chart. Perhaps he felt Jupiter's third return had finally loosened Saturn's stifling grip on him; they are, after all, trine in the natal chart, and Saturn is the more dominant planet because it's in its own sign in an angular house. Jung repeated his reference to the importance of the age of thirty-six for everyone, not just for him, in his Foreword to the fourth German edition of *Symbols of Transformation*:

> This book was written in 1911, in my thirty-sixth year. The time is a critical one, for it marks the beginning of the second half of life, when a metanoia, a mental transformation, not infrequently occurs.[49]

---

47 C. G. Jung, Letter to Upton Sinclair, 25 February 1955, in *C. G. Jung Letters*, Vol. 2 (1976), pp. 230-32.

48 For the diagram of the 'Systema Munditotius', see C. G. Jung, *Liber Novus: The Red Book* (2009), p. 363. Also see Greene, *The Astrological World of Jung's Liber Novus* (2018), pp. 143-176.

49 Jung, CW5, *Symbols of Transformation*, Forward to the fourth (Swiss) edition (1950), p. xxvi.

Jung didn't mention the Jupiter cycle in relation to this 'mental trans-formation', but he rarely expressed any specific chart interpretations in his published works.[50] Many astrologers think in terms of the transit of Uranus opposite its natal place, which remains within orb roughly between the ages of thirty-eight and forty-two, as the chief marker of 'mid-life'. But Jung's conviction that his independent thinking only began under his third Jupiter return is especially interesting because this was also the time when he began experiencing serious trouble with Freud. The formal break between the two men came in 1913, a couple of years after this third Jupiter return, when transiting Uranus had just crossed Jung's Aquarian Ascendant and opposed his natal Sun in the 7th house. But Jung was already chafing at the bit and beginning to engage in overt conflict with his mentor, challenging several of Freud's ideas which he had previously followed with apparent enthusiasm.

The fourth Jupiter return

In the year leading up to his fourth Jupiter return in 1922, Jung completed a book that was seminal to the entire edifice of his psychological theories. In this work, titled *Psychological Types*, he first used the terms 'extraversion' and 'introversion'.[51] These words have now percolated down into ordinary common speech, although often without any real understanding of the subtleties of Jung's descriptions. In the book he also discussed his theory of the four function types – thinking, feeling, sensation, and intuition – which are so valuable to our astrological understanding of the four elements. As Jung's insights developed, his psychological theories were increasingly formulated according to a symmetrical model built on opposites and their gradual integration.

Seven years prior to his fourth Jupiter return, and especially striking in relation to the planet's 8th house placement, Jung began to be overwhelmed by a series of extraordinary visions and encounters with inner figures that erupted into consciousness against his will, and which he first recorded in the diaries known as the *Black Books*. These powerful visions, peopled with mythic figures many of which have recognisable planetary associations,

---

50 An exception is his description of the natal chart of 'Miss X' in C. G. Jung, CW9i, *The Archetypes and the Collective Unconscious* (1959), ¶606.
51 C. G. Jung, *Psychological Types*, CW6 (1921).

were eventually beautifully illustrated and edited by Jung himself as the work we know as *Liber Novus: The Red Book*.

From a clinical point of view, the visions were expressions of a prolonged psychotic break extending over several years: repeating eruptions of the unconscious psyche with a consequent intermittent loss of the conscious ego's control. The Freudian analyst D. W. Winnicott, reviewing *Memories, Dreams, Reflections* in 1964, referred to Jung's experiences as evidence of a 'psychic split' and suggested that Jung had suffered from childhood schiz-ophrenia but had somehow found a way to heal himself through his inner work.[52]

The visions began in 1914, roughly three years after the third Jupiter return and around eight years before the fourth one. Their inception coincided with transiting Jupiter conjuncting natal Saturn and forming an outgoing trine to its own place, while transiting Uranus moved into opposition to its natal place in Leo. The visions continued intermittently after Jupiter had moved on. But the decision – or compulsion – to express them in verbal and pictorial form as *Liber Novus* coincided with the planet returning to its natal place. Psychosis is only one way of interpreting what happened to Jung during this time. By portraying and articulating his experiences in *Liber Novus*, Jung emerged transformed by the visions. He had, in effect, been fertilised, and he knew it; in *Memories, Dreams, Reflections* he stated that his entire life's work had been shaped by this period of his life and the insights he gained from it.[53] Jupiter returned this time without even bothering to wear a disguise.

All of Jung's psychological theories are shaped by the idea of opposites. He was convinced that the nature of the human psyche is structured according to polarities, and the process of individuation involves the necessity of their gradual integration. It's so in-your-face Libran that we couldn't make it up. Every model Jung developed – conscious and unconscious, 'superior' and 'inferior' function types, introversion and extraversion, ego and shadow, ego and Self, individual and collective – is articulated through the idea of a polarity that contains a secret unity. All his ideas focus on the integration of the opposites because this was the pattern

---

52 D. W. Winnicott, 'Review of *Memories, Dreams, Reflections*', *International Journal of Psychoanalysis* 45 (1964), 450-455.
53 Jung, *Memories, Dreams, Reflections*, p 225.

he experienced directly during his encounters with the unconscious. In the end, Jung's objective was not to cure people of their neuroses, but to help his patients become more integrated and more attuned to their inner pattern of development.

These four Jupiter returns don't seem to be linked by any immediately obvious similarity in terms of events. Exploding knives and splitting tables don't appear to have much of a relationship with a decision to study psychiatry in Zürich – unless it's a very edgy sort of psychiatry – and a vision of God dropping a giant turd on the cathedral at Basel doesn't have any clear relationship with the theories offered in *Psychological Types*. But of course the connection between all these experiences is the 8th house Jupiter in Libra. Every time Jupiter returned to its own place, yet another door opened into the 8th house realm, and it seemed to plant yet another seed that encouraged conscious understanding of a mysterious, nonrational realm full of hidden patterns that could only be truly apprehended through symbols.

Throughout *Liber Novus*, and especially in his opening comments, Jung made it clear that he felt coerced and invaded by his experiences. He was convinced that a mysterious Other – sometimes he referred to it as the 'Spirit of the Depths', and at other times as his Soul – was forcing him down a path that only later became apparent to him as the shape and ultimate purpose of his life – in Orphic terms, his *moira*. His enigmatic comment that "free will is the ability to do gladly that which I must do" reveals his long struggle to understand and willingly serve what he eventually believed to be a higher or greater reality unfolding through the whole of life, in which each individual plays a part.

Jung could easily have treated his experiences as a neurosis that needed 'curing'. Many people have strange encounters with the nonrational, visionary dimension of Jupiter, and they ignore, suppress, or rationalise what they've experienced. Some people, faced with Jupiter's inner domain medicate themselves on the advice of their doctors and family members, hoping to leave the apparent 'illness' behind. It seems we have a long way to go in terms of our collective understanding of Jupiter's mysteries.

Jupiter returns constellate all the planets that aspect its natal place. We might briefly consider these configurations in Jung's chart to get a sense of how he experienced the Jupiter cycle, how he responded to it, and why he was able to take advantage of the intuitions and opportunities, inner and outer, that arose at the time of each Jupiter return. The exact quincunx of Jupiter to Pluto emphasises the 8th house placement of natal Jupiter, since Pluto, as god of the underworld, has a relationship to the 8th house realm, whether or not we consider it to be the 'ruler' of Scorpio. Each of Jung's experiences during his Jupiter returns had a dark and sometimes frightening edge and opened a door into the underworld, usually without his consent. Some of these experiences also heralded the death of a cherished world-view. Each Jupiter return also triggered his Chiron-Neptune conjunction, so an element of pain and suffering was usually involved, as well as a stimulus for the inherent mystical inclinations of his personality.

Jung was preoccupied throughout his life in seeking transpersonal as well as clinical answers for human suffering. Every Jupiter return triggered natal Saturn and natal Mars, suggesting a powerful determination to make something tangible out of his experiences. The visions of *Liber Novus* began when transiting Jupiter trined its own place and conjuncted natal Saturn, once again triggering the natal configuration, and the subsequent Jupiter return coincided with his determination to turn the visions into concrete form. Jung pursued his goals with dogged persistence and poured tremendous energy into formulating ideas, finishing books, and completing research experiments. The natal configuration of Jupiter-Saturn-Mars reflects a passionate determination to translate his experiences into useful theories and methods that could help others as well as himself.

For some people, Jupiter returns can provide a map of critical external junctures in an individual's journey. Significant events along a route that ultimately fulfils a calling or vocation may be reflected by the Jupiter cycle. But for other people, the Jupiter cycle maps an inner journey that might not be literally mirrored in the outer world. Jung's dream of Basel Cathedral is an example of an inner event with no apparent accompanying outer occurrence. Jung's introverted nature inclined him to focus on and track inner events and their meaning because he believed them to be significant. Individuals with a different personality bias and a different house and sign placement of Jupiter will experience Jupiter returns very differently. One way of experiencing Jupiter is not 'better than' or 'superior to' another. What seems important, whatever the avenues through which we're meta-phorically, or even literally, fertilised, is that we're able to glimpse and trust the elusive footprints of a meaningful pattern.

Transits to and from Jupiter

Now I'd like to explore transits involving Jupiter. These include transiting Jupiter forming aspects to other natal planets as well as other transiting planets forming aspects to natal Jupiter. But first, let's take some time for any questions or comments you might have about the material we've looked at so far.

Push and pull

Audience: Saturn and Jupiter are near each other in my chart, not quite conjunct, but both are often touched by transits at the same time. And I often experience a 'push-pull' effect between their influences. For example, bouts of extreme optimism are followed by a period of constriction and heavy energy. Is there any way to parse which planet is doing what when trying to determine how Jupiter works in my chart? Or should I not try to separate them in this way, and simply consider them both together?

Also, Mars is in a very tight conjunction with Jupiter, which sits on my Midheaven. With Jupiter being so unpredictable and all these other planets impacting, I'm uncertain as to how I might truly examine its influence. By the way, I'm well past my third Jupiter return and still have no real career path. Jupiter is at the MC in Virgo.

Liz: The 'push-pull' response you're describing is characteristic of any natal Jupiter-Saturn aspect, and even though the two aren't conjunct in your chart, they're close together and, as you say, they'll be triggered by transits within the same time frame. Every time you have a Jupiter return, or any other planet transiting natal Jupiter, it will trigger natal Saturn as well as Mars and the MC.

All these are placed in Virgo, an earth sign, so it might be a good idea to stop trying to separate them on an abstract level and think instead about how to turn the ideas and inspirations, as well as the 'heavy energy', into an actual skill or discipline, which is what Virgo requires. You might also think about whether an unconscious fear of intellectual or professional failure or incompetence, which is often a source of anxiety for Saturn in Virgo, might be more of a problem for you than the pushing and pulling. I would also look at issues from your early life, since the MC/IC axis is the parental axis and planets close to either angle tend to reflect patterns that might have their roots in the past. How you deal with the swing between optimism and pessimism is up to you, but you might need to accept the uneven rhythm of the configuration, stop beating yourself up about it – it isn't a failing – and focus on what's required by the sign these planets are placed in, which is the glue that could bind them together.

Seeding

When Jupiter transits a natal planet, the same dynamic is at work as when transiting Jupiter returns to its natal place: the natal planet is constellated. It gets its cue and arrives on stage, where it has to engage with Jupiter's fertilising process. Something starts to emerge that was always part of the teleology of that planet, but it gets a chance to express its nature in a different, more meaningful way.

The transits of Jupiter to other planets and to the angles form a twelve-year cycle, just as the Jupiter return does. For example, if we have transiting Jupiter moving over the Sun, it will have made this same transit twelve years ago, and it will make it again in another twelve years, and so on. I want to look more carefully at these cycles and their phases in the next seminar, but that seminar will be focused primarily on Jupiter's broader historical patterns. On a personal level, if you want more insight into what Jupiter transits to natal planets might mean, track them in your own chart from your birth onward. The transits of Jupiter to another natal planet are especially important if Jupiter aspects that planet in the birth chart.

When Jupiter transits a natal planet, by conjunction or any other strong aspect, that natal planet is woken up and given a kick. Jupiter is the catalyst, but because the mythic Zeus is a master at disguise, it may sometimes seem as though the kick is anything but benefic. But whatever form the god takes, he'll fertilise the natal planet. That planet becomes pregnant with something new, and the means by which it's activated is Jupiter's widening of horizons and its revelation of meaning and connection to a larger pattern. That can occur with both joyful and painful experiences.

Jupiter's shape-shifting means that its fertilising can occur on physical, emotional, mental, or spiritual levels, or several of them at the same time. And we might not even know what's happened. In some of the stories about Zeus' amours, he seduced his lovers invisibly; when he fathered Hermes on the Titan goddess Maia, he disguised himself as a cloud of darkness. We can't expect Jupiter's arrival to take a predictable concrete form. All we might see at the time is that the natal planet is mysteriously awakened in a new and different way, with the potential to deepen, expand, and give birth to something new.

Close encounters with Jupiter can sometimes be accompanied by conflict, sorrow, and loss. A great deal depends on how the natal planet sits in the birth chart, and how aware we are of it. If we're unconscious of the patterns and needs reflected by the natal planet, we may experience Jupiter's advent as disruptive, excessive, and disturbing, regardless of the nature of the aspect. If Jupiter transits over natal Saturn, for example, and we don't have any awareness of what Saturn symbolises inside us, this might not be a particularly joyful transit because our fears and defences are likely to be triggered, internally or externally or both. But if we can be honest with ourselves about our insecurities and we're working to build an authentic sense of identity and a solid place in the world, then a Jupiter transit to Saturn might feel tough but deeply rewarding because we've built a foundation on which to stand.

But even this way of viewing Jupiter's transits is a fragile rule shot full of holes by Jupiter's refusal to accommodate any rules at all. Transiting Jupiter in hard aspect to natal Saturn may be accompanied by great material or emotional rewards even if we have no idea of Saturn's psychological complexities, and transiting Jupiter trine natal Venus might be reflected in the unhappy breakup of a relationship. The only consistent rule is that Jupiter tends to free us, one way or another, from the ties that bind so the meaning of our own journey becomes clearer – even if we didn't realise we were in bondage.

Nevertheless, when Jupiter transits natal Saturn it can help if we have a reasonable relationship with Saturn. This means at least some willingness to recognise and work with the shadow-side of the personality. That can give us the capacity to pursue life as a limited but authentic mortal rather than a smug but hollow god. If we can try to face our fears and insecurities, stop assuming we have a 'right' to be happy, make the best we can of what we are and what we have with realism and persistence, and work to build a sense of confidence based on the whole personality rather than an artificial persona or group identity, I would call that a 'reasonable' relationship with Saturn. Then Jupiter's transit to natal Saturn, even in square or opposition, might be hard going at times, but it could still be an extremely positive experience because it enhances our sense of inner authenticity.

Jupiter projected

Important transits are often embodied by other people who affect our lives in a way that changes us, and Jupiter transits to natal planets may involve the experience of Jupiter through someone else. Because Jupiter is a chameleon, the experience of the other person isn't predictable. Someone may come into our life who epitomises Jupiterian qualities, but those qualities encompass a broad spectrum. Relationships formed under Jupiter transits can be exciting, exhilarating, joyful, and life-enhancing. But it might not always be a good idea to sign anything, unless it's a prenuptial agreement. Jupiter is the archetypal *puer aeternus* who can't make a lasting commitment, but who could reveal undiscovered doors into the future.

If we're too stuck in the craving for safety and security, we may need to discover and express our own Jupiterian qualities, and one of life's most powerful ways of ensuring this is that we meet and are drawn to those qualities in someone else. That may include Jupiter's tricky, unreliable, and irresponsible dimensions. The mythic Zeus, as king of the gods, can also be authoritarian, controlling, and narcissistic. What we might need to internalise through an encounter with another person isn't always something we want to own in ourselves.

As well as experiencing transiting Jupiter through someone else, we might play Jupiter ourselves and project the natal planet Jupiter is transiting, if we feel uncomfortable with that planet. This means we're projecting qualities and expressions that belong to our own innate nature but which need to be better integrated. We often get our first glimpse of a natal planet's deeper meaning through projecting it onto someone or something outside ourselves when it's triggered by a transit.

As an example, let's say transiting Jupiter goes over our natal Saturn, and natal Saturn opposes natal Moon. Jupiter will trigger the natal opposition, but because it's a difficult aspect – is it possible to be emotionally vulnerable and emotionally defensive at the same time? – one end of the opposition may be projected onto someone else. We may experience ourselves as the sensitive, vulnerable lunar person in a difficult relationship, and it's our partner who appears to be behaving like Saturn: controlling, critical, and emotionally withdrawn. And transiting Jupiter, working inwardly through our feelings and perhaps outwardly through a new encounter, might then seem to offer the chance of a new relationship that can satisfy our emotional needs.

This kind of enactment of a Jupiter transit may turn out to be a painful experience, and it would be easy to blame others. But both natal planets – Moon and Saturn – are being triggered by Jupiter. If we identify with the Moon, we might decide to run off with someone else because we're fed up with being rejected or controlled. But if we identify with Saturn and demand too many reassurances, our partner might be the one who feels manipulated and controlled and escapes the limitations of the relationship.

This sort of scenario can turn into a hurtful mess. But something new can always come out of it. Both Saturn and the Moon belong to us, and transiting Jupiter is the catalyst, the bringer of an intuition of other possible futures which can help inspire greater awareness and integration of both sides of this complex natal aspect. We often project one end of a problematic natal configuration when Jupiter transits the natal planets. Then Jupiter may appear in our lives as someone else, disguised as either a wrecker or a saviour.

Zeus sometimes transformed himself into a poor traveller who turned up on an unsuspecting mortal's doorstep to test their character and faith. A challenge to our deepest moral convictions can be typical of transiting Jupiter. Do we do what's easy or what's right? And how do we know what's right? This is the theme of the story of Philemon and Baucis, a poor, elderly, childless couple who served as the devoted caretakers of one of Zeus' shrines. Zeus, accompanied by Hermes, knocked on the door of the couple's humble cottage, disguised as weary travellers longing for food and drink. Although Philemon and Baucis didn't realise that these tired and dishevelled strangers were in fact the king of the gods and his messenger, they still welcomed the pair and willingly shared their meagre supper. Thus they proved their fundamental kindness, decency, and compassion, and Zeus rewarded them with their dearest wish: they asked to be allowed to serve the god's shrine to the end of their days and then die at the same moment, rather than leaving the other one alone and bereft.

Jupiter may appear on our doorstep disguised as a stranger. The planet may also appear as an event. The event may be highly exciting and rewarding or highly unpleasant, or both at the same time. We have an opportunity to stretch our awareness of the natal planet and its unfoldment in our lives. If transiting Jupiter makes a strong aspect to natal Venus, a new and exciting relationship might begin, or an existing relationship might undergo an enhanced sense of the meaningfulness of loving. Equally, the same transit to Venus may herald the breakup of a relationship, or even the sad loss of a loved one. Or it may reflect an interior experience of a mystical kind, or a burst of artistic creativity, or simply a relaxed time when we're doing well financially and can afford to do some serious retail therapy. Whatever happens or doesn't happen, Jupiter's transits bring the possibility of a deepened sense of meaning.

Jupiter transits can help us to recognise that our life has a purpose: a golden thread that runs through our experiences and unites them in a single story. All those Jupiterian 'excesses' that we looked at on the first seminar – compulsiveness, gluttony, avoidance of commitment, irrespon-sibility, bombast, *hubris*, narcissism – are also likely to enter our lives, from within or through someone else. Sometimes we might need to make foolish mistakes in order to learn something about ourselves. Even the mistakes can have meaning. The same principle applies when other planets transit natal Jupiter. Jupiter then becomes the inner dynamic that's constellated – by another person, an inner experience or inspiration, or an external event or opportunity. Our need to feel our lives have meaning is constellated when natal Jupiter is awakened by a transiting planet.

Example 2: Elvis Presley

Now let's look at an example of transits to and from Jupiter. This is the chart of Elvis Presley, who might be considered as strongly Jupiterian because, although Jupiter isn't on an angle, it's the chart ruler and it sextiles natal Sun, Mercury, and Venus.

Elvis' natal Jupiter is at 18° Scorpio in the 11th house. It's also within 3° of the cusp of the 12th, and while it's unquestionably an 11th house Jupiter, it's a bit like someone looking through a doorway into another room; a planet two or three degrees away from a cusp is already eying the next house.[54] I'm inclined to look at both houses as relevant, although the 11th is clearly the most important.

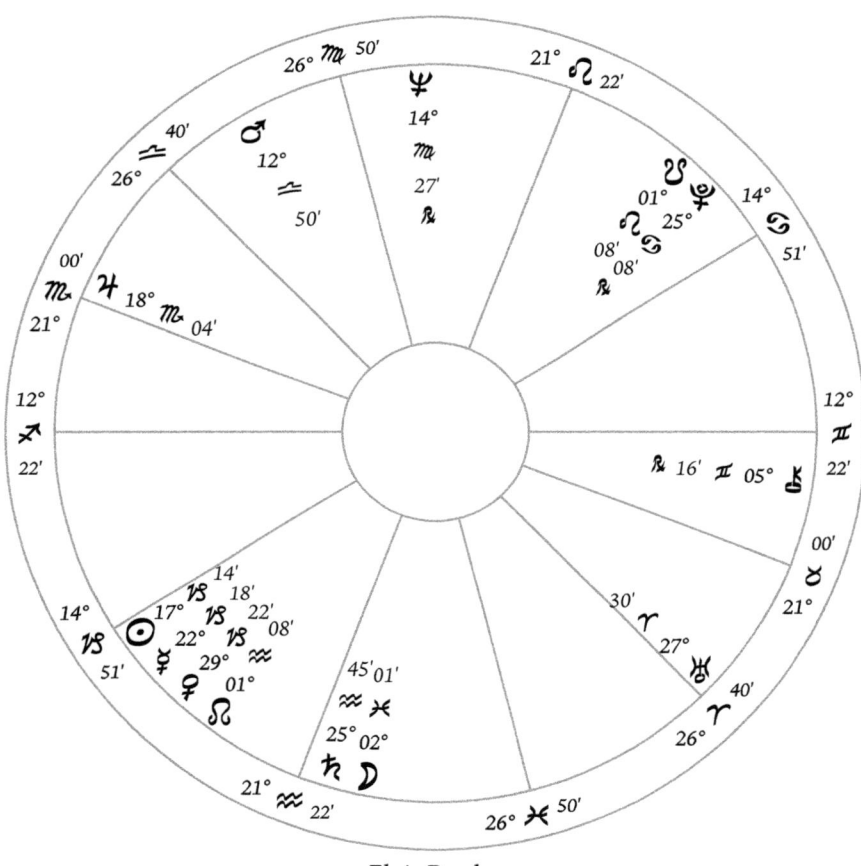

Elvis Presley
8 January 1935, 4.35 am, Tupelo, Mississippi

---

54 Elvis' birth data, available at astro.com, is given a Rodden Rating of AA – very accurate – as it was recorded on his birth certificate. Unless an astrologer is standing over the expectant mother with a stopwatch, we might need to allow for a slight gap between the actual moment of birth and the recording of the data, so recorded birth times with an AA rating are often several minutes later than the actual birth. This would mean the Ascendant is a degree or two earlier, and in Elvis' chart, Jupiter would be even closer to the 12th house cusp.

Natal Jupiter in Scorpio in the 11th house

The 11th house reflects the sphere of life where we experience a sense of meaning through the idea of a broader human family. Most typically this occurs through friendships, work colleagues, groups that share common interests, and social networks. It's through these personal, everyday linkups that we experience participation in a larger humanity and feel we can share in its development. Through planets in the 11th house, we connect with and contribute to the society in which we live, even if we don't fully realise it. We need to keep expanding our social contacts, our professional networks, and our groups of friends. We want to become an effective presence in the world through 'people power'. But we're really longing for what Plato, in the *Phaedo*, described as that specific god to whose divine choir our soul truly belongs.

As Jupiter in Elvis' chart is in Scorpio, the means by which he might experience a connection with others is through the expression of powerful emotions. Strong emotions don't necessarily have to be overtly displayed through shouting, weeping, hugging, or writing a fruity autobiography. While more extraverted personalities may enjoy sharing their feelings in obvious ways, introverted people may need a creative vehicle through which to express their emotional life. And Scorpionic feelings, which have a built-in mistrust of too much 'sharing', may be more effectively and subtly expressed through a fluid medium such as music, theatre, or dance.

An 11th house Jupiter in a water sign, however introverted the personality might be, would never be content with simply composing music for others to play, or writing a play for others to act in. This Jupiter needs to perform for an audience to feel connected. Because Jupiter is in Scorpio and not in Cancer or Pisces, Elvis' music was appropriately raw, chthonic, and sexual. And because of Jupiter's proximity to the 12th house, he also tapped into a deep frustrated longing in the collective that demanded release through an overtly primal expression of sexuality. Elvis' sense of meaning came from expressing his complex personal feelings through his music, but he was also a mouthpiece for a collective need. It's interesting that, just as he rose to fame, transiting Neptune entered Scorpio, reflecting a collective yearning for a more honest, naked, and primitive expression of emotion as a path to redemption, in stark contrast to the previous fourteen years Neptune had spent in airy, idealistic, and often emotionally constricted Libra.

Elvis Presley in 1957. Publicity photo for his film, *Jailhouse Rock*. Photo, Library of Congress..

Shy and inarticulate in early life, Elvis experienced a relationship with the collective through communicating his sexuality, his turbulent emotions, his instincts, and his imagination in forms to which everyone could relate. It's hard to listen to his music and not feel the body begin to move in time to it, unless we're deliberately forcing ourselves to sit still. And because Jupiter is in Scorpio, Elvis needed to shock, break down conventions, and free a more disruptive and primitive energy in himself and his audience. Elvis' concerts provided the arena for a shrieking, ecstatic young audience literally trying to rip the clothes off its idol in a display eerily resembling the ancient rites of Dionysos. Jupiter in the 11th can have great power in the collective through the medium of its sign, and Elvis certainly exhibited his capacity to transform collective attitudes without ever going on a protest march, waving a placard, shouting a slogan, or writing a controversial book. He just wiggled his hips and sang.

Jupiter's natal aspects integrate it comfortably with the rest of the chart. It sextiles Sun, Mercury, and Venus in Capricorn in the 2nd house, trines Pluto in Cancer in the 8th, and sextiles Neptune in Virgo in the 9th. It also squares Saturn in Aquarius in the 3rd house, the only challenging aspect between Jupiter and another natal planet. Saturn in the 3rd, in an out-of-sign conjunction with Moon in Pisces, hints at the crippling shyness, loneliness, and material deprivation that constricted Elvis' childhood, his schooling, and his efforts to communicate with his parents and his peers.

Saturn and Moon conjunct in the 3rd, and Saturn square Jupiter, suggest an ongoing struggle to express powerful and sometimes primitive feelings. Elvis couldn't do it verbally, but eventually he found a vehicle that worked for him. The square between Jupiter and Saturn may also hint at the growing gap between his fame and popularity and how he secretly felt about himself. The disconnection between the adored public image and the shy, self-deprecating child who expected to be bullied and to fail, grew larger and larger as his fame increased. It may have contributed to the way in which Jupiterian escapism, in the form of drugs and alcohol, eventually destroyed him.

For those of you who aren't familiar with his background, Elvis was born into poverty in a two-room 'shotgun house', a crude shack his father had built. He had an identical older twin who was stillborn, and if we interpret one of the more traditional meanings of the 3rd house literally, it may hint at feelings about this lost twin who, through his mother's obsession with her loss, had such a profound invisible influence on his life. Elvis was particularly close to his mother, who suffered from depression as well as a compulsive eating disorder. It seems she never got over the death of the older twin and took a variety of medications for both her depression and her compulsive eating. His father moved aimlessly from one temporary job to the next, earning very little money and apparently entirely devoid of ambition. Elvis' childhood was joyless, isolated, and bleak.

In his late teens he began experimenting with his mother's diet pills and antidepressants, and he soon became addicted. Throughout his adult life he carried with him a kit of addictive medications that included Dexedrine, Percodan, and Nembutal: pills to speed him up and pills to slow him down. In a tragic imitation of his mother, he relied on a smorgasbord of drugs to get him through each day.

Transiting Jupiter trine its own place

Elvis began his climb to fame in 1954, when he made his first recordings with Sun Studio. He was a pioneer in the musical genre known as Rockabilly, one of the earliest styles of rock and roll, which blended country and western music with rhythm and blues. During this period, transiting Jupiter in Cancer trined its own place in Scorpio. While forming this trine, transiting Jupiter also triggered all the natal planetary aspects to Jupiter, one by one.

When transiting Jupiter sets off natal configurations in this way, especially if its own natal place is also involved, opportunities may present themselves that open a clear road to the potential future inherent in those natal aspects. Perhaps because Jupiter is the chart ruler and forms so many benign aspects to other natal planets, Elvis could envision the possibilities on offer and was prepared to jump at the opportunities. And he really had nothing to lose by trying.

Transiting Jupiter conjunct natal Pluto; transiting Saturn conjunct natal Jupiter

On 6 February 1955, transiting Jupiter was at 22° Cancer, conjuncting transiting Uranus at 24° Cancer. Both planets conjuncted Elvis' natal Pluto, triggering his close natal Pluto-Venus opposition. Under these configurations, Colonel Tom Parker suddenly appeared in Elvis' life like a sleazy jinn emerging from a magic bottle. Through Parker's intervention, Elvis' recording contract was taken over by RCA Records, and this proved to be the real kickstart to his career. At the same time, transiting Saturn was moving through Scorpio, trine the transiting Jupiter-Uranus conjunction in Cancer, and it moved into conjunction with Elvis' natal Jupiter, triggering his natal Jupiter-Pluto trine. At the time of the meeting with Parker, who in the following year would become his lifelong manager, transiting Saturn was within a 2° orb of Elvis' Jupiter.

As it journeyed through Scorpio, transiting Saturn also formed sextiles to the natal planets in Capricorn, trined natal Pluto, and squared its own place at 25° Aquarius. In other words, transiting Saturn triggered natal Jupiter and all its natal aspects, and grounded them in concrete reality. From an astrological perspective, Parker himself wasn't especially Saturnian. With a Pisces Ascendant, his chart ruler, like Elvis', is Jupiter. But he acted as a kind of human embodiment of Saturn. He became the architect of Elvis' remarkable success and, according to some, also the architect of his protégé's self-destruction.

Tom Parker served as Elvis' manager for more than two decades. The synastry aspects between the two, especially those involving Elvis' Jupiter, are revealing. Elvis' Jupiter at 18° Scorpio is exactly trine Parker's natal

Mars at 18° Pisces, and closely trine Parker's natal Neptune-Venus conjunction in Cancer. The same transiting planets that triggered Elvis' Jupiter also triggered Parker's Mars-Neptune-Venus configuration. The synastry between them creates a grand water trine, constellated by the transiting planets in Cancer and Scorpio. If transiting Jupiter fertilises us with an idea, an inspiration, or an opportunity, transiting Saturn aspecting natal Jupiter may crystallise or embody that idea or inspiration, grounding something that previously existed only in potential.

Colonel Tom Parker in 1969.

When transiting Saturn arrived on his natal Jupiter, Elvis met the man who would ultimately shape his career and make it possible for him to fulfil his creative potential. He suddenly found that his life had meaning; his music actually mattered to lots of people. His social world expanded, and he could be someone of importance and express himself at the same time. And being a Capricorn with the Sun in the 2nd house, he wouldn't have turned his back on the obvious financial rewards and the possibility of finally achieving some material security. He had clawed his way out of a deprived and lonely background and arrived as a potent voice in the collective when the transits of Jupiter, Uranus, and Saturn triggered natal Jupiter.

Transiting Jupiter trine natal Uranus

Elvis' first hit single, *Heartbreak Hotel*, was released at the beginning of 1956, and it quickly reached the top of the charts. On the day of the record's release, transiting Jupiter and transiting Pluto were exactly conjunct at 27° Leo. This planetary coupling, moving through Elvis' 9th house, formed an exact trine to his natal Uranus at 27° Aries in the 5ᵗʰ house. Reinhold Ebertin, in *The Combination of Stellar Influences*, described the Jupiter-Uranus combination as 'a sudden change in destiny', and nicknamed it the "Thank the Lord!" configuration. When Pluto is thrown into the mix, Ebertin described the combination as "a strong awareness of purpose in life, a far-reaching creative activity, a sudden change of the financial circumstances".[55] It's always satisfying to see how literal the transiting aspects of Jupiter can sometimes be.

Transiting Jupiter at the Midheaven

In November 1955, transiting Jupiter entered Virgo and began its approach to Elvis' natal MC. It moved back into Leo during the first half of 1956, when it conjuncted transiting Pluto; but in the second half of the year it re-entered Virgo and then conjuncted Elvis' MC at 26° Virgo. After a brief period in Libra, Jupiter moved back over the MC in the first half of 1957. He sold ten million records during this time, and songs such as *Hound Dog, Don't Be Cruel,* and *Blue Suede Shoes* are now enshrined in musical history. Under this Jupiter-MC transit, Elvis began touring the country from coast to coast. Never one to turn down an opportunity, he appeared on a number of important American television shows, like the Steve Allen Show and the Ed Sullivan Show. He released his first movie, *Love Me Tender,* in November 1956. Transiting Jupiter arrived exactly at the MC on the day the film was released. You really couldn't make it up.

This period of Elvis' life took place under the provenance of a number of important Jupiter transits. His first single was released when transiting Jupiter and Pluto in Leo trined natal Uranus in Aries. By the time Jupiter arrived at its exact conjunction with his Virgo MC, Elvis had truly become 'The King'. But we shouldn't imagine that all this lovely Jupiter stuff just 'happened' as a manifestation of Jupiterian good luck. It required the arduous training of an innate talent, an immense amount of hard work, a willingness to seize opportunities, and an acceptance of the sometimes morally ambiguous contribution of that peculiar embodiment of Saturn's crystallising propensities, Colonel Tom Parker.

---

55 Reinhold Ebertin, *The Combination of Stellar Influences*, trans. Alfred G. Roosedale (Ebertin Verlag, 1960), pp. 162-163.

Transiting Jupiter conjunct natal Mars

Transiting Jupiter fully entered Libra in the second half of 1957, still moving through Elvis' 10th house. His next film, *Jailhouse Rock*, was released when transiting Jupiter conjuncted natal Mars at 12° Libra in the 10th. A group of fast-moving transiting planets – Mars, Mercury, and Sun – all lined up with transiting Jupiter and arrived on natal Mars at the same time. In terms of the traditional meaning of the 10th house – success, status, achievement in the world – this was, once again, a blindingly obvious expression of a Jupiter transit.

Transiting Jupiter conjunct natal Pluto, opposition natal Venus, and conjunct the Moon's south Node

On 13 September 1959, while Elvis was serving in the US army and stationed in Germany, he met and was attracted to a fourteen-year-old girl

called Priscilla Beaulieu. Tom Parker scented the possibility of a serious scandal – sex with an underaged girl could have earned his protégé a prison sentence for statutory rape – and he had no intention of allowing this kind of bad publicity to interfere with the golden promise of the future. Parker insisted on a chaste eight-year courtship (we can only imagine how this edict could have been enforced, short of locking Priscilla into a chastity belt), and she and Elvis weren't allowed to marry until 1967. The reasons for the extraordinary degree of control Parker wielded over Elvis are complex and I won't

Elvis and Priscilla at their wedding in Las Vegas on 1 May 1967. Photo, Bettmann/ Getty.

go into them now. You can all examine the synastry between the two men yourselves.[56]

When the couple finally married, transiting Jupiter had just passed an exact conjunction with Elvis' natal Pluto at 25° Cancer in the 8th house, opposed natal Venus at 29° Capricorn, and was applying to the Moon's south Node at 1° Leo, triggering his natal Pluto-Venus opposition along the nodal axis.

Transiting Jupiter conjunct natal Venus, opposition natal Pluto, and conjunct the Moon's north Node

The marriage lasted for exactly half a Jupiter cycle; Elvis and Priscilla divorced six years after marrying. Given the god's track record in myth, this timespan might be viewed as entirely predictable, and perhaps far longer than might have been expected. At the time of the divorce, transiting Jupiter arrived at 2° Aquarius, right on Elvis' lunar north Node and exactly opposite where it was when the happy couple went on their honeymoon to Palm Springs in sunny California. In the leadup to the divorce, which, not surprisingly, was rather messy, Jupiter had conjuncted Elvis' natal Venus in Capricorn and opposed natal Pluto. This mirror-image reverse of Jupiter's transit at the time of the marriage and the divorce is both striking and appropriate.

Transiting Jupiter opposition natal Moon and square natal Chiron

Elvis fathered one child with Priscilla. She was called Lisa Marie, and when she was born on 1 February 1968, transiting Jupiter at 3° Virgo had just opposed his natal Moon at 2° Pisces and was moving into square to his natal Chiron at 5° Gemini, triggering the natal square of Moon to Chiron with its suggestion of childhood vulnerability and unhappiness. Jupiter had made this same transit twelve years earlier, during the build-up to his first great successes. On both occasions Elvis no doubt experienced great joy – the transit of Jupiter in any aspect to natal Moon can coincide with a heightening and brightening of one's emotional life – but hidden within that joy was the shadow of his own early misery, along with the potential

---

56 The synastry and composite between Elvis and Tom Parker are discussed in Liz Greene, *Chiron in Love* (Wessex Astrologer, 2023).

for making peace with those childhood wounds.

The transit of Jupiter to the natal Chiron-Moon square may have triggered painful memories of his own childhood, the kind of parenting (or lack thereof) he himself had received, the kind of father he hoped to become, and the kind of father he had experienced in reality and feared he might become. But like the Jupiter transit to this natal configuration twelve years earlier, Jupiter seems to have offered a greater understanding, or at least some alleviation, of those early wounds.

Throughout his life, Elvis, like his mother, struggled with drug addiction and obesity. Towards

Lisa Marie Presley, 1 February 1968-12 January 2023, photographed at a car race in Florida in 2005.
Lisa Marie died of cardiac arrest at the age of 54, just over a year after this seminar was given.
Photo, Tech Sgt Cherie A. Thurlby, USAF.

the end he had grown enormous, weighing in at 250 pounds or, in Britain, nearly 18 stone. Also like his mother, he died of heart failure compounded by alcohol and drugs. One of the things I mentioned in our first Jupiter seminar was that Jupiter is often active at the time of death. The Romans recognised this in their belief that when a notable person died, Jupiter in the form of his eagle would descend from Olympus as psychopomp and bear the soul of the deceased up to the heavens. If the person was someone great, they would be catasterised: turned into a star or a constellation, a gift which the mythic Zeus endowed on favoured children such as Herakles. When Elvis died, transiting Jupiter made an exact quincunx to natal Venus, and transiting Venus was in turn exactly trine natal Jupiter.

These mutual Jupiter-Venus transits are gentle and benign. But Elvis' death, although peaceful at the end, was a dark mirror-image of Jupiter. His autopsy revealed a bloated liver – the organ which in traditional astrology is associated with Jupiter – and a colon that was stretched to twice its normal size. He was full of toxic levels of codeine, quaaludes, and half a dozen other drugs. Elvis lived a Jupiterian life and died a Jupiterian death, even to the extent that the organ in his body that was most damaged was the one traditionally ruled by Jupiter.

Natal Jupiter-Saturn aspects

Although the Sun in Capricorn in the 2nd house is an appropriate symbol for his ambition, his tenacity, and his wealth, Elvis lived a Jupiterian life in a very literal way. Whenever Jupiter transited one of his natal planets, it triggered some of the most fortunate configurations in the birth chart, but it also triggered the toughest one, the natal Jupiter-Saturn square. It's worth looking at this square more carefully, especially as one of you asked about Jupiter-Saturn contacts earlier, and also because this aspect, along with his natal Moon-Saturn-Chiron configuration, reflects Elvis' persistent belief that he didn't really deserve all the fame and wealth he achieved, and that, sooner or later, he would lose it all.

The way he dealt, or avoided dealing, with Jupiter square Saturn might help us to see more constructive ways of working with this combination of planets. There seems to have been a constant voice inside Elvis that kept telling him, "You're really nobody, you're just poor white trash and they'll all realise it one day, and then they'll turn on you." Saturn in Aquarius, although in dignity in its own sign, can reflect a sense of painful isolation from the group and, without enough emotional support from family and early schooling, it's easy to blame oneself. Saturn in Aquarius can often feel like an outsider who expects to be overlooked, mocked, or scapegoated. Elvis was certainly bullied and mocked as a child, and it's likely he felt it was somehow his own fault.

Natal Jupiter placed in the 11th, the house associated with Aquarius, squares natal Saturn in Aquarius. This is a kind of double whammy: the sphere where he sought meaning was also the sphere where he experienced a sharp sense of deprivation. Elvis' upbringing and experiences with his peers at school helped to engender enormous insecurity because he was always predisposed to feeling marginalised, and the greater his success, the more it ate away at him.

When we feel deprived or lacking, we may easily turn to a planet in the natal chart with which we can identify, in order to feel better. On the first seminar I talked about how we may turn to Jupiter to compensate for unconscious wounds and feelings of damage and inferiority; this is the god's role as Zeus *Soter*, 'the Saviour'. It seems Elvis turned to Jupiter – entirely understandable since it's the chart ruler and forms a benign aspect to the Sun – and tried to become the archetypal king of the gods that his fans believed him to be: a shining, omnipotent deity clothed in gold and able to have any woman he wanted. Perhaps he couldn't deal with the pain of the Jupiter-Saturn square, the Moon-Saturn conjunction, and the Moon-Chiron square. Instead of facing the pain and trying to work with it on an inner level, he just ate, drank, and medicated himself to escape, and the escape eventually led to his death.

Natal Jupiter and the national chart

There's one final point about Elvis I wanted to mention: his natal chart in relation to the chart of the country in which he first achieved fame. National heroes and national villains, whether in war, politics, religion, science, the arts, or the entertainment world, usually have strong links with the nation in which they achieve glory or infamy, and that's usually the country in which they were born. Elvis' natal Ascendant is almost exactly conjunct the US natal Ascendant at 12° Sagittarius – both Elvis and his country are ruled by Jupiter – and his natal Jupiter trines the US Sun and Mercury in Cancer and sextiles the US natal Neptune in Virgo.

Elvis was born at the same time the US was experiencing its second Neptune return, so Neptune conjuncts itself across the two charts. His natal Saturn closely conjuncts the US natal Moon as well as conjuncting his own Moon. Elvis' birth chart is woven with the collective psyche of his homeland in a powerful way that helped to ensure his immortality. He holds a place in American musical history that will never fade, because he embodied through his music and his rags-to-riches-to-tragedy story the needs, aspirations, fears, dangers, and achievements of the collective in which he was born and lived his life.

Planets transiting natal Jupiter: a brief summary

Before we move on to any questions or comments you might have, I'd like to quickly summarise some points about the transits of other planets to natal Jupiter. When another planet – especially a slower-moving one – transits natal Jupiter, our need to experience meaning and a sense of connection with a greater reality is constellated, and the planet that's making the transit acts as a catalyst. Something or someone comes into our lives that reflects the transiting planet and awakens natal Jupiter, and we get a glimpse of life being full of meaning and potential, although we might not recognise the inner dimension of the experience.

This window into a larger universe doesn't always register at the time of the transit. Sometimes it's only later that the realisation of the relevance and importance of the time begins to emerge. And 'later' might be 'much later'. When natal Jupiter is transited, in a sense the god himself is fertilised, and so is the psychological dynamic of which he's a symbol. The mythic Zeus, like the women he impregnates, can bring forth children, although they're not biological births in the literal sense. There are two stories of the god becoming 'pregnant' and giving birth. The first is Athene, goddess of wisdom, who gestated within Zeus after he swallowed her mother, and who was 'born' from his head fully armed. The second is Dionysos, god of madness and ecstasy, whose embryo was sewn into Zeus' thigh after the death of his mother Semele and was then 'born' through the agency of Hermes acting as midwife.

Transits to natal Jupiter can be experienced in a positive way: an exciting opportunity appears, a promising new idea suddenly occurs to us, or a person enters our life whom we intuitively know will prove to be important in expanding our awareness and our future. But transits to natal Jupiter can also be experienced as grinding and painful. Sometimes we wind up facing both, simultaneously or sequentially.

For example, a painful loss may be followed by a realisation of much-needed freedom, and feelings of grief and sorrow can occur simultaneously with a sense of relief. When transits involving Jupiter concern death, including one's own, it may be seen, depending on one's spiritual perspective, as both a sad ending for those left behind and a blessed release for the departed. And Jupiter's characteristic vices can also be triggered when the planet is transited. Gluttony, inflated visions of one's own importance, disregard for the consequences of one's behaviour on others, the obsessive pursuit of an idealised object, and a refusal to accept limits can all pervade our perceptions. The outcome of these 'excesses' is unpredictable because we ourselves might not know our own hearts and minds.

Saturn transits to natal Jupiter

Earlier, we looked at transiting Saturn conjuncting Elvis' natal Jupiter. At the time of the transit, Elvis met Colonel Tom Parker, the mentor and manager who shaped his life but also contributed to its destruction. This transit reflected an encounter that crystallised not only Elvis' Jupiterian dreams but also his excesses.

To get more insight into a transit like this, we need to look at Saturn's placement in the natal chart, because any transiting planet will carry the meaning of its natal placement with it like a suitcase full of clothing it's brought from home. Elvis' natal Saturn conjuncts his Moon in the 3rd house, so the transit of Saturn conjunct natal Jupiter crystallised Jupiter's meaning but also brought with it all the loneliness and constriction in communication of the natal Saturn placement. This may tell us something about why Parker was such a powerful influence. Elvis was desperate to find someone who understood him and with whom he could communicate, even if it carried a high price tag.

Transiting Saturn in strong aspect to natal Jupiter will provide flesh and bones to everything in us that's yearning to fill our lives with significance. We long to know that what happens to us means something, that our experiences aren't just random and pointless but instead hold a deeper purpose, and that our dreams and aspirations, our failures and successes, actually matter as part of some greater scheme. But crystallising our longings can also be problematic because we have to confront the worldly limits that are placed on our dreams, and cope with the recognition that experiencing meaning doesn't offer any guarantee that we'll escape difficult experiences.

Although transiting Saturn square or opposition Jupiter can challenge our faith and self-confidence, these sometimes harsh transits can still concretise Jupiter's dreams and aspirations. We may wake up to what we really long for, but the realisation can be bittersweet because we may realise we can't ever have the longed-for future in exactly the form in which we envisaged it, and the cost, while worth paying, may be high.

Chiron transits to natal Jupiter

Chiron transiting natal Jupiter can bring a more painful dimension to the quest for meaning. Jupiter may be awakened and challenged by the recognition that life involves suffering and can often be unfair: a realisation that challenges belief in any simplistic form of cosmic justice. Saturn is Chiron's father in myth, and both reflect those elements in life that threaten or limit Jupiter's unbounded quest to find meaning and joy. Both Saturn and Chiron tend to wake up Jupiter by dragging it, sometimes metaphorically kicking and screaming, into incarnation. Jupiter has to grow up, which no self-respecting *puer aeternus* would ever do unless forcibly compelled.

Any major transit from Chiron to natal Jupiter, including trines and sextiles, may reflect a time of sorrow or a feeling of restriction or victimisation, and if we're not alert to our own responses, Jupiter's propensity for inflation may ride in on a white horse to offer compensation for our suffering. Sometimes this takes the form of identifying with the archetypal Chosen Victim. But a transit of Chiron to Jupiter may also awaken the need for self-understanding as well as greater understanding of others, and we can develop compassion as a pathway to meaning through the recognition that life can be unfair to everyone and not just us, suffering is universal and sometimes unavoidable, and ultimately our pain may be as important and necessary to our teleology as our joy.

Outer planet transits to natal Jupiter

The outer planets are symbols of the great collective currents constantly at work in life, shifting and changing the collective psyche on deeper levels. Jupiter is a personal planet and our experiences of meaning are personal, although they can link us with a larger universe and a greater pattern of unfoldment. The outer planets aren't personal, but they may enter the individual's life disguised as personal upheaval or change that mirrors in microcosm the changes occurring in the collective psyche. This links our own experiences with those of the larger body of humanity. When an outer planet transits natal Jupiter, what's going on in the world 'out there' will impinge in some way on our own life in a manner that could wake us up to our connection with a broader humanity and a greater universe – if we allow it to.

Transiting Uranus aspecting natal Jupiter

Uranus reflects our collective need to progress, evolve, and fulfil our human potential. The Promethean spirit in the collective psyche triggers Jupiter's personal need for meaning, and we may suddenly feel we're part of a vast evolving life, whether we see this in spiritual, social, or ecological terms. Uranus can be highly disruptive and sometimes destructive because the individual's feelings and needs are subsumed by those of the group. But the disruption can wake Jupiter up to potentials we didn't realise we had, not only in ourselves but in the world around us.

We may experience sudden creative inspirations, or even major spiritual, intellectual, or emotional revelations. Or we may undergo sudden separations or the collapse of our secure structures and material foundations. That can obviously be frightening and generate a state of extreme anxiety. But this kind of disruption could allow us to realise that we're on a journey somewhere and that our personal journey isn't separate from the broader human journey. Uranus can awaken Jupiter through connecting us with a collective vision of human potential and unlived human possibilities. In glimpsing that deeper ongoing story, we may recognise that all of us could be more and better than what we are.

Transiting Neptune aspecting natal Jupiter

Neptune reflects our longing to merge with a greater whole and lose the sense of separateness and loneliness that makes any effort to assert ourselves as individuals a painful endeavour. We yearn to be redeemed from the harsh constrictions and suffering of mundane existence, and we hunger for being cleansed and reborn. Through merging, we lose our sense of mortal limits and the inevitable burden of human unhappiness. When transiting Neptune makes a strong aspect to natal Jupiter, this yearning for redemption flowing through the collective like a tidal wave can trigger a recognition of being part of a greater whole.

We might experience a sense of oneness through suffering, sacrifice, and deepening compassion. But Neptune transits to Jupiter can also reflect a kind of spiritual inflation: the feeling that we've glimpsed the truth and are now destined to become a messiah or a guru, often by presenting ourselves as an archetypal victim. Jupiter's propensity for inflation can be fuelled by Neptune's messianic inclinations. If this kind of *hubris* is enacted on the concrete level, the consequences to our material stability can be unpleasant. The dark side of Neptune-Jupiter is potential inflation. We and we alone have a right to win the jackpot; we've discovered the one true religion or social truth; God speaks to us and has given us a mission; and we're destined to teach our truth to others whether or not they want or need to hear it.

Neptune transits to Jupiter can open up the heart in profound ways, through empathy and the recognition of shared suffering, longings, and dreams. These transits can also reflect the opening of the imagination, providing avenues for new creative expressions. This is the alchemical *solutio*, in which the 'old king' – the corrupt and confused primal substance – is dissolved so that it can be cleansed and transformed. Neptune can disintegrate boundaries, offering a glimpse of unity but eroding a solid sense of individual identity and aspiration, and sometimes even of worldly reality. It's not unlike the experience of falling hopelessly, ecstatically in love. When we're immersed in it, it feels as though we're the only person in the history of the world ever to have experienced such heightened emotions. This is because the emotions are archetypal, and closely resemble the experience of merging with a greater Other that accompanies many mystical or 'peak' experiences. These feelings don't belong to us alone, and if we can retain enough clarity to recognise this, we might get the best from Jupiter's dissolution in Neptune's waters.

Transiting Pluto aspecting natal Jupiter

Pluto is concerned with survival: an instinctive compulsion to preserve life and perpetuate our collective as well as ourselves. This compulsion to defend life through eliminating danger and acquiring as much power as possible is often accompanied by a pervasive sense of threat, which might or might not be conscious. The creeping feeling of danger and the need to challenge it can trigger our need to find some kind of meaning and significance in what might feel like a battle with great darkness, inside or outside us.

We may experience Pluto transits to Jupiter personally through a profound loss: physical, emotional, financial, or spiritual. It's through the eruption of our human need to survive at all costs and ensure that life is worth preserving that we're impelled to rid ourselves of anything which might corrupt or poison us. Pluto transiting Jupiter reflects the emergence of a compulsive need to affirm a meaning in life and in events, because only a sense of meaning can truly ensure our survival. There's often a literal truth in that instinctive conviction, sometimes reflected in an individual's determination to survive the painful ending of a phase of life, emotional devastation, or an illness that everyone else assumes will be fatal.

Many of us may be experiencing Saturn, Chiron, or an outer planet constellating Jupiter at the moment, if not by major aspect, then by less dramatic aspects like a sesquiquadrate, a quincunx, or a semisquare. Whatever the aspect, an awakened Jupiter can offer the possibility of glimpsing some kind of meaningful pattern in the midst of the chaos and darkness that seem to be rampant in the world. When Jupiter is triggered by slower-moving planets, we can feel a connection to patterns at work both inside us and beyond us, and we might become aware of the potential birth of an entire new dimension of life.

Questions and comments

Jupiter's dark side in Jung's life

Audience: What would you say about the dark side of Jupiter in Jung's life?

Liz: If I were looking for Jupiterian darkness in Jung, I would probably look at his attitudes towards women. There were times when he seems to have treated his wife Emma in much the same way Zeus treated Hera, although we don't know how he might have really felt about his own actions. And Emma's way of dealing with it was considerably more sophisticated than Hera's. Emma Jung was neither spiteful nor inclined to throw hissy fits. But she was an Aries with a Scorpio Ascendant and a Leo Moon, and she wasn't prepared to martyr herself either. She understood intuitively how to play the long game, and she played it with consummate skill.

Jung had numerous women in his life, some of them lovers and some devoted colleagues or disciples, and he expected Emma to accept it all and tolerate his relationship with Toni Wolff even to the point of insisting that the three of them live together. Emma managed to cope because the only other option would have been to lose him, and she wouldn't take that option because she loved and believed in him and was an enthusiastic participant in his work and ideas. Jung could be arrogant in his treatment of women, and at times he could also be arrogant in his general behaviour. The conviction that he was special enough to break emotional and sexual rules without reprisal might be attributed to the darker side of Leo, which can sometimes behave in a self-entitled way. But of course it's more complicated than that.

Jung suffered from feelings of deep anxiety and a fear of what others would think of him. Unlike Freud, who had always been an outsider and was prepared to battle against the establishment and express his ideas regardless of what other people thought of him, Jung, who was accustomed to social acceptance, was afraid that if others knew how involved he was with dodgy subjects like astrology, magic, and spiritualism, they would reject him and denigrate his work. This kind of deep insecurity about the collective, especially those in his own profession, may be reflected in part by his natal Sun-Chiron square and his 1st-house Saturn in Aquarius. At such moments of self-doubt, Jupiter seems to have stepped in, as is its wont, with a dose of inflation as compensation for feelings of profound uncertainty.

But we should remember that much of Jung's sense of self-importance was justified. He viewed his gifts as a burden to be carried for posterity rather than a means of achieving praise; his ideas have profoundly altered our perceptions of human nature; and his contribution to the history of ideas is still unfolding. The cultural context of Jung's life and work has to be considered as well. The Swiss lagged behind the rest of Europe in their treatment of women and didn't grant them the vote until 1971, thirty years after the French, forty years after the Spanish, and half a century after the UK, Germany, and Austria. Jung's attitude towards marriage was typical of his cultural milieu. We might even see his views as far more advanced than those of many of his fellow psychiatrists, since Jung treated his female colleagues as equals and respected and promoted their ideas and achievements without condescension or reservation.

On intellectual and professional levels, he was more respectful in his attitudes towards women than many people are today. And we might also keep in mind that Jung's marriage to Emma remained solid throughout their lives together, and that Toni Wolff, formerly his patient, wasn't 'damaged' by their involvement. Instead, she acted as midwife for the outpourings of *Liber Novus* and experienced profound healing through their relationship. It isn't helpful for us to pass judgement on this darker face of Jupiter, just as it isn't helpful to pass judgment on the mythic Zeus. I wouldn't have wanted to be married to Jung. But then, I'm not a Swiss woman born in the late 19th century.

Example 3: Queen Victoria

This is the birth chart of Queen Victoria. Jupiter is at 16° Aquarius and, not surprisingly, in the 10th house. It's not surprising because Victoria thoroughly enjoyed the pomp and circumstance of being a queen and, as the icing on the cake, an empress, as she was also Empress of India. She may have enjoyed the role even more because of her struggle to claim the throne and demand the right to make her own decisions as a woman and a monarch, rather than serving as the puppet of the various powerful male figures surrounding her. Being Queen, and a highly popular one, was her great Jupiterian reward.

Queen Victoria's natal Jupiter is comfortable in its aspects, but the aspects are sparse. It's closely sextile Mars in Aries, and it's also sextile and trine the Moon's nodal axis. Jupiter also makes a wide square to Mercury, the only challenge it receives from another planet. Although the aspects are benign, this isn't a terribly well-integrated Jupiter, and it isn't confronted by tough characters like Saturn, Chiron, or one of the outer planets. Jupiter needs to be challenged, if not by natal aspect then by synastry aspects, in order to provoke some inner conflict and mediate the self-satisfaction that can come with a natal Jupiter that enjoys only harmonious aspects. Although her marriage to Prince Albert had its conflicts, only his natal Venus at 20° Leo formed a hard aspect to her Jupiter. Victoria's most rampant excess was her arrogance.

When Victoria was crowned Queen in 1837 at the age of eighteen, transiting Jupiter was at 17° Leo, exactly opposite her natal Jupiter and trine natal Mars, triggering the natal Jupiter-Mars sextile. At the same time, transiting Chiron arrived at 17° Gemini, forming an exact trine to natal Jupiter and a sextile to natal Mars. This Chiron trine has a strange and ambiguous feel because of Chiron's relationship with suffering and unfair injury. But perhaps it isn't that strange after all; in order to become Queen, there had to be a death, and Victoria had been very fond of her uncle, King William IV. She was only eighteen when she ascended the throne, and the burden of monarchy that suddenly descended on her involved restrictions

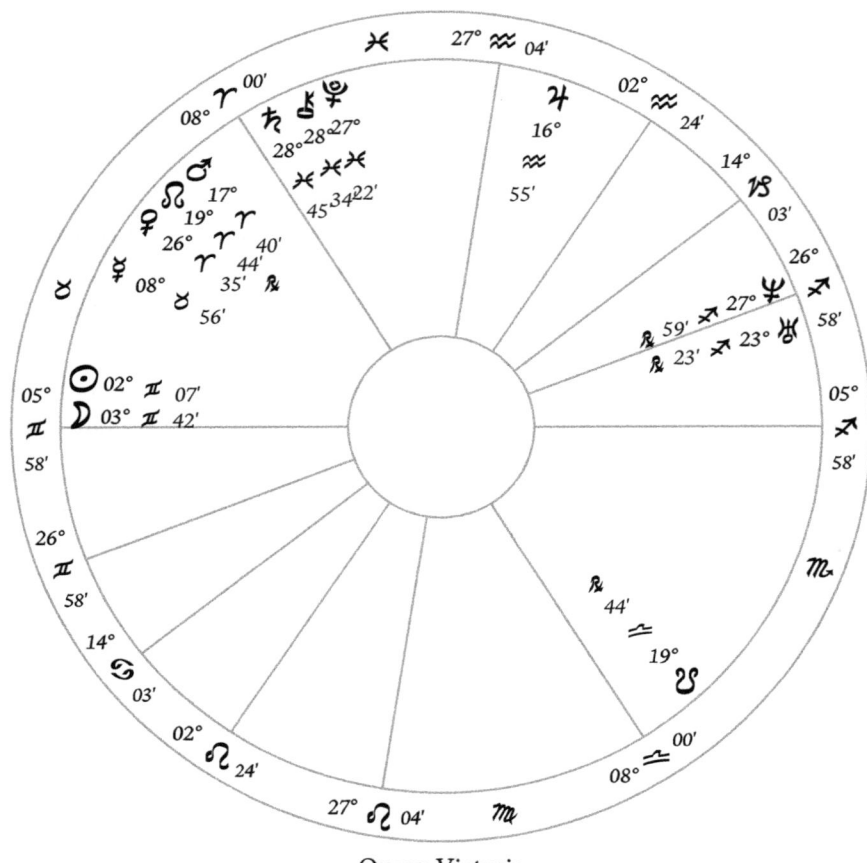

Queen Victoria
24 May 1819, 4.15 am, London

and hard decisions that she found difficult and sometimes intolerable. Although transiting Chiron's aspect to natal Jupiter is a trine, it was a painful transition for her because of her youth and the weight of responsibility now on her shoulders.

When Victoria married Albert three years later, in 1840, transiting Jupiter was at 17° Scorpio, exactly square her natal Jupiter. At the same time, transiting Pluto was at 17° Aries along with the Moon's north Node at 18° Aries, both of them right on her natal Mars and forming an exact sextile to natal Jupiter, once again triggering the natal Jupiter-Mars sextile. Her marriage was fortunate in many ways, not least because she was in love with Albert: a conjugal bonus not usually available in the arranged marriages of the monarchs of her time.

Victoria's marriage and her ascent to the throne were two of the most important events of her life. Both involved major transits to natal Jupiter and a triggering of the natal Jupiter-Mars sextile. When Albert died in 1861 after twenty-one years of marriage, natal Jupiter wasn't triggered by transiting planets, although progressed Venus at 17° Gemini, surprisingly if we expect the Greater Benefic to always behave benignly, formed an exact trine to natal Jupiter and a sextile to natal Mars. And progressed Mercury at 17° Cancer was approaching a

George Koberwein, *Portrait of Queen Victoria* (1865), Royal Collection.

quincunx to natal Jupiter as well as a square to natal Mars. Other transiting planets describe the loss of her beloved Albert more obviously. Transiting Pluto at 8° Taurus was exactly on natal Mercury in the 12th house, and transiting Neptune was sitting exactly on Victoria's natal Saturn-Pluto conjunction at 28° Pisces in the 11th house. After Albert's death, Victoria never really recovered; she isolated herself and wore mourning black for the remainder of her very long life.

Victoria's natal Jupiter reflects her absolute faith in what she believed to be a divinely given calling. For her, ruling was a sacred task; she firmly accepted the idea that a monarch was the vessel of deity, destined to serve the people as the intermediary between them and God. That's what the symbolism of being anointed with holy oil reflects, in a ritual whose roots stretch back to the ancient world. The monarch is the vessel for the deity on Earth, and Victoria took this very seriously. Being the ruler of a far-flung empire with a diverse group of nations and peoples under its umbrella suited natal Jupiter in Aquarius in the 10th house perfectly; it was where she found her meaning and her sense of being connected with a greater plan.

Not every monarch is convinced of the absolute and literal truth of the tradition, but a monarch with Jupiter in the 10th is likely to be.

Two Queens

Comparing Jupiter in the charts of Queen Victoria and Queen Elizabeth II reveals some interesting contrasts. Both were powerful women ruling in their own right rather than as consorts to a ruling king, and both enjoyed very long reigns. One had Jupiter in the 10th house, and the other Jupiter in the 1st with Saturn in the 10th conjuncting the MC. And both had natal Jupiter in Aquarius.

Ruling provided Queen Victoria with a sense of meaning, and she seems to have identified completely with the idea of the monarch as a vessel for divinity. This was reflected in her often imperious and arrogant behaviour; inheriting the crown was proof of divine favour. It may have also provided compensation for the extreme loneliness of the Saturn-Chiron-Pluto conjunction in Pisces in the 11th house. Natal Jupiter's paucity of aspects, apart from the sextile to Mars and the square to Mercury, reflects an uncomfortable discrepancy between her personal insecurities

Queen Elizabeth II visiting Queensland, Australia in 1970. Photo, Queensland State Archives.

and doubts – she was always afraid her people didn't love her – and her behaviour as a monarch.

There were really two Victorias, which is probably appropriate for someone with Sun, Moon, and Ascendant in Gemini. The first Victoria was highly sensitive, indecisive, lonely, needy, and volatile. The other Victoria was thoroughly an empress whose will was absolute, and in that role she could be quite insufferable. Her eldest son, who became King Edward VII, unfortunately experienced the second Victoria most of the time.

For Queen Elizabeth, the crown seems to have been far more onerous. With Saturn at 24° Scorpio within a degree of exact conjunction with the MC, ruling was a heavy burden as well as a passionate emotional commitment, but not something she had ever personally desired. She wasn't raised with any expectation of inheriting the throne, and only did so because of the abdication of her uncle King Edward VIII and the succession of her father King George VII to the throne in his brother's place. Being a monarch was a heavy responsibility which Queen Elizabeth steadily and meticulously discharged throughout her life, without arrogance or self-aggrandisement, although like Victoria she believed that discharging her duties as monarch was the will of God. But for her it was an act of service and self-sacrifice which she attempted to fulfil with humility, rather than something to indulge in and use for her own self-aggrandisement.

Jupiter is in Aquarius in the charts of both monarchs, suggesting that meaning for both was found through a sense of connection with a larger humanity and an ideal of social progress. Both queens seemed to gain immense satisfaction from the idea of far-flung connections with different peoples, cultures, religions, and customs. For Queen Victoria, this satisfaction came from the empire which she ruled. For Queen Elizabeth, it came from the Commonwealth of Nations, a voluntary association of fifty-six independent and equal countries, for which she had a special love throughout her life.

In Queen Elizabeth's chart, Jupiter in the 1st house squares Saturn, opposes Neptune, conjuncts Mars, and widely sextiles Chiron. The close conjunction of Jupiter and Mars suggests an independent, freedom-loving, physically and mentally active personality. Experiences of meaning came from the ability to freely exchange ideas with a wide range of people. For this Queen, meaning and joy were found in dynamic self-expression. But this expression was constantly challenged by the painful emotional realism

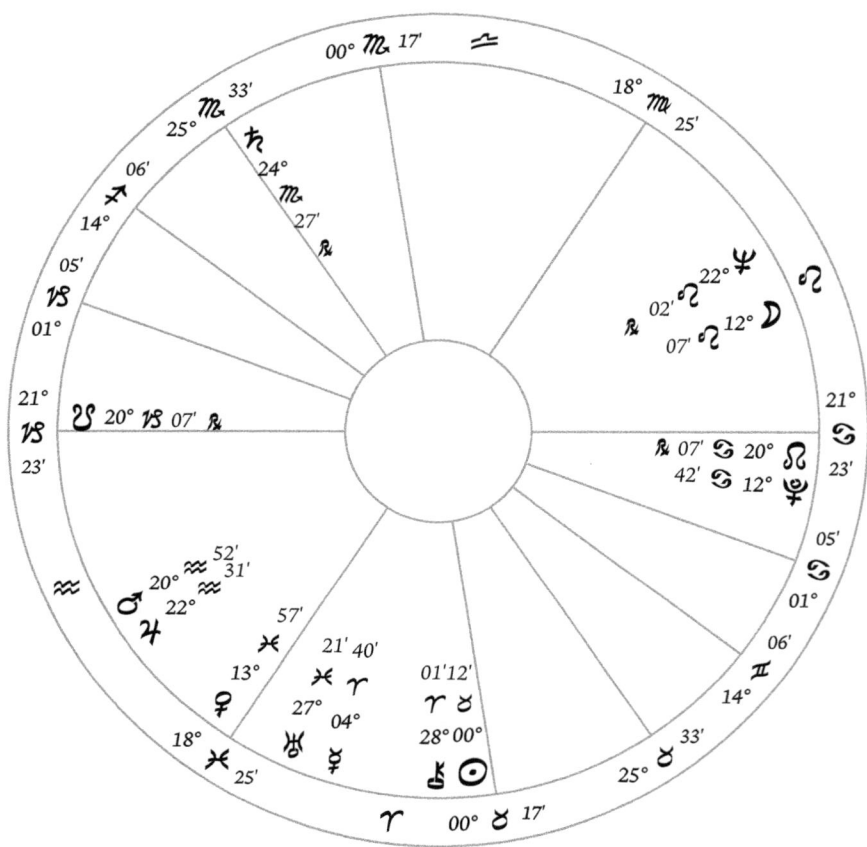

Queen Elizabeth II
21 April 1926, 2.40 am, London

of her Saturn and the sense of worldly limits imposed on an energetic, restless individual. Her need for freedom was effectively stymied, even in private, by the Queen's royal role. 'Never complain, never explain' could be the official motto of Saturn in Scorpio at the MC. Her independence was also challenged by the innate romanticism and idealism in relationship reflected by Neptune in Leo in the 7th, which demanded a high degree of emotional self-sacrifice.

These two royal women grew up and reigned at different times in history with different cultural denominators and a different collective perception of monarchy. In some ways it isn't fair to compare them, because they embodied their cultural norms and experiences as well as their individual charts. But it *is* fair to explore their different expressions of Jupiter in Aquarius, and perhaps also the possibility that hard aspects to Jupiter, although often frustrating and painful, can be immensely creative because they can generate greater insight and consciousness.

Queen Elizabeth, with Jupiter square Saturn and opposite Neptune, was internally challenged all the time and constantly sought answers to profound spiritual questions. Even the sextile to Chiron, although a benign aspect, suggests a constant awareness of and response to the suffering in life. These attitudes made her more compassionate, tolerant, and amenable to change, despite the entrenched attitudes of Sun and Moon in fixed signs. A challenged Jupiter may have helped to prevent the kind of identification with the archetype that eventually isolated Queen Victoria after Albert's death and prevented her from feeling a sense of genuine fellowship with the people she was meant to serve.

Jupiter in synastry

When we work with Jupiter in synastry, it can be helpful to view aspects between two charts in the same way we view transits. A natal planet that we've lived with all our lives, with varying degrees of consciousness, is triggered by something apparently 'outside' us; an Other appears and constellates natal Jupiter in the same way a transiting planet constellates it. The analogy isn't entirely accurate because family members may be in our lives for many decades and don't suddenly appear like a lightning bolt from heaven. But the principle of something within us being triggered by something outside us still applies.

Jupiterian relationships aren't necessarily romantic. Close liaisons and friendships can develop with synastry aspects involving Jupiter that have nothing to do with sexual attraction, and we may often see strong Jupiter cross-aspects in business relationships that are beneficial in some way or, alternatively, encourage excess, inflation, and the overestimation of possibilities.

Earlier we looked at Jupiter in Elvis Presley's chart, placed at 18° Scorpio in the 11th house, trine Colonel Tom Parker's Venus-Neptune conjunction in Cancer and also trine Parker's Mars in Pisces. A deep emotional bond existed between them, and a lot of affection – on and off, in between the vicious quarrels – that constellated Elvis' sense of having a protective parent-figure as well as an important and meaningful place in the world. Parker served as a kind of father to Elvis, replacing the one that had let him down so badly in his childhood through absence and disinterest. But although Parker contributed so much to Elvis' success, he also contributed to Elvis' inflation and eventual self-destruction.

Example 4: Winston and Clementine Churchill

These are the charts of Winston Churchill and his wife, Clementine Ogilvy Hozier.

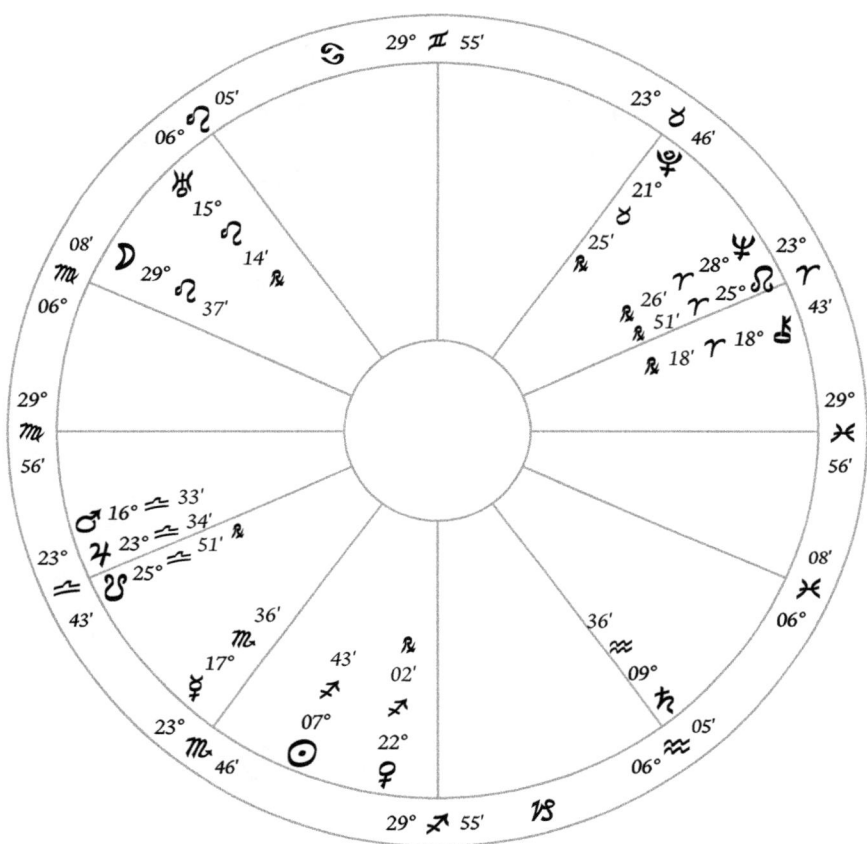

29° ♊ 55'

29° ♐ 55'

Winston Churchill
30 November 1874, 1.30 am, Woodstock, England

Winston Churchill's natal Jupiter, which rules his Sun in Sagittarius, is very busy. Placed at 23° Libra on the cusp of the 2nd house, it conjuncts Mars in the 1st and the Moon's south Node in the 2nd. Jupiter also opposes Chiron at 18° Aries in the 7th and Neptune at 28° Aries in the 8th, and it's just within range of a sextile to the Moon at 29° Leo in the 11th. It closely sextiles Venus at 22° Sagittarius and forms a semisquare to the Sun at 7° Sagittarius in the 3rd house and a quincunx to Pluto at 21° Taurus in the 8th. Jupiter is well integrated in the chart, which is dominated by the elements of air and fire. Venus in Sagittarius is in mutual reception with Jupiter in Libra; the Moon is in a grand fire trine with Neptune and Venus; and Jupiter is tightly woven into this configuration through its sextiles to Venus and the Moon and its opposition to Neptune.

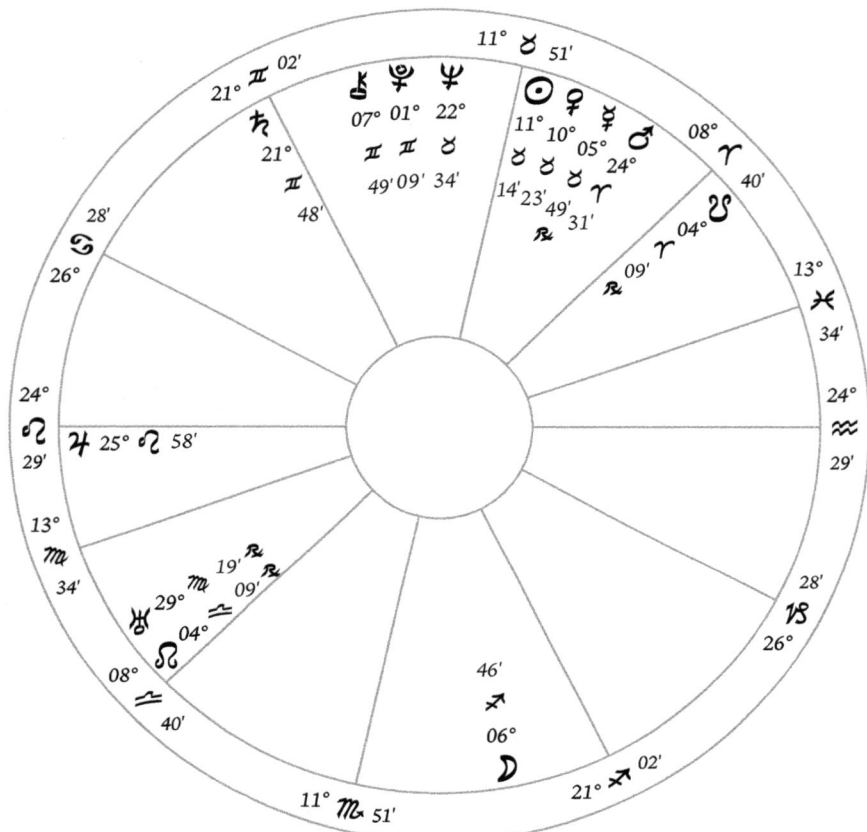

Clementine Ogilvy Hozier Churchill
1 May 1885, no time (set for 12.00 pm), London

Churchill first met Clementine Ogilvy Hozier in 1904, when he was thirty years old. He encountered her again four years later, and after a six-month courtship he married her on 12 September 1908. Transiting Pluto was at 25° Gemini at the time, slowing down to make a station retrograde at the end of the month. It trined his natal Jupiter and exactly trined the south Node. It was also within range of a sextile to natal Moon. Transiting Pluto also opposed natal Venus and formed a sextile to natal Neptune, triggering the entire fire-air configuration involving natal Jupiter at the time of the marriage.

Winston and Clementine were married for fifty-six years and had five children, one of whom died of sepsis at the age of two. Although there is no such thing as a marriage that doesn't contain conflicts and darker

Left, Winston Churchill in 1918; Clementine Ogilvy Hozier Churchill in 1915.

undercurrents, this was an enduring relationship between two highly complex, gifted people who were able to sustain a deep friendship as well as a romantic bond throughout their life together.

Clementine was born with the Sun at 11° Taurus, but we don't have a birthtime for her, so the Ascendant and house placements are unknown. Her natal Jupiter is at 25° Leo, closely sextile Winston's Jupiter, exactly trine his north Node, trine his Chiron and Neptune in Aries, conjunct his Moon in Leo, and trine his Venus in Sagittarius. Her Jupiter trines her own natal Mars at 24° Aries, which in turn closely opposes Winston's natal Jupiter, conjuncts his north Node, Chiron, and Neptune, trines his Moon, and trines his Venus. Together these synastry links form a grand fire trine interwoven with sextiles and oppositions, all involving natal Jupiter in both charts.

At the time of the marriage, transiting Pluto formed an exact sextile to Clementine's Jupiter. Meanwhile, transiting Jupiter was at 29° Leo, conjunct natal Jupiter; she was in the middle of her second Jupiter return. And transiting Chiron, which was retrograde at 19° Aquarius and moving in trine to transiting Pluto, triggered Jupiter in both charts, Winston's by trine and Clementine's by sextile.

Winston and Clementine Churchill were of enormous mutual benefit to each other in many ways, incessantly infuriating each other but also providing unwavering support and inspiration for each other's creative and political aspirations. There are other important synastry aspects between them which we could look at if we wanted a more detailed picture of the relationship, such as his natal Saturn at 9° Aquarius square her Sun-Venus conjunction in Taurus, or her Saturn at 21° Gemini opposing his Venus. These are much trickier than all those benign mutual Jupiter aspects. But these tougher contacts gave the marriage substance and depth as well as pain and conflict. The strong synastry involving Jupiter may be one of the most important dimensions of both the longevity and the mutual support and encouragement of this enduring relationship.

Laughing together

Jupiter in one chart strongly aspecting a planet in another person's chart can bring laughter into the relationship, because the absurdity of life as well as its hopefulness is part of the package that goes with Jupiter's intuitive sense of the big picture. Jupiter has a way not only of inflating us, but also of puncturing our inflation. In synastry, Jupiter aspects between two charts can inspire hope and the glimpse of new possibilities. These synastry aspects, including the trines and sextiles, can also encourage arrogance and self-entitlement. If there's already a propensity for inflation in either chart, Jupiter contacts in synastry can foster destructive and self-destructive escape routes of various kinds, including impossible aspirations, loss of reasoned judgement, a susceptibility to being duped, drug and alcohol addictions, and all kinds of gambling compulsions, whether physical, emotional, or financial.

This is the darker face of Jupiter in synastry. Excess, like misery, loves company. But other factors need to be present in the chart and in the personality to allow this dimension of Jupiter to take over in a relationship as a way of compensating for the painful limits of mortal life. And even these more destructive tendencies may be tempered by the antidote of an ironic sense of humour. Laughter is one of the most powerful elements in strong Jupiter aspects between two people, regardless of the nature of the relationship. Even if passion grows cold, the laughter will remain, and it can unlock a sense that life is meaningful, amusing, and endlessly interesting.

It isn't common to find an array of tight Jupiter aspects in synastry such as those between Winston and Clementine Churchill. The involvement of Churchill's nodal axis in the various interwoven Jupiter cross-aspects hints at a story unfolding, as though it was necessary for these people to find each other, support each other, and encourage each other's aspirations during a time when a great many people depended on their roles in the collective events unfolding in their lifetimes.

It's fashionable in the UK at the moment to focus on Winston Churchill's failings, spray graffiti on his statues, and deride him according to current social values. It might be helpful to remember that it's in large part due to the leadership qualities of this complex individual, who had a shadow-side like the rest of us, that we enjoy the freedom today to publicly complain about his failings. This kind of freedom might have been a bit more difficult to achieve under the Third Reich. But planets, unlike people, don't make political judgements. Whatever personal views we might hold about Churchill, it could be a good idea to look at these charts in as unbiased a way as possible to grasp the deeper meaning of Jupiter. The fact that Winston Churchill may have held unacceptable views on race – a reflection of the prevailing attitudes of his era – doesn't contradict the meaning of Jupiter or the synastry aspects involving Jupiter between Winston's and Clementine's charts.

It's helpful for us as astrologers to be able to distinguish between our own personal political, social, and religious views and an understanding of the meaning of an astrological planet. The importance of Jupiter in the synastry between these two charts highlights one of the most important creative contributions Jupiter can make in relationships: the encourage-ment in both people to develop faith in the unfolding of a larger pattern, optimism for the future, and an ironic sense of humour that can balance our experiences of human darkness and savagery. Without this Jupiterian vision, we would lose the will to live a meaningful existence and would fail to make any kind of creative individual contribution to the enhancement of our own and others' lives.

Jupiter in the composite chart

We might view Jupiter in the composite chart as the particular area in a relationship where a sense of meaning and connection with a greater reality can potentially be experienced by two people together – sometimes with material, emotional, intellectual, or spiritual benefits. Composite Jupiter can also reflect the area in which two people can feed each other's inflation, gluttony, and careless arrogance. The composite chart reflects the relationship as an independent entity, so it isn't quite the same as Jupiter aspects in synastry. When we're together with another person, we can experience composite Jupiter's sense of a meaningful pattern through the chemistry of the relationship. While both people have their own natal Jupiter and their own form of receptivity to a greater pattern in life, composite Jupiter reflects how this expresses itself in the relationship. And the aspects composite Jupiter makes to natal planets in both charts reflect the ways in which this dimension of the relationship affects each individual life.

Trying to make sense of a composite requires us to sit with our own chart and that of the other person and look not only at the composite itself, but also at the aspects between composite Jupiter and our own and the other person's natal planets. And we also need to explore how our own Jupiter is affected by planets in the composite. This might seem tedious, but it provides a great deal of insight into the nature of the relationship as a living entity, and the ways in which our capacity to experience meaning is enhanced by the people in our lives.

Example 5: Composite for Elvis and Priscilla Presley

This is the composite chart for Elvis and Priscilla Presley. Composite Jupiter is at 17° Libra in the 10th house, conjunct the MC at 13° Libra and the Moon's south Node at 20° Libra. In this relationship, the sense of connection with a greater design is centred on public achievement and image. These people experienced their marriage as meaningful not when they were alone together, but when they were in the spotlight enjoying public adulation. Jane Austen might have referred to such a marriage as 'advantageous'.

Composite Jupiter in Libra at the MC suggests that a sense of meaning in the relationship emerges from an ideal image of beauty and harmony, projected outward to the public eye. In other words, if the public loves you as a couple, you both feel connected to a higher purpose in life. Elvis and Priscilla were presented as a glamorous paradigm of the perfect American dream-marriage. The marriage, although it lasted for only half a Jupiter return, benefitted both of them enormously through material benefits and an enhanced public image. Priscilla enjoyed a successful acting career after her divorce from Elvis, and it's possible she might never have achieved this without her marriage to the 'King of Rock 'n' Roll'.

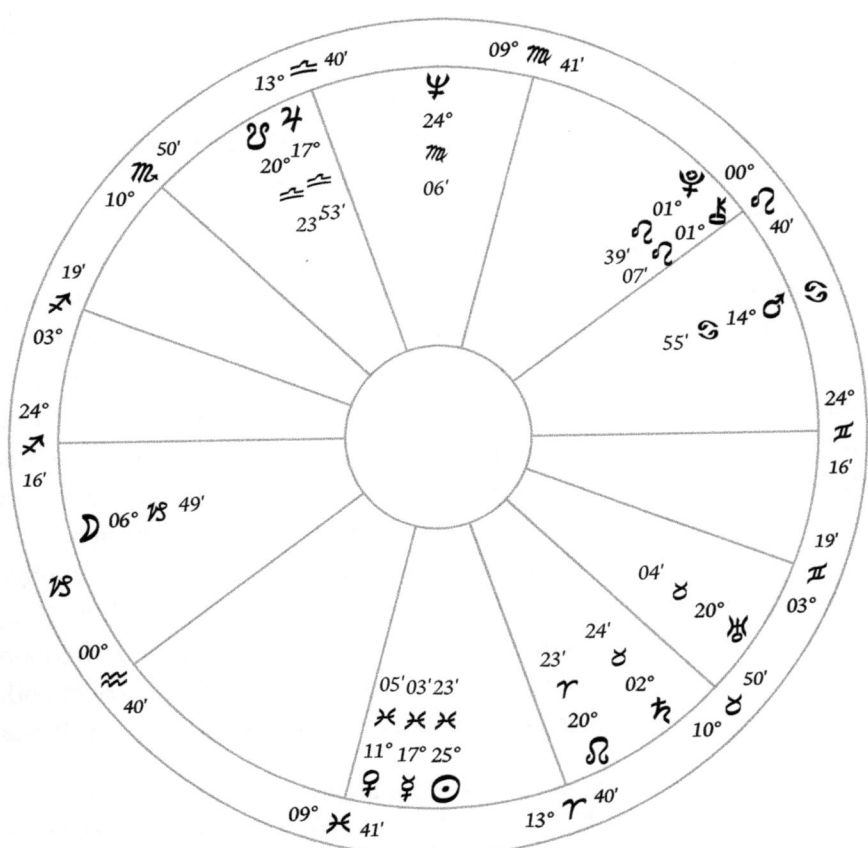

Composite for Elvis and Priscilla Presley

Interestingly, composite Jupiter isn't well integrated with the rest of the composite chart. The need to present a beautiful image to the world has a disconnected feel; composite Jupiter is a singleton in the element of air, and its aspects are sparse. Apart from a square to composite Mars in Cancer in the 7th house, its only other aspect is a quincunx to composite Mercury in Pisces in the 3rd. Jupiter's angular dominance somehow remains aloof: an image rather than an emotional reality. More cynical types might argue that this wasn't really a relationship at all, but rather, a carefully staged, stylised representation of a marriage that impressed the public and made a big impact on both people's futures but was never really anchored in flesh and blood.

Elvis and Priscilla certainly appeared to be in love in the early stages of the relationship. Trines between composite Mars and composite Sun, Venus, and Mercury suggest a strong attraction. But their well-publicised presentation of romantic love seems to have been fuelled as much by attachment to the benefits of their public image as by a passionate bond between real people. Elvis' inclination to mould Priscilla into the woman of his dreams may be part of this strangely disconnected composite Jupiter at the MC. In her autobiography, published in 1986, Priscilla described herself as "Elvis' living doll, to fashion as he pleased".[57]

The square between composite Jupiter and composite Mars at 14° Cancer in the 7th house hints at ongoing storms disturbing the relationship. Some of the conflict may be reflected in Priscilla's growing anger at being a 'living doll'; once they were divorced, she found her own identity, pursued her own dreams, and never looked back. The composite Jupiter-Mars square also reflects conflict arising from other people's influence on or interference with the relationship, since composite Mars is in the 7th house, the house of 'others'. Elvis, a true son of Zeus, was a chronic womaniser, and constant battles arose from his involvements with other women.

The composite Jupiter-Mars square may also reflect the disruptive involvement of Colonel Tom Parker in the relationship. Parker's Sun, Venus, and Neptune in Cancer all conjunct composite Mars and his Moon at 17° Libra is exactly conjunct composite Jupiter, so he fit the role of both a beneficiary of the relationship and a destructive influence on it. It was

---

57 For Priscilla's view of the marriage, see Priscilla Beaulieu Presley and Sandra Harmon, *Elvis and Me*, Berkley Publishing, 1986. A biographical drama film entitled *Priscilla* was released in 2023, directed by Sofia Coppola and starring Jacob Elordi as Elvis and Cailee Spaeny as Priscilla.

Parker, after all, who had insisted on the long waiting period between the couple's meeting and their actual marriage, and it seems that as the magic deadline approached, Elvis developed cold feet and was reluctant to legally cement the bond. He preferred his sexual freedom. But Parker, with one eye always fixed on what the world would think of his protégé, insisted that the ceremony be performed to bolster Elvis' reputation in the public eye.

These are the birth charts for Elvis and Priscilla, so we can look at some of the contacts between composite Jupiter and the couple's natal planets. Composite Jupiter conjuncts Elvis' Mars at 12° Libra in the 10th house, so the pursuit of that beautiful public image helped to energise his personal ambitions and enhance his success. But composite Mars in Cancer squares his natal Mars in Libra and opposes his natal Sun at 17° Capricorn. And composite Jupiter squares his Sun and triggers his natal Sun-Mars square.

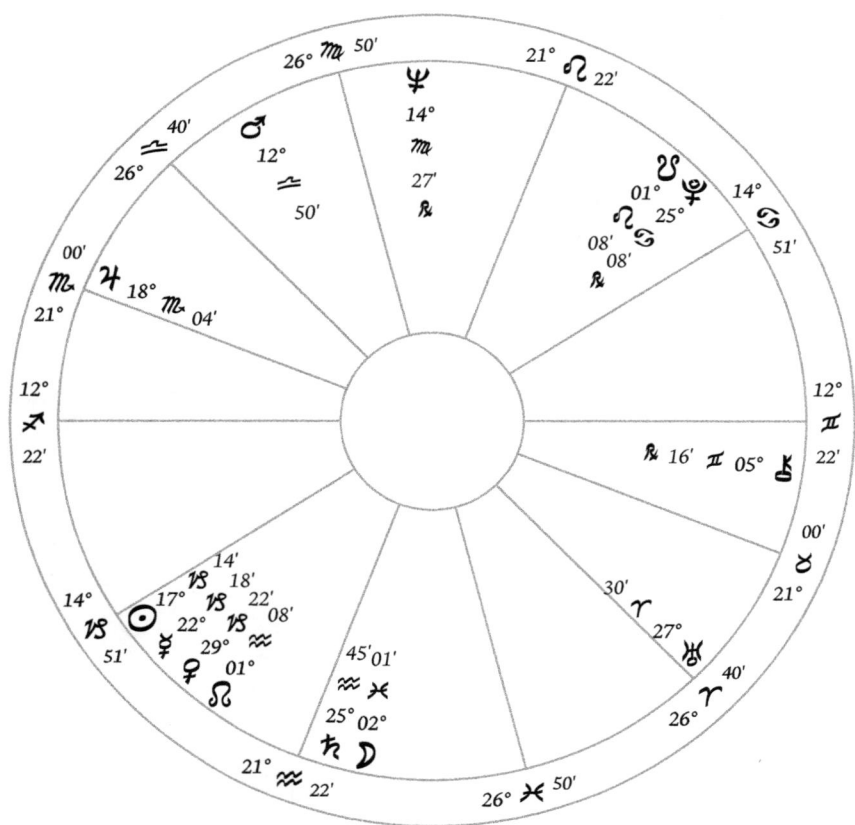

Elvis Presley
8 January 1935, 4.35 am, Tupelo, Mississippi

The combustible nature of these contacts ensured that this was never likely to be a steady, quietly supportive relationship.

Composite Jupiter opposes Priscilla's natal Mars-Venus conjunction at 16° and 22° Aries in the 3rd house, so this visually bewitching and carefully staged dream-marriage, although it brought her many benefits, also angered her, eventually constellating her fierce need for independence and her innate tendency to fight back vigorously and vociferously. On 16 November 2016, Priscilla gave an interview on ITV's *Loose Women*, in which she stated, "I did not divorce him because I did not love him, he was the love of my life, but I had to find out about the world". That's a euphemistic way of saying that while she remained with Elvis, her own development would be stifled. At the time of the divorce, transiting Saturn had returned to its natal place in her chart, at 9° Cancer in the 7th house.

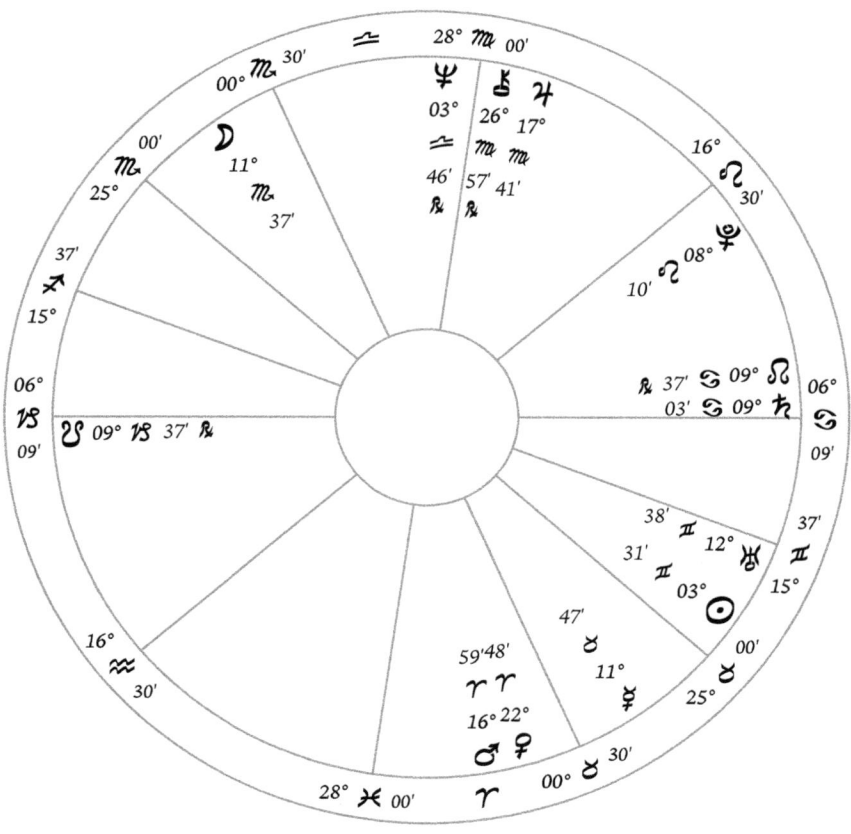

Priscilla Presley
24 May 1945, 10.40 pm, Brooklyn, NY

She was experiencing her first Saturn return and had grown up, found her own voice, and thrown aside the caricature of the 'living doll'.

Composite Mars conjuncts Priscilla's natal Saturn, so the transit of Saturn through Cancer at the time of the divorce, moving through the composite 7th house, constellated the composite Jupiter-Mars square as well as conjuncting her natal Saturn. Transiting Saturn also opposed Elvis' natal Sun and squared his natal Mars. These uncomfortable links between composite Jupiter, composite Mars, Elvis' natal Mars-Sun square, and Priscilla's natal Mars-Saturn square suggest great rage and frustration. It's not surprising that this showcase marriage between Elvis and Priscilla Presley lasted not for fifty-six years, as did the marriage of Winston and Clementine Churchill, but for only half a Jupiter cycle.

Jupiter in the progressed chart

Now I'd like to have a brief look at Jupiter in the progressed chart. Progressed Jupiter creeps rather than flying by. And that's only when the planet is direct. Many people are born with a retrograde Jupiter, or one which makes a station retrograde or direct during their lifetime. Then progressed Jupiter hardly moves at all. Even when it's positively sprinting by progressed motion, it might only cover ten to fifteen degrees of the zodiac in a lifetime. It might not form any new aspects to other planets, although it may close aspects which were already applying in the birth chart.

As all moving aspects, transiting or progressed, have orbs of applying and separating, it may be difficult to recognise the significance of the slow application or separation of a progressed Jupiter aspect, unless it's applying to complete an aspect with another planet that was already within orb at birth. However, the aspects of progressed Jupiter can be triggered by an important transit, which may be reflected in an external as well as internal expression of the progressed aspect. Transiting planets such as Venus, Mars, or Mercury making aspects to progressed Jupiter pass by very quickly, unless they make a station retrograde or direct. But transiting aspects to progressed Jupiter from the slow-moving planets may take months or even years to fully complete, particularly if the transiting planet makes a station. Then we might see a much clearer expression of the meaning of an aspect to the natal chart from progressed Jupiter.

It's often easier to recognise Jupiter's expressions when faster-moving progressed planets move into aspect with natal Jupiter. We can approach these progressions in the same way we approach the transit of a planet to natal Jupiter: Jupiter is awakened and propelled onstage. But the progressed chart seems to be more interiorised. Progressed planets reflect our psychic state at the time: the inner landscape in which we have just arrived.

The progressed chart is a snapshot of who we are now, and who we are now on an inner level may highlight, enhance, conflict, or bring to fruition the latent story of the natal chart where we began. The stage we've reached in life may be in harmony with the innate pattern of the natal chart. Equally, that current interior snapshot may reflect a time of difficulty and an activation of the individual journey through conflict. But despite the sometimes eye-wateringly obvious expressions of Jupiter that we've seen in our example charts, anything connected with Jupiter is usually unpredictable because its teleology reaches so far into the future. When progressed Venus arrived in exact trine to natal Jupiter in Queen Victoria's chart, her beloved husband Prince Albert died. This is the kind of enigma that forces us to speculate on how we evaluate our experiences, and the differences between how we feel and the deeper meaning of the time.

Example 6: Benito Mussolini

An unattractive example of Jupiter's inflationary tendencies overwhelming any sense of balance and judgement can be found in the chart of Benito Mussolini. I'd like to focus on one particular year of his life and one particular progressed planet aspecting natal Jupiter. This progressed aspect was triggered by a transit, and it illustrates rather strikingly the ways in which progressed planets aspecting natal Jupiter might be expressed.

Mussolini, like C. G Jung and John F. Kennedy, had natal Jupiter in the 8th house. His Jupiter is at 18° Cancer, the sign of its exaltation, conjunct Venus at 21° Cancer. At first glance we might think that this is a kindly, benign Jupiter. But we should be wary of jumping to conclusions about any astrological configuration, even one as apparently pleasant as this one, without looking at the whole chart and the person inhabiting it. The Jupiter-Venus   conjunction

Portrait of Mussolini as Dictator of Italy, published in 1943.
Unknown photographer; State Treasury of Poland.

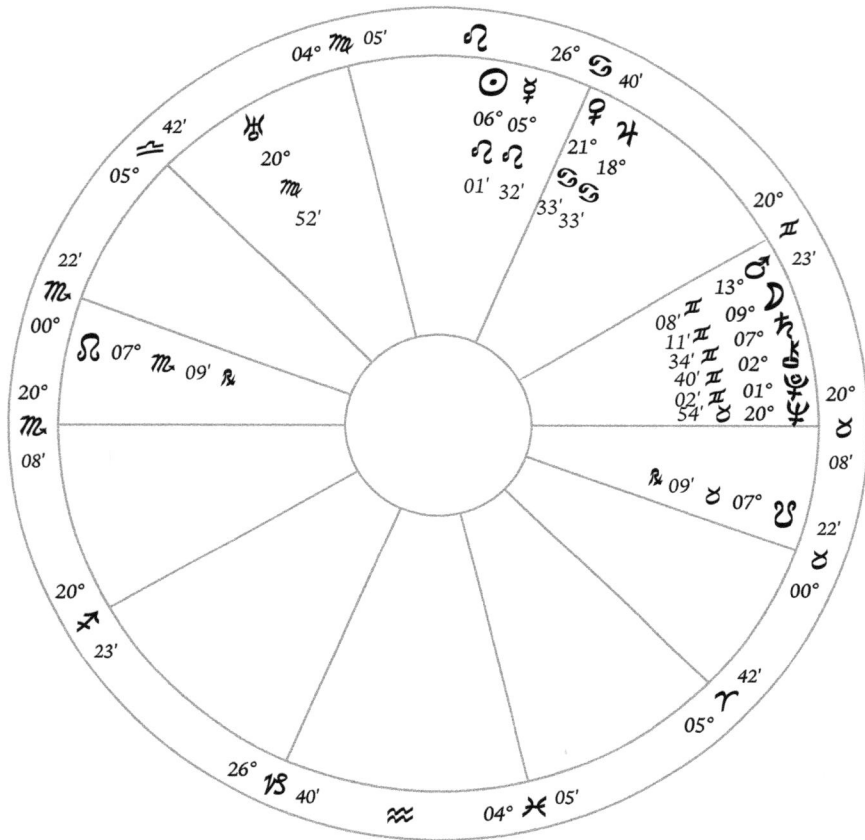

Benito Mussolini
29 July 1883, 2.00 pm, Dovia il Predappio, Italy

sextiles natal Uranus at 20° Virgo in the 10th house and sextiles natal
Neptune at 20° Taurus, exactly conjunct the Descendant.

Jupiter, immersed in a house related to the deeper levels of the
unconscious psyche, only aspects two outer planets and receives no squares
or oppositions from any other planet that might challenge it. The only
tense aspect that might help to curb Jupiter's inflationary tendencies is a
semisquare to natal Chiron at 2° Gemini in the 7th house. But Chiron is
embedded in a tight stellium with Pluto, Saturn, Moon, and Mars. Because
all these Gemini planets are clumped together in the 7th house, any conflict
suggested by the Chiron-Jupiter semisquare that might have encouraged
self-reflection is more likely to be projected onto others.

In May 1940, progressed Mars, moving from its natal position at 13° Gemini, arrived at 18° Cancer, forming an exact conjunction with natal Jupiter. On 26 May of that year, Mussolini dragged Italy into the Second World War by announcing that he would join the Germans in their battle against Britain and France. He declared that he wanted to be able to sit at the peace table "when the world is to be apportioned" following an Axis victory. He clearly thought his portion should be very large.

On the day of his announcement, the transiting north Node, moving retrograde, had reached 18° Libra and formed an exact square to natal Jupiter and progressed Mars. Many astrologers associate the Moon's Nodes with the idea of karma, or with some kind of fate at work in life. The nodal axis also tends to turn up forming strong aspects, usually close conjunctions or squares, to natal planets in quite a few of the example charts we've looked at where the individual was involved with and had an important impact on collective events.

For example, in Winston Churchill's chart natal Jupiter conjuncts the south Node, and in Elvis Presley's chart, his natal Venus-Pluto opposition is aligned with the nodal axis. Mick Jagger has Mercury conjunct the north Node in the 4th house, and in Florence Nightingale's chart the north Node is closely conjunct Pluto. Throughout their lives, individuals with this kind of planetary involvement with the nodal axis may carry the sense of an important destiny that must be fulfilled, according to the nature of the planet. Mussolini's north Node is at 7° Scorpio in the 12th house, closely square his natal Sun at 6° Leo in the 9th. He felt it was his sacred destiny to rule.

The Moon's Nodes seem to connect us with what sometimes feel like 'fated' relationships, especially relationships that involve us with larger groups and collective movements and events. The transiting Nodes can also reflect this connection. The idea of the Nodes relating to larger collective currents was emphasised by Reinhold Ebertin in *The Combination of Stellar Influences*, which I mentioned earlier in the seminar. Ebertin wasn't interested in zodiacal signs or conventional houses and aspects, but focused entirely on midpoints and combinations of two or three planets, including the Nodes, aligned through shared midpoints. His brief, keyword definitions of planets involved with the nodal axis, natally or in progressions or transits, are often highly appropriate, although perhaps lacking in psychological insight. His description of Mars-Jupiter-Node combinations, like the one I'm focusing on in Mussolini's chart, is a fine example: "Good cooperation with other people. A happy union, an engagement." Mussolini's new bromance with Hitler undoubtedly felt good to him. But it wasn't such a happy union for Italy or the rest of the world.

The transiting Nodes often reflect a sudden feeling of fate or destiny, on both personal and collective levels. I don't know whether this is 'fate' in the conventional sense or describes the karma of past lives. Perhaps this sense of destiny accompanies the inevitable fulfilment of patterns begun long before, in which individuals, as well as their families, their ancestors, and the collective of which they're a part, have made choices that bear inevitable consequences in which the individual becomes entangled. Whether it's any or all of these possibilities, both natal and transiting Nodes – and, for that matter, the progressed Nodes – can convey a sense of something that's meant to be, and this feeling can be especially strong when the transiting nodal axis forms hard aspects to natal planets.

In Mussolini's chart, the transiting Nodes in Libra/Aries formed exact squares to natal Jupiter and progressed Mars at the time Italy joined Germany and declared war on the Allies. Mussolini was already predisposed to obsessive ambition, consuming vanity, self-aggrandisement, and a craving for power. A psychiatrist might diagnose him as a malignant narcissist. Natal Jupiter was constellated by both progressed Mars and the transiting Nodes, and he believed his divine purpose and path were at last revealed through a global war and a radical expansion of his empire. One of the things I mentioned on the first of our Jupiter seminars is the way in which we tend to fall back on Jupiter to paper over the painful cracks in self-esteem described by natal Saturn and Chiron.

When we feel we've been injured, damaged, or wounded – especially if we're not conscious of those feelings of hurt and grievance – we may turn to Jupiter, particularly if it's well-aspected. If the inner damage is intractably severe, Jupiter's proclivity for narcissism and inflation may kick in and overwhelm everything else, because we believe deep down that we're actually worthless, a piece of unlovable rubbish, and that our lives are pointless. Such feelings can become unbearable. Jupiter is mobilised and charges to the rescue with its magic formula: "I'm really a terribly special, important person, even if no one has realised it yet. I'm going to be loved and admired by everyone. I have a great destiny. I was chosen to rule the world. I'm so unique and wonderful that I will be remembered forever."

Even on a less theatrical scale, Jupiter can become the means through which we try to numb a pain we need to be looking at honestly but would do virtually anything to avoid.

With this kind of pattern, we're always faced with the unanswerable question of whether severe damage can ever really be healed, even with a commitment to self-exploration. And if it can't be healed, what choices can the individual make in order to transform that damage into something that helps life rather than harming it? We're also faced with the question of whether sociopaths are 'made' or just born that way, which I mentioned when we looked at Hitler's chart.

The jury is still out on this one, and we may never reach a verdict because we're confronted with mysteries we may never rationally understand. Mussolini's chart is full of pain, but it's also full of dissociation. Mars, Moon, Saturn, Chiron, and Pluto form a tight conjunction in Gemini, a sign not inclined to confront complex emotional states. All those Gemini planets are in the 7th house, suggesting that the stellium is likely to be experienced through, and projected on, others. The emotional needs and responses of this individual seem to have been so constricted, battered, and disconnected that they were virtually unreachable, especially given the cultural values of the time.

The natal chart hints at severe, intractable wounds, and that lovely, benign Jupiter became the means by which the wound could be ignored, suppressed, and projected onto others. Natal Jupiter was triggered by progressed Mars, which suggests that on an inner level the self-aggrandising tendencies of Jupiter were gradually inflamed over a period of years, as progressed Mars gradually moved into exact conjunction with Jupiter, by the need for self-assertion and conquest. Although he had already claimed absolute power in Italy and now called himself Il Duce, Mussolini was no longer content with ruling Italy alone. He wanted an empire, in emulation of his great hero, the emperor Augustus. He joined Hitler because he believed this would provide the stepping-stone to his dream of ruling or, at the least, co-ruling the whole of Europe and north Africa. He wasn't intelligent enough to realise that he was being exploited and that, for Hitler, he was merely a useful idiot.

Inevitably, other important transits and progressed aspects were occurring at the time. Natal Jupiter triggered by progressed Mars doesn't provide the whole story. Transiting Saturn was creeping up to conjunct natal Sun in Leo, triggering the progressed MC in Scorpio, which had moved into exact square to natal Sun and aligned with the Moon's north Node. This configuration of natal Sun and the nodal axis, constellated by both progressed MC and transiting Saturn, occurred at the same time progressed Mars conjuncted Jupiter and the transiting nodal axis squared it.

So it wasn't just natal Jupiter that was constellated when Mussolini declared war on Britain and France. It was also natal Sun in Leo in the 9th, squaring the nodal axis. At its best, this can reflect profound confidence in the future, a sense of individual destiny about to be fulfilled, and a need to contribute one's knowledge to others through an individual calling. At its worst, it suggests self-obsession, the conviction of a glorious and larger-than-life destiny, and a kind of megalomaniacal insistence that one has been chosen by divine will to rule others. The contribution of progressed Mars and the transiting nodal axis aspecting natal Jupiter seems to have reflected the unstoppable engorgement of an inner dynamic that had already transgressed beyond its boundaries long before. Mussolini had been puffing up on *hubris* for years, and Jupiter's sense of connection with a higher plan or purpose appears to have fuelled the certainty that he would unquestionably achieve his dream.

This dream was to become a new Roman emperor ruling a modern, resurrected Roman empire. To that end he invested vast amounts of money and resources digging up and restoring various ancient Roman remains. In some ways he could, ironically, be seen as the father of modern Italian archaeology, because the excavation and reconstruction of Trajan's Forum, the tombs of the Appian Way, and other important Roman monuments might never have happened without his efforts. He also built the EUR just south of Rome, now a busy residential and business district but originally intended to house the 'Universal Exposition Rome' to celebrate twenty years of fascism. It was built to mimic Roman imperial town planning, full of bombastic, heroic statues and huge, intimidating buildings designed in a brutal neoclassical style. But the Universal Exposition never took place and the original construction plan was never completed because the war intervened.

Mussolini wanted his fatherland, or, perhaps more accurately, his motherland – Jupiter is, after all, in Cancer - to be a great empire again, as it had been in Roman times, with himself at the head: crowned with laurel and riding in the triumphal chariot, perhaps transformed into a bullet-proof black Mercedes, down the newly restored Appian Way. That was his grand Jupiterian vision. Since *hubris* is inevitably followed by *nemesis*, it was ironically fitting that he didn't die heroically in battle under enemy fire. Deposed by his own people, he was caught in a village in northern Italy trying to hide from the approaching Allied armies, and was unceremoniously shot by an Italian partisan on 28 April 1945. His body was dumped like rubbish in the Piazzale Loreto in Milan and was eventually strung up by the feet from the girders of a petrol station in a corner of the square. As they say, *sic transit gloria mundi*.

Some concluding thoughts on Jupiter in transits and progressions

The ruler of Olympus is easily bored, and he's endlessly creative in his shape-shifting transformations. And he never stays with any lover for very long – just long enough to fertilise her and move on to the next object of his desire. In ancient Greece this propensity earned him the epithet Zeus *Hyes*, which means 'the fertilising one'.

The fate of the lover and her newborn child isn't always easy and comfortable; that appellation of 'Greater Benefic' can be misleading if we take it literally. Sometimes Jupiter reflects obvious 'good fortune'. Equally often the gestation and birth may involve pain, struggle, and loss. This mythic dichotomy is especially relevant when we look at transits and progressions involving Jupiter, because the assumption that something wonderful will 'happen' at the time of a Jupiter transit or progression may sometimes lead to disappointment. Time tends to reveal most things, including a hint of the nature and purpose of Jupiter's imaginal children. But in our culture we've become so used to instant gratification that we perpetually risk misunderstanding Jupiter's meaningful process.

When Jupiter transits natal planets, the moment of seeding may be so quick that we barely notice it. Sometimes it takes place in darkness, as does Zeus' seduction of Maia, the mother of Hermes and we remain unconscious of it. And sometimes the god is in disguise. A Jupiter transit may last for nearly a year, but when it comes to that crucial moment of fertilisation, we can blink and it's gone. But the foreplay can take a long time, filling the entire period when the transit is within orb of the natal planet. All the groundwork is being laid, and sometimes a flash of intuition might hint that there could be progeny further down the road. That glimpse of the future might require us to be open to new possibilities, but they might lie outside our comfort zone or challenge our emotional security, and we may ignore the hint that the wind is blowing in a new direction.

Some people are naturally attuned to the changing psychic wind patterns, and remain open to intuitive hunches and visions. Others are more focused on the Earth-world. That doesn't mean Jupiter's progeny won't come to fruition, but the meaning may be lost if we remain too earthbound. Elvis missed the bigger picture behind his remarkable material opportunities, and he became addicted to them at great personal cost. It might be argued that Elvis lived the life he needed to live, and introspection would have interfered with his music. Who knows? Nevertheless, it might be helpful for each of us to try to cultivate at least a little receptivity to hearing the words that aren't spoken and recognising the chain of connections. It can give us the chance to make choices that could encourage a greater sense of trust in a deeper reality, whether we attribute that reality to a deity or to our own psyche. With Jupiter transits we won't ever be able to see too far ahead. We have to take the planet on trust. We might need to shift our way of viewing Jupiter and accept the fact that the ruler of Olympus doesn't like being second-guessed.

Questions and comments

We're approaching the end of the seminar now, so are there any questions or comments?

A stationary progressed Jupiter

Audience: Could you say something about what might happen when Jupiter goes stationary and changes direction by progression?

Liz: When Jupiter makes a station and changes direction, it can sit in the same degree for a month, which, translated into secondary progressed motion, means thirty years. The day – or, in progressed time, the year – in your life that it makes its station may feel especially full of significance, although the significance isn't likely to reflect some new revelation. But Jupiter won't move much further in your lifetime, unless it makes that station just after your birth. Any aspects progressed Jupiter forms to natal planets will remain more or less the same as in the birth chart, moving a bit forward or backward to tighten or widen the orb of the natal aspect.

Progressed Jupiter making a station in a particular year of your life won't herald anything new in terms of its aspects to other planets. But it may intensify its natal configurations, and the year of its station may also be heightened by any transits that might also trigger it. Faster planets like Mercury and Venus will move a lot further by progressed motion after a station. Although Jupiter is turbocharged compared to Saturn, Chiron, and the outer planets, a stationary Jupiter barely moves by progressed motion. Look at the year in which it goes stationary and watch for an intensification of whatever aspects it makes in the natal chart, and pay extra attention to any important transits to its position at the time of the station.

Jupiter and the entire chart pattern

Audience: Jupiter, as king of the gods, is perhaps the one who reveals their intentions in our lives most.

Liz: Thank you, that's a very good point. Jupiter seems to reveal meaning, and that includes meaning in every area of our lives, including the teleology of all the planets working together to describe our broader pattern of development. The Sun symbolises the vessel of the Self around which the other planets orbit and weave their story, but Jupiter can give us the insight to recognise that there *is* a Self and that there *is* a story.

Jupiter unaspected

Audience: How do you interpret an unaspected Jupiter? Mine is unaspected in its own house, the 9th, and it's a kind of paradox. What is the challenge here?

Liz: I sometimes think of an unaspected planet as someone who's living in our house, but we don't know they're there. They hide in the basement so we never see or hear them, and we have no idea there's anyone down there unless we deliberately make the descent and have a careful look around. But then they get fed up with being confined, and they rip up the floorboards and take over the house for a while. That's what an unaspected planet does from time to time when it's triggered by a transit, a progressed aspect, or another person's planets in synastry. The unaspected planet dwells beneath the surface and reveals itself primarily through the unconscious – dreams, fantasies, moods, and even illnesses – but sooner or later it will erupt and take over, sometimes on a cyclical basis. If it's a big eruption, it can overwhelm everything in quite an obsessive way. Sometimes remarkable gifts emerge which aren't quite under the control of the conscious ego. Sometimes darker elements emerge. And sometimes the entire spectrum of the planet can reveal itself at once.

A 9th house Jupiter can hide very quietly, and much of the time you might not be particularly drawn to the traditional Jupiterian spheres such as travel, higher education, or spiritual and philosophical pursuits. And then the planet makes a sudden entrance on the stage when it receives a powerful aspect from a transiting or progressed planet, and its revelations can be huge and transformative. I would expect an unaspected 9th house Jupiter to incline to sudden major spiritual breakthroughs or philosophical insights, or what Plato referred to as recollection – deeper knowledge you didn't know you had – or exceptional gifts in the educational sphere. But you might need to keep an eye on unconscious fanaticism and the certainty that you and you alone have discovered the Truth.

Eruptions of an unaspected natal Jupiter can happen every time a major transit constellates it and, to a lesser degree, also when a minor transit conjuncts it. An unaspected planet waits patiently for a trigger before it makes its entry into your conscious life. You might also be drawn into relationships with people whose natal planets form major aspects to your Jupiter, because projection – experiencing our own inner psychological dynamics through someone else who provides a 'hook' – is the psyche's characteristic way of ensuring that all of what we potentially are can wake up and enter consciousness.

Jupiter-Pluto and plutocrats

Audience: Bill Gates has a Jupiter-Pluto conjunction.

Liz: Yes, Bill Gates has a virtually exact Jupiter-Pluto conjunction in Leo in the 2nd house. We'll be looking at his chart in the next seminar. Gates is what we call a plutocrat, and the word is related to the mythic Pluto, guardian of the Earth's underworld riches, including its natural resources and its precious metals and gemstones. The Greek word *ploutos* means wealth, while *kratos* means power. A plutocrat is someone whose power derives from their wealth. Once again, Jupiter can be so transparently obvious that we can only go away shaking our heads and smirking.

Great expectations

Audience: So I should stop 'expecting' a lottery win as transiting Pluto approaches my natal Jupiter, which is retrograde at 27° Capricorn?

Liz: There's no rule book that says you shouldn't play the lottery under a Pluto transit to natal Jupiter. And Pluto's transits take a very long time. You never know – you might even win and become a plutocrat. But it's not a good idea to *expect* to win. Play with amusement and laughter, spend only what you can afford, and anticipate nothing. It's not wise to expect anything from Jupiter, who will always make fun of us if we try. If you understand the psychology of the *puer aeternus*, the archetypal 'eternal youth', you'll know that the fastest way to get this elusive figure to make a quick exit through the nearest open window is to expect a binding promise.

Even though the Jupiterian temperament possesses the gift of optimism about the future, concrete expectations seem to annoy Jupiter. Think of all those abandoned women calling after him, "But darling, you haven't given me your mobile number. When will I see you again?" It's characteristically Jupiterian to expect big things, but it's not helpful to assume any specific outcome from a Jupiter transit. Honour the god with something he likes, such as humour, joy, and spontaneity, and once you've bought your lottery ticket, put it in a drawer, laugh at yourself, and focus your mind on something else.

Transits versus progressions

Audience: Can you speak about transits versus progressions? Are they both equally important, or should progressions be weighted more heavily when considering all the astrological influences in a person's life? I tend to discount progressions when interpreting current astrological influences because I don't really understand them.

Liz: I'm not sure anyone really understands them. Secondary progressions are based on a symbolic calculation and not on the actual movements of the heavenly bodies. In secondary progressions, one day of planetary motion, which varies according to the speed of each planet, is equal to one year of life, symbolically conflating the daily motion of the Sun in its apparent passage around the Earth with the annual apparent passage of the Sun around the zodiac. Secondary progressions are, in effect, rooted in solar symbolism and seem to be related to the inner development of the individual. We begin with a pattern and a teleology, and the progressed planets reflect how far along the journey we've come and where we are at any particular moment in time.

Solar arc progressions, which also symbolically equate the diurnal motion of the Sun to one year of life, aren't based on each individual planet's rate of speed. These progressions involve not only the Sun but all the planets and angles moving at the same rate of speed as the progressed Sun – hence the name 'solar arc'. Because all the planets are progressing at the same rate of speed, they retain their natal aspects to each other but form new aspects to the planets in the birth chart as they move along. Many astrologers prefer solar arc progressions to secondary progressions, and sometimes I'll look at both, although for me, secondary progressions seem more nuanced and more amenable to psychological insights.

The important thing about progressions is that, unlike transits, they aren't based on planetary positions along the ecliptic as viewed from the Earth. They're based on symbolic movements that are unique to a particular individual and reflect the deeper meaning of the Sun's teleology as the centre of the personality. I don't think progressions are more important than transits, or vice versa. They're different ways of slicing an orange; the pattern of the segments looks entirely different depending on how you cut it. Secondary progressions portray a highly individual interior roadmap that seems to reflect the pattern of our inner unfoldment. Transits relate us to what's happening in the collective psyche and in the world. This is why transits triggering a progressed aspect seem to be so important: they reflect the world impacting on the ongoing story of our inner development.

Transits appear to be 'out there' in the 'real world', although of course that's only from a geocentric point of view, and the definitions of 'real world' and 'out there' are open to debate. Transits mirror the movements of the collective psyche and are relevant to everyone, although they may make specific aspects to particular planets in the individual birth chart. Progressions are highly individual because progressed motion begins at birth and is relative to the speed of each planet in a natal chart. Your progressed Jupiter isn't in the same degree of the same sign and making the same aspects to natal planets as anyone else's progressed Jupiter at the moment. But transiting Jupiter in the heavens is in the same degree of the same sign for everyone.

Transits symbolise the collective psyche impinging on our individual lives. Progressions symbolise the patterns of unfoldment we carry within us, like the acorn which gradually unfolds to become an oak tree according to its own hidden design. It isn't a question of weighting one over the other. We need to look at them together, and to look especially closely at transits to a natal planet when there's also a progressed planet making an aspect to that same natal planet. The example of Mussolini that we looked at earlier illustrates this quite clearly.

When a transit, a progressed planet, and a natal planet link up, they tend to reflect the most significant moments in our lives. We can view our lives as the world happening to us and our responses to it, or we can look at our lives as the unfolding of our *moira*, our individuation process: becoming what we're innately meant to be. The progressed chart is the symbolic portrait of the unfolding of that inner pattern, and the world will impinge on it every moment of our lives in a complex dance.

Jupiter and the Hierophant

Audience: It's a bit off topic, but could you elaborate on the relation of Jupiter and the Hierophant in the Tarot?

Liz: It isn't off topic at all. The images of the Tarot are relevant to astrology because they're symbolic images that describe the same journey of unfoldment that the natal chart does. But exploring the connections depends on how you interpret the cards and which Tarot deck you're working with. Many people associate the Major Arcana card of the Hierophant with a conventional religious figure, usually the Pope, which is how the card is represented in A.E. Waite's deck. That isn't surprising because Waite was a devout Catholic, albeit a deeply mystical one who was involved in ritual magic.

In older versions of the cards like the 'Marseilles' deck, which originated no later than the mid-17th century and may be much older, the Hierophant is portrayed as La Papesse, the 'female Pope', based on the legendary 9th-century figure of Pope Joan. She was said to have climbed to the top of the papal hierarchy and reigned as Pope for two years disguised as a man until she became pregnant and inconveniently gave birth during a religious procession. The irony of this rather heretical portrayal may reflect the artist's unflattering views about the Church at the time. Or it might

Left, The Hierophant in A. E. Waite, *The Pictorial Key to the Tarot* (1910). The design was painted by Pamela Coleman Smith at Waite's instruction. Right, La Papesse in a version of the 'Marseilles Deck', c. 1760.

suggest something subtler and more complex: an apparently conventional religious image concealing a forbidden, fertile secret.

In more conventional interpretations of the Tarot, the Hierophant represents morality and religious teaching. That could certainly be applied to the traditional understanding of the astrological Jupiter. But some Tarot researchers, perhaps like the unknown creator of the Marseilles deck, understand the Hierophant to represent the revelation of mysteries not confined to conventional religious frameworks. The word itself comes from the Greek *hieros*, meaning 'sacred', and *phaino*, meaning 'to reveal'. The Hierophant is someone who reveals sacred secrets. But what constitutes 'sacred'? Unlike the card of the High Priestess, whose underworld secrets can be dark and obscure, the Hierophant reveals the teleology of the cosmos, like Zeus in his Orphic role as Divine Mind.

Divinatory interpretations of the Hierophant inevitably vary. Some authors suggest that the card stands for tradition, convention, moral right-eousness, and orthodoxy. Jupiter can certainly show that face. But he can also be unashamedly unorthodox and amoral. If the card turns up in a

spread, the individual may actively begin to seek answers of a philosophical kind, which might involve conventional religious paths but might
equally open more unconventional and even 'heretical' doors to the inner
world. The card may reflect a deep commitment to a quest for meaning in
life. If the Hierophant appears as an external figure, it might be an analyst,
a psychotherapist, a priest, a rabbi, a spiritual healer, or even an astrologer,
to whom we turn for help and insight.

There's certainly a relationship between the Hierophant and the
astrological Jupiter, as there is between every Major Arcana card and the
planetary gods. But astrology and Tarot are different symbolic systems
that describe the journey of individuation in different ways. I'm very
much in favour of astrologers becoming familiar with the imagery of the
Tarot because it can enhance and deepen our understanding of both. But
we can't really draw exact parallels. The mythic Jupiter is an archetypal
pattern interwoven with other archetypal patterns in complex ways. Each
card in the Major Arcana may reflect more than one mythic figure, and a
mythic figure – not always a planetary one – may shed light on more than
one card.

Some dimensions of the Emperor, for example, are reflected by Jupiter
as king of the gods. But other dimensions of this card are reflected by
Saturn as lawgiver, by the Sun as the life-source, and by Uranus as the
primal father of the cosmos. The Fool can be interpreted as Neptunian
because he's off with the faeries and pays no attention to where he's going,
but he can also be Jupiterian because his faith in the future allows him to
take a terrifying risk as he walks off the cliff. Rather than trying to find a
precise one-to-one equivalent between a Tarot card and a planet, it's more
helpful to look at the connections in a looser, more intuitive way.

Jupiter and the 9th house

Audience: Would you say that Jupiter in the 9th tends to feel 'comfortable',
considering the 9th is its natural house?

Liz: 'Comfortable' is a good way of describing it. 'Too comfortable' might
sometimes also be applicable. Planets that are comfortable usually reveal
their most pleasant face, but they can also be lazy. They don't always
display the richness of all their potential facets because there isn't enough
to deepen and challenge them. Jupiter is certainly happy in its natural

house because the 9th is concerned with the search for meaning and the expansion of understanding – hence its traditional associations with travel, philosophy, and higher education as vehicles for that quest. Making intuitive connections with a greater design often comes easily to Jupiter in the 9th, and so does an unquenchable faith in the future. But it might be a good idea to avoid becoming so comfortable that we begin to take for granted the fact that everything will always work out splendidly if we just smile and think positively.

Jupiter in the 9th is often blessed with indestructible optimism and the ability to grasp connections that others miss. That's a wonderful asset that can provide great resilience and faith. But it can also lead to a kind of impervious complacency that's oblivious to the complexities of others' confusion and pain, as well as a baffled helplessness during those times when life makes ugly faces at us. It depends on Jupiter's sign and aspects to other planets. If there are no hard aspects to it natally, transits, progressed aspects, and synastry will provide them sooner or later, and that can challenge, deepen, and enrich Jupiter's strengths.

Sadly, I think we've now run out of time and have come to the end of the seminar. Thank you so much for your questions and your participation.

Part Three: Jupiter's Cycles in History

Open your mouth and shut your eyes and see what Zeus will send you.
– ARISTOPHANES

This seminar was given online for students from the Centre for Psychological Astrology and the Mercury Internet School of Psychological Astrology on 4 December 2021.

Introduction

Today's seminar is the third and last of our series on Jupiter, and we'll be exploring Jupiter's cycles in history. Since Jupiter takes only a year to move through one zodiacal sign, we won't be focusing on the Jupiter cycle alone as an historical marker because the planet moves too quickly to reflect larger movements in the collective. Instead, we'll be looking at Jupiter's cycles in combination with the slower-moving planets – Saturn, Chiron, Uranus, Neptune, and Pluto.

These cycles vary in their timing, depending on the speed of the slower-moving planet. Some, like Jupiter-Saturn conjunctions, form a regular rhythmic drumbeat. Others, like Jupiter-Pluto and Jupiter-Chiron conjunctions, are less uniform in their intervals because of Pluto's and Chiron's elliptical orbits. But all the conjunctions of transiting Jupiter with a slower-moving planet, each of which marks the beginning of a new cycle, seem to combine Jupiter's aspiration to connect to a greater plan or design with the archetypal collective impetus reflected by the other planet.

There's a central theme running through all these great cyclical conjunctions. We might view Jupiter's longing to connect with some kind of deeper purpose in life as 'religiosity': the sense of something meaningful or numinous that's injected into the collective urge symbolised by the slower-moving planet. That injection of meaning in turn colours the ways in which we experience and respond to the other planet's transit through a particular zodiacal sign, and the events and shifts in values that it symbolises.

When I use the word 'religiosity', I don't mean that we all throw up our hands and shout, "Hallelujah! God is at work here!" Some people may of course do precisely that, while others might perceive the handiwork of the Devil instead. But religiosity in Jupiter's sense doesn't depend on belief in a particular deity, or even on the conviction that any deity exists at all. The religious instinct can be expressed through science, politics, art, relationships, and earthly experiences such as sensual pleasure and the kind of worldly ambition we might ordinarily view as anything but divine.

When the ruler of Olympus is hovering nearby, we tend to confer on even the most mundane desires and happenings a quality of meaningful intervention or intent. When Jupiter conjuncts a slower-moving planet by transit, we may feel a sense of awe, and we might begin to believe that this new movement in the collective psyche, and the external objects and situations that symbolise it, will give us the answers to all our questions. Equally, we might perceive it as the rise of some cosmic evil that must be fought against. Whether dark or light, all the themes described by the slower-moving planet feel enlarged, full of meaning, and infused with a sense of deeper purpose.

The word 'religiosity' also doesn't imply that Jupiter's cyclical conjunctions with these slower-moving planets are morally 'good' or 'bad'. Jupiter can be either or both at once. In our two previous seminars, I stressed the idea that it isn't helpful to see the astrological Jupiter as solely a benefic or, for that matter, a malefic in disguise. It isn't either of these, although it can behave like both. Its cyclical conjunctions with slower-moving planets reflect movements and changes in the collective psyche that are punctuated by a sense of something meaningful and filled with teleology. But whether any such movement is expressed in constructive or destructive ways depends on the choices of human beings, who are its vessels and enablers.

The unfolding of each Jupiter cycle in the world proceeds according to how we as a collective react to it, and that in turn depends on how conscious we are as individuals. This can be a painful revelation if, through our own tendency to sleepwalk into crises, we've fallen into the hands of an oppressive or ideologically militant regime or experience the gradual erosion of the freedom to think and express ourselves as independent individuals. The truism that we get the government we deserve is harsh but sometimes uncomfortably accurate. But if we're willing to look back honestly at each choice we've made as individuals and as a collective, we might discern how we ourselves have invoked what we might now find so difficult in the outer world, often because we didn't bother to truly understand collective movements and our unconscious collusion with them. Collective shifts appear to erupt outside us, but they also occur inside us, and because of this we can make individual choices, however small and insignificant they might seem at the time.

Those choices affect the quality not only of our own lives but also the lives of all the people with whom we have any connection: our families and friends, our colleagues, our communities, our nation, and ultimately the entire human family. A collective is made up of individuals who respond in their own ways to the patterns symbolised by these cyclical Jupiter conjunctions. This is why, when Jupiter is making one of its cyclical conjunctions to slower-moving planets, it's never a good idea to respond by identifying blindly with any extreme ideology, regardless of which side of the political or moral spectrum it represents. In doing so, we may relinquish our right to individual choice, and then our lives are fated by a future we ourselves have unwittingly invoked.

Jupiter infuses the collective movements symbolised by the slower-moving planets with a quasi-religious fervour, making them seem especially seductive. We get a glimpse of what appears to be the Grand Plan, whether socio-political or spiritual, and we begin to make Faustian pacts. Our quest for meaning may alight on just about anything, even if it's destructive, if we believe it's necessary for our salvation. But gullibility, *hubris*, lack of genuine knowledge, refusal to think for ourselves, and wilful unconsciousness all rob us of our freedom of choice, and then we become helpless victims or mindless perpetrators rather than co-creators in the unfoldment of these great archetypal patterns.

The nature of cycles

It's helpful to think of the cycles of Jupiter with the slower-moving planets in the same way we might think of the phases of the lunation cycle. You can find this idea discussed at length in Dane Rudhyar's book, *The Lunation Cycle*, first published in 1967. Rudhyar's emphasis on the importance of cycles in astrology has been utilised and developed in different ways by many astrologers over the decades. Structurally and symbolically, all planetary cycles involving a pair of planets share the same attributes in terms of their astrological significance.

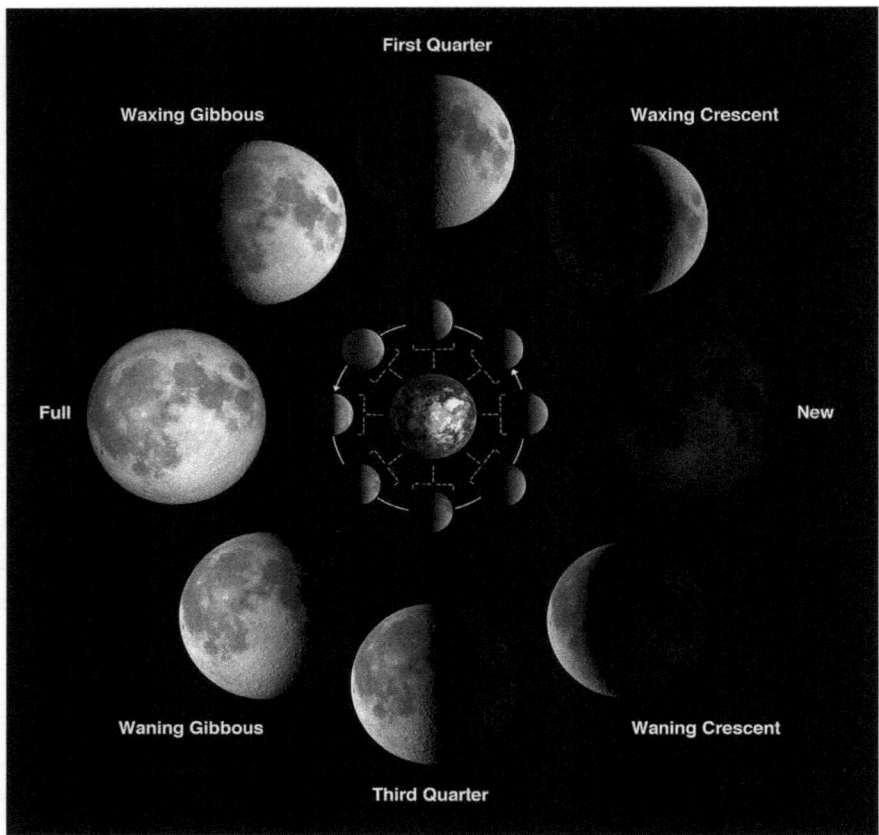

The phases of the Moon. NASA/Bill Dunford.

Every dyad cycle has a beginning, which occurs when the two planets conjunct in a particular degree of a particular zodiacal sign. The new Moon is the monthly conjunction of the Moon with the Sun, and it marks the beginning of a new lunation cycle. It's also called the 'dark' of the Moon because the Moon, the faster-moving heavenly body, is hidden by the light of the Sun at the moment of conjunction. When Jupiter conjuncts a slower-moving planet, it's like a new Moon in terms of its symbolic meaning: its fertilising function is invisible because it's 'hidden' by the other planet. While we may still see the physical planet shining brightly in the heavens, and events relevant to the meaning of the conjunction may reflect it in the outer world, we can't see what it's up to on a deeper, teleological level, just as in myth we can't see what Zeus is doing at the moment of impregnation because he's in disguise.

Each cycle of Jupiter with a slower-moving planet moves from the conjunction into a waxing phase, which includes its outgoing semisextile, semisquare, sextile, square, trine, sesquiquadrate, and quincunx to the other planet. During this waxing phase, Jupiter begins to reveal itself in an increasing sense of something 'destined': a meaningful process that feels as though it's slowly moving towards an as-yet-unknown fruition. The most powerful point in the waxing phase is the outgoing square, which reflects a struggle as the progeny of the conjunction first attempts to emerge in the world. The pregnancy has now resulted in a birth, and the symbolic child is threatened by danger as it seeks to fulfil its future potential.

This leads to the point of fruition, equivalent to the full Moon, when Jupiter is opposite its planetary partner. At this time we have a chance to understand with greater clarity what's really emerging through this particular cycle. Something reaches culmination and expresses itself fully; Jupiter comes out into the open because its child is now full-grown and visible in the world. However, we might still not recognise the full scope of what confronts us because there are more phases to go through.

Then the cycle moves into its waning phase, which includes Jupiter's incoming quincunx, sesquiquadrate, trine, square, sextile, semisquare and semisextile to the other planet. The period of Jupiter's waning is a time of harvest, realisation, and integration, symbolically equivalent to the waning phase of the Moon. The most powerful point at this stage of the cycle is the incoming square. But the struggle now is one of adjustment, acceptance, and integration, rather than efforts to manifest something new in the world.

The last period of the waning phase, known in the lunation cycle as 'balsamic', leads to the end of the cycle and the next conjunction. Of course these cycles don't really have a beginning and an end because they keep giving birth to themselves. The close of one cycle forms the beginning of the next one, like the alchemical ouroboros eating its own tail. The moment of the dark of the Moon at the end of the lunation cycle is also the moment of the new Moon at the beginning of the next cycle, and the same applies to Jupiter's cycles with slower-moving planets. It isn't until the whole cycle is complete that we can really make sense of what kind of new progeny has come out of this Jupiterian fertilisation of a slower-moving planet. And even then, the meaning might still not be clear because the cycles continue to weave their story far into the future.

We can learn a great deal by looking at these cycles in our own lives. When has a conjunction of transiting Jupiter with a slower-moving planet triggered anything in our natal chart? What was the experience like, internally and externally? Is there a theme emerging from the cycle that can be connected in meaning with the previous cycles of those two planets? In addition to this kind of exploration of our own histories, we can also get a sense of the scope of Jupiter's cycles by looking at the broader sweep of history. We might need to have at least a little knowledge of the history of social and religious cycles if we want to gain any kind of insight into Jupiter in an individual chart. Sadly, the study of history is vanishing from school and university curricula – unless it's modern socio-political and economic history with a particular ideological bias – so we have to do our own research.

Jupiter's cycles with slower-moving planets, like all transits, describe the qualities of the time. Because these qualities are occurring within us as well as outside us, the cycles reflect how we perceive what's happening in the world around us, how we respond to it, what insights and interpretations we distil from our experiences, and what choices we make. As individuals, we may justifiably feel we have no power over world events. We may be subsumed by major collective movements like wars, economic and political upheavals, pandemics, and natural disasters, and it seems at such times that the individual's will is worthless and all our actions are pointless. A huge steam roller is flattening us, and we're impotent. But on a deeper level we might still contribute something important to these cycles, even if our personal efforts seem pathetically small at the time. The ultimate expression of the cycle, and the changes it might reflect, are as much up to each of us as to the inevitable unfolding of an impersonal archetypal dance.

The Jupiter-Saturn cycle

There's a long tradition of astrological research into and speculation about the Jupiter-Saturn cycle, first described in detail by medieval Arab and Jewish astrologers as a heavenly harbinger of the rise and fall of kingdoms and kings. Since Chiron and the outer planets were unknown in the ancient and medieval worlds, Saturn was perceived as the limit of the solar system, so immense importance was placed on Jupiter-Saturn conjunctions as significators of the fate of nations and peoples. The ideas surrounding this speculation appear to be rooted in the ancient mythic battle between Zeus and Kronos: the old king of the gods is overthrown, the new king rises to power, and a new world order is inaugurated.

The rise and fall of religions and the coming of messiahs and prophets form another, related theme that medieval and early modern astrologers associated with the Jupiter-Saturn cycle, and this interpretation is still important to many astrologers in the modern world, especially in relation to the dawn of the Christian era. Jung, for example, believed Jesus had been born under a Jupiter-Saturn conjunction. He acquired this idea from earlier researchers such as Johannes Kepler, who postulated in the early 17th century that a conjunction of Jupiter and Saturn, occurring three times between 6 and 7 BCE, was the actual Star of Bethlehem that portended Jesus' birth.[58]

These interpretations of the conjunctions of Jupiter and Saturn reflect ancient beliefs about the sacred nature of kingship. There's a direct relationship between Jupiter's endless quest for meaning, its cyclical conjunctions with Saturn's drive towards embodiment, and the symbol of the anointed monarch as the representative of the divine on earth and the corporeal intermediary between the deity and the people.

---

58 For Jung's discussion of and sources for the Jupiter-Saturn conjunction at the time of the birth of Jesus, see C. G. Jung, *Aion: Researches into the Phenomenology of the Self*, CW9 ii (1951). Also see Liz Greene, *Jung's Studies in Astrology* (Routledge, 2018), Chapter 6.

This conjoining of spiritual and material was understood to be the core meaning of the conjunctions of Jupiter and Saturn. The anointed ruler, a symbol of the godhead incarnated in flesh, was both a human being and a sacred vessel, sometimes imaged as a Good Shepherd who looked after a vulnerable but wayward flock with justice and mercy, strength and compassion. I mentioned in our first seminar on Jupiter that in the ancient world, the image of the shepherd was often associated with Zeus, expressed in stories in which the god disguised himself as a humble shepherd to seduce a desired love object or test a human's faith in the divine. Kingship, in the ancient and medieval worlds, was as much a religious issue as a political one.

Jupiter is sometimes referred to in modern astrological texts as a 'social' planet, suggesting that it's concerned with the moral and legal structures of society and with the individual's relationship to those structures. The cyclical conjunctions of Jupiter and Saturn seem to reflect major changes in religious structures and attitudes which might or might not be deemed 'social'. Many modern academics argue that religion is solely a cultural product, and that gods are created by societies to embody socio-political forces.

But which comes first, the chicken or the egg? We might also argue that the socio-political structures of any culture are rooted in, and shaped by, underlying religious perceptions that can't be attributed solely to economic and social currents. These 'god-images', as Jung called them, have their own life and agency and their own cyclical timing, and their ultimate source may always remain a mystery because they're envisioned, shaped, and adapted, but not created, by humans.

One way of viewing the astrological Saturn as an archetypal dominant in the collective is that this planet reflects our fundamental human need to build permanent structures. We know instinctively that as a species we're frighteningly vulnerable, despite our big brains, our long opposable thumbs, and our aptitude for destroying each other. We experience what's known as 'prolonged immaturity': human children take a lot longer to develop physical and psychological independence than other species and require constant parental protection for far longer. Some researchers have suggested that humans are born twelve months too early; our mothers should have carried us in the womb for twenty-one months, not nine. Our infant helplessness makes it all too easy for us to be snuffed out.

Although some cultures, like the Aboriginal Australians, are nomadic and disinclined to build fixed abodes, the land itself provides the safety and permanent structure within which the group dwells, and the deep relationship with the land in turn demands its own strong social and spiritual laws. We can see the same instinctual pattern in the animal world. Even species such as the big cats, many of whom live and hunt alone, still define their permanent structures through marking and protecting the boundaries of their fixed territories.

Why do we need such permanence? Obviously our structures protect us, whether they're inner or outer, and they fulfil our need to believe that this protection will ensure our survival as individuals and as a collective. On the most fundamental level, our determination to build houses, towns, institutions, societies, laws, and religious edifices reflects our human fragility and sense of weakness in the face of terrifying internal and external powers. This is the function of Saturn. We lack the strength to defend ourselves through physical prowess and cleverness alone. Psychologically, we also lack the strength to protect ourselves from depression, misery, compulsion, hurt, envy, fear, and rage – all the 'spites' contained in Pandora's jar. Permanent structures – whether intellectual, social, emotional, spiritual, or concrete – defend and shield us against a hostile world that might control, stifle, damage, or annihilate us, as individuals and as a collective.

Saturn reflects what matters most to us in terms of our capacity to endure. What can we truly rely on? Whom or what can we trust to watch our backs? This also applies on an interior level. What inner resources do each of us depend on to build a solid, permanent core? The need to build that solid core reflects our powerful sense of vulnerability, which in turn reflects what we feel we lack. Will we survive or not? Saturn symbolises an urgent need to establish something solid so that our lives, which are limited and vulnerable, have a solid base on which to stand. As transiting Saturn enters each new sign of the zodiac, we can perceive a change in the collective perception of what's lacking, deprived, or damaged, and what needs to be repaired, strengthened, and made permanent in order to protect against weakness and vulnerability.

When Jupiter enters Saturn's world through their cyclical conjunctions, a sense of teleology, an intuition of meaning, begins to infuse what's otherwise a purely pragmatic understanding of strengths and weaknesses.

A religious dimension starts to fertilise Saturn's domain, even if we don't call it by that name, and it colours any efforts we make as individuals and as a collective to pursue the kind of security-orientated goals that are reflected by the sign Saturn is moving through. Jupiter arrives and 'overthrows' Saturn's entrenched perspective by shining a light on what's missing, revealing a deeper meaning that justifies all that effort.

It's as if Jupiter says to Saturn, "Yes, you have to build all these structures to defend yourself, but they must also *mean* something. Otherwise, what's the point of life? Why bother? There's a bigger picture. There's more to life than material needs. There's a purpose behind it all, a reason why you feel weak and vulnerable and why you're so driven to protect yourself. Look for the meaning, or your life will be enslaved by the tyranny and loneliness of endless defensiveness."

The timing of the cycle

Jupiter-Saturn conjunctions, which for centuries have been known as 'Great Conjunctions', occur every 19.9 years. Because we always need to keep orbs in mind, the conjunction doesn't suddenly become relevant when it's exact to the minute on Thursday morning at 10.00 am. The two planets remain within orb of conjunction from four months to a year, or even slightly longer, because both planets will turn retrograde during the period of the conjunction. Most of the time Jupiter and Saturn will form an exact conjunction just once, but sometimes we might see a triple conjunction, such as the Jupiter-Saturn conjunction in Pisces in 6-7 BCE that fascinated Kepler and Jung. The retrograde motion of both planets results in an exact conjunction repeating three times, each time in a slightly different degree.

Because the orbits of both planets are relatively regular, successive conjunctions, when mapped in the circle of the zodiac, create an extraordinary geometric pattern. Successive conjunctions recur in the same element of the zodiac – fire, earth, air, or water – for a period of around 240 years before they move into the next element. Occasionally, towards the end of that period, there might be a hiccup because a conjunction may fall right at the end of, say, a fire sign, and then the next conjunction will slip forward into the element of earth, and the following one will slip back into fire to complete its 240-year run in that element.

The pattern isn't perfect because the orbits of the planets aren't perfect circles. But in the main, they keep repeating for nearly two and a half centuries in the same element. Then they move into the next element following the natural order of the zodiac: from fire to earth, earth to air, air to water, and water back to fire. But successive conjunctions within one element move in the opposite direction to the usual order of the signs: from Aries to Sagittarius to Leo, from Taurus to Capricorn to Virgo, from Gemini to Aquarius to Libra, and from Cancer to Pisces to Scorpio.

The beautiful geometry of these Jupiter-Saturn conjunctions has captured the imagination of astrologers over the centuries because it seems to offer proof of an intelligent design, a confirmation of Pythagoras' vision of the 'music of the spheres' and Plato's idea that all things first emerge from the One in geometric forms. That there should be such order in the universe has offered astrologers throughout history an apparent confirmation of a greater plan or design. The entire cycle of Jupiter-Saturn conjunctions through all four elements takes nearly 800 years before they start their procession through the elements once again.

During the medieval and early modern periods, astrologers were convinced that the Jupiter-Saturn cycle, especially conjunctions that marked the shift into a new element – known as a 'Great Mutation' – underpinned all the major cycles of world history, reflecting the rise and fall of kings and empires and the birth of new religions and religious leaders. Careful attention was paid to the three different types of cycle involved in the dance between the two planets: the Great Conjunctions that occur roughly every 20 years; the Great Mutations (the first of the sequence of conjunctions occurring in a new element after 240 years); and the full 800-year cycle marking the complete passage of the conjunctions through all four elements of the zodiac.

This way of viewing history through the lens of the Jupiter-Saturn cycle has continued into today's astrological research, especially among more traditionally inclined astrologers. Later we'll look at Jupiter's conjunctions with the other slow-moving planets, which are equally important in terms of major collective shifts and movements but which, because they don't involve Saturn's concretising propensities, aren't always quite as visible on the world stage.

'Fearful symmetry'

This diagram comes from a very useful booklet by an astrologer called Astrid Fallon, published twenty years ago and, as far as I know, now out of print, called *Planetary Cycles at a Glance*.[59] Used copies might still be available and it's well worth trying to find one, especially if you favour visual images on paper over lists and graphs on a computer screen. But if you prefer the latter, there are slightly different versions of this diagram currently offered online.

I'd like to look briefly at some earlier Jupiter-Saturn conjunctions in relation to the diagram, and a few of the historical events that coincided with them. This is always an ambiguous exercise because it's so easy to select events that seem to fit the pattern and ignore those that don't. If we

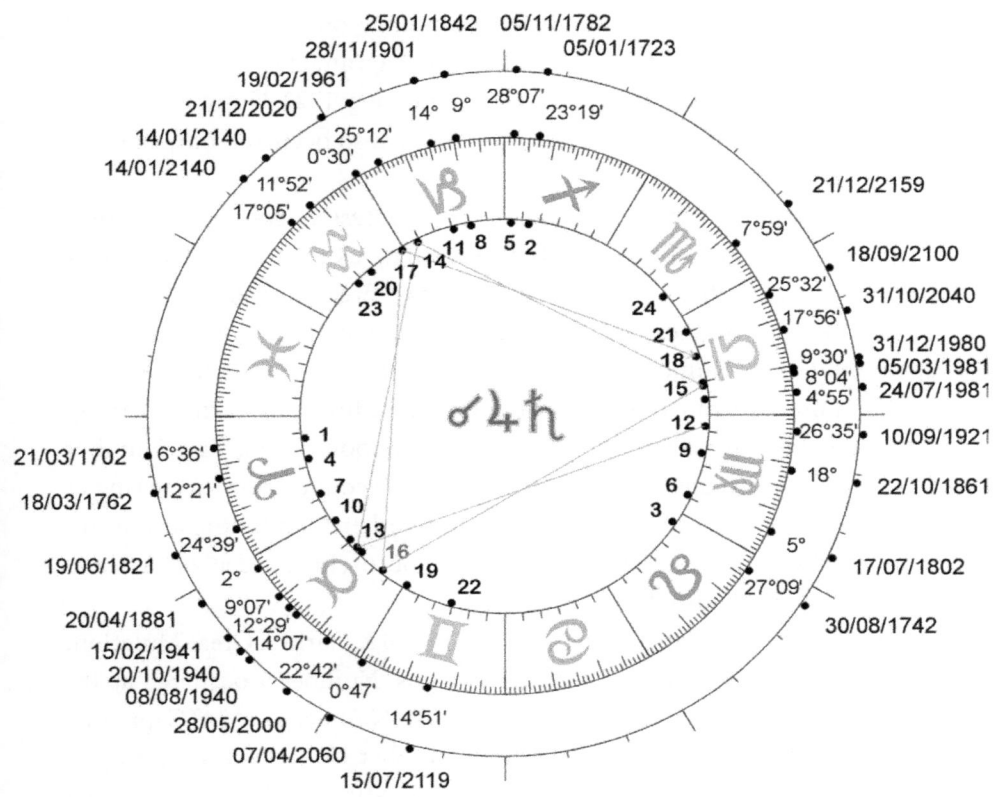

---

59 Astrid Fallon, *Planetary Cycles at a Glance* (Fallon Astro-Graphics, Sheffield, 2001. www.fallonastro.com). I'm very grateful to Astrid for providing the originals for the diagram to be reproduced in this book.

look for something amidst a mass of data, we'll almost always find what we're looking for according to our own predilections, and fail to see what we aren't interested in or don't wish to find. And sometimes collective events are subtle and interior, and concern shifts in thinking rather than obvious happenings like wars and pandemics. But sometimes the correlations are impressive.

Once you get used to the structure of the diagram, it's easy to read. Astrid Fallon's starting date for tracing Jupiter-Saturn conjunctions is the early 18th century, with a conjunction of the two planets in Aries. This conjunction was a Great Mutation: the beginning of a new conjunction cycle in the element of fire.

The diagram is set up like a flat chart, with 0° Aries on the Ascendant. Number 1, which you can find close to the Ascendant, is dated 21 March 1702. Jupiter and Saturn conjuncted only once on that occasion, at 6° Aries. Number 2, which you can find on the diagram close to the MC, also occurred only once, at 23° Sagittarius on 5 January 1723. Number 3, which you can find towards the end of the 5th house, also occurred only once, at 27° Leo on 30 August 1742.

If you connect the dots for these three successive conjunctions, they predictably form a roughly equilateral triangle as they move backwards through the signs belonging to the element of fire. After the conjunction in Leo in 1742, the next one, Number 4, occurred at 12° Aries in 1762, again only once. Number 5 occurred once at 28° Sagittarius in 1782. The conjunctions keep moving backward through the fire signs, each one falling in a different degree from the previous conjunction in that sign. Number 6 is one of the hiccups I mentioned earlier. This conjunction, occurring at 5° Virgo in 1802, slipped into an earth sign rather than falling at the end of Leo. But the next conjunction, Number 7, occurring once at 24° Aries in 1821, slipped back into the element of fire.

Number 8, occurring at 9° Capricorn in 1842, marks a Great Mutation, beginning a 240-year cycle in the earth signs. Number 9 occurred at 18° Virgo in 1861; Number 10 at 2° Taurus in 1881; Number 11 at 14° Capricorn in 1901; Number 12 at 26° Virgo in 1921; Number 13 – a triple conjunction – at 12-14° Taurus between 1940 and 1941; and Number 14 at 25° Capricorn in 1961. Number 15 constitutes another hiccup, as this triple conjunction of 1980-81 slipped forward into 4-9° Libra, changing elements briefly. But Number 16, in 2000, was back in Taurus again, at 22° of the sign. Then, with Number 17, another Great Mutation occurred at 0° Aquarius, and the conjunctions began their 240-year cycle in the element of air. We are currently right at the beginning of this new cycle in air signs; the Great Mutation at 0° Aquarius occurred in 2020.

If you keep joining the dots for each group of three conjunctions in signs of the same element, you'll see that Jupiter-Saturn conjunctions weave an eerily beautiful pattern. The successive sequence of triangles eventually creates a star with multiple points. This image was drawn by Johannes Kepler as a portrayal of the near-perfect star-shape of the Jupiter-Saturn cycle through the four elements. It was published in his *Mysterium Cosmographicum* in 1596.

You can see why the near-perfect geometric structure of these conjunctions has helped to fuel ideas of the mystical significance of the

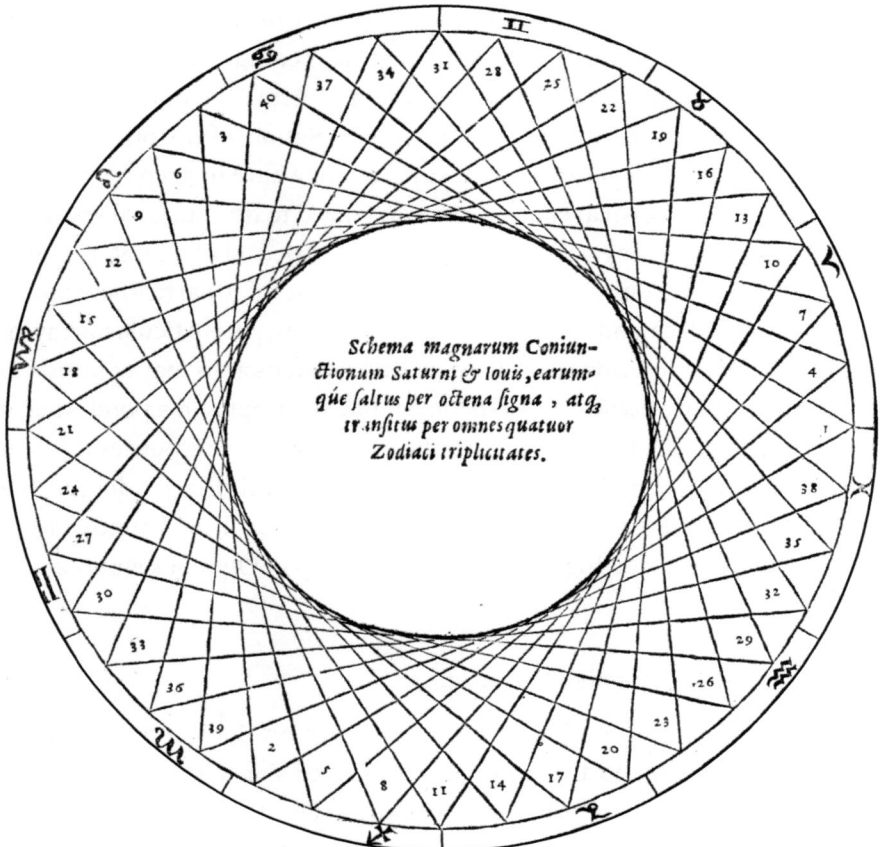

Johannes Kepler's diagram of the 800-year Jupiter-Saturn cycle in *Mysterium Cosmographicum* (1596). .

cycle and a belief in the prescient patterns of divinity expressed through it. If the essence of God manifest is embodied in geometry, as Plato suggested and Kepler believed, the Jupiter-Saturn cycle is a powerful indicator of that geometry in celestial form. Jupiter as *nous*, Divine Mind, combines with Saturn as *Rex mundi*, Lord of the World, to herald events that contain a deeper meaning and teleology and reflect the order and symmetry of the divine plan.

Some tidbits of Jupiter-Saturn history

Now I'd like to look briefly at a few of the relevant events that occurred under some of these conjunctions. Because the conjunctions are hardly rare happenings – twenty years might seem long in terms of a human life, but it's a mere blip in the context of the sweep of history – there will be a great many important historical events attending the time of each conjunction. If we trawl through any list of significant happenings in any given year, we'll inevitably find some that we feel are pertinent. The ones I've picked out strike me as appropriate, but the interpretation of history is always subjective – that's why historians always feel they have to keep rewriting it according to their own agendas – and you'll need to do your own research.

We can look at any year coinciding with the period of a Jupiter-Saturn conjunction and sometimes get the strong sense of a particular *kind* of event taking place and, perhaps more importantly, a particular array of perceptions and reactions to that event. The repercussions may continue to resound for many decades or even longer, like the ripples in a pond when a stone is thrown in. The core of both the events and our responses to them often reflects a deeper political, social, or religious shift according to the sign in which the conjunction takes place. Zeus fertilises Kronos rather than simply overthrowing him, and the rulership of Olympus enters a new phase.

The War of the Spanish Succession

The Great Mutation of 1702, exact at 6° Aries on 21 March, marked a new cycle of Jupiter-Saturn conjunctions in fire signs. This was the first conjunction in Aries for nearly eight centuries. Less than two months later, on 14 May, the War of the Spanish Succession erupted, triggered by the death of the childless King Charles II of Spain. Britain, the Dutch Republic, and the Holy Roman Empire declared war on France and Spain. As a result of this war, major changes in the boundaries of nations were established that have remained in place to this day, including Britain's much-contested claim to the island of Gibraltar.

When expansionist wars occur under Jupiter-Saturn conjunctions, which they almost always do, it isn't particularly helpful to jump up and down screaming 'Colonialism!' and hurl abuse at a nation – including one's own – because its values and aspirations once differed from our current ones. Current values may be far closer to those of the past than we wish to admit, but the objects on which Jupiter's aspirations are projected may have changed and may concern ideas and beliefs rather than territory. Expansion of boundaries, intellectual and spiritual as well as material, is an obvious and literal dimension of Jupiter conjoined with Saturn, and perhaps a more nuanced understanding of the deeper meaning of the conjunction, and a recognition of both the dark and light dimensions of the conflicts coincident with it, might help us to develop a less simplistic and more constructive perspective.

We shouldn't be surprised that a major war coincided with the 1702 conjunction of Jupiter and Saturn in Aries. In myth war was an inevitable facet of the relationship between these two kings of the gods. Also, the conjunction took place in a sign ruled by the war-god Mars. Nor is it surprising that the traditional Jupiter-Saturn theme of the 'rise and fall of kingdoms' was reflected in the changes wrought by this particular war. Wars occur all the time, and not all of them break out under Jupiter-Saturn conjunctions. And there are different kinds of war, not all of them fought on battlefields. We might think of the 'Cold War', whose tensions lasted for over forty years without any physical fighting, or our current 'culture wars', which can be as cruel and mindless on subtler levels as the Battle of the Somme. Some physical wars, such as the Thirty Years War and the Hundred Years War, go on and on and encompass more than one Jupiter-Saturn cycle. But the conflicts that erupt under the conjunctions seem to generate permanent changes on multiple levels that shape the future in ways we can't foresee.

One of the features of wars that cluster around Jupiter-Saturn conjunctions is that they seem to be fuelled by a new ideological or religious vision. They're not solely a grab for territory, wealth, or power, although the expansion of material boundaries is often involved. Most of all, these wars are rooted in *belief*. Often there's an unshakeable conviction that God – or moral 'Right' in some form – is on the group's or nation's side. This usually winds up pitting two different gods against each other, which always poses a thorny theological problem.

The prevailing collective belief tells us that the conflict *must* happen because it's necessary, right, and fitting, and part of some kind of grand plan for the group's, nation's, or even planet's destiny. Usually the ways in which the battle unfolds don't adhere to anyone's plan and aren't welcomed by either side. But the outcome reflects a permanent change in thinking as well as boundaries. We're back to all those mythic stories about Zeus' children, each of whom carries a special destiny that may be obscured and overlooked in the midst of the trouble and conflict of the conception and birth.

The War of the Austrian Succession

In 1742, when Jupiter and Saturn conjoined in Leo, the War of the Austrian Succession erupted, which resulted in the rise of Prussia as a major European power. Prussia's emergence led to a sequence of profound territorial and cultural changes over the next century, culminating in Bismarck's absorption of formerly Habsburg-ruled Bavaria, the Franco-Prussian war, and the vision of an expanded and united Germany, which ultimately led to the Second World War. The long-term consequences of Jupiter-Saturn conjunctions aren't always pleasant. But the cycle keeps on running, and only with hindsight can we see how history unfolds in both creative and destructive ways, moving towards distant goals it seems we always fail to anticipate, no matter how hard we try.

The American War of Independence

Under the Jupiter-Saturn conjunction in Sagittarius at the end of 1782, a war ended rather than commenced. Like other Jupiter-Saturn struggles, this one had profound and permanent repercussions. The American and British governments met in Paris after the American War of Independence to negotiate preliminary peace articles, which in the following year, on 3 September 1783 – just after the conjunction had moved out of orb – were formalised in the Treaty of Paris, officially granting American independence. We usually date the birth of the US to the signing of the

Declaration of Independence. But the Jupiter-Saturn conjunction of 1782 heralded international acceptance of that birth: a sort of formal christening that gave legitimacy to what previously had been viewed by much of the world as an illegitimate child.

Benjamin West, *American Commissioners of the Preliminary Peace Agreement with Great Britain* (1783), Winterthur Museum, Delaware. From left to right, the signatories are John Jay, John Adams, Benjamin Franklin, Henry Laurens, and William Temple Franklin, Benjamin Franklin's grandson.

This painting by Benjamin West appears to portray a group of people in wigs hanging about looking bored. The most interesting thing about it is that it was left blank on the right side. This is because, when West was working on it in 1783, the final conditions of the Treaty of Paris hadn't been agreed on and the British delegation refused to pose. The only negotiators portrayed are the Americans, so the painting remained incomplete.

The First Anglo-Afghan War

On 25 January 1842, another Great Mutation occurred, this time in the element of earth, at 9° Capricorn. As with the conjunction of 1782, a war was concluded rather than begun: the First Anglo-Afghan War, which formally ended within two days of the exact conjunction. The war itself had erupted three years earlier and was fought between Britain and the Emirate of Afghanistan. This conflict became known as the Disaster in Afghanistan. A furious backlash against the war continued to erupt from its inception to its end, and long afterwards. Many political voices in Britain criticised the fighting, declaring it to be rash, pointless, and the result of an imaginary rather than a real threat from Russia, whose influence in the region was perceived as menacing. Does this sound familiar?

This war was especially bloody at its conclusion because, as the British troops were retreating from Kabul in 1842, while the conjunction was within orb, they were massacred. The 44th Regiment was wiped out, and the British Army withdrew shortly afterwards. You may draw any conclusions you like about this ignominious event. But whatever else it might have been, it reflected, like so many other Jupiter-Saturn wars – whether fought on the battleground or through subtler means – an expansionist vision that seemed to justify on the mundane level a belief in the divine rightness of national destiny. We never seem to learn anything from history.

This work by William Barnes Wollen, painted more than half a century after the event and titled *The Last Stand*, portrays the massacre of Lord Elphinstone's 44th Regiment at Gundamuck during the British retreat from Kabul. We might catch a glimpse of Jupiter's dark, ironic humour in the fact that, in the year following the most recent Jupiter-Saturn conjunction in December 2020, exact at 0° Aquarius – a Great Mutation in the element of air – American troops withdrew from Afghanistan after years of bloody fighting against Taliban insurgents. The abrupt and badly organised withdrawal, which had been planned while the Jupiter-Saturn conjunction was within orb, has received scathing criticism ever since because the clumsy handling of the evacuation process resulted in panic, unnecessary deaths, and the eventual collapse of the Afghan National Security Forces. Years of fighting had achieved nothing. As Mark Twain purportedly once wrote, history might not repeat itself, but it does like to rhyme.

William Barnes Wollen, *The Last Stand of the 44ᵗʰ Regiment at Gundamuck, 1842* (1898), Essex Regiment Museum, Chelmsford.

The many levels of Jupiter-Saturn wars

We usually think of war as a dimension of Mars. But the mythic Zeus was just as warlike and was usually engaged in a battle of one kind or another. Ares, after all, was the son of Zeus. The Titanomachy, the Gigantomachy, the battle with Typhon, and the ongoing struggle with humanity are mythic stories that portray a god who could be as cruel and violent as his ferocious son. And Zeus and Kronos were not exactly BFFs; they were bitter enemies who engaged in a great cosmic battle which Zeus ultimately won. There's a battle inherent in these planets' relationship, and it seems to be reflected in the way their conjunctions are mirrored by historical events. But Jupiter-Saturn conjunctions sometimes preside over the ending of a war rather than its beginning, and sometimes they herald a bloodless change in regime, or the defeat or overthrowing of a particular political party or political system.

A good example of the latter occurred when Jupiter and Saturn conjuncted on 28 May 2000 at 22° Taurus. Within a few months of the exact conjunction, Slobodan Milošević, the Serbian President, was ousted in Belgrade following a presidential election on 24 September, resulting in the downfall of his government. This event was accompanied by thousands of protestors converging on Belgrade and the partial burning of the parliament building, so it wasn't an entirely peaceable coup. It's sometimes referred to as the '5 October Overthrow' or the '5 October Revolution'. In the following spring, Milošević was detained by Serbian police and transferred to The Hague to be prosecuted for war crimes.

Subtler forms of war can sometimes wreak as much havoc as literal wars. In this context it's useful to look at the recent Jupiter-Saturn conjunction in Aquarius. This conjunction, as well as presiding over the American withdrawal from Afghanistan, also encompassed one of the darkest periods of the Covid-19 pandemic. The language employed about Covid by governments worldwide was the language of war, with words like 'battle', 'front line', 'victory', and 'defeat' constantly utilised to both frighten and mobilise a shocked and confused public. The period of the conjunction was punctuated by lockdowns in virtually every country – a form of martial law – resulting in severe economic and psychological damage to world finances, productivity, education, social interaction, and prevailing views of social and political morality. Zeus' battlegrounds, when the conjunctions occur in the element of air, can often be found in the domain of ideas, information and, inevitably, misinformation.

This current Jupiter-Saturn cycle is still in its waxing phase. The first quarter phase might be described as the struggle to manifest whatever new 'king' was conceived at the time of the conjunction. But don't assume we can work out the nature of that new king before the cycle is complete. Whenever we're confronted by Jupiter, nothing is ever quite what it seems, and this cycle, like the night, is still young. The first quarter was exact when Jupiter in Gemini reached its outgoing square to Saturn in Pisces in August 2024.[60] This was a triple square; the planets were exactly square again in December 2024 and, for the third time, with Jupiter at 1° Aries and Saturn at 1° Cancer, in June 2025. Since we're currently in the waxing phase of the

---

60 The first of the three exact squares of Jupiter to Saturn in August 2024 occurred a month after the election in the UK of the first Labour government for fourteen years. A month before the second exact square in December 2024, the US presidential election saw Donald Trump win not only the electoral college but also the popular vote, upending predictions that he would never achieve a second term in power. The results of further elections in Germany and France suggest that the political and social turmoil accompanying this outgoing series of squares will continue to upset collective assumptions and expectations until the time of the opposition between the two planets in 2030.

cycle, we can't really predict how it will unfold over the next eight or nine years, although it's probably safe to suggest that, in light of current political and social turmoil, we're witnessing the early stages of a vast ideological war on many fronts, on many levels, and in many nations. We might see its meaning more clearly when Jupiter in Sagittarius opposes Saturn in Gemini in 2030, the moment of the 'full' or fruition point of the cycle.

'Changes in religious structures'

'Changes in religious structures' is an expression sometimes used to describe the collective shifts occurring under Jupiter-Saturn conjunctions. Because the cycle has always been associated with religious themes, endless speculation has occurred about the timing of the birth of the major religions. When did Buddhism begin? When did the birth of Christianity occur? What about Judaism and Islam? Or Hinduism, Sikhism, Shinto, or Zoroastrianism? Is it even possible to define the 'beginning' of a religion, or does the rhizome quietly form underground long before the plant appears? Can it be traced to the birth of a leader, teacher, or prophet who founds a religious movement, or to the formal foundation of a religious institution? And if the birth of a religious leader provides the significant date, how do we distinguish between myth and history in relation to these often quasi-mythic and perhaps sometimes entirely mythic figures?

William Butler Yeats described the Buddha as a 'Jupiter-Saturn influence'. Yeats was fascinated by astrological speculations about the rise of religions and religious leaders, not only in the context of the Jupiter-Saturn cycle but also in terms of the astrological aions or 'ages'. His poem, *The Second Coming*, is a terrifying and, as it increasingly seems, prophetically accurate and deeply unsettling description of the advent of the Aquarian aion, with its human-headed, lion-bodied 'rough beast' – an image of the Aquarius-Leo polarity – 'slouching towards Bethlehem to be born'.

One of the many speculations about the Buddha's birth that interested Yeats was that it may have taken place under a Jupiter-Saturn conjunction in Taurus in 563 BCE. But that's not the only Jupiter-Saturn date offered by astrological authors. There are two other conjunctions that are sometimes put forward as possible birth dates for the Buddha. All that Yeats was certain of was that the Buddha was a 'Jupiter-Saturn influence'.

Yeats described the eight-century cycle of Jupiter-Saturn conjunctions through all four elements as a 'vivification of old intellect'.[61] He believed

---

61 William Butler Yeats, *A Vision (1937)*, p. 208.

this great cycle symbolised a rebirth, incorporating and transforming older worldviews into something 'new'. That was how he understood the beginning of every new religious dispensation: the same underlying archetypal pattern, which Jung described as the god-image, emerging in new clothes, wearing a new face, and adapted for a new era. Jupiter-Saturn cycles do often coincide with the beginning of new religious forms, but the emerging dispensation is built on and from the materials of what came before. Christianity has sometimes been called a marriage of Athens and Jerusalem because it used the building blocks of both Judaism and the Greek philosophers to create its 'new' dispensation. In the same way, the early Church appropriated the geographical sites, stone walls, and columns of ancient pagan temples to construct many of its own places of worship.

Just as there's been speculation about the birth of the Buddha, there's been even more speculation about the birth of Jesus. Some astrologers have felt it was profoundly important to discover when individuals such as Jesus and the Buddha were born, as though this might help to explain their enormous power. If Jupiter-Saturn conjunctions reflect shifts in religious consciousness, then individuals born under the conjunctions would embody the spirit of the conjunction and serve as its mouthpiece, and an especially gifted person might be viewed as a prophet or messiah. The birth charts of great religious leaders, if we could access them, might not validate the 'truth' of any particular religion, but they might shed light on the particular collective vision reflected by the conjunction and its subsequent cycle, which colours the perception and interpretation of the god-image of the time.

As we've seen, one of the most prevalent ideas about the birth of Jesus is that he was born under a triple Jupiter-Saturn conjunction in Pisces between 6 and 7 BCE. The symbolism of the fishes, ubiquitous in early Christian writings and iconography, seems to confirm this idea to its adherents. Jung was intrigued by the concept and wrote extensively about it in *Aion*. Like Kepler and many astrologers today, Jung was convinced not only that Jesus had been born under this conjunction but also that the 'Three Wise Men', bearing the costly royal gifts of gold, frankincense, and myrrh, were not themselves kings. They were astrologers, tracking what they believed to be a major astrological portent: the conjunction of Jupiter and Saturn, heralding the birth of a new king.

The astrological Jupiter as a symbol of our human need to make a connection with a larger, more purposeful universe, combined with Saturn as the symbol of our need to create enduring structures and embody our ideas and visions in permanent form, certainly hints at some kind of spiritual revelation that, over time, could solidify as a formal religious edifice. Jupiter's new spiritual vision overthrows the old Saturnian rule just as Zeus overthrew the rule of Kronos. And inevitably the new vision begins to crystallise and become rigid as it ages, embodied in concrete physical and political structures that themselves then require renewal under another Jupiter-Saturn dispensation.

'Mummy wheat'

In 1934, Yeats wrote a short poem titled *Conjunctions,* in which he declared:

> If Jupiter and Saturn meet,
> What a crop of mummy wheat! [62]

'Mummy wheat' refers to the popular belief, current at the time Yeats wrote his poem, that the seeds of grains found in Egyptian tombs, if moistened, would still sprout after four millennia. Sadly, they didn't. But archaeological discoveries in Egypt during the 1920s and early 1930s had powerfully influenced the collective imagination. Tutankhamun's tomb with its extraordinary treasures was uncovered in 1922, along with a number of sarcophagi containing mummies filled not with human remains but with grain seeds, usually wheat or corn. These mummies wore a wax mask of Osiris in order to encourage the god to favour the next year's harvest.

Yeats' lines refer to the Egyptian myth of Osiris as the first mummy; he used the ancient story as a symbol of his idea of the 'vivification of old intellect' reflected by the Jupiter-Saturn cycle. Yeats, like Jung, was also fascinated by the interface between particular Jupiter-Saturn conjunctions and the shifting of the astrological aions. If a Great Conjunction occurred – especially a Great Mutation into a new element – and this conjunction coincided with the shift of the equinoctial point into a new constellation, a new religious vision would emerge that would eventually, over the course

---

62 William Butler Yeats, *The Variorum Edition of the Poems of W. B. Yeats,* (1957), Part 10, p. 562.

of two millennia, become a dominant theme in human perceptions of the divine. As Jung understood it, the god-image would emerge from the depths of the collective psyche in a new form.

The myth of Osiris

The myth of the resurrection of Osiris dates back to at least 2400 BCE and was first described in the *Pyramid Texts*. Son of Geb, the Earth, and Nut, the Sky – the Egyptian predecessors of Ouranos and Gaia – Osiris was said to be the first divine king of Egypt, married to his sister Isis. But Set, one of his brothers, secretly coveted his throne.

Set ruled the desert, and presided over disorder, violence, war, chaos, and storms. He was called the 'Instigator of Confusion' and was sometimes associated with the planet Mercury, but more often with Mars. He could often be benign, but he was both a trickster and a violent and frequently malevolent deity. Set was usually portrayed in human form with the head of a mysterious animal, referred to by Egyptologists as the 'Set animal' because it can't be identified with any known species. It vaguely resembles a jackal, but the squared-off ears and peculiar anteater's snout defy classification.

Determined to claim the throne for himself, Set murdered Osiris and tore his brother's body into fourteen pieces, which he scattered across the whole of Egypt. Isis patiently collected the dismembered fragments, consecrating as sacred each site where she discovered a part of her brother-husband's body. Eventually she found all the pieces except the phallus, which was irrevocably lost because it had been eaten by a fish. Despite this bit of bad luck, Isis magically recreated the body from the pieces, wrapping it in bandages to create the first mummy. She replaced the missing phallus with one made of gold and, taking the form of a bird, she breathed life into the mummy and then copulated with it, resulting in the conception of their son Horus, whose symbol was the hawk.

At the moment of Horus' birth, tiny green shoots of wheat began to sprout from Osiris' inert mummy, heralding a renewal. Meanwhile, Isis had to flee to protect herself and her new-born son from Set, and she hid in a papyrus thicket in the Nile Delta until Horus was old enough to defend her. After a series of terrible battles, Horus finally defeated Set and became ruler of Egypt in his father's place, while Osiris, now fully restored, became ruler of the realm of the dead, presiding over the Hall of Judgement in which each human heart was weighed against a feather on the scales of Ma'at, goddess of justice.

Horus was associated with the rising Sun and Osiris with the Sun at midnight. Osiris was thus reborn as the young Horus, just as the Sun is reborn at dawn: the 'vivification of old intellect' in a new form. Osiris was often portrayed as green-skinned after his resurrection, symbolising his association with the cycles of nature and vegetation: the mythic justification for the corn and wheat mummies found in Egyptian tombs. On this corn mummy from the Ptolemaic period, the mask of Osiris was placed where the head of the deceased would normally be. There were no human remains in the mummy wrapping; it was filled entirely with seeds.

The story of Osiris' dismemberment and resurrection may seem a long way from the world of Greek myth, with little relevance to the Jupiter-Saturn cycle. There is no association in Egyptian texts between either planet and this strange story of rebirth. Osiris and his son are solar deities; Set was associated with Mercury and Mars; and Isis was usually portrayed with the lunar crescent on her head. But Yeats thought the myth was relevant to the Jupiter-Saturn cycle and that makes it worth considering, as his prophetic insights are so uncomfortably accurate.

An Egyptian corn mummy from the Ptolemaic period, c. 4000-2000 BCE, originally filled with corn seeds and wearing a mask of Osiris. Metropolitan Museum of Art, NY.

Yeats' association of Jupiter-Saturn with the Osiris myth suggests there is a kind of dismemberment that occurs at the time of a Great Conjunction of Jupiter and Saturn. This is the 'dark' phase of the cycle. Yeats wrote in *The Second Coming*:

> Things fall apart; the centre cannot hold; mere anarchy is loosed upon the world.

The poem describes the imminent changing of the astrological aions from Pisces to Aquarius, which, in Yeats' view, will be heralded by a Great Conjunction, and perhaps even a Great Mutation. As we've seen, the latter occurred in December 2020 at 0° Aquarius. I don't know whether Yeats was thinking of this conjunction when he wrote his poem. But perhaps we should be thinking of it ourselves.

After the dismemberment, the process of collecting the pieces begins; what has been damaged, on material, spiritual, and psychological levels, needs to be reassembled and restored. The missing phallus can't be replaced because it's vanished forever, but something else can be put in its place that might be even more precious. Osiris, although he's a god, can still be destroyed – at least temporarily – and the creative power symbolised by the phallus can be lost. But gold, in myth and alchemy, is the only planetary metal that's incorruptible and immortal. All the others – silver, lead, tin, iron, copper, and quicksilver – oxidise and eventually decay, but gold is indestructible. It's an archetypal image of divinity and of the life-force itself, and its worth is eternal; it symbolises values that can never be corroded by time, change, or the current *zeitgeist*.

The restored mummy is then wrapped up, briefly animated, and left dormant while a hidden new life begins in the darkness of Isis' womb. Something new, secret, and invisible has quickened. This mythic tale might tell us something about the way Jupiter-Saturn cycles work on both individual and collective levels, and it may also reveal insight into why Jupiter transits sometimes initially feel like a dismemberment rather than a time of joy and abundance. When we can't find anything at all benefic about a Jupiter transit to our natal planets, especially when it also forms a hard aspect to transiting or natal Saturn, we might do well to remember mummy wheat.

Jupiter-Saturn and the birth of Jesus

Writing about the Jupiter-Saturn cycle, the 8th-century Arab astrologer Mash'allah observed that if Jupiter is stronger than Saturn, it will signify good, but if Saturn is stronger, it will signify detriment. On this basis, the triple conjunction of 6-7 BCE was 'good' because Jupiter was in its own sign of Pisces, but the conjunction that occurred in December 2020 was 'detrimental' because Jupiter was in Saturn's sign of Aquarius, giving the power to Saturn. Given the way in which world events have developed since that conjunction, it's hard to argue with Mash'allah's interpretation.

Mash'allah also stated that if the conjunction takes place in a fire or air sign, dryness, sterility of the earth, and severity of cold will follow. If it takes place in an earth sign, it signifies famine and the destruction of seeds. In water signs it indicates excessive rain and pestilence. And if the conjunction is near an angle at the moment it's exact, it signifies the appearance of a king or prophet from the direction of that sign. The conjunction of 21 December 2020 occurred at 0° 29' Aquarius, right on the Descendant at 0° 45' Aquarius, at 6.20 PM GMT, Greenwich, England. So perhaps we should expect the imminent arrival of a king or prophet. Or perhaps not. Unfortunately, Mash'allah didn't give us any pointers on how we might distinguish between a 'true' and a 'false' leader. Since there currently seem to be a lot of candidates belonging to the latter category, I won't be holding my breath in hopeful anticipation.

Abu Ma'shar al-Balkhi, writing in the 9th century, developed his own theories about the Jupiter-Saturn cycle, and he articulated them in greater detail. He distinguished between three different kinds of conjunction. A 'Great Conjunction' occurs roughly every twenty years, falling in signs of the same element over a period of 240 years. Abu Ma'shar suggested that any of these Great Conjunctions can indicate the elevation of kings and the rise of prophets, but if such an event occurs, it tends to be local rather than regional or global. However, a 'greater' conjunction (a Great Mutation), which occurs when the planets meet in a new element after nearly two and a half centuries, indicates major political and religious changes in a larger region of the world. Based on this idea, that's presumably what we can expect from the recent Great Mutation in Aquarius as it unfolds during its 20-year cycle.

It takes eight centuries for the Great Conjunctions to move through all four elements, and then a new cycle begins. According to Abu Ma'shar, the first conjunction in Aries initiating that new cycle is the 'greatest' conjunction, describing major changes in empires and kingdoms as well as floods and earthquakes that can decimate entire populations. The conjunction in Aries in 1702 was one of these 'greatest' conjunctions. The War of the Spanish Succession with its long-term consequences certainly reflected major changes in particular European nations, but it didn't live up to Abu Ma'shar's global expectations. Nor did the death in Britain of King William III, known as 'Dutch' William, which occurred under the same conjunction. William's demise eventually led to a new dynasty on the British throne: the German House of Hanover, which reached its cultural and political peak during the reign of Queen Victoria and ultimately became the present-day House of Windsor.

As for floods and earthquakes, in March 1702 an earthquake occurred near Benevento in Italy that killed 400 people, and the Changbaishan volcano erupted on the Chinese-North Korean border in April of that year. These events were certainly devastating locally, but this kind of natural disaster tends to occur in vulnerable areas of the world with great frequency and without any help from a Jupiter-Saturn conjunction. Perhaps we need to be less literal than Abu Ma'shar in our understanding of the Jupiter-Saturn cycle.

The ideas of these two great Arab astrologers about the significance of the Jupiter-Saturn cycle continued to reverberate through subsequent centuries. In the 9th century, the Christian Arab astrologer Ibn Hibinta attempted to combine Mash'allah's earlier interpretations of Jupiter-Saturn with the idea that a conjunction of the two planets must have occurred at the birth of Jesus. But he didn't offer a specific date or time for the birth, only the possibility of two different years: 25 BCE and 2 BCE. Perhaps he got his calculations wrong, as there was no Jupiter-Saturn conjunction in either of those years. Abu Ma'shar, writing slightly later than Ibn Hibinta, suggested that Jesus had the first decan of Virgo on the Ascendant, perhaps in part because this sign rising in the east encapsulated the symbolism of the Virgin Birth.

Although he didn't calculate a complete chart for Jesus, Abu Ma'shar's work was translated into Latin in the 12th century and exercised great influence on Western Christian astrologers. In the 13th century, Albertus Magnus, a German Dominican friar, astrologer, and alchemist, created a speculative birth chart for Jesus in his *Speculum astronomiae*, in which he took up Abu Ma'shar's suggestion of a Virgo Ascendant. So did the

14th-century French cardinal and astrologer Pierre d'Ailly, who offered 8° Virgo as the Ascendant degree.

In the 16th century, Gerolamo Cardano, an Italian astrologer and polymath, offered his own speculative birth chart for Jesus in *De iudiciis astrorum*, published in 1554. Albertus Magnus and Pierre d'Ailly had based their charts on the traditional birthdate of 25 December and the traditional time of midnight. They seem to have subordinated accurate calculation to faith by relying on the symbolism of a Virgo Ascendant reflecting the Virgin Birth. Cardano, a child of the Italian Renaissance, accepted the traditional date and time of 25 December and the traditional time of midnight, but he didn't depend on either the Virgo symbolism or the traditional year. He calculated the chart for 1 BCE, arriving at a 2° Libra Ascendant with Jupiter at 8° Libra conjunct the Ascendant and square the Sun in Capricorn exactly on the 4th house cusp. However, none of these three authors – not even Cardano – refers to a Jupiter-Saturn conjunction, since the conjunction nearest the dates they used had already occurred in 6-7 BCE.[63]

Kepler seems to have been the first astrologer to fully depart from official Church doctrine and insist that the birth of Jesus must have occurred in 6-7 BCE at the time of the Jupiter-Saturn conjunction in Pisces. Jung had explored the work of earlier Christian sources like Albertus Magnus and Cardano, as well as those of Mash'allah and Abu Ma'shar. But he was more impressed by Kepler's calculations, and was also convinced that the third 'hit' of this triple conjunction, which occurred while Mars was in opposition from Virgo in 7 BCE, was 'exceptionally large and of an impressive brilliance'.[64] In *Aion*, he wrote:

> Christ was born at the beginning of the aion of the Fishes. It is by no means ruled out that there were educated Christians who knew of the *coniunctio maxima* of Jupiter and Saturn in Pisces in the year 7 BC, just as, according to the gospel reports, there were Chaldaeans who actually found Christ's birthplace.[65]

---

63 For more detail on these charts and their authors, see James Holden, *Early Horoscopes of Jesus*, in *Journal of Research*, American Federation of Astrologers, Vol. 12, No. 1, Spring 2001.
64 See C. G. Jung, *Aion*, CW9ii, Part Two (Routledge & Kegan Paul, 1951), ¶130.
65 Jung, CW9ii, ¶172.

Gerolamo Cardano's speculative birth chart for Jesus in
De iudiciis astrorum (1553).

He parted ways with tradition even further by following the calculations
of the German astrologer Oswald Gerhardt, who had proposed 29 May 7
BCE as the correct birth date of Jesus: the day on which the configuration
of Jupiter-Saturn opposite Mars had been exact.

Jung believed that the incoming Aquarian aion would not involve the
advent of an actual religious leader or avatar, as did the incoming Piscean
aion coinciding with the Great Conjunction of 7 BCE. Instead, he was

certain the emergence of the god-image of the new aion would be a gradual inner process: a dawning recognition of the divine within each individual, and a hard-won internalisation of previously projected perceptions of God and the Devil as divine potencies existing somewhere 'out there'. Good and evil, according to Jung, are not attributes that belong solely to other people or to principalities and powers operating independently in and on the external world. They are within the human collective psyche and within each individual, and they're our own responsibility.

Jung seems to have been inspired by Yeats' work, and it's possible that the prophecies expressed in Yeats' *The Second Coming* as well as *A Vision* influenced Jung's own thinking about the new aion.[66] He was convinced that as this Aquarian aion begins to unfold, it won't look much like the age of 'love and brotherhood' so hopefully portrayed in the 1968 musical *Hair*. Instead, perhaps for as long as a century, its 'teething' period will involve painful and sometimes horrific collisions with the shadow-side of our own natures, the shadow-side of the collective psyche, and the shadow-side of divinity which Jung first glimpsed in his childhood vision of God dropping a giant turd on Basel Cathedral.

The extreme political, social, and religious polarisations we're currently experiencing were predicted by Jung as well as Yeats a long time ago, and both men took their cues from the changing of the astrological aions coincident with a Great Conjunction of Jupiter and Saturn. The imminent confrontation with the shadow might, after a long, painful birth, result in the gradual realisation that blaming governments, nations, and racial, religious, social, or political groups for the world's evils is a futile exercise. The advent of Phanes, Jung's spherical, enigmatic god of the new aion whom he named after the Orphic primal creator-god, would only be achievable within each individual through conscious awareness, internalisation of our projections, and direct inner experiences of both the diabolical and the divine.

---

66 William Butler Yeats, *A Vision: An Explanation of Life Founded upon the Writings of Giraldus and upon Certain Doctrines Attributed to Kusta Ben Luka* (T. Werner Laurie, 1925).

Questions and Comments

Before we move on to the cycles of Jupiter with Chiron and the outer planets, are there any comments or questions?

Audience: If the archetypal gods are always fighting in myth and never seem to grow psychologically, and given that they're alive within us, does this help explain why we humans never seem to learn from experience or history except through work on a personal level? Or do we only learn so slowly socially and collectively that it may not be enough before we exterminate ourselves and all other living beings, including our Earth, through climate change and/or nuclear war?

Liz: I wouldn't assume that archetypes never grow. Mythic figures like Zeus and Kronos are god-images that belong to the world of archaic pre-classical Greece. Their stories reflect a particular culture at a particular epoch of history, although they're still relevant to us now because they reflect innate human psychological dynamics. But they're archetypal images, not the archetypes themselves.

Even within the time-span of the Greco-Roman world, perceptions of the gods changed as the culture changed. The Greek Ares was perceived as far more dangerous and untrustworthy than the Roman Mars, who reflected a different cultural attitude to war; and the Roman Jupiter, as head of the Capitoline Triad and patron god of Rome, was more stable and benignly paternal than the Greek Zeus. The archetypes themselves are living patterns inherent in life itself, and we can only access them through images generated by the unconscious psyche and perceived through the imagination. We can't really get any kind of handle on an archetype except through its images, which is why the Neoplatonic philosophers of late antiquity were so insistent that the imagination is the bridge between the human and the divine.

Everything living grows and changes. Archetypal images acquire new expressions over millennia, and they seem to be capable of their own form of transformation, of which we humans are a part, consciously or not. Just as we ourselves change, so do the gods. Our changing perceptions of and interactions with the archetypal patterns symbolised by the gods seem to alter the expression of these patterns in our individual lives. Some underlying themes seem to remain the same. The compassion of the Greek virgin lunar goddess Artemis as protectress of children, for example, is perpetuated in the compassion of the Virgin Mary, who is often portrayed with her feet on a crescent Moon. But other attributes seem to develop and alter, perhaps in tandem with the gradual enlargement of human consciousness.

Your entirely valid observation that we don't seem to learn anything from history may reflect the fact that the human psyche is frighteningly snail-like in its development. We learn so terribly slowly, and the incremental changes in our god-images – as Jung put it, what we deem to be of the 'highest value' – reflect that slowness. There's a branch of psychology known as 'evolutionary' psychology (not to be confused with 'evolutionary' astrology) which basically trashes the idea that the human psyche makes wonderful progress every decade.

We've certainly made great progress technologically, and our ideals of a fair society – at least in some parts of the world, although not in others – might be more advanced in some respects than they were in ancient Babylon or Ottoman-ruled Turkey. But socially we're still tribal creatures, and human emotional and instinctual responses haven't altered much since the Neanderthals died out. Technology and legislation don't make a blind bit of difference on that level; they only give us the illusion that our psyches have radically changed. Our glacier-like progress towards integration and wholeness makes a mockery of the idea that we're so much more advanced than our ancestors because we have iPhones, social media, antibiotics, supersonic missiles, and AI.

Human consciousness does change, and so do the expressions of archetypal patterns and perhaps the archetypes themselves. But it takes an enormous amount of time – tens of millennia rather than the lifespan of a new government or a new scientific invention – and as humans we seem to have to experience an enormous amount of suffering and wretchedness before we learn even the smallest lesson. I have no idea whether we have enough time before we destroy ourselves, if that's indeed where we're headed, which is open to debate. I suspect collective human destiny is up to each individual, and in the end it might rest on whether each of us can avoid destroying ourselves and each other through personal anger, resentment, greed, envy, apathy, a craving for approval, a hunger for power and control, or a determination to blame everyone else for our own personal mess.

It's not very helpful to sit around saying, 'If only people would do something.' As a collective it's true we haven't learnt much from history.

Even when we believe we've made a great leap of progress by vociferously repudiating some 'evil' of the past, we may find ourselves secretly behaving like the very people we're condemning. And the work still has to be done by each individual, and the only place to begin is in our own backyard.

Audience: So the facing of the shadow might be associated with the predominance of Saturn in the conjunction of December 2020?

Liz: I don't think it's quite that specific. Consciousness is an ongoing process that isn't defined by any particular astrological configuration, and I wouldn't necessarily relate it to the Jupiter-Saturn cycle. This astrological pairing seems to be concerned with the infusion of meaning into our practical efforts to establish safety and stability, and it usually begins with a struggle or a major change as old structures are replaced by new ones that can encompass and facilitate the vision of a 'destined' future plan or design. The dominance of Saturn in the conjunction of 2020 might support Abu Ma'shar's suggestion that when Saturn has the power in a Great Conjunction, the effect is 'detrimental'. Expressions of human darkness have certainly been highlighted during and since that conjunction.

Jung's idea of the facing of the shadow in the context of the Aquarian aion is related to his understanding of the meaning of Aquarius in contrast to Pisces. He perceived Pisces as a dual sign with an innate internal split or dichotomy. Therefore the struggle for consciousness, which isn't limited to any specific astrological aion and might well not be limited only to human life, would inevitably be projected during the Piscean aion through the polarisation of Christ and Satan, good and evil, saint and sinner, body and spirit, 'true' religion and heresy, religion and science and, in modern politics, Left and Right, socialism and capitalism, democracy and dictatorship. Jung understood the Piscean aion to be one in which the god-image emerged in the collective as a sometimes destructive and sometimes creative collision between apparently irreconcilable opposites projected 'outside'. But any individual's quest for greater consciousness isn't limited by the prevailing god-image in the collective psyche.

Aquarius isn't a dual sign. It's symbolised by a human figure pouring water from a jug, and to Jung it represented an integration of the opposites of the Piscean aion. In Babylonian myth Aquarius was associated with the water-god Ea, who was often portrayed holding an overflowing jug of water. The Greeks sometimes associated the figure with Deucalion, the son of Prometheus who survived Zeus' Great Flood, but more often with Ganymede, the beautiful youth abducted by Zeus to become cupbearer for the gods. Alan Leo, in the early 20ᵗʰ century, interpreted Aquarius as an image of humanity itself, and Leo's interpretation seems to have been important in Jung's understanding of the sign. You can see how the equation of humanity with the god-image could invite some serious problems, not least the hubristic belief that, being divine, we can do whatever we like.

The integration of the shadow isn't only concerned with Saturn, although that seems to be where we often have to start. Although Jung did associate Saturn with the shadow, especially in its role in alchemy as an image of the *nigredo*, he felt the integration of the shadow in the Aquarian epoch needed to be reflected in a growing recognition of the deeper nature and task of being a full human. Every planet has a shadow-side, and all of them are inside us.

Jung didn't write anything about the Great Conjunction in Aquarius in 2020 – at least not in any published work or private document that I've had access to. I have no idea whether he thought it was relevant, and he might not even have had access to an ephemeris that far ahead. He did state – although he began to question his own conclusions later – that 1941 was the year in which, through the precession of the equinoxes, the solar equinoctial point reached the first star in the constellation of Aquarius, which represented the 'official' start of the new aion.[67]

This timing coincided with a Great Conjunction, although it wasn't a Great Mutation. On 15 February 1941 Jupiter was exactly conjunct Saturn at 9° Taurus, and both planets were within orb of conjunction to Uranus in May of that year. Although he didn't mention Uranus, Jung was convinced that this juxtaposition of a Jupiter-Saturn conjunction with the shift of the equinoctial point marked the first labour pains of what would be a long and difficult birth; he assumed, no doubt rightly, that – as you say – we learn very slowly, and only when we're subjected to great suffering.

The process of interiorising our projected polarities of good and evil, in Jung's view, would begin with severe splitting and the unleashing of a great deal of darkness as we're gradually forced to come to terms with the fact that we contain and generate evil as well as good within ourselves. He

---

67 See Greene, *Jung's Studies in Astrology*, pp. 166-68, for Jung's correspondence with the Dutch astronomer Rebekka Biegel about the timing of the new aion.

predicted fanaticism, intense divisiveness, and violent collisions between opposing movements, forces, and ideologies. In the manner of all good prophets, he, like Yeats, seems to have nailed it. It may be that recognising these opposites within ourselves, individual by individual, is the only key we have to our survival as a species.

Audience: I hadn't noticed that humanity is moving forward on a collective level.

Liz: No, it's rather hard to spot. It's a bit like watching a stone grow. Actually, stones do grow and mature as they accrue different mineral inclusions and form a crystalline structure and pass through their sedimentary, igneous, and metamorphic stages. It takes a few million years for an agate to form, so we're not likely to notice that it's moving forward and making progress.

Audience: So you're talking about a changing of the gods in the sense of internalising multiplicity and divinity. It's *in* us and *on* earth?

Liz: I've been talking about a changing of the god-image, rather than a changing of the gods. The gods themselves, whatever they are or aren't, symbolise archetypal patterns. We perceive the divine through our images of it, which change as we ourselves do. God-images arise spontaneously from the collective unconscious when their time has arrived. We don't consciously make them up, and any efforts to construct them artificially would have no lasting power. Political and religious leaders have often attempted this throughout history, but their efforts succeed only if they're in accord with an emerging archetypal image.

The varying faces of the god-image are reflected in the myths and iconography of the aion. The god-image of the Piscean aion looks like Pisces. That doesn't mean the god appears as a fish with fins, scales, and goggle-eyes, although fish symbolism does permeate early Christian texts and iconography. But it's the underlying themes of Pisces – sacrifice, suffering, compassion, submission to divine will, redemption and forgiveness – that shape the god-image and its attributes.

In Christian iconography, Jesus is never portrayed as a warrior or a firm, determined leader, nor is he ever shown having a good time. No one is laughing in portrayals of the Last Supper. His face is invariably sorrowful and compassionate. He's imaged as suffering on the cross, or as a vulnerable infant, or in the act of healing the sick. Think of the words of the hymn:

'Gentle Jesus, meek and mild/ Look upon a little child'. And the opposite fish, his dark twin, is usually portrayed either as Satan with a terrifying goat's face, horns, hoofs, and tail, or as fierce, proud Lucifer, full of rage and spite.

What might an Aquarian deity look like? Aquarius is related to the faculty of reason and the acquisition of knowledge, not just through the rational intellect, but also in the sense of Plato's definition of reason. That includes comprehension of the whole, arising from synthesis, forethought, and a recognition of the interconnecting patterns that underpin all systems and structures. The water-bearer carries water, but he himself isn't a watery creature. What does he do with the water? On a really good day, perhaps he waters the earth to nurture its growth through understanding, and washes away the illusion of separateness from living things to reveal the patterns of their interconnectedness.

In the *Red Book*, Jung painted the water-bearer more than once. In one image, he's pouring water from his jug onto seven growing plants with strange humanoid faces. Perhaps these plants represent humanity, although the number could also suggest the seven planets, whose expression as symbols of archetypal patterns is enhanced through conscious awareness. Knowledge thus becomes the water of life if it's utilised in life-giving ways. The challenge is to work out what constitutes 'life-giving' rather than 'life-stifling' or 'life-destroying'. Jung's painting is symbolic, so it's open to many different interpretations.

Audience: Jonathan Haidt sees the current level of polarisation as a return to the norm after the long post-war consensus.

Liz: Polarisation may indeed be 'the norm' because all life polarises on a cyclical basis. It's a prerequisite for synthesis and new growth, and we can see its symbolism in the Jupiter-Saturn cycle from conjunction to opposition and back to conjunction. Political parties have always polarised; it's one of the fundamental principles of democracy, which in its best forms can offer us choice. Totalitarian states offer no choice, and create the illusion of unity by simply eradicating the opposition. As Joseph Stalin once said, "No man, no problem."

I can understand at least some of what Haidt means. The Second World War shocked people into a greater willingness to agree with each other and with their governments out of fear that the same disaster might happen again. But efforts to establish a consensus out of fear rather than greater consciousness aren't prone to success, and sooner or later the polarisation will begin to wreak havoc again. There's a different flavour in each form of polarisation, and we can sometimes link them with planetary symbols. Jupiter's flavour carries a religious quality. We're impelled to act not from simple greed, fear, or desire, but because we have a vision, a sense of the rightness of something as part of an unfolding plan. So we polarise against those who seem to oppose or thwart our vision, even if their vision, viewed from outside the arena, might be equally valid and important.

Jupiter and Saturn are polarised in myth. And extreme polarisation may be characteristic of the shifting of every astrological aion into the next one. The opening centuries of the Piscean aion, if we consider the framework of the aions to be a valid perspective, were certainly accompanied by extreme polarisation as the waning social, philosophical, religious, and scientific inheritance of the classical world collided with an early Church which displayed an often fanatical violence in asserting the supremacy of its beliefs. If you want to experience a moving and deeply disturbing illustration of this, watch the 2009 film *Agora*, with Rachel Weisz and Max Minghella. It's set in Alexandria in the dying days of the pagan world and focuses on the persecution and murder of one of the last Neoplatonic scientific philosophers, Hypatia. It could all be happening now, in different forms but with the same underlying pattern.

Haidt is a social psychologist, and he has a valid point. But I'm inclined to look past the impact of socio-economic forces and consider the structure of the human psyche itself, which seems to develop and grow through polarisation. No consensus can ever remain stable, nor can it ever be perfectly balanced, because individuals will always shatter it sooner or later. Every one of us is lopsided, as is every birth chart, and the 'centre' will always keep shifting. Perhaps a great deal depends on how we handle our polarisations, and whether we're capable of recognising the importance of individual responsibility and individual choice.

The Jupiter-Uranus cycle

Uranus is a symbol of our collective urge to progress towards an ideal of perfection. Whether 'progress' is understood as social, psychological, physical, scientific, spiritual, economic, or technological, Uranus reflects the Promethean spirit, which generates a vision of potentials that could ultimately flower in a perfectly functioning human unit within a perfectly functioning society and a perfectly functioning world. In myth, Ouranos is the 'starry heaven': the universal matrix of ideas of what could and 'should' unfold.

With the exception of the Orphic figure of Phanes, the primal deity in Greek myth was usually identified as Ouranos, emerging with his sister-wife Gaia, along with Ananke or Necessity, from the inchoate womb of Night and Chaos. Ouranos was the progenitor of all the other gods and the spirit of divine potential, with a plan for the perfect universe contained within him but not yet incarnated. Only when he mated with Gaia, the Earth, could the manifest cosmos take shape. But then, when it did, Ouranos rejected it because it wasn't as perfect as he'd envisaged.

Prometheus, the grandson of Ouranos, bears a name which means 'forethought'. We humans are gifted with forethought, or we want to believe we are. We look into the future and devise a plan for what we could become. The plan isn't always the same for every individual or for every epoch of history. But the Promethean spirit always insists that we could be more than what we are. Life could be so much better. We could eradicate social evils, poverty, starvation, war, and disease; we could foresee and prevent pandemics; we could have perfect bodies with perfect genes. We could create world peace and level all inequalities; we could avoid ageing and even live forever. Uranus tells us that whatever we've achieved, we have to continue to pursue the vision because we haven't yet fulfilled our potential.

Uranus is the father of all social, scientific, and political ideologies of any persuasion which focus on progress. But because it's an outer planet beyond the boundary of Saturn, the progressive spirit of Uranus is a collective vision that takes no account of the individual. Eggs, in the view of Uranus, must inevitably be broken to create omelettes. There's no point in worrying about the suffering of any individual egg if breaking it serves what's perceived to be the greater good. And some eggs might have to be removed altogether if they're deemed to be 'inferior'. The recognition of individual suffering or individual aspirations that might challenge the plan isn't really part of Uranus' frame of reference.

When Jupiter conjuncts Uranus, our collective vision of progress, filtered through the sign in which Uranus is transiting, is infused with a sense of religiosity. Our aspirations aren't limited to making things better in practical ways like building new health clinics, inventing new vaccines, developing new technologies to improve productivity, or repairing disintegrating roads and railways. We're convinced we must make the world better on every level, including how and what we think, because we're destined to become something greater. Viewing the world though this lens, politics and science can become religions, religions can tamper with politics and interfere with science, and social causes can become infused with a religious fervour that justifies the persecution of heretics in the name of collective progress. The positive impact of Uranian progressive ideas on human life is obvious. The negative impact is often rationalised or ignored.

The timing of the cycle

Jupiter-Uranus conjunctions occur every 13.8 years, and they form a great cycle of 83 years. This timing is very close to the 84-year cycle of Uranus, so the first conjunction of each new great cycle tends to recur within a few degrees of the first conjunction of the previous cycle. Jupiter-Uranus conjunctions can remain within orb from three months to a year because of the retrograde motion of both planets. Unlike Jupiter-Saturn conjunctions, which repeat in one element for two and a half centuries before moving into the next element in a Great Mutation, each successive Jupiter-Uranus conjunction occurs in a sign sextile to the previous one. Instead of creating equilateral triangles like the Jupiter-Saturn cycle, the Jupiter-Uranus cycle creates hexagons.

This is Astrid Fallon's diagram of the Jupiter-Uranus cycle. If you connect the successive conjunctions of a great cycle, you'll see that they

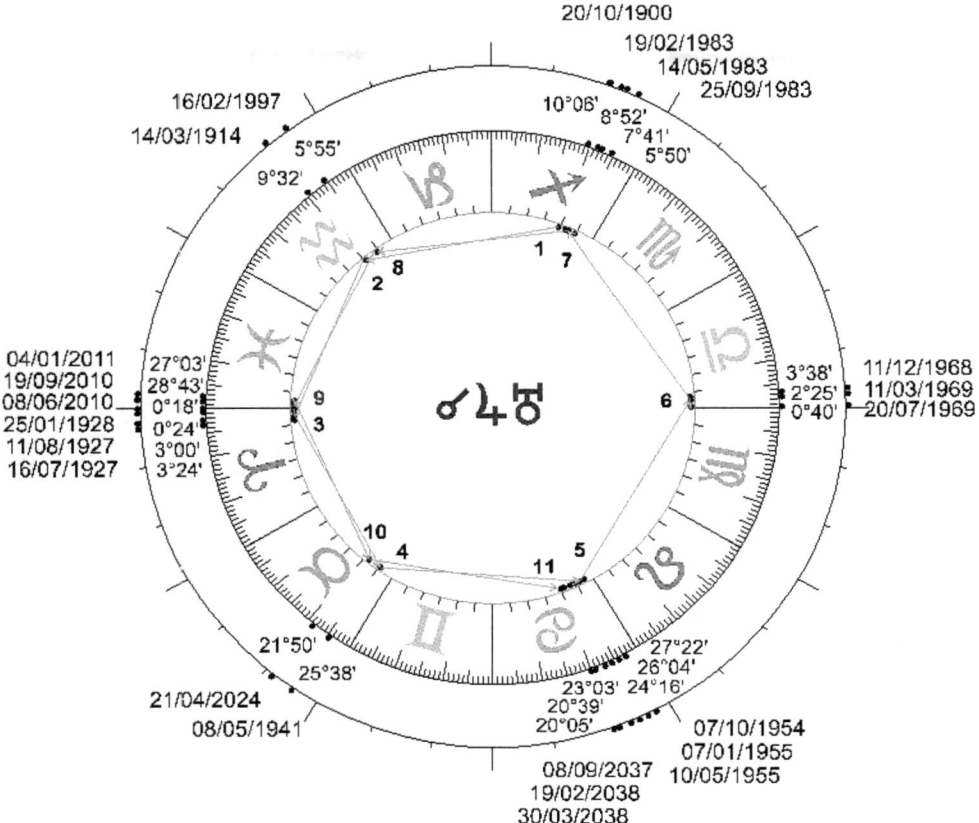

create a six-sided figure. Number 1 in the diagram marks a conjunction at 10° Sagittarius, which occurred in October 1900. Number 2 occurred at 9° Aquarius in March 1914, forming a close sextile to the previous conjunction fourteen years earlier. Number 3 was a triple conjunction from 0° to 3° Aries, occurring between June 1927 and January 1928. The latter two of the three conjunctions were just within orb of a sextile to the previous conjunction. Number 4, exact at 25° Taurus in May 1941 and sextile the previous conjunction, was particularly significant because the two planets also conjuncted Saturn, marking a new cycle for both Jupiter-Uranus and Jupiter-Saturn. This is the Jupiter-Saturn conjunction that Jung associated with the first birth pangs of the new aion.

Number 5 was a triple conjunction from 24° to 27° Cancer, occurring between October 1954 and May 1955 and closely sextile the previous conjunction in Taurus. Number 6, another triple conjunction, occurred from 0° to 3° Libra between December 1968 and July 1969, once again sextile to the previous conjunction although out of sign. Number 7, yet another triple conjunction, occurred from 5° to 8° Sagittarius between February and September 1983, and we're more or less back where we started after a complete cycle of 83 years. Number 8 occurred at 6 degrees Aquarius in 1997, in the same degree as the conjunction 83 years earlier. And Number 9, a triple conjunction occurring between 27° Pisces and 0° Aries in 2010-2011, fell close to the triple conjunction between 0° and 3° Aries in 1927-28, 83 years earlier. You can see how each successive conjunction sextiles the previous one, and the complete 83-year cycle ends very close to where the preceding one did.

The next conjunction, Number 10 on the diagram, was exact in April 2024 at 21° Taurus. The 'full' phase of this new cycle – the time of fruition – will occur in January 2031 when Jupiter is at 19° Sagittarius opposite Uranus at 19° Gemini. The diagram finishes with Number 11, a triple conjunction that will occur from 20° to 23° Cancer between September 2037 and March 2038.

Some tidbits of Jupiter-Uranus history

When Jupiter-Uranus conjunctions combine with other slow-moving planets, a potent cocktail of powerful collective movements tends to erupt. I mentioned that 1941 was especially important because it marked not only a new Jupiter-Uranus cycle but also a new Jupiter-Saturn cycle. This coincided with what's often viewed as the most horrific year of the Second World War. Germany invaded and occupied Denmark, Norway, Belgium, the Netherlands, and France; Hitler signed his Axis pact with Mussolini; the Blitz destroyed huge swathes of London; the Japanese bombed Pearl Harbour, dragging the US into the war; and the largest concentration camp, Auschwitz-Birkenau, was opened in Poland, where over a million people would be murdered in the next four years. This conjunction of Jupiter, Saturn, and Uranus also formed incoming trines to Neptune in Virgo, adding a mystical and messianic flavour to the mix.

The conjunction of these three planets fused together the Uranian need for progress, the Saturnian urge to strengthen and protect existing structures, and the Jupiterian sense of a higher purpose or meaning. Occurring in an earth sign, its expression might be expected to be mirrored in worldly events and struggles over territory and resources. We might recall those older definitions of Jupiter-Saturn that equated the conjunctions with the rise and fall of kings and empires.

The Jupiter-Uranus conjunction of 1941 was expressed through stark polarisation, probably inevitable because collective movements of an extreme kind invariably call forth their opposite. Hitler's Third Reich was driven by the vision of a perfect Aryan society cleansed of its 'inferior' elements, and by an obsession to extend its territory on the basis of the quasi-religious idea of the *Volksgemeinschaft*, the Germanic 'folk soul'. Although the Nazi regime rejected any form of denominational religion, a kind of religious fanaticism coloured all its goals and symbols. The nations who opposed this dark vision of 'progress' were inspired by an equally fervent determination to champion the concept of democratic freedoms, to go to battle on behalf of an ideal of enlightened civilisation, and to fight against a tyranny perceived as a cosmic evil. Without that absolute, quasi-religious conviction, it's possible the Allied nations might have struggled to find the will to go on fighting.

Echoing the great battles of myth, like those of the Babylonian god Marduk against the monstrous sea-serpent Tiamat, or Zeus against the similarly monstrous sea-serpent Typhon, the war during which this 1941 conjunction occurred assumed the proportions of a great cosmic battle of light against darkness. Yet we're still confused by the fact that light could be found, albeit often secretly, in every Axis nation, and darkness could be found, sometimes more openly, in every Allied nation. Every Allied country had its own Nazi movement, like Oswald Moseley's British Union of Fascists and Fritz Kuhn's German American Bund; and every Axis country had its outstandingly courageous Resistance fighters. As usual, where Jupiter is concerned, nothing is ever quite as simple as it seems.

The 'Arab Spring'

The Jupiter-Uranus triple conjunction of 2010-11 at the end of Pisces and the beginning of Aries coincided with what became known as the 'Arab Spring': a series of anti-government protests, uprisings, and armed rebellions that spread across most of the Middle East. This movement, full of hope and progressive vision at its outset, inadvertently ended up creating a power vacuum that invited the rise of fanatical terrorist groups such as

Al Qaeda and Islamic State, as well as rebellions, religious conflicts, and civil wars in Syria, Yemen, and Lebanon that continue to rumble on with varying degrees of violence. Nature abhors a vacuum, and so do human societies. It remains to be seen what sort of omelette will emerge from all those broken eggs.[68]

Growing awareness of environmental disaster

Another striking dimension of the Jupiter-Uranus conjunction of 2010-11 was a series of natural and human-made disasters: two major earthquakes in Haiti and Chile, the eruption of the volcano Eyjafjallajokull in Iceland, and a disastrous BP oil spill in the Gulf of Mexico, the worst oil spill in US history. These events helped to energise an already growing concern for the fragility of human infrastructures in the face of vast natural forces, and the devastating effects of human carelessness on the natural environment. But Jupiter-Uranus, although often gifted with inspired ideas, isn't a combination inclined to favour moderation or common sense.

The progressive vision emerging in many Western countries to counteract the threat of environmental destruction has begun to tip, in some quarters, into a form of religious fanaticism that may ultimately do more harm than good. Once again we can see the tendency to polarise between 'good' and 'evil' inherent in this planetary combination. Jupiter-Uranus can easily overdose on a Promethean zeal utterly disconnected

---

68 In the six months preceding the conjunction of Jupiter and Uranus in April 2024, the Middle East once again found itself seriously destabilised and on the threshold of a full-blown war, the trigger this time being the terrorist attack on Israel by Iran-backed Hamas on 7 October 2023. In November 2024, seven months after the conjunction, renewed rebellions against the government of the Syrian President Bashar al-Assad, who had been kept in power by Russia and Iran during the earlier fighting under the Jupiter-Uranus conjunction of 2010-2011, resurrected the spirit of the 'Arab Spring'. Western countries currently refer to a new 'axis of evil', a term first used by President George W. Bush in 2002 when Jupiter in Leo was opposing Uranus in Aquarius, to describe the governments of Iraq, Iran, and North Korea. Today's 'axis of evil' is now understood to comprise Iran, North Korea, and Russia, with China sometimes included as well. The outgoing square or first quarter phase of the current cycle will occur in 2027 when Jupiter in Virgo squares Uranus in Gemini, and the opposition or fruition phase will occur in 2031, when Jupiter in Sagittarius opposes Uranus, still in Gemini. The cast of characters keeps changing, but Jupiter-Uranus's tendency to extremism and polarisation appears to remain consistent.

from human reality. Ironically, neither Jupiter nor Uranus was known in myth for any abiding love of the actual Earth and its creatures. It's the *idea* that matters, along with a demand for immediate solutions sometimes divorced from the potential suffering too much urgency can generate.

Earthquakes happen all the time, and so do volcanic eruptions. These kinds of events aren't limited to Jupiter-Uranus, nor are human-engendered environmental disasters. But when the conjunction does coincide with events, we tend to perceive those events in a particular way. They become part of an urgent need for progress that demands drastic remedies for everything we define as wrong or evil in society. We view them through a certain lens, connect the dots, and demand a course of action that's grander and more meaningful than the purely practical challenges of constructing better flood defences, resurfacing the roads, and rebuilding the villages with improved drainage and stabler houses.

Events take on a teleological importance under Jupiter-Uranus; they become meaningful in the context of a bigger picture of a better future that shimmers just over the horizon. Our Promethean spirit gets high on adrenalin, and in problematic situations we begin to perceive inspiring challenges, opportunities for progress, and the possibility of creating a more perfect world. This perception grows and develops as the new cycle moves through its phases and reaches a conflict, a culmination, a period of integration, and finally some kind of resolution before the next cycle begins. We might be able to truly make things better. Equally, we might make them much, much worse through extremism or simple lack of common sense, and that ultimately depends on each of us.

The Jupiter-Neptune cycle

Neptune reflects the human longing for redemption through merging with a source greater than oneself. This longing can take many different forms. It may be expressed through religious or spiritual aspiration; it can reflect the experience of the artist immersed in a creative vision; it could come through an imagined future world in which there's no suffering, loneliness, or separateness; or it might be expressed through a social vision of equality, fellowship, and the levelling of all racial, economic, sexual, and cultural differences through a heartfelt recognition of our shared humanity. These are the classic utopian dreams of Neptune, and they all mirror our yearning to free ourselves of the sense of a separate self with its accompanying pain, struggle, loneliness, and inevitable demise.

Neptune's dreams aren't the same as Uranus' visions of progress. They arise from our feelings rather than our minds. From Neptune's point of view, there can be no redemption as long as we're separate beings trapped in Saturn's bleak world of physical incarnation. The Neptunian longing isn't always immediately recognisable as a mystical longing. It often takes an ideological form. But Neptune's ideologies aren't rooted in rational understanding. They express a need to merge, to lose ourselves, and to relinquish individual autonomy in the yearning to be cleansed, redeemed, and returned to the source.

Jupiter infuses this archetypal Neptunian longing with a striving towards knowledge of the divine as well as immersion in it. Jupiter's perspective requires thoughtful participation; we want understanding as well as experience, although the understanding can be intuitive rather than scientific or pragmatic. This is the Sagittarian dimension of Jupiter. We long to understand the numinous, to make sense of it, to see a cosmic plan rather than simply having blind faith in something we can't see or comprehend. We don't just want to lose ourselves in it. Jupiter is a personal planet, not a collective one. We want to participate in its wisdom and contribute to its unfolding as individuals.

Jupiter's quest for meaning, even if it expresses itself on a purely material level, acquires a mystical flavour when it cohabits with Neptune. Each new Jupiter-Neptune cycle reflects a new vision of humanity's path towards redemption from the isolation and bitter limitations of mortal life. Even if this yearning wears the clothing of a political movement, the mystical longing permeates the ideology. Compassion as well as delusion may be part of that yearning. It lacks the chilly detachment of Jupiter-Uranus; collective suffering matters to Jupiter-Neptune. But individual suffering and individual differences may be as insignificant in Neptune's world as they are in Uranus'. The pain of an individual is unimportant compared to the pain of the larger group with which one identifies.

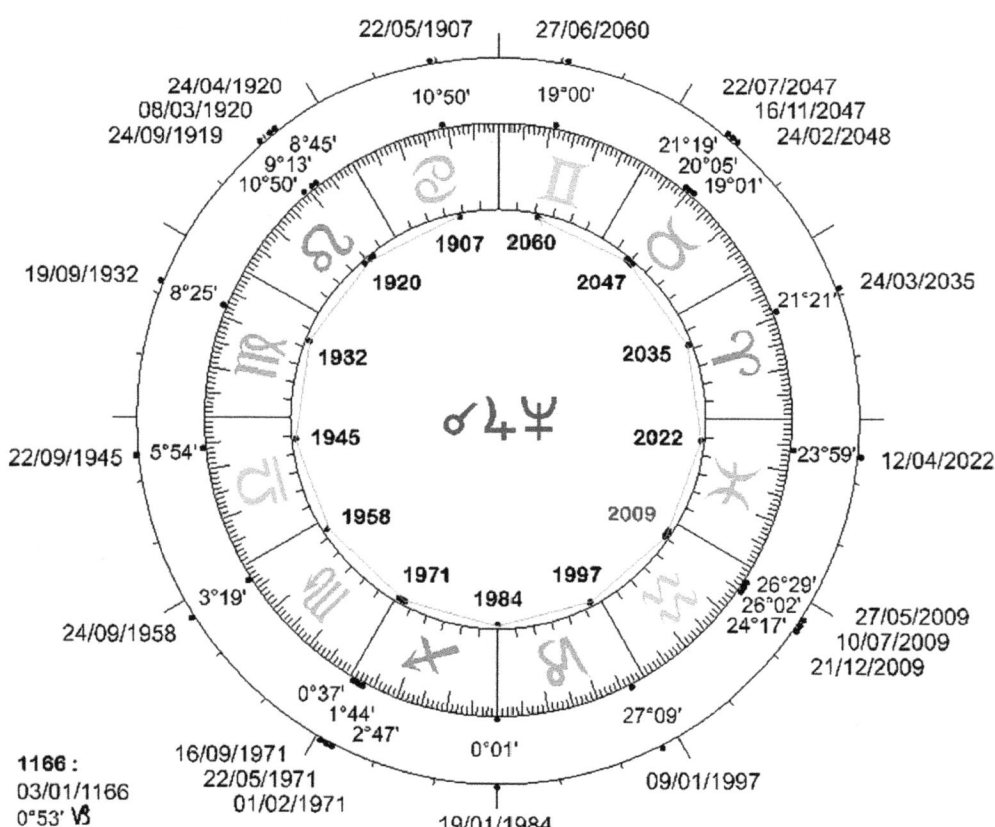

The timing of the cycle

The Jupiter-Neptune cycle takes 12.8 years to complete. The conjunctions form a great cycle of 166 years before they return to the same zodiacal sign, and they follow each sign in sequence. Unlike Jupiter-Saturn's triangles and Jupiter-Uranus' hexagons, the geometric pattern formed by successive Jupiter-Neptune conjunctions is a twelve-sided figure called a dodecagon. The orb of conjunction lasts for two to eight months depending on the retrograde cycle of each planet, and sometimes, as with Jupiter-Saturn and Jupiter-Uranus, a triple conjunction may occur. Each new cycle reflects a new collective dream of the path towards redemption as the fulfilment of a greater plan, coloured by the sign in which the two planets are placed.

Some tidbits of Jupiter-Neptune history

Astrid Fallon's diagram covers Jupiter-Neptune conjunctions from 1907 to 2060. You can see how they follow the zodiacal signs in order. I'd like to look at a couple of these conjunctions in the context of the events of the time.

Peace in our time?

On 22 September 1945, an exact conjunction of Jupiter and Neptune occurred at 5° Libra. The Second World War had officially ended on 2 September 1945, twenty days earlier, when Jupiter was at 1° Libra and already close to the exact conjunction. After the horrors of the war, the collective was understandably swept up in an idealised vision of peace and harmony between nations, and unanimous in its fervent belief that such horrors could and should never happen again. This reflects the idea suggested by Jonathan Haidt that one of you mentioned earlier: the collective urge for a 'post-war consensus'.

Of course these horrors can happen, are already happening, and will happen again in one form or another. But from this conjunction of 1945, dreams emerged that have proven to be enduring if not entirely achievable, including the belief that it might be possible to create political and social structures to ensure that the world can never go to war again on such a scale. Although this has already proven to be an untenable vision, nevertheless

Celebrations at the end of the Second World War, 2 September 1945, with Jupiter at 1° Libra applying to the exact conjunction with Neptune at 5° Libra. Photo, National WWII Museum, New Orleans.

it's unquenchable, and the belief has led to important changes in how we view the obligations of societies and nations to each other.

The emergence of the dream of a united Europe is a direct descendent of this vision, along with a number of groups and organisations whose function is to preserve international peace. The fact that some of these organisations have often been shockingly remiss in implementing the vision, and are sometimes prone to serious corruption, unashamed *hubris*, and flagrant religious and racial bias, doesn't detract from the beauty and elegance of the dream. Perhaps it's fitting that the exact conjunction occurred in Libra.

An element of disillusionment invariably arises when we swim in Neptune's waters because our redemptive dreams can never be matched by reality, even if – and sometimes because – Jupiter's quest for meaning infuses and inflames them. Saturn's world will always intervene and demand a more sober recognition of the complexity of human nature and the inevitability of individual differences and conflicts. This doesn't mean that Jupiter-Neptune's visions are 'false', and sometimes they come tantalisingly close to fulfilment and leave enduring changes in their wake.

But there will never be a perfect match between the vision and the reality, any more than when an artist envisions something and then tries to paint it. The painting never quite matches the inner image; the moment something is incarnated in form, it suffers a kind of forcible amputation, like the unfortunate travellers bound to Procrustes' mythic bed. Neptune can be as much of a tyrannical, ruthless perfectionist as Uranus. The boundless realm of the creative imagination, and the sense of meaning that this imaginal domain can convey, will inevitably collide, sooner or later, with Saturn's limits.

'ET phone home'

In 1971, a triple conjunction of Jupiter and Neptune occurred between 0° and 2° Sagittarius. This conjunction coincided with important advances in space exploration. We might expect this kind of scientific innovation from Jupiter-Uranus conjunctions; the first Moon landing, not surprisingly, occurred on 20 July 1969 under an exact Jupiter-Uranus conjunction at 0° Libra. But the collective motive behind the Jupiter-Neptune space explorations seems to have been different.

Under the 1971 conjunction, NASA's Apollo 14 mission to the Moon, the third successful mission of its kind, was launched on 31 January; the Soviet Union launched the first space station, Salyut 1, into low Earth orbit on 19 April; and the Mariner 9 spacecraft became the first to enter the orbit of another planet – in this case, Mars – on 14 November, having been launched on 30 May when the conjunction was exact. Perhaps the conquest of outer space under this Jupiter-Neptune conjunction in Sagittarius wasn't simply a nationalistic display of superior technology, but was inspired by the vision of a larger humanity united through an experience of touching the transcendent. There's more than a little of the flavour of Steven Spielberg's 1982 film *ET* in Jupiter-Neptune's yearning. Like ET, we long to phone home, and under Jupiter-Neptune conjunctions we may strive to use our scientific knowledge to find the means to achieve it.

Neptune has a special relationship with fashion, glamour, music, and the magical world of film; these spheres of life can vividly express our shifting Neptunian dreams and yearnings in imaginal form. The first *Star Wars* film, *A New Hope*, was released in May 1977 when the opposition of Jupiter in Gemini to Neptune in Sagittarius – the 'full' phase of the cycle that began with the 1971 conjunction – was nearly exact. In November of that year, Spielberg's *Close Encounters of the Third Kind* was released. By then the two planets had moved out of opposition, but production took place while they were within orb.

Films like *Star Wars* and *Close Encounters* belong to Jupiter-Neptune's world, and their appearance at the time of the conjunction mirrors the hidden collective currents behind the remarkable acceleration in space exploration that occurred in 1971. Jupiter-Neptune asks: are we truly alone on Earth? Are there life-forms on other planets, in other solar systems, in other galaxies? If so, are they benign or malignant? Are they wiser than we are? Are they part of a greater divine plan? Can they teach us anything? Uranus might be the 'starry heaven', but Neptune is the encircling cosmic stream of the mythic Okeanos: the boundless, inchoate realm of primal substance, full of endless unformed possibilities, that lies within, beneath, around, and beyond the Earth.

The Jupiter-Pluto cycle

Pluto reflects our instinctual urge to survive at any cost, and the accompanying determination to control or, if necessary, destroy anything that might interfere with that survival, whether internal or external, psychological or physical. The survival instinct is expressed in its most primal form on the biological level, and it exists in every living thing. Due to our hubristic assumption of human superiority, we haven't yet learned enough about other species to know whether they, like humans, struggle to survive on an emotional level. However, it's obvious to anyone who lives with an animal companion and pays attention that our fellow creatures, including dogs, cats, horses, sheep, guinea pigs, rats, monkeys, and parrots, can be extraordinarily intelligent, complex, subtle, highly manipulative, and as determined as humans to gratify their emotional as well as their physical needs.

Pluto's urge may also include intellectual survival – the life-supporting right to think for oneself – as well as the survival of tribes, groups, institutions, collectives, and nations. The notorious possessiveness and need to control associated with Pluto seem to spring from the conviction that a particular person, place, object, or idea is necessary for our survival. Without that source of safety, we might cease to exist. This obsessive determination to remain alive, hardwired into every one of us, lies at the root of Pluto's sometimes ferociously destructive tendencies. Even when expressed in covert ways, it's an 'eat or be eaten' approach to life, and a great deal depends not only on our ethics but also on what we perceive as a threat.

The astronomical Pluto, now demoted to the category of 'dwarf planet', is miniscule compared to Jupiter, the great gas giant. It's a tiny dot when measured against Jupiter's 'Red Spot', the huge storm that's been raging for centuries on the planet's surface. But when it comes to the preservation of life, size, as they say, doesn't matter.

When these planets conjunct, Jupiter infuses Pluto's chthonic survival instinct with a sense of teleology. As a collective – and as individuals, if

we're born under the conjunction or one of the critical phases of the cycle – we become convinced that there's a deeper, higher plan at work which infuses a sense of meaning and purpose into our existence and validates our determination to survive. This can sometimes confer a sense of rightness on any behaviour, however excessive or ruthless, through an 'ends justify means' approach.

Jupiter-Pluto can be immensely creative and courageous because of its refusal to be cowed or beaten. And its determined preservation of life may lead to important scientific and psychological discoveries that can help to make our lives longer, healthier, and more meaningful. For example, the smallpox vaccine, the very first vaccine to be created and the only one effective enough to have entirely eradicated a disease, was discovered by Dr. Edward Jenner in May 1796, just two months after an exact Jupiter-Pluto conjunction at 28° Aquarius and while the two planets were still within orb.

Jupiter-Pluto's relentless determination is fuelled by the belief in an ultimate purpose or meaning. But this kind of teleological approach to survival can also provide justification for the most appalling collective behaviour. Our group, tribe, community, or nation is 'meant' to survive, regardless of the cost to others. It's divinely ordained, even against terrible odds, and if that means the total control or elimination of whatever we perceive as a threat to our continuing existence, well, it's all part of a greater plan. Each new Jupiter-Pluto cycle is expressed in the collective through a new determination to root out anything that might threaten the survival of our divinely ordained needs, coloured by the sign in which the conjunction occurs.

The timing of the cycle

The Jupiter-Pluto cycle takes 12.5 years from one conjunction to the next, and the orb of conjunction lasts between two and eight months. A great cycle occurs every 237 to 249 years. Like the conjunctions of Jupiter and Neptune, those of Jupiter and Pluto occur in sequence through the zodiac signs. But because of Pluto's elliptical orbit, over the period of a great cycle more conjunctions tend to occur in Aries, Taurus, and Gemini, which Pluto takes longer to transit, while fewer conjunctions occur in Libra, Scorpio, and Sagittarius, which Pluto moves through more quickly.

Pluto spends only eighteen years in Scorpio, but it languishes in Taurus for thirty years. While it's plodding doggedly through the sign of the Bull,

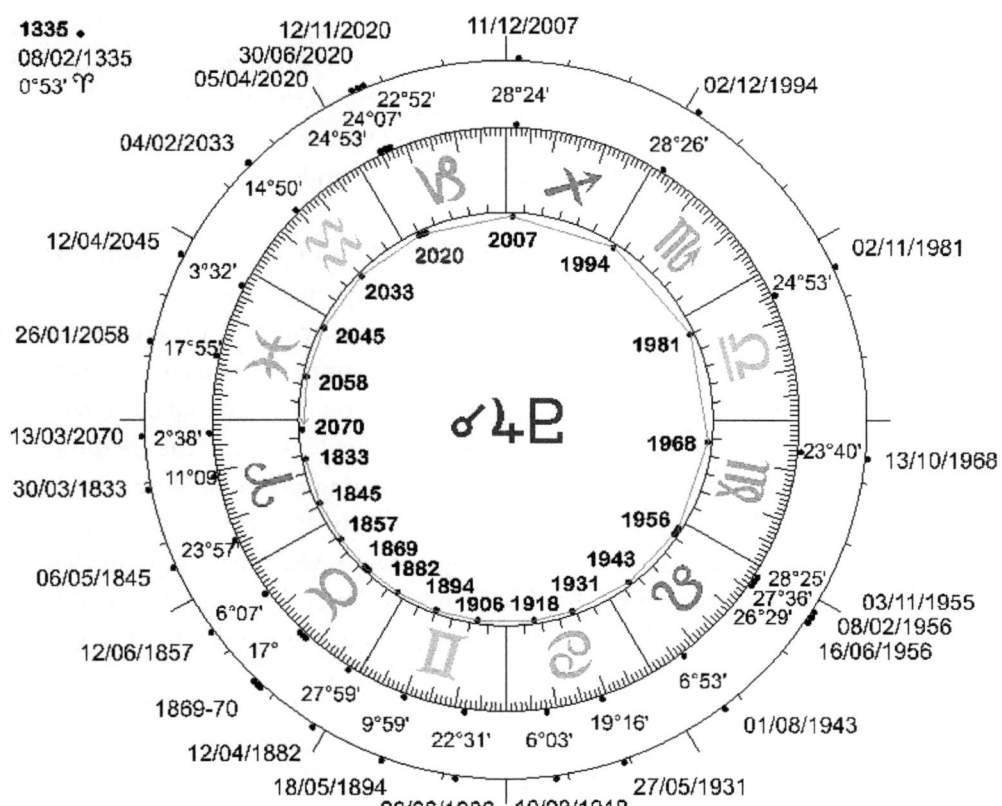

Jupiter will return for a close encounter every twelve years. This can mean quite a few clandestine meetings. You can see in Astrid Fallon's diagram, which covers Jupiter-Pluto conjunctions from 1833 to 2070, that the last time Pluto transited Taurus during the second half of the 19th century, Jupiter conjuncted it five times: once in 1857, three times between 1869 and 1870, and once in 1882. In contrast, the last time Pluto was in Scorpio, Jupiter only conjuncted it once, in 1994. But frequency, like size, apparently doesn't matter to Jupiter-Pluto. No doubt, from Jupiter's perspective, there's a deeper meaning in this apparent inequality of conjunction frequencies. But I have absolutely no idea what that meaning might be.

Some tidbits of Jupiter-Pluto history

When two outer planets conjunct, they can take a very long time doing it, and Jupiter may at some point catch up and conjunct them both within the same time frame. This was the case in 1894. Neptune and Pluto were within orb of conjunction in Gemini for roughly ten years; the conjunction was exact three times during 1891 and 1892, at 8° Gemini on 2 August 1891, 8° Gemini on 6 November 1891, and 7° Gemini on 30 April 1892, but was still within close orb in 1894. In that year Jupiter arrived at the party, conjuncting Pluto first at 9° Gemini in mid-May and then Neptune at 13° Gemini on 1 June.

Outer planet conjunctions reflect the beginning of vast shifts in the collective psyche, and their cycles can take up to five centuries to complete. Social and political upheavals often coincide with the time of the conjunction, like the marches, riots, and immense social changes coincident with the Uranus-Pluto triple conjunction in Virgo that occurred in the mid-1960s, or the final collapse of the Soviet Union and the creation of the European Single Market under the triple conjunction of Uranus and Neptune in Capricorn in the late 1980s and early 1990s. But the deeper significance of these outer planet pairings never reveals itself fully in the course of any single human lifetime. And how they unfold in the world during the cycle depends on human choices as much as the meaning of the planets themselves.

Jupiter, Neptune, and Pluto throw a party together

Jupiter, Neptune, and Pluto coming together in 1894 fused Pluto's obsessive determination to survive with Neptune's longing for redemption and Jupiter's quest for a meaningful pattern in life, all expressed through the lens of a sign concerned with knowledge, education, and communication. It seems that this conjunction of the mythic Jupiter with his two brothers presided not only over blatantly Geminian events, like the patent for the first motion picture film and the installation of the first battery-operated telephone switchboard, but also over an entire era in which collective ideas about the nature of science, religion, politics, class, marriage, and sexuality were being overturned and transformed. We're only in the outgoing sextile phase of that Neptune-Pluto cycle at the moment, and we still can't see what it might ultimately mean for human society and human development.

Jupiter-Pluto conjunctions are sometimes associated with major shifts in financial markets. The mythic Pluto presides over the riches of the earth; I mentioned earlier that his name is derived from the Greek *plouton*, meaning 'wealth'. But Pluto, as we all know, isn't always a pleasant, polite deity. Death-gods rarely are. Often a way of life, rather than life itself, must come to a permanent end to make way for something entirely new.

Plagues and pandemics

A triple conjunction of Jupiter and Pluto occurred from 22° to 24° Capricorn between 5 April and 12 November 2020, and this conjunction coincided with both planets conjuncting Saturn, which was also transiting through Capricorn. Although the Jupiter-Saturn conjunction wasn't exact until December 2020 and occurred in the first degree of Aquarius, the three planets were within orb of conjunction in Capricorn for virtually the whole of 2020. The entire period coincides with the first wave of the Covid-19 pandemic and the extreme responses to it, with all their physiological, psychological, and economic consequences.

Saturn's need to protect and strengthen vulnerable defences and structures, combined with Pluto's compulsive survival instinct, were infused by Jupiter with a quest for meaning and a determination to find answers in the face of a global threat in which many people were, and still are, dying because of a constantly mutating disease that no one, even now, fully understands. We began asking Jupiterian questions at the outset and we're still asking them, although the answers aren't always forthcoming.

We're asking questions such as "Why did this happen? Is it the fault of humans, animals, the malignance of fate, nature's way of thinning the population, deliberate biological warfare, an accidental spill in a laboratory, or just bad luck? Can we find a permanently effective vaccine, like we did with smallpox? How much toilet paper should we stockpile? Why have so many young people died of it, and others with only mild symptoms inexplicably suffered for years from 'long Covid'? Is there an environmental component? A genetic one? Are pandemics such as Covid due to the *hubris* we display towards the natural environment? Could we be better prepared in the future?" Despite the absolute certainty invariably exhibited by those given over to extremes of thinking, we still have no real answers to these questions.

This combination of Jupiter-Saturn and Jupiter-Pluto doesn't, of course, literally indicate a pandemic, nor does Jupiter-Pluto on its own. Outbreaks of disease can occur under any planetary combination, or none at all. The Spanish flu pandemic, which killed an estimated 50 million people globally, first erupted in February 1918 when there were no conjunctions or hard aspects between any of the outer planets, and no strong aspects between any of them and Jupiter. Saturn made an exact conjunction with Neptune in Leo on 1 August 1917, and this conjunction, although the orb was wide and separating, coincided with the first appearance of the flu in the following year. And by September of that year, Chiron transiting through Aries had moved into square with Pluto in Cancer. But it isn't helpful to assume that such aspects 'cause' or even 'signify' a pandemic.

The first outbreak of bubonic plague – fondly known as the Black Death – killed the same number of people as the Spanish flu, roughly a third of the world's population at the time, and occurred between 1347 and 1351. A conjunction of Uranus and Pluto was exact in Aries between 1343 and 1344, and it was still within wide orb at the time of the outbreak of the plague. These kinds of aspects occur cyclically throughout history, and with hindsight we can always find some relevant event within the time frame. But we seem to be unable to pin down the precise nature of the events occurring at the time, and we certainly can't assume the outbreak of disease.

Transits reflect changes in the collective psyche, and sometimes these changes are synchronous with external events. What seems to be described with precision is our perceptions of and responses to such events, rather than the events themselves. Like the images in a dream, inner and outer may mirror each other in symbolic if not literal ways. What happens to us as a collective is also what we're becoming and where we've arrived at a particular moment in time. The Jupiter-Saturn-Pluto conjunction in Capricorn in 2020 could teach us a great deal about why we responded to Covid as we did and what kind of consequences might ensue, rather than heralding the pandemic itself. It's a great pity those who govern us consistently fail to avail themselves of such insights.

The Jupiter-Chiron cycle

Chiron reflects our urge to heal, transform, or, if we find we still can't cope, simply disconnect from feelings of being irrevocably wounded, damaged, and victimised by life, people, society, or fate. Jupiter infuses this experience of something that we desperately wish to 'fix' with the urgent need to discover a meaning and a purpose in our suffering. Even if we know and accept that 'fixing' might not really be an option, we may still have a powerful sense that the experience of wounding has an ultimate teleology and can lead to something greater, for others if not for ourselves. When Jupiter enters Chiron's world, we strive to understand why painful, unfair things happen to us, and what we can learn from them.

If this urge for connection with a deeper meaning behind our pain fails to achieve its goal – perhaps because we don't trust any 'evidence' other than our senses and our rational intellect – Chiron's rage and bitterness may be inflamed by Jupiter's determination to experience the sense of a deeper meaning in life. That can result in identification with the archetypal victim and an accompanying desire for revenge on those we blame for our suffering. The darkest dimensions of both Jupiter and Chiron can begin to poison our faith in life and, consequently, our treatment of ourselves and others.

In our first seminar on Jupiter, we looked at the chart of Adolf Hitler, who had a Moon-Jupiter conjunction in Capricorn opposite Chiron in Cancer. This is a chilling example of a natal Jupiter-Chiron aspect gone badly wrong. Equally, the best of both planets may emerge, and the conviction that suffering has meaning and purpose may generate a powerful desire to heal. Jung, like Hitler, had a natal Jupiter-Chiron opposition, but the way he expressed the aspect was rather different. Pope John XXIII, the 'good Pope' who displayed a genuine tolerance and spiritual inclusivity unseen in any previous or subsequent Pope, had an exact Jupiter-Chiron conjunction in Taurus, which also conjoined both Pluto and Neptune. Jupiter-Chiron conjunctions often reflect a time when the extremes of the conjunction are visible on a collective level and in the individuals born under the conjunction.

The timing of the cycle

Chiron, like Pluto, has an elliptical orbit, so it spends longer in some signs than in others. But Chiron moves much more quickly through the zodiac than Pluto, taking a mere fifty years compared to Pluto's 248-year cycle. As a result, Jupiter-Chiron cycles are irregular, making it difficult to create a diagram demonstrating any kind of orderly geometric pattern. Although Astrid Fallon included a graphic presentation of the Chiron cycle in her book, she didn't provide one for the Jupiter-Chiron cycle. Perhaps by now someone has constructed a diagram that offers a visual image of the cycle. But so far I haven't been able to find one online, and I don't have the technical expertise to create one myself. So you'll have to just visualise it yourselves.

The conjunctions of Jupiter and Chiron occur anywhere between 13 and 20 years apart. They're more frequent in Pisces and Aries because Chiron spends longer in these two signs than in the others, so Jupiter can catch up for a second or even a third meeting. There are fewer conjunctions in Virgo and Libra, the signs through which Chiron moves most quickly. Jupiter-Chiron conjunctions don't follow the zodiac signs in a sequential way, unlike Jupiter's cycles with Saturn, Uranus, Neptune, and Pluto, and they can avoid some signs for centuries. No conjunction between them has occurred in Virgo for over two hundred years.

To give you some idea of the irregular nature of the cycle, let's look at some dates. In 1821 the two planets were conjunct in Aries, and in 1834, thirteen years later, they conjoined at 29° 34' Taurus. In 1853-54, fifteen years later, a triple conjunction occurred between 18° and 20° Capricorn. In 1868, a conjunction occurred at 27° 34' Pisces. In 1881, Thirteen years later, a conjunction occurred in Taurus. That one was aligned with Neptune, which was also transiting through Taurus. Between 1899 and 1901, eighteen to nineteen years later, a triple conjunction occurred from 29° Sagittarius to 0° Capricorn; this conjunction was exact at 0° Capricorn in January 1901. In 1915, fourteen years later, in the midst of the First World War, another conjunction occurred in Pisces, the first in this sign since

1868: an interval of forty-seven years. The Jupiter-Chiron cycle is nothing if not erratic.

Some tidbits of Jupiter-Chiron history

Let's look at some examples of the kind of events and human responses that seem to reflect Jupiter-Chiron conjunctions.

The stock market crash of 1929

On 17 August 1928, an exact Jupiter-Chiron conjunction occurred at 10° 10' Taurus, the first in that sign since 1881 after a gap of forty-seven years. Although by May of the following year Jupiter and Chiron were well out of orb of conjunction and by June Jupiter had moved into Gemini, the meeting of the two planets seems to have been a herald of the Stock Market Crash which began in September 1929. The fact that the conjunction occurred in Taurus, a sign concerned with material stability and security, seems disturbingly appropriate. But the conjunction took place a full year before the crash and not only didn't 'cause' it in any literal sense; it didn't seem to coincide with it either. But that meeting of Jupiter and Chiron seems to have reflected collective perceptions and, most importantly, collective actions made before the Crash that led directly to it. It's an uncomfortable illustration of the way in which planetary configurations reflect attitudes, attitudes provoke choices, and choices result in consequences.

The most important 'before' factor, while Chiron was moving through Taurus and Jupiter came to meet it in the autumn of 1928, was the rapidly growing conviction among the American public that even a very poor person could miraculously become wealthy. Hundreds of thousands of Americans invested heavily in the stock market, often borrowing money to do it. Over $8.5 billion was out on loan, more than the entire amount of money circulating in the country at the time. Healing of the wounds of financial hardship seemed to be at hand with only a very small financial commitment. Anyone could buy shares; speculation wasn't limited to rich people; markets would continue to rise and the economy would continue to boom; and everyone could leave poverty and suffering behind them and find their lives transformed. Albert H. Wiggin, the president of the Chase Manhattan Bank, commented at the time of the crash:

We are reaping the natural fruit of the orgy of speculation in which millions of people have indulged. It was inevitable, because of the tremendous increase in the number of stockholders…that the number of sellers would be greater than ever when the boom ended and selling took the place of buying.[69]

Hindsight comes easily, but foresight is harder to acquire. The Jupiterian promise of the rewards of financial gambling, combined with Chiron's dream of healing the wounds of generations of hardship and poverty, fuelled an overheated economy and was one of the chief causes of the economic crash. Chiron is linked with the wounds of bitterly disappointed ideals and expectations; the greater the expectations, the more painful the disillusionment. There is a subtle but clear connection between how we perceive things as individuals, the choices we make based on those perceptions, and the events that happen on a collective level as both the product and the reflection of those perceptions and choices.

The aftermath of war

Seventeen years after the 1928 conjunction in Taurus, an exact conjunction of Jupiter and Chiron occurred at 11° Libra in October 1945. The conjunction had been applying during the summer of that year and remained within orb until October 1946, and it also conjuncted Neptune. Earlier we looked at the Jupiter-Neptune conjunction of 1945 in relation to the ending

---

69 Albert H. Wiggin, 'Second Crash', published in the *Sydney Morning Herald*, Sydney, Australia, 30 October 1929, p. 17.

of the Second World War. The addition of Chiron to the mix seems to have reflected not only the profound redemptive yearning for peace and the poignant belief in a hopeful future that emerged at the end of the war, but also a horrific dawning realisation of the appalling damage and destruction that had been wrought on so many levels. Throughout 1945, one concentration camp after another was liberated in Germany, Austria, and Poland, and under this Jupiter-Chiron-Neptune conjunction, the full scale of the Nazi horrors which the Allied troops discovered finally came to the attention of a shocked global public.

A Soviet soldier walking through a mound of victims' shoes piled outside a warehouse at the concentration camp at Majdanek, Poland. Photo, Archiwum Akt Nowich.

Healing collective wounds

In 2009, a triple Jupiter-Chiron conjunction occurred between 22° and 26° Aquarius, exact on 23 May, 22 July, and 7 December of that year. Jupiter and Chiron also conjuncted Neptune, as they had at the end of the Second World War. This alignment of Jupiter with Chiron and Neptune happened to conjunct the Moon at 27° Aquarius in the US natal chart, coinciding with the inauguration of Barack Obama to the office of President of the United States in January 2009: the first person of colour ever to be elected President.

It's interesting to explore how a conjunction of Jupiter with a slower-moving planet might affect the natal chart of a nation directly involved in the collective changes reflected by the conjunction – always assuming it's possible to obtain such a national chart, which it often isn't. This kind of exploration can give us a glimpse of the ways in which Jupiter's cycles fertilise the development not only of individuals, but also of a particular collective entity at a particular time in history.

In Barack Obama's chart, the Moon's nodal axis is at 27° Leo-Aquarius, aligned exactly with the US natal Moon, so his nodal axis was also triggered by the Jupiter-Chiron-Neptune conjunction. For many people, with or without astrological knowledge, it was difficult to avoid the conclusion that some deeper plan or higher destiny was at work. It seemed that the long and painful history of racism in America might finally be on the brink of some kind of healing, and feelings of great hope for the future accompanied the time of this conjunction. In some ways that hope might be seen as genuinely inching towards fulfilment. In other ways, since that conjunction in Aquarius, the collective wound has become even more bitter as politics become more divisive, ideological perspectives have solidified and become rigid doctrines, and the collective hunger for scapegoats has sought an ever-widening range of targets.

The next Jupiter-Chiron conjunction occurred between 2022 and 2023 and was exact at 14° Aries on 12 March 2023. This was a single conjunction which wasn't aligned with any other slow-moving planets except for a semisextile to Uranus in Taurus. But that didn't seem to diminish its importance. Queen Elizabeth II died on 8 September 2022 while Jupiter was beginning to apply to the exact conjunction, and her eldest son took the throne as King Charles III. His official coronation was celebrated on 6 May 2023, while Jupiter at 27° Aries was still within a 10° orb of Chiron at 17° Aries. The collective feeling in Britain and elsewhere in the world was a mixture of grief, mourning, hope for the new reign, and the sense of an entire era coming to an end, accompanied by an intimation of imminent and immense cultural change that didn't necessarily bode well and was welcomed by some but not others.

On 7 October 2023, after Jupiter had moved out of Aries into Taurus, Hamas terrorists, breaking a ceasefire agreement that had been in place since 2021, attacked Israel, torturing, raping, and murdering 1200 people including young children and the elderly, and abducting another 250, many of whom were subsequently tortured and killed in the Hamas tunnels. Although the event didn't occur under the Jupiter-Chiron conjunction in Aries, the attack had been meticulously planned a long time before the event took place, and its final preparations must have been put in place under the conjunction.

This event, followed by Israel's inevitable retaliation and the fiercely divided responses of the international community, have led to the threat of a full-blown Middle Eastern war and a huge rise in antisemitic attacks, anti-Israeli propaganda, and divisive sectarian politics in virtually every Western country, helped along by the ideological extremes of the Jupiter-Uranus conjunction in April 2024. A pervasive sense of depression, impotence, rage, and hopelessness, exacerbated by the ongoing war in Ukraine, increasing violence in the Middle East, galloping inflation, pressures from mass migration, and acrimonious political polarisation everywhere, has undermined collective optimism since that conjunction in Aries, with the spirit of grievance and resentment triumphing over hope, and an absence of any sense of an underlying meaning emerging – yet. The outgoing square of this Jupiter-Chiron cycle, a triple conjunction exact in October and December 2025 with Jupiter at 22-24° Cancer and Chiron at 22-24° Aries and again in July 2026 with Jupiter at 0° Leo and Chiron at 0° Taurus, demonstrates the characteristic pattern of a struggle to manifest the meaning of the conjunction in the world.

Jupiter-Chiron conjunctions can sometimes show humanity's best face, but sometimes they also coincide with a display of some of the least attractive human attributes. And they aren't always literal or obvious in their expression. Their time frame can encompass the emergence of attitudes and choices that result in events which occur quite a long time after the period of the conjunction has passed. The Stock Market Crash of 1929 following the conjunction of 1928 in Taurus is an example of this kind of delayed unfoldment of concrete events. Equally often, specific events emerge at the time of the conjunction that seem to embody its meaning, such as Obama's election to the US Presidency in 2009 when the two planets, along with Neptune, conjuncted in Aquarius.

Jupiter-Chiron conjunctions may reflect the upsurge of a particular aspiration to salvage or heal or, in their more unpleasant forms, a pervasive sense of, and even an active pursuit of, unfair wounding and oppression. The repercussions may be initially invisible but ultimately profound. We get a glimpse of both the potential for compassion and healing and the potential for human rage, spite, and cruelty under Jupiter-Chiron conjunctions, and it's up to us whether we can find meaning and creative possibilities through our realisations, or whether we steep ourselves in hatred and make things a great deal worse.

Individuals born under Jupiter conjunctions with slower-moving planets

Individuals born under a Jupiter conjunction with Saturn, Chiron, Uranus, Neptune, or Pluto embody the qualities of the conjunction under which they were born. This also applies to those born under the subsequent phases of a particular Jupiter cycle, especially the major aspects: sextile, square, trine, and opposition. Although trines and sextiles seem to reflect less tension and intensity, the individual with these 'easy' aspects in the birth chart is no less a part of the unfolding pattern of the cycle. We contain not only our own history, but the history of the world at the moment of our birth, as well as the future as it unfolds through the phases of these cycles.

Example 7: H. P. Blavatsky
and the Jupiter-Uranus conjunction of 1831

A good example of someone born under a Jupiter-Uranus conjunction who expressed the conjunction in obvious ways is Helena Petrovna Blavatsky, who created the Theosophical Society in 1875. Blavatsky's extensive legacy of written works merges ideas from Hindu philosophy with many of the tenets of late antique Neoplatonism, spiced with bits and pieces from disparate sources including the Kabbalah and ancient and medieval ceremonial magic, all filtered through her highly individual interpretation of 'progress'.

Blavatsky rejected the tenets of Christianity, and her Russian Orthodox upbringing was thrown on the bonfire with all the rest. But unconsciously it seems she remained deeply influenced by its doctrines. Her work focuses on the spiritual evolution not only of the human race but of the entire cosmos. The operative word here, in keeping with the spirit of the Jupiter-Uranus conjunction in Aquarius under which she was born, is *evolution*. *The Secret Doctrine* and *Isis Unveiled* present a progressive spiritual vision clothed in the garb of the scientific language of Victorian England. The goals of the Theosophical Society are explicitly aimed at the potential fusion of science and religion as an essential step in the story of human progress.

Blavatsky's ideas have inspired and influenced many so-called 'New Age' currents. Some of these ideas, like her Christianised interpretation of karma and reincarnation, still have great agency and attractiveness to many people involved in contemporary spiritualities because they combine a Uranian vision of social progress with Jupiter's quest for meaning.

In Helena Blavatsky's chart, Uranus is at 12° Aquarius conjunct Jupiter at 17° Aquarius, both placed in the 8th house. This separating

Helena Petrovna Blavatsky in 1877. Photographer unknown; Blavatsky Archives.

conjunction, exact five months before her birth, aligns with the Moon's nodal axis at 21° Leo-Aquarius, opposes the Sun at 18° Leo, and squares Chiron at 16° Taurus. Each of us is a paradigm of the values and responses of our generation group, reflected in the outer planet placements and configurations at the time of our birth. Blavatsky was no exception.

Her ideas present an individual interpretation of a much greater collective shift in ideas that began at the time of the conjunction, and for which, in mid-life, she provided a mouthpiece. But the ideas that emerge under Jupiter-Uranus conjunctions aren't limited to the particular cycle in which they begin. In true Jupiterian fashion they can reflect a fertilisation that unfolds over many Jupiter-Uranus cycles, with critical moments occurring not only under the conjunctions but also under other important phases of the cycle, especially the squares, trines, and oppositions.

Jupiter-Uranus conjunctions occur every 13.8 years. The next conjunction of the two planets after Blavatsky's birth was exact at 3° Aries in February 1845, conjunct her natal Pluto in the 10th house and opposing a Venus-Moon conjunction in Libra in the 4th. Not much is known of

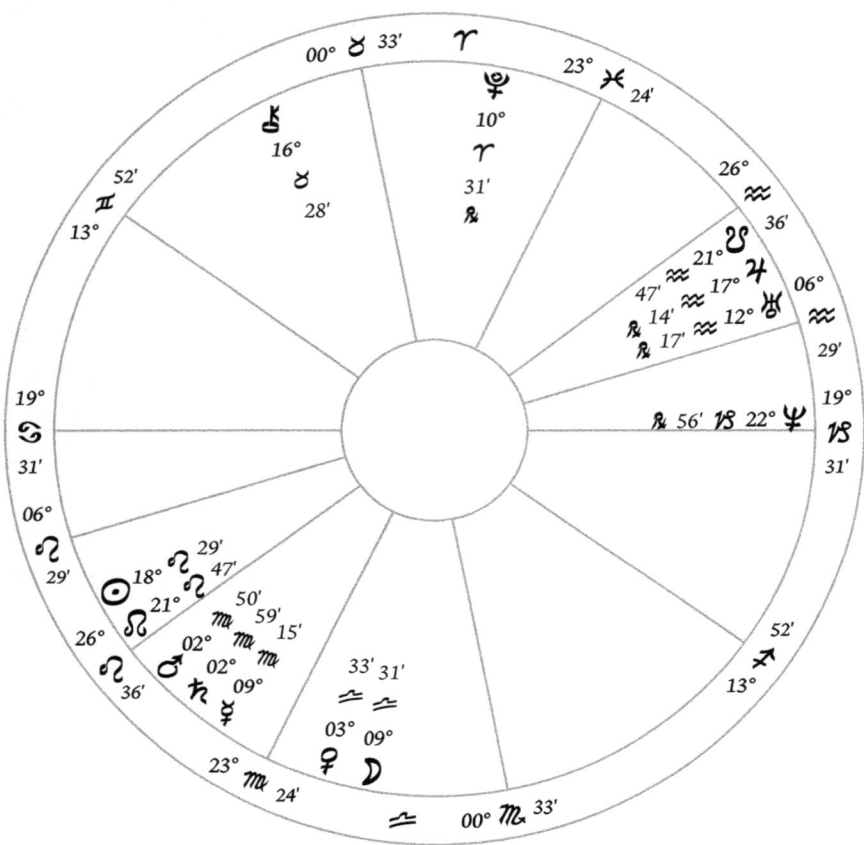

H. P. Blavatsky
12 August 1831, 2.17 am, Ekaterinoslav, Ukraine

her life at this time, although it seems she travelled extensively with her aristocratic family. In June 1848, after Jupiter had moved into Cancer and formed its outgoing square to Uranus, still in Aries, she married Nikifor Blavatsky. But she left him a few months later.

Then, in 1849, as Jupiter moved into Leo and made its outgoing trine to Uranus, she embarked on a series of journeys alone, culminating in a trip to India. Here she claimed she met a group of spiritual adepts – the 'Masters of the Ancient Wisdom' – who sent her to Tibet, where she received her first real training in the synthesis of religion, philosophy, and science. Like Jung's 8th-house Jupiter, Blavatsky's 8th-house Jupiter seems to have opened doors to the realm of the nonrational. But while Jung experienced his Jupiter as an inner journey to the depths of the psyche, Blavatsky experienced hers as a vertical ascent to higher spiritual planes. Both, with natal Jupiter in an air sign, were impelled to formulate their experiences as a system of ideas.

The third conjunction of Jupiter and Uranus after Helena Blavatsky's birth was exact in May 1858 at 29° Taurus. Under this conjunction she returned to Russia to visit her family and seek a divorce from her husband. The divorce never materialised. The fourth conjunction of Jupiter and Uranus occurred at 28° Cancer in June 1872, three years before the founding of the Theosophical Society, her most significant progeny.

This conjunction, which opposed her natal Neptune at 22° Capricorn, coincided with her first vision of a global organisation that could disseminate her ideas. According to her own narrative, she was living in Philadelphia at the time and became ill with a seriously infected leg. While in a state of feverish delirium she experienced a 'spiritual transformation' and conceived the idea of the Theosophical Society. Although it might not always be wise to accept Blavatsky's biographical statements as incontestable facts, the timing is entirely appropriate. Apparently the previous conjunctions were quietly laying groundwork, and the real fertilisation of her natal Jupiter-Uranus conjunction occurred under this conjunction in Capricorn. After a three-year pregnancy, the Theosophical Society was born. In the natal chart of the Society, which we'll look at in a moment, Jupiter is at 14° Scorpio, forming its outgoing square – the phase of struggling to manifest what was conceived at the time of the conjunction – to Uranus at 19° Leo.

This outgoing square of Jupiter to Uranus triggered Blavatsky's own natal Jupiter-Uranus conjunction. Transiting Jupiter squared it and transiting Uranus opposed it. If we're born under a configuration such as Jupiter-Uranus, each new cycle of the dyad will usually prove significant in the unfolding of the story, even if the two planets in the new cycle aren't directly aspecting natal planets. In Blavatsky's case, they did directly constellate the natal conjunction. What came to fruition in Blavatsky's life at the time of her Uranus half-return also came into manifestation as a new idea expressing an intensely individual interpretation of a collective vision of progress first seeded at the time of her birth.

The Theosophical Society

This is the seal of the Theosophical Society. Its creator is unknown, although Blavatsky would have had a major input – if she didn't create it herself – and given it her stamp of approval.

The seal incorporates a variety of religious and esoteric symbols meant to reflect the Society's idea of spiritual synthesis. The ankh is an ancient Egyptian hieroglyph signifying life. The Star of David is both a Jewish symbol representing the connection between God, Israel, and the Torah, and an ancient magical symbol of wholeness reflecting the interweaving of 'above' and 'below'. The swastika, drawn in the opposite direction to the Nazi emblem, is an ancient solar symbol found on Mesopotamian coinage and in Sanskrit texts; it signifies well-being and good fortune. The Aum, or Om, is one of the most important Hindu symbols, representing ultimate reality. The ouroboros belongs to the Greco-Egyptian magical tradition of late antiquity and was especially important in alchemy; it symbolises eternal cyclic renewal. Christian references seem to be missing. Although the Society claimed to be inclusive in terms of religion, Blavatsky not only railed against Christianity but frequently indulged in overtly antisemitic outbursts, as did many of her followers. It seems vociferous inclusivity can sometimes display its own form of exclusiveness.

The natal chart for the Theosophical Society contains not only that outgoing square of Jupiter in Scorpio to Uranus in Leo following their conjunction in Cancer in 1872, but also an incoming square of Jupiter to Saturn in Aquarius and an applying opposition of Jupiter to Pluto in Taurus. Jupiter, Saturn, Uranus, and Pluto, along with Mars, form a grand fixed cross, echoing and constellating the fixed T-cross in Helena Blavatsky's own birth chart.

Jupiter in the Society's chart is a lively participant in a major outer planet configuration: the outgoing square of Uranus in Leo to Pluto in Taurus, following a triple Uranus-Pluto conjunction at 28-29° Aries between 1850 and 1851. Uranus-Pluto conjunctions are irregular in their frequency and occur between 113 and 141 years apart, and they seem to be signatures of a new cycle of major social and scientific innovation, upheaval, and change.

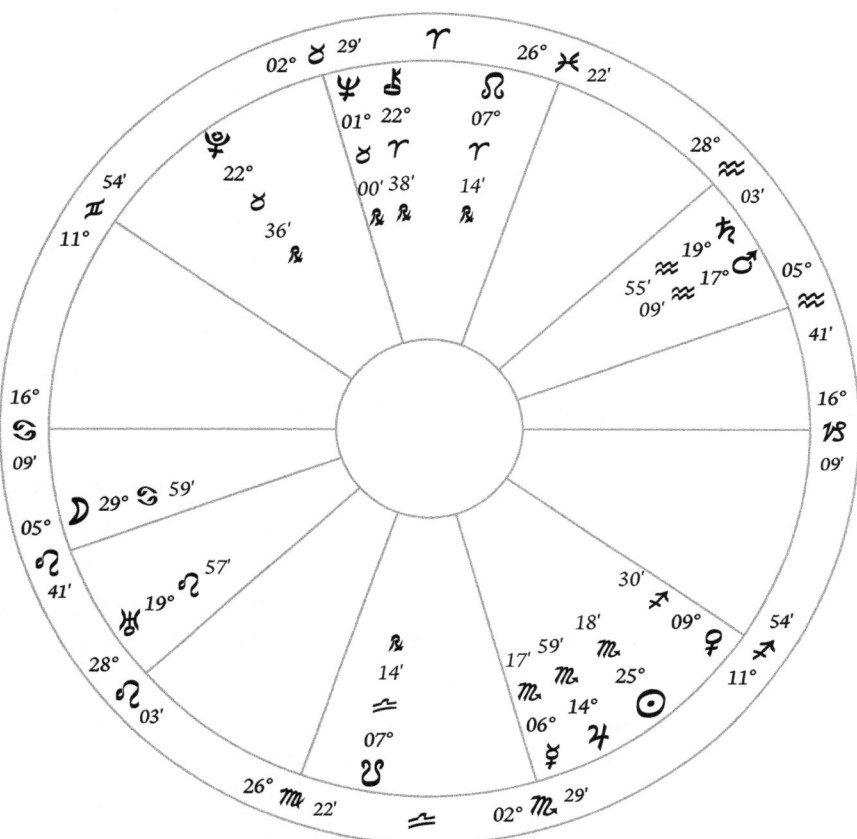

Theosophical Society
17 November 1875, 8.00 pm, New York

Apart from the usual wars and revolutions erupting in various parts of the world, which don't require a Uranus-Pluto conjunction to provide justification, the UK's Great Exhibition of 1851, which offered a showcase of 'the Works of Industry of All Nations' and heralded the golden age of Victorian industrial and social innovation, is an apt symbol.

The darker side of that Uranus-Pluto conjunction in Aries was mirrored in the Great Famine in Ireland, which lasted from 1845 to 1852. The worst year was 1847, when Uranus and Pluto had been within orb of conjunction for over a year and Jupiter, transiting through Cancer, formed outgoing squares to them both. A million people died during the Famine and a million more emigrated to other countries, resulting in major changes in Irish society and radically altering the future history of the British Isles as well as that of the US. Under the conjunction, Patrick Kennedy, John F. Kennedy's great-grandfather, escaped the Famine by sailing from Ireland with his wife Bridget Murphy in 1849, founding his dynasty in Boston.

Jupiter-Uranus and the Victorian era

Queen Victoria's reign lasted from 1837 to 1901, a period of 64 years, although the Victorian 'era' isn't definable with quite such precision. Many of the new ideas associated with the time, such as those that inspired the Arts and Crafts Movement, are still alive and well in the 21st century, and many progressive social and religious currents identifiable as 'Victorian' had begun to form before Victoria took the throne.

Jupiter-Uranus ideas of meaningful progress were also bursting out elsewhere in the world under the successive conjunctions of this era. Freud, who was born in 1856, produced two of his most important and influential works – *The Interpretation of Dreams* and *The Psychopathology of Everyday Life* – just before and during a Jupiter-Uranus conjunction at 10° Sagittarius in 1900, a year before Victoria's death. And in May 1907, when Jupiter opposed Uranus from 12° Cancer to 12° Capricorn – the 'full' phase of that same cycle – Jung met Freud in Vienna for the first time and went home to found the first psychoanalytic group in Zürich, the foundation stone of what eventually became 'analytical psychology', his own approach to the human psyche. Neither Freud nor Jung was born with a natal aspect between Jupiter and Uranus. But both had the Sun in strong aspect to an outer planet – in Freud's case, Sun conjunct Uranus, and in Jung's, Sun square Neptune – and it seems they were receptive to, and willing to serve as mouthpieces for, the emerging collective currents of their time.

Several Jupiter-Uranus conjunctions occurred just before, during, and immediately after the Victorian era, the first being the conjunction in Aquarius at the time of Blavatsky's birth, six years before Victoria began her reign. Other important planetary configurations, particularly the Uranus-Pluto conjunction which was within 10° orb of conjunction between 1847 and 1854, and the Neptune-Pluto conjunction in Gemini, exact in 1891-92, reflected a deeper, slower, and longer-lasting impetus for major collective change, providing a backdrop for the Jupiter-Uranus cycles. Jupiter-Uranus isn't the only show in town, and its cycles need to be viewed together with that underlying drumbeat of the slower-moving outer

wealth isn't only a means for him to achieve worldly goals and satisfaction. It's also a necessity for his own survival and, in his eyes, the survival of the society in which he lives. In contrast, his involvement in philanthropic ventures, his willingness to 'seed' the potentials of individuals and companies, and his inclination to gamble on high stakes, reflect the Jupiterian half of the conjunction. Although he isn't a flamboyant personality in the way many people with Jupiter in Leo are, his career is a means of creative self-expression and a way of affirming his sense of con-

nection with a greater purpose in life. Gates is a Catholic who claims his religious morality is the inspiration for his charity work. Whatever your views on him might be, Gates has exercised a massive influence on our modern, technologically driven world.

On 4 April 1975, when Jupiter was at 4° Aries opposing Pluto at 7° Libra, Gates, who was nineteen years old at the time, founded Microsoft with his childhood friend Paul Allen. We all know how that gamble worked out. This opposition was the 'full' phase of a conjunction of Jupiter and Pluto at 23° Virgo that was exact in October 1968, when Gates was 13 years old, and continued within orb through the first half of 1969. This conjunction

Bill Gates at a European Union Commission conference in 2023. Photo: Lukasz Kobus for the EU Commission.

in Virgo had little direct impact on Gates' chart, only forming a sextile to his natal Saturn at 21° Scorpio. But the subsequent opposition of the two planets in 1975 fell right across his MC-IC axis at 4° Aries-Libra. The opposition also triggered his natal Uranus, Moon, and Mars. Like H. P. Blavatsky, this is another example of the ways in which successive cycles of Jupiter with a slower-moving planet can reflect successive stages in the unfolding of the natal configuration.

In September 2000, another exact opposition occurred from Jupiter at 11° Gemini to Pluto at 11° Sagittarius, repeating in May 2001 at 14° Gemini-Sagittarius. This opposition was the fruition phase of a Jupiter-Pluto conjunction at 28° Scorpio in December 1994. The conjunction in Scorpio formed an exact square to Bill Gates' natal Jupiter-Pluto conjunction at 28° Leo; the opposition was widely conjunct his Moon's nodal axis at 18° Sagittarius-Gemini. On 1 December 2000, under the opposition of Jupiter and Pluto, Gates and his wife Melinda created the Bill and Melinda Gates Foundation, one of the largest charitable foundations in the world.

As with Blavatsky's chart, we can see how successive conjunctions and critical phases of these Jupiter cycles can mark major turning points in the individual's life that faithfully reflect the unfolding of the natal configuration. Perhaps the feeling of meaningful opportunity that often accompanies Jupiter's cycles with slower-moving planets provides an individual with the energy and impetus to make the choice of voluntarily pursuing that unfolding. But from Jupiter's perspective, it's one's *moira*. As the Romantic poet Novalis declared, character and fate are two names for the same principle.

Example 9: Johannes Kepler and the Jupiter-Pluto conjunction of 1571

Here is one more example of natal Jupiter conjuncting a slower-moving planet, and the ways in which its cycles play out in an individual's life. Johannes Kepler was born with Jupiter at 18° Pisces in the 10th house conjunct Pluto at 21° Pisces close to the cusp of the 11th. This conjunction is particularly important because both Jupiter and Pluto form squares to Neptune at 23° Gemini in the 12th house, just a degree behind the Ascendant.

Kepler's natal Jupiter is bound up with one of the great Neptune-Pluto cycles that reflect vast shifts in collective attitudes and values, especially evident in the sphere of religious structures and aspirations but relevant to any domain of life where humans seek an experience of redemption. I've already talked a bit about the Neptune-Pluto conjunction in Gemini in 1891 and 1892, whose waxing phase we're living under now. The conjunctions of these two planets occur 493 years apart, with a great cycle of 25,000 years – almost unimaginable in terms of human history.

The outgoing square of Neptune to Pluto under which Kepler was born is the first quarter phase of a conjunction that was exact between 2° and 4° Gemini in 1398 and 1399. The conjunction was already within orb by 1390, when both planets were still in Taurus, and it remained within orb until 1407. This period was reflected in Western Europe by the eruption of profound mistrust in the Catholic Church, exacerbated by the Great Schism which resulted in two rival Popes who reigned in opposition at Rome and Avignon for nearly forty years.

The Church and its earthly representatives were increasingly perceived as corrupt and ripe for change if not actual destruction. Under this conjunction, the first green shoots of the Italian Renaissance, with its revival of the philosophy, art, science, and occultism of the Hellenistic

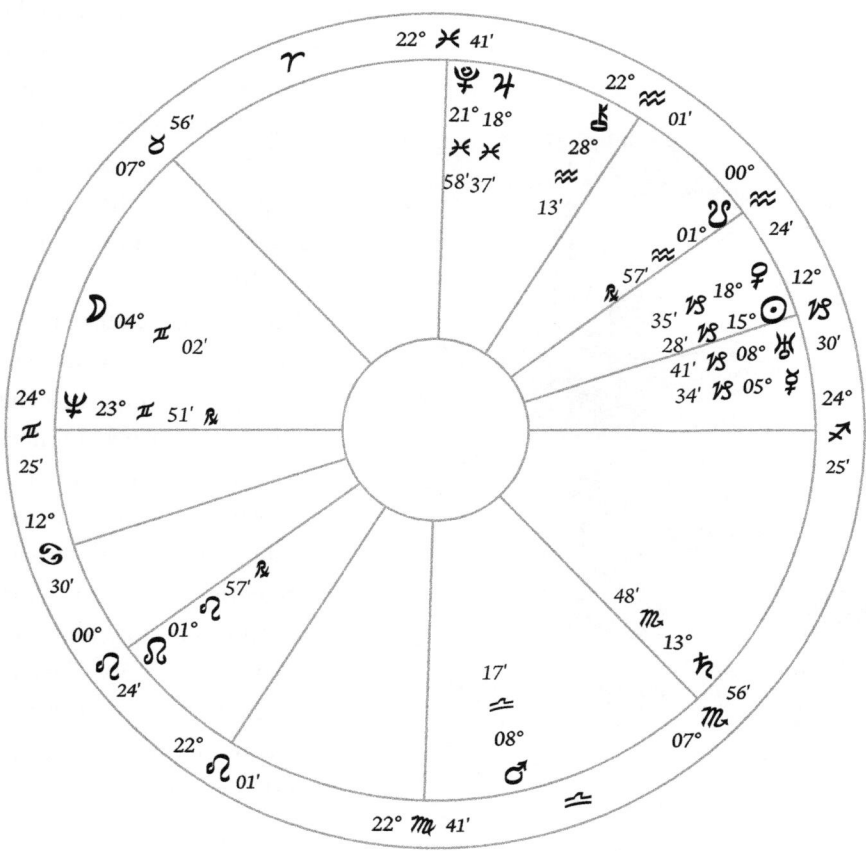

Johannes Kepler
27 December 1571, 2.37 pm, Weil der Stadt, Germany

age, had just begun to emerge. Kepler, born under the outgoing square of Neptune to Pluto – the phase of struggling to manifest the spiritual and scientific regeneration seeded at the time of the conjunction – was one of its most wholeheartedly committed children.

The Neptune-Pluto cycle is concerned with the destruction and regeneration of spiritual values and ideals. The outgoing square under which Kepler was born was reflected in the eruption of the Wars of Religion in northern Europe, the strengthening grip of Protestantism, and new ideas about the nature of kingship and its relationship with the godhead and the people. The prologue for these changes was the terrible impact, spiritually as well as physically, of the Black Death between 1347 and 1353, during which a third of the world's population died. The aftermath was the cracking of the previously impregnable edifice of the Catholic Church. Jupiter conjunct Pluto and square Neptune in Kepler's chart suggests that he believed he was 'meant' to be part of this struggle to restore and enhance an older, more tolerant world-view in which knowledge, spiritual and scientific, would be freely available to all and not controlled or suppressed by the dictates of any single dogmatic religious edifice.

Unlike Bill Gates' focus on wealth and resources with Jupiter-Pluto in the 2nd house, Kepler's Jupiter-Pluto conjunction in the 10th, with Pluto close to the cusp of the 11th, describes his relentless determination to disseminate his ideas to a larger community despite life-threatening opposition. This conjunction in Pisces suggests a deep sense of connection not only with the survival, renewal, and purpose of humanity, but also

August Köhler, *Portrait of Johannes Kepler* (1910), after an original painted in 1627. Kepler-Museum, Weil der Stadt, Germany.

with what he experienced as a higher spiritual source.   But he couldn't find that source in any doctrinal religious institution, although he tried. He began his life as a devout Lutheran, but he was excommunicated by the authorities of his own church and persecuted by the Catholics for his 'heretical' heliocentric theories.

In 1596, at the age of forty-five, during another Jupiter-Pluto conjunction at 18° Aries that also conjuncted transiting Uranus and closely squared his Sun-Venus conjunction in Capricorn in the 8th house, Kepler wrote *Mysterium Cosmographicum,* his most important work. The book is firmly rooted in Plato's cosmology as described in the *Timaeus,* and proposes that the five Platonic solids underpin the structure of the universe and reflect God's plan through the geometry of the planetary orbits. The starlike diagram of the Jupiter-Saturn cycle that I showed you earlier, based on the equilateral triangles formed by successive conjunctions, comes from *Mysterium Cosmographicum.* Here's another diagram from this work, portraying Kepler's Platonic solids model of the solar system.

Twelve and a half years later, during the next Jupiter-Pluto conjunction which occurred in Taurus in 1608, Kepler wrote a novel called *Somnium.* This work, considered to be the first scientific treatise on lunar astronomy, was also one of the earliest works of science fiction ever written. It was published posthumously by Kepler's son in 1634, four years after his father's

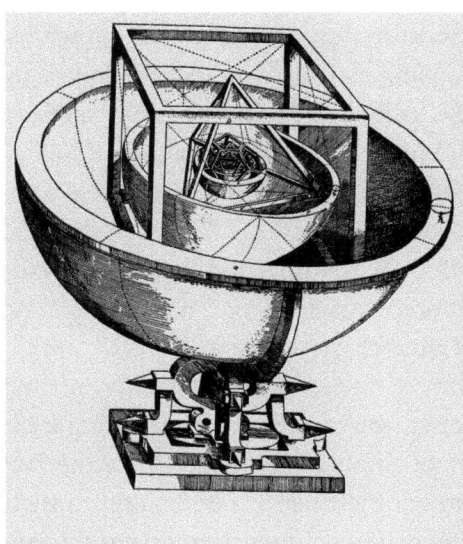

Kepler's Platonic solids model of the solar system based on the tetrahedron (pyramid), cube, octahedron, dodecahedron, and icosahedron, all contained within spheres representing the planetary orbits. Each planet – Mercury, Venus, Mars, Jupiter, and Saturn – is represented by a Platonic solid. Jupiter is symbolised by the pyramid, formed by four equilateral triangles which Plato, in the *Timaeus,* associated with fire. Saturn is symbolised by the cube, formed by six squares, which Plato associated with earth. From *Mysterium Cosmographicum* (1596), *Tabula III.*

death. The novel describes how the Earth would look when viewed from the Moon, and the main characters are an Icelandic boy, his witch-mother, and a *daimon* from the world of Greek myth. We can glimpse in this extraordinary work, which seamlessly blends science with the imaginal world, the involvement of a rising Neptune in Gemini with that natal conjunction of Jupiter and Pluto. In the same year, on a more overtly Taurean note as befitted the conjunction, Kepler also invented his own refracting telescope, known as the Keplerian telescope.

In 1620 and 1621, during the next Jupiter-Pluto conjunction, which also occurred in Taurus – Pluto moves more slowly through this sign and there's often more than one conjunction – Kepler wrote *Three Laws of Planetary Motion*. In this work he improved on Copernicus' heliocentric theory of planetary orbits, describing how the planets move in slightly elliptical rather than perfectly circular orbits around the Sun. Kepler insisted that this irregularity, applied to the Earth's orbit, explained why the time between the spring and autumnal equinoxes was unequal to the time between the autumnal and spring equinoxes. Today we do our calculations using astrological software programmes, which Kepler probably would have enthusiastically adopted and improved on. But as astrologers we're all regularly confronted with the fact that although absolute geometric perfection can't be found in our physical universe, it comes disturbingly close.

These three books are Kepler's most important and influential works, and all of them were produced during Jupiter-Pluto conjunctions following the one under which he was born. It's well worth spending time exploring your own chart, not only if you were born under a conjunction of Jupiter with Saturn, Chiron, Uranus, Neptune or Pluto, but also if you were born under any of the phases of one of these Jupiter cycles. And even if you're aspect-free, the transiting conjunctions will still reflect critical currents in the collective psyche and therefore in each of our individual lives, depending on where they fall in the natal chart.

If you're born under any aspect of Jupiter to these slower-moving planets, whether incoming or outgoing, you're part of the unfolding cycle that preceded your birth, and part of the history of the time. The fact that a great many people are born under these aspects doesn't mean their significance is any less for each individual's own nature and development. If you're born at a later phase of the cycle, such as the incoming trine, square, or opposition, you might think about what this phase might mean – it's always useful to remember the lunar phases – and look at when the conjunction preceding your birth took place and what was happening in the world at the time. You might discover some very interesting things about the ways in which you view and respond to life, and the ways in which the course of your own journey, and the meaning you discover in it, is part of a larger collective current unfolding within you as well as in the world around you.

Questions and Comments

Some concluding thoughts

Jupiter's conjunctions with Saturn, Chiron, and the outer planets, each marking the beginning of a new cycle, reflect the emergence of archetypal patterns seeking to emerge in the collective psyche in new ways. Some of these seedings may coincide with major world events, sometimes specific to or focused on a particular nation depending on how the conjunction aspects the birth chart of that nation. Sometimes the events are global. Sometimes a conjunction is mirrored by catastrophes such as wars, earthquakes, or pandemics. Sometimes it can coincide with a breakthrough in science, art, medicine, or technology, or herald great social, political, or religious changes.

But literal correspondences aren't guaranteed. When they do occur, they're usually unpredictable, although with hindsight, external events do tend to be vivid symbolic reflections of the inner pattern described by the conjoining of the two planets. Each new seeding, as well as sometimes coinciding with outward expressions that synchronously mirror it, marks the beginning of an unfolding story that continues to develop with each subsequent cycle. These conjunctions aren't isolated occurrences. They're unique, but they're also chapters in a never-ending tale.

Jupiter's cycles with slower-moving planets might also be seen as descriptions of the collective perceptions of the time, infusing the archetypal pattern symbolised by the slower planet with Jupiter's spirit of inspiration, discovery, exploration, meaning, teleology, and sometimes – on a collective as well as an individual level – an arrogance that arises from an inflated identification with divinity. Collectives, like individuals, can puff up with *hubris*, often in compensation for a pervasive sense of failure or weakness. An historical example of this reactive process is the rise of Nazi Germany as a form of collective compensation for the nation's humiliation after the First World War through the impact of the Versailles Treaty and its dire economic and social consequences.

Transiting Jupiter's conjunctions with slower-moving planets, when they trigger a placement in the individual chart, may be experienced as exciting, inspiring, and life-changing. They may also be experienced as highly unpleasant, painful, and even disastrous at the time of their occurrence. But even the difficult expressions can eventually yield a major change in perception: a metaphorical offspring, inner as well as outer, that allows us to connect our personal lives with the sense of a deeper meaning and teleology behind the patterns and movements of time and history.

What happens to us as a collective is also what we've become as a collective – the present point at which we've arrived – and that in turn depends on the choices every individual makes. While we might personally feel as if we're being subsumed by a frightening collective tidal wave or volcanic eruption, and are denied any real choices, we always have a choice as individuals about what attitudes we take and how we respond to these currents in our daily lives. It may be hard, but sooner or later each of us may need to come to terms with the fact that we are, paradoxically, unique individuals and also part of a larger unity.

Often these opposites end up on a collision course, and the individual whose personal views conflict with the prevailing collective *zeitgeist* can feel persecuted and victimised. And we *are* often impotent and trampled by collective currents. But I would never underestimate the power of one person's attitude to affect changes, positive or negative, in their immediate environment. We may not see the ultimate effect of our choices and actions in our individual lifetimes. But exploring Jupiter's cycles in history, and glimpsing the connections between events and experiences through time, can help us to realise that conscious awareness is far more powerful than we might realise, that our individual lives are full of meaning, and that the ongoing story doesn't ever stop. The astrological Jupiter symbolises our capacity to grasp this eagle's-eye view of the process of human development and the importance of the role individual consciousness plays.

Now let's take some time for any questions or comments any of you might have.

The question of orbs

Audience: Liz, do you still use a 10° orb with the conjunctions regarding their transits to natal planets?

Liz: Yes, I use 10° orbs, not only for major aspects from these cyclical conjunctions to natal planets, but also for transiting Jupiter conjuncting another transiting planet. Jupiter's cycles with Saturn, Chiron, and the outer planets don't suddenly become relevant when the conjunction is exact. They have a long prologue and a long epilogue while they're within that 10° orb of conjunction. Sometimes we tend to bracket events too rigidly and see them as isolated, unconnected occurrences because that makes it easier to explain them in literal, causal terms. We fail to see how all the threads, psychological as well as physical, are already weaving the pattern long before the cloth is visible, so we miss the connections and shared symbolism between world events and apparently disparate happenings and phases in our individual lives.

I've found that wider orbs work, often in obvious ways. I'm always happy to shift my perspective on any astrological symbol or technique if I can see in actual practice that my understanding has been too limited. But the operative term here is 'actual practice', not the insistence of someone else who has a different point of view. Astrologers will always have different points of view – it comes with the astrologer kit – which is why I keep talking about forming your own conclusions based on your own experience. None of us can ever see the entire picture because every one of us is temperamentally lopsided. As Jung pointed out, we see only what we're inherently predisposed to see. Pure objectivity can only ever be an ideal towards which we aspire.

The orb of conjunction when planets are near each other, natally and by transit, is, in my view, wider than many astrologers accept. But as with everything else in astrology, you need to do your own research, look at lots of charts, come up with your own conclusions, and use them in your work if they demonstrate their validity to you, rather than simply accepting something I or anyone else might tell you. As Psalm 34 advises us, "Taste and see."

Pluto and survival

Audience: I'd see Pluto as the necessity for new life to keep emerging, rather than just survival of what is.

Liz: Yes, that's a fair comment; Pluto is indeed concerned with the necessity of new life emerging. But for me the term 'survival' in relation to Pluto encompasses both. It's a paradox, like the alchemical ouroboros, the serpent that forever devours itself and forever gives birth to itself. Something ends and something new emerges, but at the same time, an essence survives because of that process.

On one of the ancient Orphic *lamellae* which I talked about in the first seminar, there's a phrase that states: "Out of a human you will become a god." This is part of a list of instructions given to the soul of the deceased on how to deal with the underworld guardians. The wording is precise. 'Out of' tells us that the god was always present within the human and will be revealed after the death of the mortal body. Physical death is followed by new life. But there's also the continuity of something eternal. The divine always was, is, and will be within mortal forms, just as Zeus is described in the Derveni Papyrus.

All living things die, so you're right: the survival of life can't occur without a constant cycle of new birth. But the continuity of life depends on something that remains constant: the life-force itself, which exists as an indestructible essence in the midst of the cyclical birth and death of its incarnate expressions. In Pluto's world, *this* is what must survive; otherwise there can't be any new birth. This idea lies behind biological evolution: species go extinct, but life itself survives and generates other, more adaptable forms. It's also the idea behind some of the more sophisticated interpretations of reincarnation. An individual lifetime ends, and the individual personality dies along with, or soon after, the mortal body. But a unique essence remains – whether we call it soul, spirit, immortal spark, energy, or whatever – throughout successive incarnations. Plato expressed this paradox on a cosmic level when he wrote that time, symbolised by and embodied in the planetary cycles, is 'a moving image of eternity'.[70]

---

70 Plato, *Timaeus* 37c-e.

Neptune or Jupiter as ruler of Pisces?

Audience: Liz, could you please comment on why you only consider Jupiter as Pisces' ruler? I know some astrologers do, but I'm not sure I understand the rationale behind it.

Liz: I don't consider Jupiter as the only planet *connected* with Pisces. There's clearly an important relationship between Neptune and Pisces. But when we apply specific techniques to a chart, such as viewing a planet 'ruling' or 'governing' the sign on a particular house cusp as an indicator of the affairs of that house, and we then try to apply an outer planet to this tight geometric scheme, there's a disturbing dissonance between two different modes of thinking that don't seem to work well when forced together. One approach is symmetrical and highly structured – that's the nature of the astrology we've inherited from the Hellenistic period – and the other is more intuitive and fluid.

I believe both approaches are valid. Neptune can tell us about important dimensions of Pisces that aren't easily expressed through the symbol of Jupiter. But I'm not entirely happy assigning this outer planet as a 'ruler' in the technical sense. For me, Jupiter rules Pisces in the context of the structure of the birth chart, but both Jupiter and Neptune as symbols reflect different dimensions of the sign. I do draw the line at abandoning Jupiter as the ruler of Pisces and replacing it with Neptune, as some astrologers do. I have the same problem with abandoning Mars as the ruler of Scorpio and only using Pluto as its ruler, and abandoning Saturn and replacing it with Uranus as the ruler of Aquarius. The Martial dimension of Scorpio is obvious, as is the Saturnian dimension of Aquarius. So is the Jupiterian dimension of Pisces.

I can't be categorical about whether Neptune 'co-rules' Pisces. As I said, there's a profound affinity between Neptune and Pisces, and I've learned a great deal about the sign from exploring Poseidon and older images like the Greek Okeanos, the Sumerian Enki, and the Babylonian Tiamat, and making connections between these mythic images and the dynamics of the sign. There are so many different layers in astrological symbolism, and some of them work on one level and not another. If I want to describe Pisces, I'll think of both planets. If I want to discuss the ruler of a chart in which the Ascendant is Pisces, then I'll look at Jupiter.

Jupiter-Saturn-Pluto and mistrust of authority

Audience: I was born in 1956, when the Jupiter-Pluto conjunction in Leo was nearly exactly square Saturn in Scorpio. Since the 2020 Jupiter-Pluto conjunction, I've been struggling to find meaning and purpose in my life, besides compulsively tracking and responding to the evolving Covid pandemic and the bungled government response to it.

Liz: Your compulsive tracking of the progress of a dangerous disease is certainly redolent of Saturn-Pluto. It reflects a deep instinctive determination to survive in the face of a very real threat. Your suspicion of government responses also seems characteristic of Saturn-Pluto, which is a survivor – profoundly suspicious of authority and even more suspicious of collective group-think, especially if the group seems to be sliding into authoritarianism. You're compelled to rely only on yourself to find the truth. You must become your own authority.

It sounds as though your Saturn-Pluto square has taken over at the moment, and Jupiter isn't able to contribute its sense of meaning and hope for the future. It's only adding its favourite ingredient, excess. But I suspect this is true of many people, and not just of you. You're especially sensitive because you were born under this combination of planets. The collective psyche seems to be submerged in a kind of depressive breakdown – a sort of alchemical *nigredo* – since the recent Jupiter-Saturn-Pluto conjunction. This conjunction appears to be dominated by Saturn's pessimism and focus on material events and causes, emphasised by its presence in Capricorn, Saturn's sign. It also opens the door to more authoritarian political ideologies, which may move in to fill the vacuum. It feels as though Jupiter isn't allowed a look-in except to exaggerate the anxiety and gloom. In the end, though, the mythic Jupiter always manages to fertilise the object of his desire, even if he's convincingly disguised at the time as a Saturnian prophet of doom.

If you were able to shift your focus from tracking Covid on a purely concrete level to looking more deeply at what's emerging in the collective psychologically, and what kind of purpose might be found in all the depression, resentment, and cynicism, you might discover a more profound level of meaning in what's occurring in the world as well as within yourself, and you might find more creative ways of working with those insights. You might also think about your own personal history and the experiences that have fed the darker dimensions of the natal configuration. Covid may be more than a threatening disease to you. It might also be a symbol of powerlessness in the face of an insidious force that threatens to control or crush you.

Jupiter-Pluto conjunctions, whether natal or in a transit cycle, emphasise the necessity to ensure survival because a sense of meaning is embedded in that survival and its ability to generate new life. But when Saturn enters the equation, there's often a long family history of feeling oppressed, threatened, disbelieved, or undermined. The recent Jupiter-Pluto conjunction combined with Saturn seems to have evoked the extremes in a great many people, and it's especially relevant to anyone born with a configuration of these three planets in their natal chart.

We might all need to look at the recent conjunctions and think about what it's continuing to bring out in each of us. Even though the time of the conjunctions has now passed, it marked the beginning of a new cycle of all three pairs of planets – Jupiter-Saturn, Jupiter-Pluto, and Saturn-Pluto – in which we're continuing to experience their underlying meaning and unfoldment. How can we deal with these collective patterns in a way that's more conscious and less a knee-jerk polarised reaction? Have we all been too hopelessly naïve about human nature and too willing to believe in our own moral superiority, and might we need to find a better balance between idealism and realism?

Every government bungles sooner or later, as does every human being. Your suspicion and resentment might be entirely justified, but it might also be rooted in something much deeper that needs careful exploration so you can glimpse a more meaningful pattern at work. Try to understand your emotional responses and what they might reveal about your past experiences. That might help you to discover how you can make the most creative use of the probing intensity and fierce demand for truth that Saturn in Scorpio square Jupiter-Pluto reflects in your natal chart. You might discover Jupiter's golden thread if you don't use up your energy feeling powerless and blaming people and institutions in the outside world.

Jupiter-Neptune and totalitarianism

Audience: You said earlier that we can only speculate about these Jupiter cycles. But don't you think the Jupiter-Neptune conjunction coming up in Pisces in 2022 could give some type of collective movement somehow related to totalitarianism in the name of a pure ideal?

Liz: Yes, it certainly could.[71] But 'totalitarianism' is a concept that's used very loosely at the moment. *Oxford Languages* defines it as a form of government that's 'centralised and dictatorial' and requires 'subservience to the state'. If we believe all the pronouncements on social media, many of which are rarely clean and honest even at the best of times, any authority, governmental or otherwise, that demands respect for a particular set of laws or stands in opposition to one's own ideas is called 'totalitarian'. All the planets can display a totalitarian quality because they reflect archetypal patterns that strive to fulfil their own unique teleology. Left alone, they'll all fight to achieve this through any means available. This is what lies at the core of any hard planetary aspect. The irresistible force meets the immovable object, and it's up to individual consciousness to find a way to mediate and get them to stop fighting – at least some of the time – and find some points of compromise.

The outer planets can certainly display more than their share of what we might call totalitarianism because they reflect collective currents that are not concerned with individual development. Collective movements by their nature demand absolute subservience and the sacrifice of individual will. The mythic deities after whom these planets are named rule boundless, mysterious, impersonal realms: the heavens, the sea, the underworld. In the face of such vastness, the individual is a tiny, irrelevant speck.

---

71 It did. Jupiter and Neptune were in exact conjunction at 23° Pisces in April 2022. Two months earlier, on 24 February 2022, just as Jupiter came within 10° of Neptune, Russia invaded Ukraine. This might be seen as a totalitarian movement justified as a 'pure' ideal – the 'restoration' of a fantasised Russian Empire – although it's doubtful that Vladimir Putin himself believed in the ideal. For him it's more likely to have provided a useful marketing tool to sell the bitter cost of the invasion to the Russian people and any available useful idiots in the West. We might also consider the political shifts to more extreme ideological positions in the UK, Europe, and the US in 2024, as Jupiter in Gemini began its outgoing square to Neptune in Pisces following that conjunction.

The inner planets are more relatable. It's easier to understand Mars with his belligerence, his me-first attitude, and his aggressive antics on the battlefield, or Venus with her self-indulgence, her vanity, and her seductive wiles, because we can see our own individual human qualities in these mythic images. Neptune's utopian dreams are anything but compassionate and forgiving if any individual dares to oppose its demand to submerge individual self-expression in the mass – despite the fact that those driven by Jupiter-Neptune ideals often claim the moral high ground as 'caring' individuals.

In that sense I agree with you. Jupiter-Neptune can be extraordinarily compassionate and, in terms of collective movements, the combination can reflect emerging social and political ideals aimed at helping suffering in the world. This was the case under the Jupiter-Neptune conjunction that occurred at the end of the Second World War. But at the same time, Jupiter-Neptune may try to annihilate opposition in the name of its vision. Two interesting examples of individuals born under Jupiter-Neptune conjunctions are Pope John XXIII, the 'Good Pope', who, as I mentioned earlier, had the conjunction in Taurus, and Elon Musk, who was born under an out-of-sign conjunction of Jupiter at the end of Scorpio and Neptune in early Sagittarius. I leave it to you to decide where on the spectrum of totalitarianism versus compassion these individuals might lie. Sometimes distinguishing between the two extremes isn't always as simple as we imagine.

James Hillman suggested in *A Terrible Love of War* that the cruellest, most brutal wars usually arise from *belief*, and that religion and ideology are secretly the same: they're both rooted in fixed beliefs rather than in what Hillman understood as a deep, 'mythic', fluent, and broad-based understanding of human experience.[72] Neptune can certainly be brutal in the pursuit of its ideals, and Jupiter can certainly inflame it and bring the waters to boiling point. This is the spirit of the Inquisition, torturing and killing heretics and forcing religious conversions in the name of saving their souls. But the power of any collective movement depends on how each individual responds to it and what that individual chooses to do in their own life. Rather than trying to predict the rise of a totalitarian movement 'out there' because a Jupiter-Neptune conjunction is about to

---

72 James Hillman, *A Terrible Love of War* (Penguin, 2004).

arrive, perhaps we need to ask ourselves whether we're aware of our own totalitarian attitudes, and whether we ourselves are unwitting participants in these collective currents, unconsciously adopting destructive beliefs because it's so much easier than thinking for oneself.

I know I keep talking about individual consciousness as the ultimate arbiter of our future. But it's really the only effective tool we have. As individuals we might not be able to stop wars and terrorist attacks enacted in the name of an ideal, or eco-warriors blocking ambulances on motorways and destroying works of art, or governments imposing higher and higher taxes, or supermarkets jacking up prices on bread and eggs. We might be fastidious about recycling our yoghurt containers to 'save the planet', but as individuals we can do nothing about the nations who contribute the most to climate change. But we can respond in our own lives with better understanding, rather than becoming helpless, enraged pawns on someone else's chessboard. We don't have to be useful idiots. We can learn to think and choose for ourselves.

We tend to sit around waiting for something to happen to us rather than taking responsibility for our own choices. I sometimes think that as astrologers we're more prone to this than many other people because we persist in seeing the planets as 'doing' something to us. And then we wait for the lucky win, the disaster, or the superhero to ride to the rescue. We might become militant and join a noisy, violent protest, but aggressive responses never really change the collective psyche; they just create more polarisation, hatred, and frustration. But the way each of us treats the other people in our lives each day actually does change something, and it would be a mistake to assume it's too small an effort to matter. We think of our suffering in terms of 'me', but we think of changing things in terms of 'them' or, in the case of identity politics, 'us'. But change, like charity, has to begin at home in our own psyches if we want to work with Jupiter cycles in a creative way.

Perhaps we need to make more of an effort to reflect on what's emerging inside us, because we're part of the collective and we all make a contribution, consciously or not. I can't predict whether the upcoming Jupiter-Neptune conjunction in Pisces is going to be expressed in the collective as a compassionate vision or enacted through some kind of totalitarian levelling of individual differences – or both, which is often the case. Neptune is the master of illusions, and just when we feel most smug about our compassion and moral superiority, we're likely to have a lot of unnoticed dirt under our fingernails. All any of us can do as individuals is take responsibility for our choices and actions, and recognise our own handiwork in the consequences.

Circles and spirals

Audience: How does a recurring conjunction 'evolve' in one's life? The next time we undergo the same conjunction in our lives, what does it bring that is new?

Liz: I assume that by 'the same conjunction' you mean the repeating conjunctions of two planets, like Jupiter and Saturn, which form a sequence of cycles. Consecutive cycles don't move in a circle; they act like a spiral, which never returns to exactly the same point. The cycles of Jupiter with a slower-moving planet never come back to exactly the same degree of the same sign, and even if they did, the collective, and you yourself, would have changed and moved on in the interim. A different chapter unfolds in a never-ending story. Although the characters might be the same, they alter through experience and can express themselves in new ways as a result of their interactions with each other.

Each time the conjunction repeats, it will be in a different degree and probably a different sign, and it will form different aspects to the other transiting planets. It will offer a new dimension of its meaning and open up new possibilities. Whether we like it or not, our experiences change us and alter our consciousness. On the most basic level, a mature person will respond differently from a small child to the same planetary combination because the body itself has changed. We might reconnect with issues we didn't deal with the last time the cycle came around, or reap the rewards of earlier efforts, and we may respond to challenges differently. We may discover dimensions of ourselves that hadn't yet emerged at the time of the previous conjunction. There's always a difference.

Other transiting planets will form different relationships with each other and with the natal conjunction each time the cycle recurs. Earlier we looked at the chart of Bill Gates, with a Jupiter-Pluto conjunction in Leo in the 2nd house. He and his wife created the Bill and Melinda Gates Foundation in December 2000 under a transiting Jupiter-Pluto opposition, the 'culmination' phase of the previous conjunction. Jupiter and Pluto were in a different aspect and in entirely different signs from Gates' natal conjunction; Jupiter was transiting through Gemini and Pluto through Sagittarius. They were in opposition rather than conjunction, suggesting a time of flowering rather than seeding. And the other planets were transiting in different signs at that time and making entirely different aspects to the natal and progressed chart. Transiting Saturn, in December 2000, was moving retrograde through the last degrees of Taurus, square Gates' natal Jupiter-Pluto conjunction in late Leo. Although there's a major life theme unfolding once again in relation to natal Jupiter-Pluto in the 2nd house, it's not a repeat performance.

We could say the same about the cycle of a single planet. The second and third Saturn returns are entirely different experiences from the first Saturn return – not only because we're nearly thirty years older each time, but because we're building on experiences and memories that have shaped us and through which we've been formed according to circumstances and prior choices. The first Saturn return occurs at a time when we're at our physical peak, still young but old enough to have accrued some valuable experience and knowledge. The second Saturn return occurs when we're still in our prime but facing the gradual slowing down of the body as well as the consequences, emotionally and materially, of decades of choices. The third Saturn return, if we manage to reach it, occurs when we have to face the body's increasing frailty and the inevitability of mortality. The entrance door is a distant memory and the exit door is disturbingly close. Our experiences, memories, and character form not only from these Saturn cycles but from other transits and progressed aspects as well.

If we reflect on our lives from an inner perspective and don't focus merely on events, an underlying theme can be discerned in all our Saturn returns as well as in the hard and soft aspects transiting Saturn makes to its natal place between those returns. But that theme, whose essential nature is portrayed by Saturn's natal sign, house, and aspects, isn't static. It develops and unfolds like a plant growing from seed to maturity, or a novel in which the same characters develop and change from the first to the last chapters. In the second seminar we looked at the sequence of four of Jung's Jupiter returns, and the ways in which an essential pattern unfolded through disparate but related experiences in his life. The events that accompany transit cycles may be entirely different and apparently unconnected each time. It's a process of development rather than a repeat performance.

We're back to Hillman's 'acorn' theory. The acorn eventually develops into an oak because that's its essential nature. During its lifetime the oak will be influenced and shaped by climate, soil, insects, fungi, birds, rabbits, squirrels, nearby trees, and the unpredictability of human intervention. But it remains an oak. This is why I prefer to use the charts of people who are older or long dead as examples in these seminars. We can see the scope of a fully lived life, and the patterns as well as the choices emerge more clearly. Although the chart of a young person would certainly be of great interest, it won't tell us enough about how these patterns unfold over a lifetime.

If you have Jupiter conjunct Pluto natally, you'll experience the re-emergence of an underlying theme each time the conjunction cycle and its phases repeat in the heavens, regardless of the signs they're in. But it's the unfolding of a developing story rather than a constant rereading of the first chapter. You'll be different because you're a living being, psychologically as well as physically. You aren't static. Nothing in heaven or earth is static; even planets, stars, and galaxies are born and eventually die, even if they take a very long time doing it. Jupiter and Pluto will be in different signs each time they come around. The other transiting planets will also be following different dance steps, and the progressed planets will be making different aspects. The natal conjunction reflects a consistent archetypal theme, but each cyclical journey we make to it takes us on a different road.

Now I'm afraid we've run out of time and have reached the end of today's seminar. I hope all three of these seminars have contributed something to your understanding of the enigma of Jupiter. Thank you for your questions, and thank you all very much for participating.

Bibliography

Aeschylos, *Prometheus Bound*, trans. E. H. Plumptre (P. F. Collier & Son, 1909).

Alvarez, Marco Antonio Santamaria (ed.), *The Derveni Papyrus: Unearthing Ancient Mysteries* (Brill, 2019).

Athanassakis, Apostolos N. (trans.), *The Orphic Hymns: Text, Translation, and Notes* (Scholars Press, 1977).

Aquinas, Thomas, *Summa theologica Prima Pars*, trans. Fr. Laurence Shapcote OP (Aquinas Institute, 2023).

Aquinas, Thomas, *Summa contra gentiles*, Books III & IV, trans. Laurence Shapcote OP (Aquinas Institute, 2019).

Barrie, J. M., *Peter and Wendy* (Hodder and Stoughton, 1911).

Betegh, Gábor, *The Derveni Papyrus: Cosmology, Theology and Interpretation* (Cambridge University Press, 2004).

Bierce, Ambrose, *The Devil's Dictionary* (Bloomsbury, 2004).

Bloomfield, Morton W., 'The Origin of the Concept of the Seven Cardinal Sins' (*Harvard Theological Review*, 1941).

Bloomfield, Morton W., *The Seven Deadly Sins* (Michigan State College Press, 1952).

Cicero, M. Tullius, *Somnium Scipionis*, in *Cicero's Political Essays*, trans. C. W. Keyes (William Heinemann, 1928).

Cook, Arthur Bernard, *Zeus: A Study in Ancient Religion*, 3 volumes (Cambridge University Press, 1914).

Cordovero, Moshe, *Shi'ur Qomah*, Modena MS 206b, in Daniel Matt, *The Essential Kabbalah: The Heart of Jewish Mysticism* (Castle Books, 1997).

Cumont, Franz, *The Oriental Religions in Roman Paganism* (Open Court Publishing, 1911).

Cumont, Franz, *Astrology and Religion Among the Greeks and Romans* (G. P. Putnam's Sons, 1912).

Ebertin, Reinhold, *The Combination of Stellar Influences* (Ebertin Verlag, 1960).

Evelyn-White, H. G., (trans.), *The Homeric Hymns and Homerica* (William Heinemann, 1957).

Fallon, Astrid, *Planetary Cycles at a Glance* (Fallon Astro- Graphics, 2001).

Ganz, Timothy, *Early Greek Myth: A Guide to Literary and Artistic Sources* (Johns Hopkins University Press, 1993).

Graf, Fritz and Sarah Iles Johnston, *Ritual Texts for the Afterlife: Orpheus and the Bacchic Gold Tablets* (Routledge, 2007).

Greenbaum, Dorian Gieseler, *Temperament: Astrology's Forgotten Key* (Wessex Astrologer, 2005).

Greene, Liz, *Jung's Studies in Astrology* (Routledge, 2018).

Greene, Liz, *The Astrological World of Jung's Liber Novus* (Routledge, 2018).

Greene, *Chiron in Love* (Wessex Astrologer, 2023).

Hesiod, *Works and Days*, trans. H. G. Evelyn-White (William Heinemann, 1914).

Hesiod, *The Homeric Hymns and Homerica*, trans. H. G. Evelyn-White (William Heinemann, 1914).

Hillman, James, *The Soul's Code: In Search of Character and Calling* (Random House, 1996).

Hillman, James, *A Terrible Love of War* (Penguin, 2004).

Hillman, James, *Senex and Puer: Uniform Edition of the Writings of James Hillman*, Vol. 3:03 (Spring Publications, 2005).

Holden, James, *Early Horoscopes of Jesus, American Federation of Astrologers Journal of Research*, Vol. 12, No. 1 (Spring 2001).

Hone, Margaret E., *The Modern Textbook of Astrology* (Fowler & Co., 1972).

Jung, C. G., *Studies in Word-Association: Experiments in the Diagnosis of Psychopathological Conditions* (William Heinemann, 1918).

Jung, C. G., *On the Psychology and Pathology of So-Called Occult Phenomena*, in Jung, C. G., *Psychiatric Studies*, CW1 (Routledge & Kegan Paul, 1957).

Jung, C. G., *Symbols of Transformation*, CW5 (Routledge & Kegan Paul, 1952).

Jung, C. G., *Psychological Types*, CW6 (Routledge & Kegan Paul, 1971).

Jung, C. G., *The Archetypes and the Collective Unconscious*, CW9i (Routledge & Kegan Paul, 1959).

Jung, C. G., *Aion: Researches into the Phenomenology of the Self*, CW9ii (Routledge & Kegan Paul, 1951).

Jung, C. G., *C. G. Jung Letters*, 2 volumes (Routledge & Kegan Paul, 1973-76).

Jung, C. G, *Memories, Dreams, Reflections* (Vintage Books, 1965).

Jung, C. G., *Liber Novus: The Red Book* (W. W. Norton, 2009).

Kepler, Johannes, *Mysterium Cosmographicum* (Erasmus Kempfer, 1596).

Kingsley, Peter, *Ancient Philosophy, Mystery and Magic: Empedocles and Pythagorean Tradition* (Clarendon Press, 1995).

Kirk, G. S., J. E. Raven, and M. Schofield (eds. and trans.), *The Pre-Socratic Philosophers* (Cambridge University Press, 1983).

Klein, Melanie, *Envy and Gratitude: A Study of Unconscious Sources* (Basic Books, 1957).

Kouremenos T., G. M. Parassoglou, and K. Tsantsanoglou (eds.), *The Derveni Papyrus* (Libri Antichi Arezzo, 2006).

Laks, André and Glenn W. Most (eds.), *Studies on the Derveni Papyrus*, 2 volumes (Oxford University Press, 2001-2022).

Macrobius, *Commentary on the Dream of Scipio*, trans. William Harris Stahl (Columbia University Press, 1990).

Miller, Alice, *The Drama of the Gifted Child: The Search for the True Self* (Basic Books, 2008).

Nietzsche, Friedrich, *Human, All Too Human: A Book for Free Spirits*, trans. A. Harvey (Charles H. Kerr & Co., 1908).

Plato, *Plato in Twelve Volumes*, trans. Harold North Fowler (William Heinemann, 1966).

Plotinus, *The Enneads*, trans. Stephen MacKenna (Faber & Faber, 1969).

Powys, John Cowper, *Porius: A Romance of the Dark Ages* (Macdonald, 1951).

Presley, Priscilla Beaulieu and Sandra Harmon, *Elvis and Me* (Berkley Publishing, 1986).

Rudhyar, Dane, *The Lunation Cycle* (Llewellyn, 1967).

Von Franz, Marie-Louise, *The Problem of the Puer Aeternus* (Spring Publications, 1970).

Waite, A. E., *The Pictorial Key to the Tarot* (Rider, 1910).

Wiggin, Albert H., 'Second Crash', *Sydney Morning Herald*, Sydney, Australia, 30 October 1929.

Winnicott, D. W., 'Review of *Memories, Dreams, Reflections*', *International Journal of Psychoanalysis* 45 (1964), pp. 450-455.

Yeats, William Butler Yeats, *A Vision: An Explanation of Life Founded upon the Writings of Giraldus and upon Certain Doctrines Attributed to Kusta Ben Luka* (T. Werner Laurie, 1925).

Yeats, William Butler, *The Variorum Edition of the Poems of W. B. Yeats* (Macmillan, 1957).